Fides Christi: The Justification Debate

Fides Christi

THE JUSTIFICATION DEBATE

Paul O'Callaghan

FOUR COURTS PRESS

This book was set in 10.5 on 12.5 point Ehrhardt
by Woodcote Typesetters for
FOUR COURTS PRESS LTD
Fumbally Lane, Dublin, Ireland
and in North America for
FOUR COURTS PRESS
c/o ISBS, 5804 NE Hassalo Street, Portland, OR 97213.

ISBN 1-85182-316-6

A catalogue record for this title
is available from the British Library.

Printed in Great Britain
by The Martins Printing Group, Bodmin, Cornwall

For Lucas F. Mateo-Seco, with gratitude

Foreword

This book appears at a crucial moment in the development of closer relations between the Roman Catholic Church and Lutheran Churches world-wide. In the Spring of 1997 the *Joint Declaration on the Doctrine of Justification* was submitted to the Roman Catholic Church and the member churches of the Lutheran World Federation (LWF). This Declaration was jointly elaborated by representatives of the Pontifical Council for Promoting Christian Unity and the LWF. In its concluding paragraphs the *Joint Declaration* states: 'The understanding of the doctrine of justification set forth in this Declaration shows that a consensus in basic truths of the doctrine of justification exists between Lutherans and Catholics. In the light of this consensus the remaining differences of language, theological elaboration and emphasis in the understanding of justification ... are acceptable'. The significant agreement referred to here has an important consequence: 'Thus the doctrinal condemnations of the sixteenth century, in so far as they relate to the doctrine of justification, appear in a new light: the teaching of the Lutheran churches presented in this declaration does not fall under the condemnations of the Council of Trent; the condemnations in the Lutheran Confessions do not apply to the teaching of the Roman Catholic Church presented in this Declaration' (*Joint Declaration on the Doctrine of Justification*, *LWF*, Geneva 1997, paras. 40 and 41). It is hoped that the churches involved will respond by May 1998 (or in any case before the year 2000) whether they are able to accept these conclusions.

The first member church of the LWF to respond was the Evangelical Lutheran Church in America at its Assembly in August 1997. There, the delegates accepted the *Joint Declaration* by a majority of 97.5 per cent of the votes. If the other churches would follow this example the acceptance of the *Joint Declaration* would constitute a step of historic significance. It would signal that the deepest theological differences from the time of the Reformation, which have been at the root and centre of the divisions within Western Christianity, have been overcome. It would create a new atmosphere of trust between our churches in the awareness that we have reached a consensus, on the deepest level, in our efforts to understand our commitment to proclaim God's unmerited but life-changing grace and salvation.

This *Joint Declaration* does not present the results of a new dialogue on justification, but is a summary and evaluation of over twenty-five years of official Lutheran-Roman Catholic dialogue on international and national level, and also of historical and theological investigations of individual Roman Catholic and

Lutheran theologians. The book by Professor O'Callaghan is an important contribution to and commentary on this remarkable process from mutual condemnation to common affirmation. We find here a most valuable source of information and interpretation of the history of understanding the place, role and content of the doctrine of justification from Martin Luther to the present day. The book contains a detailed overview of the theme of justification in different ecumenical dialogues with special attention to the Lutheran-Roman Catholic ones. And, perhaps most importantly, in its second part it provides an extremely helpful contribution to the Lutheran-Roman Catholic dialogue on the criteriological and hermeneutical function as well as the content of the doctrine of justification.

This dialogue has not come to an end with the *Joint Declaration*. Rather, the basic consensus on justification now being reached and the acceptance of the remaining differences of theological explanation and emphasis concerning specific points of this doctrine represent an enormous encouragement for the task according to which the 'Lutheran churches and the Roman Catholic Church will continue to strive together to deepen this common understanding of justification and to make it bear fruit in the life and teaching of the churches' (Joint Declaration, par. 43). For this task the book offers thoughtful suggestions and reflections which, in my Lutheran perspective, can help Lutherans free their understanding of justification from a tendency towards certain narrow and individualistic perspectives. That there is an openness among Lutheran theologians to broaden traditional positions is shown by the lively and productive activity of the newly emerging Finnish school of Luther research. The studies coming out from this school seek to complement the obvious and essential personal and existential emphases of Martin Luther's theology by a rediscovery of the ontological strands in his understanding of salvation explicated by the message and doctrine of justification. The way in which Professor O'Callaghan opens up the wider and richer context of the doctrine of justification by indicating its ecclesiological and social dimensions and its relation to God's good creation redeemed by Jesus Christ provides directions for further fruitful dialogue.

Geneva, September 1997
Günther Gaßmann,
Director of the Commission of Faith and
Order of the World Council of Churches, 1984-1994.

Contents

Abbreviations

CJ   Lutheran-Roman Catholic Joint Commission, Declaration *Church and Justification* (1993)

CT   *Concilium Tridentinum: diariorum, actorum, epistolarum, tractatuum nova collectio*, Societas Görresiana, Freiburg i. B. 1901

DH   J. Denzinger, *Enchiridion symbolorum definitionum et declarationum de rebus fidei et morum*, ed. P. Hünermann, Freiburg i. B. 1991

EO   G. Cereti, S.J. Voicu and J.F. Puglisi (eds.), *Enchiridion Œcumenicum*, 4 volumes, Bologna 1986–1996

LV   K. Lehmann and W. Pannenberg, 'The Justification of the Sinner' (1986), in *The Condemnations of the Reformation Era. Do they still divide?*, Minneapolis 1990, pp. 29–69 (English translation of *Lehrverurteilungen – kirchentrennend?*)

USA   H.G. Anderson, et al. (eds.), 'Justification by faith' (1984), in *Lutherans and Catholics in Dialogue VII*, Minneapolis 1985, pp. 8–74

WA   M. Luther, *Dr Martin Luthers Werke: Kritische Gesamtausgabe*, Weimar 1883ff.

Preface

At the beginning of the sixteenth century, a quiet revolution began. An unknown monk at an Augustinian monastery in Erfurt in Germany accused the Church and Christendom at large of having fallen prey, in its life and spirituality, to a disastrous form of practical Pelagianism: ousting our merciful Saviour Jesus Christ from the Church he founded, destroying the freedom he won for us by shedding his blood on the Cross, manipulating his saving and comforting word and sacraments. The spiritual sparks scattered by Martin Luther ignited a bonfire which swept across the whole of Europe in the space of a few short years. And the entirety of his message was centered on a seemingly abstruse theological concept which, though in itself thoroughly Pauline, had traditionally occupied quite a modest place in Christian thought: the doctrine of justification by faith.

Luther made this doctrine the *articulus stantis et cadentis ecclesiae*, the only doctrine capable of explaining the true nature of Christianity, of adequately discerning and identifying where Christ's Spirit is present and active. According to the Reformer, Christianity and the Church, in their many manifestations, must highlight one thing and one thing only: the unconditioned and magnanimous quality of God's pardoning love towards humans, his wayward children. The concrete expression of human response to this unconditioned pardoning love should involve a joyful recognition of God's creating and saving action, a true repentance of sin, and, most significantly, complete detachment from one's own good works and undertakings. And this is what Luther's doctrine of justification expresses: we are saved by *God alone*, that is, by *grace alone*, on account of *Christ alone*, by *faith alone*. And for Luther 'faith alone' means not placing any trust whatsoever in our own works, or virtues, or capacities, or projects, or undertakings. Luther took it that his own and others' 'search for a gracious God' was being seriously obstructed by a practical insistence on 'works-righteousness' in Church life and spirituality. He considered that certain ordinances and teachings of the Church, certain elements of piety and sacramental life, instead of facilitating the word and power of God being transmitted in a visible and structured way through the word and sacraments, tended to act as obstacles to the magnanimous promise of divine pardon in Christ.

Four hundred and fifty years have gone by since the death of Luther, and the doctrine of 'justification by faith alone' no longer plays, in the mind of most Christians, the rôle it once did. Four hundred and fifty years have also passed since the Council of Trent, in reply to Luther's challenge, promulgated its extensive decree on justification.[1] Of course things have changed considerably since then. Factors of

1 Trent's decree on justification, prepared at the sixth session of this ecumenical council, was

a social, political and economic kind which facilitated the breaking up of Christendom in the sixteenth century no longer apply. More than anything else, faced with
the challenge of a world in full flight from God, a deep and urgent desire is felt on
both sides to overcome the differences that once divided the minds, hearts and
allegiances of Europeans. And of course, *abusus non tollit usus!* Christians have come
to appreciate the futility of any attempt to condition or obstruct the saving power of
God in a serious and definitive way: *non est abbreviata manus Domini* (Is 59:1), God's
power and saving grace has not been lessened or weakened with the passing of time
or the sinfulness of humans.[2] Yet the world needs the united testimony of Christians, 'so that it may believe' (cf. Jn 17:21).

Recent years have been rich in attempts to find a common way for Christians,
and especially for Roman Catholics and Lutherans, in the fundamental area of justification. Common ecumenical statements related to this doctrinal area have
abounded.[3] Besides, there seem to be good prospects in the relatively near future for
the drawing up and approval of a joint common declaration on justification by the
highest authorities of the Roman Catholic Church and the Lutheran World Federation.[4]

This book, fruit of several years teaching Christian anthropology to under-gradu-
ate and post-graduate students at the Pontifical Atheneum of the Holy Cross in
Rome, and of a recent symposium on justification organized at the same university,[5]
has a double purpose. Firstly it intends to present a series of significant episodes in

---

promulgated on 13 January 1547. See chapter 3 below.   2 ' "The arm of the Lord has not been
shortened". God is no less powerful today than he was in other times; his love for man is no less
true. Our faith teaches us that all creation, the movement of the earth and the other heavenly
bodies, the good actions of creatures and of all the good that has been achieved in history, in short
everything, comes from God and is ordered to God' (Blessed J. Escrivá, *Christ is Passing By*, Dublin 1982, no. 130; cf. ibid., no. 50; idem., *The Way*, Dublin 1987, no. 586). This awareness of divine
fidelity, of the abundance and definitive character of the saving power of God, at the heart of the
doctrine of justification, brought the founder of Opus Dei to fully appreciate and promote a deep
awareness of the message of the universal call to holiness: all Christians, no matter how varied be
their circumstances and personal situation, can live Christian lives to the full, for external circumstances, no matter how adverse, are no obstacle. This doctrine was taught by Vatican Council II (cf.
especially Const. *Lumen gentium*, 39–42). Pope Paul VI, in his Motu Proprio *Sanctitas clarior* (19
March 1969, *Acta Apostolicae Sedis* 61 (1969) 150) stated that the doctrine of the universal call to
holiness was the most characteristic feature (*proprietas*) and ultimate purpose of Vatican II teaching. Cf. also the final report of the Special Synod of Bishops on the twentieth anniversary of the
conclusion of the Council (1985), II, a), 4. On the relationship between the universal call to holiness and the 'holiness' of the Church, cf. P. O'Callaghan, 'The Holiness of the Church in "Lumen
Gentium" ', in the *Thomist* 52 (1988) 673–701, especially 678–683.   3 Cf. chapter 4 below.   4 Cf.
H.-A. Raem, 'I rapporti con i Luterani nell'anno 1995', in *Osservatore Romano*, 22–23 January,
1996. A possible first draft of such a document has already appeared in French, German and other
languages: 'Konsens in Sicht? Der Entwurf einer lutherisch-katholischen Erklärung zur
Rechtfertigungslehre', in *Herder Korrespondenz* 50 (1996) 302–306. For the time scale of an even-
tual agreement, cf. ibid., p. 547.   5 Cf. J.M. Galván (ed.), *La giustificazione in Cristo* (Atti del II
Simposio Internazionale della Facoltà di Teologia del Pontificio Ateneo della Santa Croce, 14–15
marzo 1996), Vatican City 1997. Cf. P. O'Callaghan, 'L'uomo giustificato, nuova creatura in Cristo.
Una riflessione intorno all'attuale dibattito ecumenico', in ibid., pp. 129–164.

the history of the debate on justification (the teaching of Luther, that of some of his followers, of the Council of Trent, the ecumenical consensus statements on justification over the past thirty years). This historical overview comprises the first four chapters. Secondly, taking advantage of important advances made throughout this century on the exegetical, hermeneutical, historical and theological fronts, we will see to what degree recently-growing consensus on the topic of justification between Lutherans and Catholics can become profound and lasting. This topic will be examined in chapters 5 and 6. The analytic part proper of the work begins in chapter 5.

At the same time it should become clear that agreements reached, such as they are, constitute not only a significant point of arrival for the ecumenical movement, but also a point of departure for further study and dialogue. Specifically, I hope it will become clear that theological tensions remaining between both sides on the anthropological and ecclesiological front point at heart to more fundamental questions relating to the theology of creation and sin, and ultimately, of course, to Christology. Specifically I believe that future developments in a theology of a truly ecumenical kind must come to grips with a Christologically-based vision of being and reality,[6] and set the basis for an authentically 'Christian' metaphysics.[7]

Those whom I wish to thank for their help in preparing this text are far too numerous to mention. In the first place, I wish to thank my colleagues at the Pontifical Atheneum of the Holy Cross in Rome, especially Professors Aranda, Blanco, Galván, Reale, Estrada-Barbier, Tanzella-Nitti, Tabet and Ducay, able and willing theological sparring partners, without whose encouragement and suggestions it would have been impossible for me to begin and to finish these pages. I also acknowledge the real contribution made by the 1996–7 Theology Licentiate class at the Atheneum who patiently sat through a course on the topic of justification, and brought me back to reality (both human and ecclesial) when, as often, this was necessary. I am very grateful to Fr James F. Puglisi SA, Sister Mary Peter Froelicher SHCJ and the staff at the ecumenical Centro pro Unione in Rome, for their encouragement and for having given me access to the extensive library facilities of the centre. I wish to express a particular debt of gratitude to Professor A.E. McGrath of the University of Oxford, for the material he has made available in his extensive study *Iustitia Dei*, which I used liberally throughout these pages. And so many others whom I consulted and with whom I conversed on justification and related topics in preparing the text: Professors Luigi Sartori of Padova, Gianni Colzani of Milan, Sergio Rostagno of the Waldensian Theological Faculty in Rome, Romano Penna and Brunero Gherardini of the Lateran University, Jared Wicks SJ of the Gregorian University, Hans-Martin Barth of Marburg, Harding Meyer of Strasbourg, Günther Gaßmann, of the Faith and Order Secretariat of the World Council of Churches,

---

6 Such an attempt is to be found for example in W. Pannenberg's *Systematic Theology*, vol. 2, Edinburgh 1994. cf. the presentation of and comments on this work by G.L. Brena, 'Teologia della creazione e della redenzione', in *Civiltà Cattolica*, quad. 3490 (1995/IV) 366–378.   7 Cf. P. O'Callaghan, 'Il realismo e la teologia della creazione', in *Per la filosofia* 12 (1995) 98–110.

especially for his kindness in writing the foreword to this book, Pedro Rodríguez, Dean of the Faculty of Theology of the University of Navarre, and Lucas F. Mateo-Seco of the same Faculty. My thanks also to Dr Thomas Heilbrun for his assistance in correcting the manuscript and checking the bibliography, and to Michael Adams, Ronan Gallagher and staff at Four Courts Press in Dublin for their invaluable suggestions and expertise in publishing the text.

However, my most heartfelt thanks go to Blessed Josemaría Escrivá, founder of Opus Dei. He helped me more than anyone else to appreciate Luther's precious insights into the magnanimity of divine pardon in Christ. However, his life and teachings also brought me understand that God's unconditional pardon is not limited, as it were, to humans being sinners and God, in Christ, being their merciful Saviour. Christian experience of magnanimous divine pardon speaks fundamentally of the eternal Fatherhood of a God who wished, in the Incarnation of his eternally begotten Son, to convert us from being sinners into being his sons and daughters, heirs to eternal life. Besides, in taking the logic of the Incarnation to its ultimate consequences, he appreciated more than most the divine delicacy of putting a human face on his unconditioned pardon by administering it through the Church in the Sacrament of Reconciliation.

25 March 1997

Feastday of the Incarnation of God's Word
in the heart and womb
of the Blessed Virgin Mary.

PART ONE

Elements of the History of the Doctrine of Justification

CHAPTER ONE

Luther's contribution to the doctrine on justification

THE CENTRALITY OF JUSTIFICATION IN LUTHER'S DOCTRINE

Any debate on the theology of justification should by right begin with at least a summary presentation of the great variety of different understandings of this doctrine arisen throughout the history of Christianity. Those of Paul, Augustine, the predestinationist controversies of the ninth and tenth centuries, Thomas Aquinas, Duns Scotus, Ockham and the Nominalists, come particularly to mind.[1] The reason why Luther's doctrine is being considered first is because, in its various interpretations, it is situated at the very heart of the debate that concerns us; it constitutes the soul of the Protestant Reformation. For Luther himself, indeed, justification was the *articulus stantis et cadentis Ecclesiae* (he does not use this exact term),[2] the core article of Christian faith, without which Christianity would simply not be Christ's: *hoc amisso amittitur Christus*.[3]

And he is the one who put it on centre-stage. Not only was it important for him in the sense that by insisting on it he wished to correct what he perceived to be a gravely unbalanced understanding of the reality of sin and of pardoning grace common in the late medieval Church. He considered this doctrine, whose full description would be something like 'the justification of the sinner by faith alone', to be critically determinative of every single aspect of Christian faith and life: God, Christ, man, Church, sacraments, ethics etc. He said: 'This article can never be sufficiently considered and inculcated. If it is driven away, if it falls into ruin, all knowledge of truth is driven away, and falls into ruin. If it flourishes, all good things flourish: religion, true cult, the glory of God, sure knowledge of all situations and all things.'[4]

It should be added, however, that the doctrine of justification, in Luther's mind, may not be presented in a purely descriptive way; it is not simply a more important doctrine among others. In other words, he regards justification as the central article of Christian faith not only for its thematic content, but principally insofar as it acts as a kind of global criteriological principle which serves to interpret the entire gamut

---

1 For general surveys of this material, cf. for example, G.H. Tavard, *Justification: An Ecumenical Study*, New York 1983, pp. 5–48; A.E. McGrath, *Iustitia Dei. A History of the Christian Doctrine of Justification*, 2 vols, Cambridge 1986. 2 Even though Luther used an expression of this kind in some of his works (e.g. 'quia isto articulo stante stat Ecclesia, ruente ruit Ecclesia' *Exp. in Ps. 130*, 4 (1538): WA 40/3: 352), the exact formula is to be found in later authors: by the Protestant theologian J.H. Alsted in his *Theologia scholastica didacta*, Hannover 1618, p. 711, and by the Lutheran V.E. Löscher in his work against the Pietists, *Timotheus Verinus*, Wittenberg 1718. Cf. USA 27. 3 M. Luther, *Exp. in Ps. 130* (WA 40/3: 355). 4 Idem., *In ep. S. Pauli ad Galatas Comm.* (1531–35: WA 40/1: 39).

of doctrines and practices that go to make up the Christian whole: God's saving action, the reality and life of Jesus Christ, the practice and action of the Church, especially in its sacraments and preaching, Christian anthropology, spirituality and ethics, etc. And the point is that Luther's unshakable conviction that man (the sinner) is justified (or pardoned) by faith *alone*, that is *independently of* works, *critically determines* his very understanding of God, of Christ, of the Church, of Christian life. It expresses in a concise and unequivocal way the exact nature of the relationship between God and man. 'The proper subject of theology', he says, 'is man guilty of sin and condemned, and God the justifier and Saviour of man the sinner (*homo reus et perditus* and *Deus iustificans ac salvator*). Whatever is asked or discussed in theology outside this subject is error and poison'.[5]

Before presenting his doctrine on justification, two general observations could be usefully made, one methodological, the other historical.

1. Luther's point of departure in explaining justification is *God's nature and action as experienced by man*.[6] Everything begins and ends with God's free, merciful, gracious initiative, grasped and lived by man. *Sola experientia fit theologum*,[7] he said. In that sense, the reality of justification, for Luther, is simple, pure, lineal: God is the sun whose rays spill into the universe in uninhibited profusion, the sun in which man basks. Yet Luther's reflection, intensely human and personal, is by definition a conditioned and subjective one, though this need not be taken in a pejorative sense. His reflection is conditioned, that is, by the very one who experiences and receives the undeserved gift of justifying grace, the one whose being and thought and action is being renewed in this very moment by the God who justifies, yet who personally contributes nothing to being justified, and is, besides, though just, a sinner. The *subjectum theologiae* for Luther, is *homo peccator* and *Deus iustificans*, man the sinner and God the justifier.[8]

Any reflection made on the lineal and pure quality of Luther's understanding of the justification process/event, starting with God who gives everything and ending with the sinner who can only receive, must needs be tempered and modified critically by the awareness that it is man himself, within his sinfulness and remaining a sinner, who attempts to describe, in his own (sinful?) categories, the process he is undergoing and experiencing. Thus the following question must be kept in mind: does Luther's depiction of the justification process/event, in offering his reader a 'pure', unsullied description of God's saving action, transparently and faithfully express and reflect the relationship between God the Saviour and man the sinner, or does it in some way colour and distort the very reality it is attempting to describe?

---

5 Idem., *En. in Ps. 51* (WA 40/2: 328). On this critical text, cf. the analysis of G. Ebeling in chapter 5: pp. 161–168 and 203–205f.   6 In the words of G.H. Tavard, (*Justification . . .* , op. cit., p. 62) the focus used by Luther to throw light on all theological assertions is 'the experience of being justified by faith'.   7 WA *Tischreden* 1: 16 (1531).   8 Cf. *En. in Ps. 51* (WA 40/2: 328).

Of course the specificity and richness of Luther's personality is at issue here,[9] as is his peculiar theological method, centered on the *theologia crucis*.[10] For Luther, divine revelation and redemption are expressed definitively and defined exactly only in relation to the cross of Christ; they should not therefore be understood in purely rational and simplistic terms, as a *theologia gloriae*, but in a consistently apophatic way, that is, as an *opus sub contrario absconditum*.[11]

Perhaps the following rule of thumb may be of some use: 'Anyone wishing to study Luther would indeed be in no peril of going astray were he to follow this simple rule: never believe that you have a correct understanding of a thought of Luther before you have succeeded in reducing it to a simple corollary of the thought of forgiveness of sins'.[12]

2. Luther's own understanding of justification developed considerably during his lifetime.[13] Due to his schooling at Erfurt, in his early years he uncritically accepted the Pelagian-tinged teaching on grace of the Nominalist school (the so-called *via moderna*), thus coming under the influence of Gabriel Biel,[14] to some degree Gregory

---

9 For a rich pen-picture of Luther's personality, spirit and style, cf. G. Ebeling, *Martin Lutero. L'itinerario e il messaggio*, Torino 1988, pp. 78–88. 'Without his wanting it, [Luther's] person became the paradigm of his doctrine' (ibid., p. 82).   10 Cf. especially W. von Löwenich, *Luther's Theologia Crucis*, Witten 1967; J. Vercruysse, 'Luther's Theology of the Cross at the Time of the Heidelberg Disputation', in *Gregorianum* 57 (1976) 523–548; B. Gherardini, *Theologia crucis: l'eredità di Lutero nell'evoluzione teologica della Riforma*, Rome 1978; A.E. McGrath, *Luther's Theology of the Cross*, Oxford 1985; H. Blaumeiser, *Martin Luthers Kreuzestheologie: Schlüssel zu seiner Deutung von Mensch und Wirklichkeit*, Paderborn 1995. Luther's Christology is centered predominantly on the Cross of Christ as distinct from his Incarnation, hidden or public life and Resurrection (which of course are not excluded). Hence his theology is based on the notion that 'the sign does not represent reality by analogous and homogeneous expression, but instead stands in contrasting discrepancy with reality' (J. Wicks, 'Justification and Faith in Luther's Theology', in *Theological Studies* 44 (1983) 3–29, here p. 10). He considered the Incarnation as a hiding of God, and speaks of the '*sapientia incarnata ac per hoc abscondita*' (*Die Vorlesung über den Römerbrief*, 1515–16: WA 56: 237, on Rom 3:11). Luther's 'negative' definition of the theologian is well known: in the Heidelberg Disputation of 1518 (theses 19–20), he says: 'The one who beholds what is invisible of God (*invisibilia Dei*) through the perception of what is made is not rightly called a theologian, but rather the one who perceives what is visible of God, his back [cf. Ex 33:23], by beholding the sufferings and the cross (. . . *qui visibilia et posteriora Dei per passiones et crucem conspecta intelligit*)' (WA 1: 354). For Luther the *visibilia et posteriora Dei* are 'the very opposite of the invisible. They are the humanity, stupidity, madness and weakness of God' (ibid., p. 362). Leaving aside whether or not this antithesis between the visible and the invisible forms the structural principle of Luther's Christology (cf. T. Beer, 'La "theologia crucis" de Lutero', in *Scripta Theologica* 16 [1984] 747–780), it seems clear that the centrality of the *theologia crucis* makes the rôle of visible things in Revelation and salvation somewhat ambiguous.   11 M. Luther, *Dicata super Psalterium* (1513–16, on Ps 90: WA 4: 77).   12 E. Billing, *Our Calling*, Philadelphia 1964, p. 4.   13 Cf. A.E. McGrath, op. cit., vol. 2, pp. 3–20; J. Wicks, 'Justification and faith in Luther's Theology', op. cit.; G.H. Tavard, *Justification...* op. cit., pp. 49–69.   14 Cf. C. Feckes, *Die Rechtfertigungslehre des Gabriel Biel und ihre Stellung innerhalb der nominalistischen Schule*, Münster 1925; L. Grane, *Contra Gabrielem: Luthers Auseinandersetzung mit Gabriel Biel in der Disputatio contra scholasticam theologiam 1517*, Copenhagen 1962; H.A. Oberman, *The Harvest of Medieval Theology: Gabriel Biel and Late*

of Rimini,[15] and even of Eckhart, Tauler, Gerson and the German mystical school.[16] However, as he began to write and teach, Luther's understanding of theology and specifically of justification took on a consistent, established profile which he maintained for the rest of his life, virtually at the opposite extreme of what he had held at the beginning. Though many elements of his characteristic teaching are to be found in writings over the period 1514–1516 (*Lectures on the Psalter*, on *Romans*, on *Galatians*), his definitive position (expressed for example in his final *Commentary on Galatians* (1531/1535) which will be cited extensively in the coming pages) is already delineated for example, in his *Commentary on Galatians* (1519), his *Sermon on Good Works* (1520), the *Rationis Latomianae confutatio* (1521). Scholars disagree however as to the exact date of the radical change-about, and in spite of Luther's own references to a clearly dated Tower Experience, prefer to map a gradual evolution in his thought patterns.[17]

As a result the following observation may be made: Luther's turn-about is both

---

Medieval Nominalism, Cambridge, (Mass.) 1963; M. Santos-Noya, *Die Sünden- und Gnadenlehre des Gregor von Rimini*, Frankfurt a. M. 1990. Oberman holds that when Biel speaks positively of the aphorism *facienti quod est in se, Deus non denegat gratiam*, he may be referring to a purely natural action of the will (cf. ibid., p. 138). Others, such as H.J. McSorley ('Was Gabriel Biel a Semipelagian?', in L. Scheffczyk (ed.), *Wahrheit und Verkündigung (Festschrift M. Schmaus)*, Munich 1967, vol. 2, pp. 1109–1120) and W. Ernst (*Gott und Mensch am Vorabend der Reformation*, Leipzig 1972, pp. 310–320; 332 f.) tend to hold that Biel was Pelagian or semi-Pelagian. McGrath (*Iustitia Dei . . .* op. cit., vol. 1, pp. 76–78), reflecting on the pact theology of Biel, holds he should not be considered, strictly speaking, as Pelagian or semi-Pelagian (Massilian).   15 Cf. L. Grane, 'Gregor von Rimini und Luthers Leipziger Disputation', in *Scottish Journal of Theology* 22 (1968) 29–49. It would seem that Luther's knowledge of Gregory's ideas dates from 1519, that is, when the former's doctrine on justification was well established. Cf. M. Luther, *Resolutiones Lutherianae super propositionibus suis Lipsiae disputis* (WA 2: 394–396).   16 Several authors have identified elements of Luther's thought on justification in the teaching of the German Mystics, especially Tauler, e.g. A.V. Müller, *Luther und Tauler auf ihren theologischen Zusammenhang neu untersucht*, Berne 1918, p. 25. Tauler's discussion of human nature shows an anthropological pessimism not unlike Luther's: man is introverted, poisoned, fallen. The key difference lies however in the fact that salvation for Tauler 'is understood in terms of a direct, unbroken and unmediated mystical fellowship with God . . . Tauler's essentially neo-Platonist anthropological and theological presuppositions lead to his conceiving salvation in terms of a substantive union between God and man. Luther's insistence upon the exclusive location of all soteriological resources outside man stands in diametrical opposition to Tauler's concern to promote the *Seelengrund*, and Gerson's concern to enhance the soteriological possibilities of synderesis' (A.E. McGrath, op. cit., vol. 2, p. 20). cf. S.E. Ozment, *Homo spiritualis: a comparative study of the anthropology of Johannes Tauler, Jean Gerson and Martin Luther (1509–16) in the context of their theological thought*, Leiden 1969; M. Vannini, 'La teologia mistica', in G. Occhipinti (ed.), *Storia della Teologia, vol. 3: da Pietro Abelardo a Roberto Bellarmino*, Bologna 1996, pp. 263–290.   17 Luther himself, in a justly famous 1545 autobiographical fragment (*Preface to Latin works*: WA 54: 185), indicates that by 1519 his position was already firmly established. Yet an analysis of his lectures on the Psalter (1513–15), on Romans (1515–16) and on Galatians (1516–17), makes it clear that at this stage his theology of justification was definitely altered from the one he (said he) held beforehand.

rational (or at least reasoned), and historically conditioned.[18] This intellectual, spiritual and social 'localization' of his work is of considerable importance.

LUTHER'S UNDERSTANDING OF JUSTIFICATION

I shall attempt to present Luther's understanding of justification in three stages:[19] (1) his doctrine of God, fountain and basis of all justification, and Christ, in whom God's saving power and mercy is revealed and communicated; (2) his understanding of faith which *alone* justifies; (3) his understanding of the relationship between justification on the one hand, and sanctification and 'good works' on the other.

1. *God who justifies man in Jesus Christ*

'Iustitia Dei' The key issue of the nominalistic 'pact-theology' of the *via moderna* that characterized Luther's early training,[20] lies in its particular interpretation of the medieval axiom *facienti quod est in se est Deus non denegat gratiam*: 'God does not deny grace as long as man does his best'.[21] The understanding of this phrase com-

18 It was primordially a 'theological breakthrough' rather than a 'reforming discovery' (cf. A.E. McGrath, *Iustitia Dei* . . . op. cit., vol. 2, p. 9). 19 Bibliography among Protestants on Luther's doctrine of justification is very ample. Of particular interest and value are the following works: H.J. Iwand, *Rechtfertigungslehre und Christusglaube: eine Untersuchung zur Systematik der Rechtfertigungslehre Luthers in ihren Anfängen*, Munich 1966 (original 1930); M. Kröger, *Rechtfertigung und Gesetz: Studien zur Entwicklung der Rechtfertigungslehre beim jungen Luther*, Göttingen 1968; G. Ebeling, *Luther, Einführung in sein Denken*, Tübingen 1964 (English translation: *Luther: An Introduction to his Thought*, London 1970); V. Subilia, *La Giustificazione per Fede*, Brescia 1976; A. Peters, *Rechtfertigung*, Gütersloh 1984. Among studies by Catholic authors on Luther's doctrine of justification, cf. for example D. Belluci, *Fede e giustificazione in Lutero. Un esame teologico dei 'Dicta super Psalterium' e del Commentario sull'Epistola ai Romani (1513-1516)*, Rome 1963; A. Bellini, 'La giustificazione per la sola fede', in *Communio* (ed. it.) 38 (1978) 30–73; J. Wicks, 'Justification and Faith in Luther's Theology', in *Theological Studies* 44 (1983) 3–29; G.H. Tavard, *Justification* . . . op. cit., pp. 49–69; G. Bof, 'Giustificazione', in *Nuovo Dizionario di Teologia, Supplemento*, Cinisello Balsamo 1983, pp. 1992–2004; F. Buzzi, 'La teologia di Lutero nelle "Lezioni sulla lettera ai Romani" (1515–1516)', in *La Lettera ai Romani*, Cinisello Balsamo 1991, pp. 5–180; B. Gherardini, 'Articulus stantis et cadentis ecclesiae', in *Annales Theologici* 10 (1996) 109–117. 20 Cf. for example his *Dictata super Psalterium* (1513–15: WA 4: 262). For Luther's later rejection of the *via moderna*, cf. L. Grane, *Contra Gabrielem*. . ., op. cit., pp. 369–385. 21 On the Patristic interpretation of this axiom, cf. J. Rivière, 'Quelques antécédents patristiques de la formule: "facienti quod est in se" ', in *Revue de Sciences Réligieuses* 7 (1927) 93–97; G.H. Tavard, *Justification* . . . , op. cit., pp. 18 ff. Cf. also J. Trütsch, 'Facienti quod in se est Deus non denegat gratiam', in *Lexikon für Theologie und Kirche*, vol. 3 (1959), 1336 f.; A.M. Landgraf, *Dogmengeschichte der Frühscholastik, I/1: Die Gnadenlehre*, Regensburg 1952, pp. 249–264; H.A. Oberman, 'Facientibus quod est in se est Deus non denegat gratiam. Robert Holcot O.P. and the Beginnings of Luther's Theology', in *Harvard Theological Review* 55 (1962) 317–341; M. Flick and Z. Alszeghy, *Il vangelo della grazia*, Firenze 1964, pp. 236–242; A.E. McGrath, *Iustitia Dei* . . . , op. cit., vol. 1, pp. 83–91.

mon to Luther's time – one which Aquinas[22] and others might well have found unrecognizable – was essentially linked with a particular notion of *iustitia Dei*, God's justice or righteousness.

It was commonly held over this period that God is considered *just* insofar as he offers justifying grace or favour to those who have done what is in their power to do; by the same justice, he punishes those who do not do so. Thus the divine attribute of justice is expressed and exercised on the basis of the individual *possessing* a quality which God would be in some way 'obliged', in his equity and justice, to recognize and reward. However, since the Christian tangibly experiences spiritual weakness and ineptitude, he or she must at least offer to God this humiliation (*humilitas fidei*)[23] as a preconditioning token payment (*quod est in se*) necessary for justification. Such humility is a kind of *accusatio sui*, 'an active imitation of the humility of Christ',[24] performed without the assistance of grace as such. In fact Luther himself spoke in this way in his 1515–16 *Commentary on Romans*, holding that *humilatate et fide opus est*, 'both humility and faith are needful',[25] a position not out of keeping with the canons of the *via moderna*.[26]

However, the possible effects on spirituality and Christian life of this vision, certainly if taken to the letter, were patently and painfully obvious to Luther: in his better moments man would allow himself be filled with complacent and sterile self-contemplation, in his weaker periods, he would be devastated by scruples and a terrorized conscience in realizing he was not doing enough to deserve divine favour. Of the axiom *facienti quod est in se Deus non denegat gratiam* Luther commented in

22 Cf. Thomas Aquinas, *Summa Theologiae I-II*, q. 112, a.3. 'Cum dicitur homo facere quod in se est, dicitur hoc esse in potestate hominis secundum quod est motus a Deo' (ibid., q. 109, a. 6, ad 2). In earlier works (*II Sent.*, D. 28, q. 1, a. 4 and *De Veritate*, q. 14, a. 11, ad 1), the axiom is applied to man in the 'natural' state. For the medieval period interpretation of the axiom, cf. G.H. Tavard, *Justification* . . . , op. cit., pp. 36–48.   23 Cf. M. Luther, *Dicata super Psalterium* (WA 3: 588; 4: 127 & 231); *Die Vorlesung über den Römerbrief* (WA 56: 282). This linkup between justification and humility dates in Luther from 1513–14.   24 V. Subilia, *La Giustificazione per fede*, op. cit., p. 130. cf. M. Kröger, *Rechtfertigung und Gesetz* . . . , op. cit., pp. 38–62; J. Wicks, 'Justification and faith in Luther's Theology', op. cit., pp. 4ff.   25 M. Luther, *Die Vorlesung über den Römerbrief* (WA 56: 218).   26 In confirmation of this interpretation of Luther's early writings, cf. G. Miegge, *Lutero*, vol. 1, Torre Pellice 1946, p. 138; E. Bizer, *Fides ex auditu. Eine Untersuchung über die Entdeckung der Gerechtigkeit Gottes durch Martin Luther*, Neukirchen 1958; A. Gyllenkrok, *Rechtfertigung und Heiligung in der frühen evangelischen Theologie Luthers*, Uppsala 1952; H. Bornkamm, 'Zur Frage der "Iustitia Dei" beim jungen Luther', in *Archiv für Reformationsgeschichte* 52 (1961) 16–29; 53 (1962) 1–60. On particular works of Luther (principally earlier ones), cf. R. Prenter, *Der barmherizge Richter. Iustitia Dei passiva in Luthers 'Dictata super Psalterium' 1513–1515*, Copenhagen 1961; M. Lienhard, 'Christologie et humilité dans la "Theologia Crucis" du Commentaire de l'Epître aux Romains de Luther', in *Revue d'histoire et de philosophie religieuses* 42 (1962) 304–315. For a summary of the controversy on Luther's development cf. especially O.-H. Pesch, 'Neuere Beiträge zur Frage nach Luthers "Reformatorischer Wende" ', in *Catholica* 37 (1984) 66–133; V. Subilia, *La Giustificazione per Fede*, op. cit., pp. 129–134; F. Buzzi, 'La teologia di Lutero nelle Lezioni sulla lettera ai Romani. . .', op. cit., pp. 5–14.

1519: 'Whether they do what is in them or not, all should despair of themselves and put their trust only in God'.[27]

The turnabout lies in a radically new understanding of divine justice, which, according to Luther, not even Augustine had appreciated,[28] and is recounted by Luther himself in the following autobiographical sketch written the year before he died:

> I greatly longed to understand Paul's Epistle to the Romans and nothing stood in the way but that one expression, 'the justice of God' [Rom 1:17], because I took it to mean that justice whereby God is just and deals justly in punishing the unjust. My situation was that, although an impeccable monk, I stood before God as a sinner troubled in conscience, and I had no confidence that my merit would please him. Therefore I did not love a just and angry God, but rather hated and murmured against him. Yet I clung to the dear Paul and had a great yearning to know what he meant . . . Night and day I pondered until I saw the connection between the justice of God and the statement that 'the just shall live by faith' (Rom 1:17). Then I grasped that *the justice of God is that righteousness by which though grace and sheer mercy God justifies us through faith.* Thereupon I felt myself to be reborn and to have gone through open doors into paradise. The whole of Scripture took on a new meaning, and whereas before the 'justice of God' had filled me with hate, now it became to me inexpressibly sweet in greater love. The passage of Paul became a gate to heaven.[29]

Divine justice, he says, is 'that righteousness by which though grace and sheer mercy God justifies us through faith'. Leaving aside for the moment whether or not Luther's discovery is as momentous as he thinks it is,[30] the message resounds unequivocally: the Christian should not consider and confide in the *attribute* of divine justice (*iustitia Dei* in subjective genitive), against which he might *calibrate* his own justice and act accordingly, but rather the *action* of God justifying (*iustitia Dei* in objective genitive), the *iustitia qua nos Deus induit, dum nos iustificat.*

Righteousness or justice, in other words, is simply a gift from God which man accepts in faith, joy and gratitude, without any need for 'preliminary' or preparatory works. God *himself* meets the precondition that man cannot fulfill; in other words, *God* makes the sinner just.

---

27 M. Luther, *In ep. Pauli ad Galatas Comm.* (1519: WA 2: 539). And in 1518 at the Heidelberg Disputation (thesis 16, WA 1: 354), he said: 'The man who thinks he comes into grace by doing what is in his power, adds sin to sin, and becomes doubly a sinner'. 28 Cf. idem., WA Tischreden 2: 138 (1532). 29 Idem., *Preface to Latin Works* (1545: WA 54: 185 f.). Emphasis added. 30 H. Denifle, in a study on the use of Rom 1:16-17 by sixty doctors of the Western Church (*Die abendländischen Schriftausleger bis Luther über 'Iustitia Dei' [Röm I.17] und 'Iustificatio',* Mainz 1905), shows that not one of them, from Ambrosiaster onwards, understood the term *iustitia Dei* in the sense rejected by Luther.

The God who justifies the sinner   Completely transcending all beings, above any law, dominating the whole of creation, God is considered by Luther in fundamentally dynamic terms, as incessant activity, continual operation. 'If God must be represented', Luther states, 'then he should be depicted as the one who, in the abyss of his divine nature, is entirely fire and ardour, that is, love for humankind. Love as such is not a human thing, nor is it angelic, but divine; it is God himself.'[31] And elsewhere he says: 'Gottes natura est, quae omni dat et juvat. Si haec agnosco, habeo pro Deo vero . . . Hoc est esse Deum: non accipere bona sed dare.'[32] 'This is God's being, not to receive good things but to give them'.

In the words of Bellini, for Luther 'God's being is to act, to give and not to receive, insofar as God cannot be given anything that is not already his; his is to place wisdom where wisdom is not to be found, to put justice where there is no justice, . . . salvation where there is none . . .'[33] In such a context, it is easy to appreciate that any doctrine of justice and justification based on human works, on human action which might enter into competition and conflict with divine dynamism, is to be considered simply as idolatry,[34] as a denial of the divinity of God.

The inevitable corollaries of this doctrine are two: that human free will in any *active* or *contributive* sense is no longer meaningful in the religious sphere; and that justification is always a *justificatio impii*, a justification 'of the sinner' who, incapable of obtaining any justice for himself, remains perpetually in divine debt, truly a sinner in his own right. In his work *De servo arbitrio* Luther says: 'God's "turning" . . . is that most active working of God which a man cannot avoid or alter, but under which he necessarily has the kind of will that God has given him, and that God carries along, by his own momentum (*rapit suo motu*).'[35]

And in his final commentary on the Letter to the Galatians: 'we teach that all men are wicked, we condemn all free will (*liberum arbitrium*), human strength, wisdom and justice in man, all willful religion, and everything that is good in the world. In short, we say that there is absolutely nothing in us sufficient to merit grace and the remission of sins, but we preach that this grace and this pardon can be obtained by the pure, unique mercy of God alone.'[36]

Christology and justification   For Luther God's justifying action and Christ's are one and the same thing. Accordingly, in the same way as a 'justice of works' would compromise the justice of God (that is, God's justifying action) and constitute an act of idolatry, by the same token would it 'obscure the benefit of Christ',[37] imply that 'Christ is of no benefit',[38] and therefore 'make useless his death, his resurrec-

---

31 M. Luther, *Sermon no. 1*, 1532 (WA 36: 424).   32 Idem., WA 17/1: 233 & WA 4: 269.   33 A. Bellini, 'La giustificazione per la sola fede', op. cit., p. 34.   34 Cf. *In ep. S. Pauli ad Galatas Comm.* (1531–35: WA 40/1: 224) and *Exp. in Ps 130* (WA 40/3: 352).   35 M. Luther, *De Servo Arbitrio* (1525: WA 18: 747).   36 Idem., *In ep. S. Pauli ad Galatas Comm.* (1531–35: WA 40/1: 121).   37 M. Luther, *In ep. S. Pauli ad Galatas Comm.* (1531–35: WA 40/1: 252).   38 Ibid. (WA 40/1: 251).

tion, his victory, his glory, his kingdom, heaven, earth, God himself, his majesty and everything else.'[39]

More specifically it could be said that the righteousness of God, his active, self-donating, unconditional mercy towards the sinner, *is revealed and made present* in Christ, especially on the Cross. The reality and life of Christ *is* the power of God's grace *for us*; Christ's action and life is one and the same thing as God's out-going, justifying self-donation.[40]

Christ is God, undoubtedly, overflowing with all the treasures and wisdom of the divinity (cf. Col 2:3.9), but in a sense he is not only that: Christ is *Deus pro me*, God giving-himself-to-the-Christian, the tangible human manifestation and reality of God's mercy and enduring, personal love. In that sense it could be said that Luther's Christology is strictly *functional*, not metaphysical. Glossing Col 2:20, Luther calls Christ 'the Son of God who sacrificed himself for me and offered himself to God in sacrifice for miserable sinners like us, to sanctify us for all eternity; he [like God] did not do this on account of some merit or justice of ours, but out of pure mercy and love.'[41] Jesus 'is not a rent-collector or legislator, but *the one who gives grace*, the Saviour, the merciful one who is, no more and no less, pure and infinite mercy: *mercy given and mercy giving*.'[42]

In Christ therefore '*you will see the love, the goodness, the sweetness of God*; you will see the wisdom, the power and the majesty of the sweet God placed at your disposition.'[43] Thus Christ is 'the joy of man frightened and disturbed, he is sweetness itself, he is, as the luminous title given to him by Paul has it, the one who loves me and has sacrificed himself for me. In fact, Christ is the one who loves those who are in anguish, in sin and in death.'[44]

The life of a Christian is thus one of dynamic interchange or *admirabile commercium* between God and himself, centered on and made possible by the life and action of Christ the Saviour, God and man, who has become our justice before God.

2. *'Faith alone justifies'*

Faith, God's gift and work   When Luther speaks, as he does frequently, of faith *alone*, he is referring in the first place to the *exclusion of works*. He intends to warn Christians to avoid seeking, in the upright human actions they carry out, anything

---

39 Ibid. (WA 40/1: 307–308).   40 On Luther's Christology, cf. Y.M.-J. Congar, 'Regards et réflexions sur la christologie de Luther', in A. Grillmeier and H. Bacht, *Das Konzil von Chalkedon, Geschichte und Gegenwart*, vol. 3, Würzburg 1954, pp. 457–486; idem., *Martin Luther. Sa foi, sa réforme. Etudes de théologie historique*, Paris 1983, pp. 121–133; J.D.K. Siggins, *Martin Luther's Doctrine of Christ*, New Haven 1970; M. Lienhard, *Au coeur de la foi de Luther: Jésus Christ*, Paris 1991; G. Iammarrone, 'Gesù Cristo Riconciliatore e Redentore in Martin Lutero', in *Miscellanea Francescana* 96 (1996) 425–454.   41 M. Luther, *In ep. S. Pauli ad Galatas Comm.* (WA 40/1: 298).   42 Ibid.   43 Ibid. (WA 40/1: 79).   44 Ibid. (WA 40/1: 299).

that could smack of complacency and self-seeking, anything that might 'contribute' to their salvation or justification. But he is also very careful to point out that faith itself is not a 'work', which might in some way supplement God's saving power and our justification, but in every sense it is *God's own gift*, the only one capable of receiving or accepting justifying grace. Otherwise, it would be a work, a human contribution to God's grace. In fact, the innermost reality of faith pairs off perfectly with the sovereign action of God in Christ. For Luther faith is, in the words of Althaus, 'the only kind of human behaviour that corresponds to the essence of God, to his divinity'.[45] Faith is 'the specific manner in which the Word, and God with him, is present in man'.[46] 'God and faith always go together':[47] this formula, according to Ebeling, goes to the very core of Luther's theology. Faith is the exact correlate in man of the action of God who promises salvation through his Word, in such a way that 'where the promise of God is absent, so also is faith.'[48] *Fide accipitur promissio*.[49] Faith is defined and constituted by the divine word of promise.

Undoubtedly faith is experienced as an acceptance of and confidence in God's word, it implies an expecting from and an attribution of everything to God, praising him and giving him glory.[50] But the point is that *even the experience of this reality* in the life of the Christian is the fruit of divine grace, which man lives, or better, which man lives off and passively experiences. God, in other words, justifies man *in making him a believer*. In the words of Bellini, 'man of himself has nothing to place him in contact with God: he can only be taken by God in the manifestation of the power of his grace, allowing God to act, and grasping and holding on to what God has done for him. Faith is this *being taken by God*, allowing him to act.'[51]

Clearly therefore, faith according to Luther is on no account an autonomous 'human' act of knowing God in an objective fashion, the actualization of a kind of a latent 'faith register' in human nature, complementary to the 'natural' human access to God through the use of reason. Rather faith is simply to be *identified* with the personal *rapport* that results from God's justifying grace being received by man. It is not an action, so much as a passion (*leiden*).[52] According to Luther, 'faith is a work of God, not of man . . . Other faculties act with us and through us. Only this one acts in us but without us (*in nobis et sine nobis*).'[53]

---

45 P. Althaus, *Luther und die Rechtfertigung*, Darmstadt 1971, p. 24. Luther states: 'Si quidem haec duo, fides de Deus, una copula conjungenda sunt. Jam in quacunque re animi tui fiduciam et cor fixum habueris, haec haud dubio Deus tuus est' (*Der Große Katechismus I*, 3, cit. in *Bekenntnisschriften der evangelisch-lutherischen Kirche*, Göttingen 1967, p. 560).   46 P. Althaus, *Die Theologie Martin Luthers*, Gütersloh 1962, p. 52.   47 G. Ebeling, *Luther, Einführung in sein Denken*, Tübingen 1964, p. 288. cf. also R. Marlé, *Parler de Dieu aujourd'hui. La théologie herméneutique de G. Ebeling*, Paris 1975, pp. 88ff.   48 M. Luther, *Ein Sermon von dem Neuen Testament, das ist von der heilige Messe* (1520: WA 6: 363).   49 Idem., WA 39/2: 207. cf. O. Bayer, *Promissio. Geschichte der reformatorischen Wende in Luthers Theologie*, Göttingen 1971, p. 276.   50 Cf. M. Luther, *In ep. S. Pauli ad Galatas Comm.* (WA 40/1: 360); *Exp. in Ps 125* (WA 40/3: 154).   51 A. Bellini, op. cit., p. 45.   52 Cf. idem., *Enn. in Genesis* (1535—: WA 40/2: 452).   53 Idem., *De captivitate Babylonica Ecclesiae* (1520: WA 6: 530).

Faith as a psychological and subjective experience by which man finds himself saying 'yes' to God, exists, of course, but has no value whatever before God; 'God has nothing whatever to do with such faith'.[54] Instead, the nature and reality of man's faith response is determined entirely by God's essence and donating action, and can be encumbered or nullified only by self-complacency in one's own works. Faith is, in Luther's graphic expression, *creatrix divinitatis*, creator of the divinity, not of course within God himself, but in *us*;[55] faith is 'all-powerful, like God himself';[56] it produces a 'divinization' in us not unlike that present in the humanity of Christ.[57] And in order to believe, Luther insists time and again, man's only 'contribution' is to decisively exclude any other cognoscitive or volitive faculty as an *alternative* means of knowing or loving God.[58]

Perplexity arises, of course, in respect of what exactly faith produces in the believer: if the agent and object of faith is God himself, if faith does not really 'touch' or involve human reality and response, or so it might seem . . . what does it consist of *in man*? What can it respond to conceptually in him, what is its thematic content? How can it avoid sooner or later becoming a 'work'?

Luther's reply to this question must be vouched for in *christological* terms. Here in fact is to be found the core of Luther's intuition, the true understanding of his doctrine of the *admirabile commercium*,[59] according to which the sinner is at one and the same time really *united with Christ*, and *interchanged with him*. When Luther says that 'Christian justice consists of two elements, faith in the heart and imputation by God',[60] this must be taken in a Christological sense. Justice in the Christian consists of a real union with Christ, a belonging to him, an appropriation of his justice; yet the believer never comes to acquire or possess this justice, for it always remains a *iustitia aliena*. Let us examine the two elements (belonging to Christ, never possessing grace) one by one.

Union with Christ, 'inherent' justice   Faith produced by God in man directs the latter, as we saw, to *God's concrete word of promise*, and brings him to accept it and trust it. But since Christ is God's own saving and justifying Word proffered to man, faith is directed thematically towards him: justification is union with Christ, faith in Christ. In Luther's key phrase, commenting Rom 3:22,[61] 'righteousness is to believe in Jesus Christ', *iustitia est fides Jhesu Christi*, taken in the objective genitive sense.[62]

---

54 Idem., *Sermo no. 36* (1522: WA 10/3: 214).   55 Idem., *In ep. S. Pauli ad Galatas Comm.* (WA 40/1: 360).   56 Ibid. (WA 40/1: 229).   57 Cf. ibid. (WA 40/1: 366). 'In theology, faith is perpetually the divinity of works, and is so present in the works as the Divinity is in the humanity of Christ' (ibid., 417).   58 According to W. von Löwenich, *Theologia crucis . . .* , op. cit. (from the Italian translation, Bologna 1975, pp. 69–120).   59 Cf. M. Lienhard, *Au coeur de la foi de Luther: Jésus Christ*, op. cit.; T. Beer, *Der fröhliche Wechsel und Streit*, Einsiedeln 1980; R. Schwager, 'Die fröhliche Wechsel und Streit', in *Zeitschrift für katholische Theologie* 105 (1983) 27–66.   60 M. Luther, *In ep. S. Pauli ad Galatas Comm.* (WA 40/1: 364).   61 'The righteousness of faith through faith in Jesus Christ (διὰ πίστεως Ἰησου Χριστοῦ) for all who believe' (Rom 3:22).   62 M. Luther, *Die Vorlesung über den Römerbrief* (WA 56: 255; 298; 482); also *Die Glossen über den Römerbrief* (WA 57: 69).

Justification becomes a holding on to Christ, his person, his work, his very presence, or better, *being held onto and drawn along by Christ*,[63] for 'Christus . . . actuosissimus est in nobis'.[64] Righteousness received, says Luther,

> consists in doing nothing, in attempting nothing, in knowing nothing of law or works, but in knowing and believing in only one thing: *that Christ has gone to the Father's side* and is no longer to be seen; that he sits in the heavens at the right hand of the Father, not as a judge, but that by God *he has been made for us* wisdom, justice, sanctification and redemption; in short, he is our priest, who intercedes for us, who reigns over us and in us by grace.[65]

Faith, what Luther terms *fides Christi* (which at one and the same time means faith due to Christ, and the presence of Christ in the believer), has as its object this active interceding, protecting presence of Christ before God in our favour: *Christus apparuit vultui Dei pro nobis*.[66] 'Christian faith is not an idle quality', Luther says. 'If it is true faith it is a certain, sure trust of the heart and firm assent, in which Christ is apprehended, so that Christ is the object of faith, though not really the object but rather, so to speak, Christ is present in faith itself. Faith is therefore a certain knowledge or darkness which sees nothing, and yet in this darkness Christ, apprehended in faith, sits, as God at Sinai and in the temple sat in the midst of darkness.'[67]

The Christian's true dignity consists in having faith: 'On account of this gift [of faith], the Christian is greater than the whole world . . . [faith is] a gift small in appearance, yet the very smallness of the gift which [the Christian] has in faith is greater than the heavens and the earth, for Christ is greater, Christ who himself is this very gift.'[68]

Living under the veil of Christ: 'imputed' justice Faith, though consisting of and producing an intimate union with Christ and a real belonging to him, lays hold of a righteousness which never comes *under the dominion*, as it were, of the human person, for it always remains a *iustitia Christi aliena*. Man's new-found dignity as a Christian, as a believer, though stable, is perpetually 'on loan'. This is the other side of the Christian's justified state: 'imputation by God'.[69] Faith as we saw is certainly a *fides apprehensiva*, a faith which seizes Christ and holds him fast.[70] Thus man is justified not so much on account of his faith (*propter fidem*), but on account of Christ

---

63 On the essentially Christocentric nature of faith in Luther, cf. D. Olivier, *La Foi de Luther*, Paris 1978. 64 M. Luther, *Sermo die S. Matthiae* (1517: WA 1: 140). cf. J. Wicks, 'Justification and faith in Luther's Theology', op. cit., pp. 13f. On the actuality of Christ in the new life of the believer, cf. W. Joest, *Ontologie der Person bei Luther*, Göttingen 1967, especially pp. 365–391. 65 M. Luther, *In ep. S. Pauli ad Galatas Comm.* (WA 40/1: 47). Emphasis added. 66 Idem., *Die Scholien über den Römerbrief* (WA 57: 215). 67 Idem., *In ep. S. Pauli ad Galatas Comm.* (WA 40/1: 228f.). 68 Ibid. (WA 40/1: 235 f.). Emphasis added. 69 Ibid. (WA 40/1: 364). 70 Cf. idem., *Thesen de fide* (1535: WA 39/1: 44 f.).

(*propter Christum*): the believer holds *Christ* fast in faith.[71] But of course, since Christ is *Deus pro me*, Christian faith in his saving action can never be expressed as dominion, as possession; it can never be expressed *coram Deo* as an 'autonomous' human action, for man is just in God's eyes exclusively on account of his beloved Son. The following text from Luther's major commentary on Galatians offers a synthetic view of his understanding:

> Christian justice should be properly and accurately defined as trust (*fiducia*) in the Son of God, or trust in the heart of God through Christ. Here one should add this specific note: this faith is imputed as justice for the sake of Christ. *These two elements*, as I have said, make Christian justice perfect: one, faith (*fides*) itself in the heart, which is a gift divinely given and formally believes in God; the other, that *God considers this imperfect faith to be perfect faith for the sake of Christ*, his Son, who suffered for the sins of the world, in whom I have begun to believe. And *for the sake of this faith in Christ, God does not see the sin which is still left in me* . . . And imputation does this for the sake of the faith by which I have begun to apprehend Christ, *for whose sake God considers imperfect justice to be perfect justice*, and sin not to be sin although it is truly sin. Thus *we live under the veil of the flesh of Christ*.[72]

In approximate terms, it could be said that *Christ becomes ours by taking our place before the Father*, in such a way that the two elements of our relationship with Christ (being united with him, being accounted for or protected by him) relate to one another dialectically yet inseparably. If we were not intimately united with him, his intercession for us would be meaningless and the doctrine of imputed justice mere extrinsicism. Conversely if our justice were our very own and not received and imputed, we would not be united with him, but simply with ourselves. This dialectic is at the very heart of Luther's spiritual and theological vision.

3. *Justification, sanctification and the value of 'works'*

'Solus Deus', 'sola gratia', 'solus Christus', 'sola fides': four concepts that come to mean the same thing for Luther: 'solus Deus', for God alone makes man just; 'sola gratia', *only God* gives man justice, and he does so as an *unmerited* gift, without works; 'solus Christus', the gift is *God's alone* and his *giving of it* is identified with the life and action of Jesus Christ; 'sola fides', even man's *acceptance* of that gift is exclusively God's work in him, not the synergistic confluence of God's work and man's.[73]

---

71 'The Christ who is grasped by faith and lives in the heart is true Christian righteousness, on account of which God counts us righteous and grants us eternal life' idem., *In ep. S. Pauli ad Galatas Comm.* (WA 40/1: 229).   72 Ibid. (WA 40/1: 366f.).   73 G. Ebeling states: 'The "alone" [Luther] continually adds [grace alone, faith alone, Christ alone] takes on a fundamental theologi-

In such a context, of course, the question must needs arise as to the meaningfulness of the doctrine of justification in human life. Does justification really make a difference? Does it effect any transformation of man's being and activity? Does it not involve any human contribution or cooperation in its genesis and development? We shall examine the question under three headings: 1. The extrinsic character of justification; 2. Justification, works and concupiscence; 3. Justification, conversion and sanctification.

The extrinsic character of justification   Luther states repeatedly that justification is entirely *extra nos*; in its origin and formality it is a *iustitia aliena*, completely on God's side. *Ubi sapientia, ubi iustitia, ubi veritas . . . ? non in nobis, sed in Christo, extra nos in Deo*,[74] he exclaims. According to Luther man cannot love God as such; to 'love' God would only be possible in the sense that we could *recognize* the goodness or lovableness of God,[75] not that we could conceivably offer him something in return for his gifts, which he had not given us in the first place. Grace in man is simply 'God's favour, but not a quality of the soul';[76] it is simply the act by which God pardons our sins by not taking them into consideration[77] on account of Christ whose justice has redeemed us: *justitia nostra nihil aliud est quam reputatio Dei*.[78] In other words man is righteous with a righteousness that is not won by his own strength or merit. Man's true being, his 'being Christian', in God's sight, is literally an 'extasis'; it exists outside of himself, of his freedom, of his human reality.[79]

Yet for Luther, paradoxically, the fact that man attains fullness and perfection only *outside himself*, is, at one and the same time his true life, his authentic life, *his own life*. Man redeemed by Christ is, as it were, greater than himself. Again Luther understands this true (justified, redeemed) state of man in Christological terms. Man lives *in Christ*, says Luther, paraphrasing Paul's 'It is no longer I who live but Christ who lives in me' (Gal 2:20); or more correctly, Christ lives in him: Christ's life in man is the man's true life.

> When he [Paul] says: 'Now I live', some kind of personal resonance may be detected, as if Paul was speaking of his own person. But immediately he rectifies, saying 'but it is no longer I', that is, it is no longer I who live in my own person, but 'it is Christ who lives in me'. The person lives on, undoubtedly, but

cal significance, that is, that in everything that is said about God, it must be remembered that *it is God who speaks . . .* and whatever does not let God be God must be excluded' (G. Ebeling, *Luther, Einführung in sein Denken . . .*, op. cit., p. 285).   74 M. Luther, *Sermo die S. Matthiae* (WA 1: 139). 75 'Altius ascendam et dicam, amare ejus modi semper iniquum esse, dum fuerit in seipso, nec esse bonum nisi extra seipsum sit in Deo' (*In ep. S. Pauli ad Galatas Comm.*, 1519: WA 2: 581).   76 Idem., *Rationis Latomianae confutatio* (1521: WA 8: 106).   77 '. . . quia justitia nostra divina est ignorantia, remissio gratuita peccatorum nostrorum' (*Exp. in Ps 130*: WA 40/3: 350). 78 Idem., *Vorlesung über Iesaias* (1527–30: WA 31/2: 439).   79 'I attribute everything to God, nothing to men . . . It is true that the doctrine of the Gospel takes away from man all glory, all wisdom, all justice, etc., attributing them to the Creator alone' (*In ep. S. Pauli ad Galatas Comm.*: WA 40/1: 131f.).

not in himself, or in his quality of being a person. So, who is this 'I' of whom it is said 'it is no longer I who live'? This 'I' is the one who has the law and which must do good works: in some sense it is the person separated from Christ. Paul rejects this 'I' as a person distinct from Christ and belonging to death and hell. This is why he says: 'It is not I who live, but Christ who lives in me', *Christ* who is for me like the *form who adorns my faith*, like the colour and the light adorn the wall ... Christ, he says, attached to me, cemented to me, abiding in me, lives in me the life which I lead; and not only that: the life that I live, as such, is Christ himself.[80]

The concrete life that the individual lives is but apparent, for under it 'there lives another, Christ, who is truly my life. You do not see it, but you hear it, as you hear the wind blowing, but you do not know whence it comes or whither it goes [cfr. Jn 3:8]. And so you see me speaking, eating, acting, sleeping, and yet you do not see my life, because this time of life which I live, I live it undoubtedly in the flesh, but I do not live it as coming from the flesh nor according to the flesh, but in faith, on the basis of faith and according to faith.'[81]

The logic of the Incarnation, the *admirabile commercium* between God and man, is repeated in the case of the individual believer: *qui credit in Christum, evacuatur a se ipso.*[82] In the words of Wolf, 'Christ himself is the person of the new man'.[83] 'What Christ has lived is mine, what he has worked, said, suffered, died, as if I had lived it, had worked it, had said it, had suffered it, as if I had died.'[84]

Man, in believing, forms a unity with Christ; between Christ and the believer there is an *inhaerentia*, a *conglutinatio*, an *inhaesio*[85] in such a way that they become 'one person that cannot be divided', they 'form one single flesh'.[86] Justification takes place in that very transplant or transfer. Hence the justice of God and of Christ are present 'in my person and in my substance', the justice 'by which Christ lives in us, not that which would be present in our person'.[87] Justice is present in us, but never becomes part of our being and our action, in such a way that we could cherish and admire it in ourselves as our own possession. Only in faith can we contemplate the justice of God in us, and faith is not in man nor from man, but is referred exclusively to God and Christ, and to the acceptance of the divine promise. Hence righteousness in man is, as it were, extrinsic (*aliena*) and attributed (*imputata*);[88] it is not a personal possession over which man retains disposition, it is not a way of being or of acting that belongs to the human person, nor a quality or intrinsic form of man's being.[89]

'You are just, you are holy from without', Luther states. 'You are just by mercy

---

80 Ibid. (WA 40/1: 283). Emphasis added.   81 Ibid., 288.   82 Idem., *In ep. S. Pauli ad Galatas Comm.* (1519: WA 2: 564).   83 E. Wolf, 'Die Rechtfertigungslehre als Mitte und Grenze reformatischer Theologie' (1949), in *Pereginatio*, vol. 2, Munich 1965, pp. 11–21 (here p. 16).   84 M. Luther, *Serm. de duplici iustitia* (1519: WA 2: 145).   85 Cf. idem., *In ep. S. Pauli ad Galatas Comm.* (1531–35: WA 40/1: 283f.).   86 Ibid., 285 f.   87 Ibid., 282.   88 Cf. ibid., 370f.   89 'The Christian quality is not a form that inheres' (ibid., 225); 'it is not a form that inheres in the heart' (ibid.); 'it is not an infused quality' (ibid., 370).

and pardon. This is not a *habitus* of mine, nor a *qualitas* of my heart, but we know that our sin has been remitted from outside, that is, by divine mercy, and that we live in his mercy and in his abundant and great pardon.'[90] 'When we speak of Christian justification, we must put the person completely aside. In fact, if I stay with or speak of the person, it becomes, whether I like it or not, a doer of works (*operarius*), subject to the law.'[91].

Traditional Lutheran insistence on the extrinsic (forensic or declarative) character of justification intends above all to emphasize the gratuitousness and transcendence of grace, in the face the danger of Christians developing a self-contemplating complacency in respect of their good works or talents or achievements, and, as a result, of their falling into despair under the assault of a troubled conscience, seeing themselves unable to achieve everything they consider they must.

However, Luther's pastoral and spiritual problem soon became a theological one. The antagonism between 'extrinsicism' and 'intrinsicism' in the domain of grace and justification became, from Luther's time onwards, the principal contentious issue dividing Lutherans and Catholics, fuelling considerable mistrust and a wide variety of misunderstandings on both sides. We will come to the historical development of the issue in the next chapter. Suffice it to say for the moment that *for Luther himself* the emphasis on the 'extrinsic' quality of justification, on the justice of Christ as a *iustitia aliena* meant neither:

— that the concrete moral actions of Christians are indifferent to justification or grace, as some of his more enthusiastic antinomistic followers (the *Schwärmer*) held,

— nor that man was not sanctified or transformed by justifying grace.

We shall briefly examine these two issues (ethical responsibility, and the link-up between justification and sanctification) in the following sections.

Justification, works and concupiscence   Luther insisted to such a degree that works were useless and worse than useless for being saved (faith alone is sufficient) that in some of his writings he went as far as to say that man does nothing else but sin in everything he does, and in others quite the opposite: that the Christian cannot actually sin no matter how he behaves.

1. In his *Commentary on Romans* (1515–16) he claimed that 'everyone without faith, even if he behaves well, sins . . . not because he acts against his conscience, but because he does not act out of faith: that is why he sins . . . because the defect of faith always remains'.[92] In the 1517 *Disputation against Scholastic Theology* he taught that the unjustified can only will and perform evil.[93] In the *Heidelberg disputation* the following year he said openly that 'free will after sin is a mere title (*res est de solo*

---

90 M. Luther, *Enn. in Ps.* 2 (1532-: WA 40/2: 253).   91 M. Luther, *In ep. S. Pauli ad Galatas Comm.* (WA 40/1: 282).   92 Idem., *Die Vorlesung über den Römerbrief* (WA 56: 237).   93 Idem., *Disputatio contra theologia scholastica*, thesis 4 (1517: WA 1: 224). This work was directed in fact against the theology of G. Biel, not against all Scholastic theologies.

titulo), and when it does what is in its power, it sins mortally.'[94] This position seems
to be even more radical and entrenched in his 1525 anti-Erasmian work *De Servo
Arbitrio* which seems to teach that God himself is the author of sin: *Deus operatur et
mala opera in impiis.*[95]

2. In writings of the same period, strangely enough, Luther also states that the
Christian cannot sin no matter how he behaves. In his 1520 work *On the Babylonian
Captivity*, for example, he affirmed that one baptized, even if he sins, cannot lose
grace as long as he does not renounce faith.[96] Some years later, in the *Smalcald
Articles* (1537), he clarified his position, rejecting the mistaken interpretation the
Schwärmer gave to his words: 'once the Spirit and the pardon of sins has been re-
ceived, or once one had become a believer, one perseveres in the faith even when
sinning afterwards, in such a way that such a sin harms them no longer'.[97]

In spite of these clarifications, the impression does linger in some of his writings
that concrete sin is no longer possible or meaningful, and, understandably, the teaching was taken up at the Council of Trent in its 1547 decree on justification, and
rejected.[98]

This paradoxical and at times contradictory way of speaking about sin and grace,
very characteristic of Luther, must be understood in its context. In fact it reflects a
living or existential dialectic at the very heart of his teachings, that may be expressed
succinctly in his famous phrases *pecca, et pecca fortiter* and, in particular, *homo simul
iustus et peccator*. It brings us to reflect on a decisive aspect of Luther's anthropology, according to which he considers man's sinfulness (or *concupiscentia*) as inherent, intrinsic, unhealable; sin is what most authentically defines man 'on his own'.[99]
'What then is original sin?', he asked. 'According to the subtleties of the scholastic
theologians, it is the privation or lack of original justice . . . But according to the
Apostle and the simplicity of Christian discourse, it is the privation, total, complete
and universal of the rectitude and of the power for good in all the energies of body
and soul, in the whole of man, interior and exterior.'[100]

In man there is a *peccatum in substantia*, a radical sin, *cordis peccatum occultissi-
mum*,[101] 'a complexive corruption of nature in all its members'[102] which makes man
a thorough-going egoist, continually turned in on himself, or as Luther says, *cor
incurvatum in seipsum*.[103] This deeply rooted sinful infection (one might say, what is
most authentic to man *on his own*) is not pure weakness or sensuality; nor is it the final
outcome of a dissolute life. Man is constitutionally a sinner, in such a way that,
faciens quod est in se, he sins, and sins gravely.

94 Idem., *Heidelberg Disputation*, thesis 13 (WA 1: 354).   95 Idem., *De Servo Arbitrio* (WA 18:
709).   96 Cf. idem., *De captivitate Babylonica Ecclesiae* (WA 6: 529).   97 Cf. idem., *Artic.
Smalcaldae III*, 3 (1537–8: WA 50: 225f.). cf. USA 41; 61.   98 Cf. DH 1540; 1573.   99 Cf. M.
Luther, *Heidelberg Disputation* (WA 1: 374); *Dicata super Psalterium: Ps CVI* (WA 4:
207).   100 Idem., *Die Vorlesung über den Römerbrief* (WA 56: 312f.).   101 Idem., *Rationis
Latomianae confutatio* (WA 8: 105).   102 Ibid., 104.   103 *In ep. S. Pauli ad Galatas Comm.* (WA
40/1: 282). Cf. idem., *Die Vorlesung über den Römerbrief* (WA 56: 305; 325).

'Before everything else', Luther says, 'man loves himself, he seeks himself in everything he does, loves everything for himself, even when he loves a neighbour or friend, because in the other he seeks only the things that concern him.'[104] Even man's 'love for God' is perverted and self-seeking: 'our nature by the effect of the first sin, is so deeply folded in on itself (*in seipsam incurva*), that not only does it twist towards itself the best of God's gifts drawing advantage from them . . . but it uses God himself to obtain those gifts, and is unaware it is seeking all things, even God, for himself, in a manner so iniquitous, tortuous and perverse.'[105] 'To love God for his gifts and for self-comfort is to love him with depraved love, that is, by concupiscence. This means using God, not taking our complacency in him.'[106]

Luther's understanding of course is not merely the result of observation, whether of his own or of others' experience. He considers his discovery to be an entirely Christian and theological one: man is truly a sinner *in God's sight* insofar as he instinctively seeks to be justified on the basis of his own resources. He is constituted *coram Deo*, that is theologically – not just anthropologically, in relation to himself and others – in terms of a living opposition between *caro* and *spiritus*, between flesh and spirit, understood in the Pauline sense: *homo simul et spiritus et caro.*[107]

Caro is the fleshly, sensual, worldly side of man, what man is *outside* of Christ, while *spiritus* represents man's higher nature, oriented towards God, that is, insofar as he lives in Christ by faith and is moved by his Spirit through the preached word. 'Flesh' means justice, profane wisdom and the thoughts of the mind, all of which wish to be justified by the law. Paul calls 'flesh' everything that is best and most excellent in man, that is, 'the supreme wisdom of reason and the very justice of the law.'[108] 'Flesh' 'is not only the sensual man with his concupiscences etc., but in general everything that is outside the grace of Christ . . . *Hence all justice and wisdom that is outside grace is flesh and carnal.'*[109]

This living hostility, interwoven into human existence, remains in the whole man (*totus homo*) who thus remains subject to a double servitude,[110] one towards God, the other towards sin, and is therefore *simul iustus et peccator.*[111] And this seemingly tragic situation of constitutional tension cannot be healed or cancelled even by Baptism.

---

104 M. Luther, *Die Vorlesung über den Römerbrief* (WA 56: 482).   105 Ibid., 304.   106 Ibid., 307.
107 Ibid., 350. cf. V. Subilia, op. cit., pp. 141f.; E. Schott, *Fleisch und Geist nach Luthers Lehre unter besonderer Berücksichtigung des Begriffs 'totus homo'*, Leipzig 1928; P. Althaus, *Die Theologie Martin Luthers . . .*, op. cit., pp. 138ff.; G. Ebeling, 'Disputatio de homine', in *Lutherstudien*, vol. 2, Tübingen 1977 ff. cf. also H.-M. Barth, 'L'uomo secondo Martin Lutero. Alcune osservazioni sulla 'Disputatio de Homine' (1536)', in *Studi Ecumenici* 1 (1983) 209–228; and M. Cassese, 'L'uomo nuovo e le buone opere secondo Martin Lutero', in ibid., pp. 247–276.   108 Idem., *In ep. S. Pauli ad Galatas Comm.* (WA 40/1: 347).   109 Idem., *Die Glossen über den Römerbrief* (WA 57: 77). Emphasis added.   110 Cf. idem., *Die Vorlesung über den Römerbrief* (WA 56: 347).   111 Cf. ibid. (WA 56: 270; 272; 343; 351). On Luther's doctrine of *simul iustus et peccator*, cf. R. Hermann, *Luthers These 'Gerecht und Sünder zugleich'*, Gütersloh 1960; R. Kösters, 'Luthers These "Gerecht und Sünder zugleich" ', in *Catholica* 33 (1964) 48–77. According to Joest, 'the *simul* is not the equilibrium of two mutually limiting partial aspects but the battleground of two mutually exclu-

Justification, conversion and sanctification However, according to Luther, such sinfulness is truly *covered* over by God's justice, displaced and destroyed by Christ's living in man, taking his place, acting in his stead. Due to Baptism, sin remains, but as a *peccatum regnatum*, no longer a *peccatum regnans*,[112] it is 'a sin without anger, without the law, a dead sin, a harmless sin'. The Christian therefore is a perpetual penitent: *semper peccator, semper penitens, semper iustus*,[113] is always turning back to Christ, is always beginning afresh, *semper a novo incipere*.[114]

Yet the Christ we carry within us moves us to live a new life, and in doing so we are gradually healed, or sanctified. 'In fact he who believes in Christ', says Luther, 'is just, not fully as yet, but in hope (*nondum plene in re sed in spe*). He has begun to be just and to be healed (*sanari*) . . . In fact God is the one who justifies and heals.'[115]

God's gift in us, as it gradually works out our sanctification, is entirely the fruit of 'first justice', the justice God attributes to us in Christ, 'its fruit and outcome'.[116] Yet this healing power must always be attributed to Christ, at least in the sense that the believer must exclude any security based on the work of justification being carried out in his own life (sanctification).[117] Works, therefore, must be considered simply as *the necessary and passive fruits of righteousness*. H.J. Iwand explains that

> Luther defends himself on two fronts: on that of the *extra nos*, that of Christ against the transferal to the person of values obtained by grace, and on that of the *in nobis*, against the destruction of the unity of being between God and man through the interposition of moral concepts. With the former man is held from calling himself just without reference to God, with the latter from calling himself just without reference to himself. With the former, the unity of value is based on Christ, with the latter, it is based on the unity of being. In fact God

sive totalities. It is not the case that a no-longer-entirely sinner and a not-yet-completely-righteous one can be pasted together in a psychologically conceivable mixture; it is rather that real and complete righteousness stands over real and total sin . . . The Christian is not half free and half bound, but slave and free at once, not half saint, but sinner and saint at once, not half alive, but dead and alive at once, not a mixture but a gaping opposition of antitheses.' (W. Joest, *Gesetz und Freiheit: Das Problem des tertius usus legis bei Luther und neutestamentliche Paränese*, Göttingen 1956, p. 58). 112 Cf. M. Luther, *Rationis Latomianae confutatio* (WA 8: 96). The link-up established by Luther between the concepts of *peccatum regnans* and *peccatum regnatum*, on the one hand, and consent and non-consent to sin, on the other, is highly significant. 113 Idem., *Die Vorlesung über den Römerbrief* (WA 56: 442); cf. *Rationis Latomianae confutatio* (WA 8: 109). 114 Idem., *Die Vorlesung über den Römerbrief* (WA 56: 259). 115 Idem., *Disputatio Johannis Eccii et Martin Lutheri Lipsiae habita* (1519: WA 2: 249). 116 Idem., *Rationis Latomianae confutatio* (WA 8: 107). cf. E. Iserloh, '*Gratia et donum*, giustificazione e santificazione secondo lo scritto di Lutero contro il teologo lovaniense Latomus (1521)', in Various authors, *Lutero e la riforma. Contributi a una comprensione ecumenica*, Brescia 1977, pp. 129–153. On the link-up between justification and sanctification, cf. J. Lutz, *Unio und Communio. Zum Verhältnis von Rechtfertigungslehre und Kirchenverständnis bei Martin Luther. Eine Untersuchung zu ekklesiologisch relevanten Texten der Jahre 1519–1528*, Paderborn 1990. 117 Cf. ibid., p. 111.

has made man just in Christ; hence, whoever believes in Christ cannot call God just if he does not call himself just.[118]

In sum, one could say that the performance of concrete 'good works' is by no means in an ambivalent or conflictive relationship with grace; rather, such works are purely and simply the fruit and natural/necessary outcome of grace and faith;[119] in Luther's words, such works 'reveal salvation'. 'If works do not follow [faith], it is certain that this faith of Christ does not reside in our heart, but is dead . . . Works are necessary for salvation, but do not cause salvation, because only faith gives life . . . Works are a necessary effect in the Christian, who is already saved in faith and hope, and nonetheless tend in this hope to reveal salvation (*ad salutem revelandam*).'[120]

Luther spoke in fact of two dimensions to justification, 'one of faith before God, the other of works before the world',[121] understanding the latter (works) as an exterior and necessary confirmation or demonstration of the former (faith). Likewise he distinguished between abstract faith and living faith,[122] and paired off the relationship between faith and works with that obtaining between the divinity of Christ and his humanity.[123] He even went so far as to speak of faith 'growing fat' by works as it makes its presence felt in man's life.[124] Luther states that 'works save us externally, that is, they testify to our being just and that faith, which is what saves from within, is present in man . . . External salvation shows up the good tree, as its fruit; it shows there is faith.'[125]

In some of his writings, Luther even waxed eloquent on the need to perform good works, clarifying however their true theological value and measure: 'When I have this righteousness within me, I descend from heaven like the rain that makes the earth fertile. That is, I come forth into another kingdom, and I perform good works whenever the opportunity arises.'[126]

The rôle of works as a sign and fruit of justifying grace may be clarified further by noting that, for Luther, Pauline 'conversion' or *metanoia* does not mean so much a turning away from evil actions, but rather a complete change of mind and attitude.

---

118 H.J. Iwand, *Rechtfertigungslehre und Christusglaube: eine Untersuchung zur Systematik der Rechtfertigungslehre Luthers in ihren Anfängen* . . . , op. cit., p. 37.   119 Cf. M. Luther, *Disputatio de fide infusa et acquista* (1520: WA 6: 94). On the continuity between faith and works in Luther, cf. P. Manns, 'Absolute and Incarnate Faith: Luther on Justification in the Galatians' Commentary of 1531–1535', in J. Wicks (ed.), *Catholic Scholars Dialogue with Luther*, Chicago 1970, pp. 121–156; G. Ebeling, *Luther. Einführung in sein Denken* . . . , op. cit., pp. 177–197.   120 M. Luther, *Thesen de fide*, no. 30 (WA 39/1: 44); *Die Disputation de iustificatione* (1536: WA 39/1: 96); *Die Promotionsdisputation von Palladius und Tileman* (1537: WA 39/1: 254).   121 Idem., *Die Promotionsdisputation* . . . , op. cit. (WA 39/1: 208).   122 He contrasted *fides abstracta vel absoluta* (without works) with *fides concreta, composita seu incarnata* (active in good works), giving value to good works done in faith: cf. *In ep. S. Pauli ad Galatas Comm.* (WA 40/1: 414–416). cf. J. Wicks, 'Justification and Faith in Luther's Theology', op. cit., p. 25.   123 Cf. P. Manns, 'Absolute and Incarnate Faith: Luther on Justification in the Galatians' Commentary of 1531–1535', op. cit.   124 M. Luther, *De loco iustificationis* (1530: WA 30/2: 659).   125 Idem., *In ep. S. Pauli ad Galatas Comm.* (WA 40/1: 96).   126 Ibid. (WA 40/1: 51).

Μετανοῆτε, which literally means 'after the mind', can also be taken, and was done so by Luther, as *trans-mentem*. Christian conversion therefore came to mean for him a *transmutatio mentis: mentem et sensum alium induite*,[127] to 'put on another mind and meaning', to see things the other way round.[128]

And he claims that 'this is the reason why our theology is certain: because it takes us out of ourselves and places us outside ourselves, in such a way that we do not confide in our strength, in our conscience, in sentiment, in the person, in our works, but we confide in what is outside ourselves, that is the promise and the truth of God, who cannot deceive.'[129]

What remains quite clear is that, whether justified or not, man for Luther must never cast a complacent side-glance at his own works, seeking assurance in his heart that he has in some ways crossed the 'favour barrier' between himself and his Creator. In God's sight he always remains a creature and sinner. In fact, it is fair to say that Luther did not wish as such to 'fight against works . . . but against the *present-ability* of works before God.'[130]

Catholics, of course, would be happy enough with much of that. But the fact remains that however much emphasis Luther places on sanctification as a necessary follow-up to justification, and on good works as the inevitable fruit of salvation, it is hard to shake off the impression that human reality (what Luther terms 'the person'), in its stable ontological consistence (reason, will, freedom, faculties), is simply left out of the picture. Man *himself* is not really freed by grace; he simply appropriates the *iustitia Christi aliena*, partaking of Christ's life.

Thus God justifies, God sanctifies, and he does so dynamically or 'actualistically' and directly, taking over in Christ the reins, as it were, of human reality; 'good works' seem to be little more than 'works of Christ's Spirit in man'. The topic will come up again later on.[131] Yet for the time being, Bellini's observation on the matter is pertinent:

> When the Reform affirms that sanctification follows on necessarily from justification, or, as Calvin teaches explicitly, that sanctification is a part of justification, in such a way that the latter cannot be said to exist without the former, it does not intend to speak of a sanctification of man in his being, an *ontological sanctification*, as Catholic theology would hold, but rather a *moral sanctification*. In other

127 Cf. M. Luther, *Resolutiones Disputationum et indulgentiarum virtute* (1516: WA 1: 525; 526; 530). **128** Here Luther sees a link-up between Christ's calls to repent (Mt 4:17, Mk 1:15) and the Pauline texts Rom 12:2 ('Do not be conformed to the world but be transformed *by the renewal of your mind*') and Gal 5:24 ('And those who belong to Christ Jesus have crucified the flesh with its passions and desires'). cf. his *Resolutiones Disputationum et indulgentiarum virtute* (WA 1: 530-532). Cf. J. Wicks, 'Justification and faith in Luther's Theology', op. cit., pp. 5f. **129** M. Luther, *In ep. S. Pauli ad Galatas Comm.* (WA 40/1: 589). **130** R. Hermann, 'Willensfreiheit und gute Werke im Sinne der Reformation', in *Gesammelte Studien zur Theologie Luthers und der Reformation*, Göttingen 1960, pp. 44-76, here p. 64. **131** Cf. pp. 227-228 below.

words man under God's grace, in whom Christ inhabits, alongside the divine declaration that he is just, must also perform works of justice, which would be, as it were, sign of the grace of God over him and of Christ present in him with his Spirit who has begun to renew man, and also a sign of that new and future life to which every man has been destined by God.[132]

132 A. Bellini, op. cit., p. 69. We shall consider the relationship between these two understandings of 'sanctification' in the last chapter.

CHAPTER TWO

Interpretations of Luther on justification

INTRODUCTION

There is something highly attractive, yet noticeably paradoxical, about Luther, his personality, his life, his writings. Perhaps his theology and spirituality (inseparable, of course, one from the other) could be characterized as 'extreme and consistent', or perhaps better 'dialectical and consistent', in the sense that his violent and seemingly intolerant 'extremes' are habitually and disconcertingly countered, though not 'balanced' or diplomatically 'explained away', by an astonishing abundance of warmth, gentleness, reasonableness, tenderness, humanity. He 'could scold like a fishwife . . . and be as gentle as a sensitive maiden'.[1] And at the same time, Luther's recurrent dialectical 'countering', which at times makes it difficult to give coherent and definitive expression to his thought, responds neither to a superficial eclecticism nor to mental weakness. Luther is volcanic: his eruptions are powerful, unpredictable, even frightening, but the fountainhead is unitary and white-hot: his own heart and mind. That Luther himself would insist that the only source of his theological reflection is God's own word in Jesus Christ, and not himself,[2] does not take away from this. His reflection is undoubtedly rooted in the divine word of promise. The point is that, whatever may be said of the validity, the truth-value or otherwise of his theology, it is quite clear that it is his theology, his own reflection on the word of God.

This I say not in a negative or pejorative sense, among other reasons because any theology that is not personally assimilated, lived and expounded has little to offer for good or for ill. Perhaps it could be put slightly differently: whereas it is difficult to map Luther's *consistent thought forms*, at least in certain areas, it is much easier to relate to *him* and empathize with his personality humanly and existentially (perhaps positively, perhaps negatively). He establishes an immediate *rapport* with his listener or reader because he is speaking *about truth* (perhaps more or less successfully), about values worth living and dying for. Maybe for this very reason – he is sounding out the richness and 'otherness' of truth – he is hard to grasp *at a single sweep*, that is, it is virtually impossible to obtain a *single exact interpretation* of his theology. He reflected upon the word of God as a fighting, living Christian, within the coordinates his own circumstances and limitations. And because of this vital

---

1 H. Heine, *Religion and Philosophy in Germany*, Boston 1959, p. 46, quoted by J. Pelikan, *Jesus through the Centuries. His Place in the History of Culture*, New Haven 1985, p. 160.   2 'Consider the words, and forget my insignificant person', Luther said in 1532 (*Sermo 36*: WA 36: 265).

link-up with his concrete personal and social situation, his theology is authentic, human, and in that sense highly communicable . . . though at the same time, it is very personal, very unique, strangely incommunicable, hard to pin down, to comprehend, to share. It would be unjust to say that Luther's theology reflects exclusively the tormented and sinful aspects of his life and character. But it is fair to say that it is a very personal theology, producing in his followers and students deeply personal and at times strongly divergent reactions.

Serious and serene studies of Luther's theology abound today, and considerable convergence seems to exist on his vision of the doctrine of justification. Reference was made to some of them in the last chapter. Difficulties arise, however, when one attempts to draw from his reflection practical consequences of an ecclesiological, spiritual or ethical kind. *His paradoxes seem to explode on coming in contact with everyday situations.* One of the proofs of this is to be seen in the fact that in Luther's own lifetime, and certainly afterwards, several widely diverging and even opposing understandings of his fundamental teachings developed.[3] Was this due to the living, fighting quality of his reflections? Was it due simply to the constant internal contradictions of his teaching? Was it the result of systematic misrepresentation of his thought?

Hopefully the second part of this work should cast some light on these questions, making it clear that Luther's doctrine of justification did not and does not merely provide a systematic understanding of a notion that goes to the heart of Christianity (the 'doctrine' of justification), but constituted and constitutes a whole way of looking at the Gospel, at man's life and the Church's reality (the 'message' of justification). It will never be possible to come to an agreement on the value and usefulness of Luther's systematic or dogmatic theology of justification if it is not taken principally for what he wanted it to be: a fundamental methodological or critical principle for guiding the action and life of the Church, for directing and inspiring Christian spirituality and ethics.

For the moment it should be sufficient to present briefly four visions of the doctrine of justification and related matters inextricably and dialectically related to Luther's teachings. Other interpretations,[4] such as those of Erasmus,[5] Bucer,[6]

---

3 On the difficulty of connecting Luther's own theology and Reformation theology in general, cf. for example H.A. Oberman, 'Headwaters of the Reformation: Initia Lutheri—Initia Reformationis', in H.A. Oberman (ed.), *Luther and the Dawn of the Modern Era*, Leiden 1974, pp. 40–88.   4 Cf. A.E. McGrath, *Iustitia Dei* . . . op. cit., vol. 2, pp. 32–39. For a theological and historical overview of the period, cf. J. Vercruysse, 'Da Lutero a Calvino', in G. Occhipinti (ed.), *Storia della Teologia, vol. 3: da Pietro Abelardo a Roberto Bellarmino* . . . op. cit., pp. 389–404.   5 Cf. E.-W. Kohls, *Die Theologie des Erasmus*, Basel 1966, vol. 1, pp. 143–158; G. Chantraine, *Érasme et Luther, libre et serf arbitre*, Paris-Namur 1981.   6 Cf. F. Krüger, *Bucer und Erasmus: Eine Untersuchung zum Einfluß des Erasmus auf die Theologie Martin Bucers*, Wiesbaden 1970; W.P. Stephens, *The Holy Spirit in the Theology of Martin Bucer*, Cambridge 1970; M. Greschat, 'Der Ansatz der Theologie Martin Bucers', in *Theologische Literaturzeitung* 103 (1978) 81–96.

Zwingli,[7] Karlstadt,[8] Staupitz,[9] Calvin,[10] etc., are of considerable interest on their own account, but the following authors and movements, I think, are of particular interest because they offer an ample range of *live interpreters* of Luther, taking him as an authoritative starting point, though ending up, in some cases, rationalizing, reducing and even contradicting him. Furthermore, they illustrate the point I have discussed earlier: that Luther's paradoxical though consistent theological reflection was capable of spawning a wide variety of heterogeneous and even opposed theologies, philosophies, political, social and religious systems. The four areas I intend to examine are the following: 1. The antinomian spiritualism of the Enthusiasts (or *Schwärmer*). 2. Extrinsic justification, Melanchthon and the *Confessio Augustana* (1530). 3. Inchoate justification, Osiander, the Gnesio-Lutherans and the *Formula Concordiae* (1577). 4. Pietism and the Enlightenment critique of orthodox justification doctrine.

Later, in chapter three, we will look at a critical point of reference for appreciating the development of Lutheranism, that is, the fullest statement of Catholic Magisterium on justification, made in the context of the spread of Lutheranism, at the Council of Trent in 1547.

THE ANTINOMIAN SPIRITUALISM OF THE 'SCHWÄRMER'

Luther's message came across forcefully as a shout for freedom. As he saw things, the Church of his time, in the name of Christ, not only interfered immoderately and even scandalously in the life and workings of society, but above all, through aberrant sacramental practices, had tyrannized the consciences and sapped the spiritual energies of many Christians. On the institutional side, the inner core of the Christian message, based on simplicity and joy, had been lost. The awareness of God's grace, he said, is meant to 'make us joyful, fearless and playful before God and all creatures through the work of the Holy Spirit in faith. Hence man becomes willing, unhindered, happy to do good to everyone, to serve everyone, to bear all things.'[11]

7 Cf. A. Rich, *Die Anfänge der Theologie Huldrych Zwinglis*, Zürich 1949; H. Schmid, *Zwinglis Lehre von der göttlichen und menschlichen Gerechtigkeit*, Zürich 1959. 8 Cf. F. Kriechbaum, *Grundzüge der Theologie Karlstadts: Eine systematische Studie zur Erhellung der Theologie Andreas von Karlstadts*, Hamburg 1967. 9 Cf. A.E. McGrath, *Luther's Theology of the Cross*, Oxford 1985, pp. 27–40; 63–71; E. Wolf, *Staupitz und Luther: Ein Beitrag zur Theologie des Johannes von Staupitz und deren Bedeutung für Luthers theologischen Werdegang*, Leipzig 1929. 10 Cf. A. Bellini, 'La giustificazione per la sola fede', op. cit., passim; A.E. McGrath, *Iustitia Dei . . .* , op. cit., vol. 2, pp. 36–39 (based on Calvin's 1559 *Institutiones*); H.P. Santmire, 'Justification in Calvin's 1540 Romans Commentary', in *Church History* 33 (1963) 294–313; W.M. Thompson, 'Viewing Justification through Calvin's Eyes', in *Theological Studies* 57 (1996) 447–466. Note that Calvin's theology of justification is already well developed in his commentary on Romans; J. Boisset, 'Justification et sanctification chez Calvin', in W.H. Neuser (ed.), *Calvinus Theologus: Die Referate des Congrés Européen des recherches Calviniennes*, Neukirchen 1976, pp. 131–148. On the Scottish reformed tradition, close to Calvin's, cf. T.F. Torrance, 'Justification: its radical nature and place in reformed doctrine and life', in *Scottish Journal of Theology* 13 (1960) 225–246.

This attitude and spirit of Luther's, taken alongside his insistence on the doctrines of *servum arbitrium* (freedom enslaved), the priority of faith over works, and the unlimited confidence in God's pardon, brought some of his more enthusiastic followers (the *Schwärmer*, or enthusiasts) to dispense with good works altogether, and proclaim open antinomianism in his name, holding that God's law was no longer applicable to those who believe. Their interest in the Christian message centered exclusively on the grace of Christ, who frees us once and for all from our sins, and provides consolation for sinners.[12] The commandments, especially insofar as they are linked with the Church's preaching, no longer apply. We have already seen instances of how Luther's teaching could (and did) give rise to this mode of thinking. However, the double-front on which he reacted to and soundly rejected this reading of his doctrine, mainly in later writings, is of quite some interest and provides a significant criterion for interpreting his teachings.

1. *Faith and works*

As regards the relationship between faith and works, Luther makes it clear time and again – as we saw above – that if works are absent, faith is necessarily non-existent. 'Faith is never without works . . . It is impossible that faith be present in the absence of constant, many and great works'.[13] 'Faith without works is nothingness and vanity . . . it is a fanatical abstraction, pure vanity and a dream of the heart, it is false and does not justify'.[14] His position is made quite clear in the *Smalcald Articles* (1537) and in his *Von den Konziliis und Kirchen* (1539), works clearly directed against the *Schwärmer*. In the latter work he explains how his adversaries flee from the consequences of justification (sanctification or the new life in Christ) as they would from the devil himself.

The *Schwärmer* proclaim, he says: 'You are an adulterer, a fornicator, a miser, in any case, a sinner . . . Only believe, be happy, have no fear of the law; Christ has fulfilled all things.'[15] But Luther goes on to say: 'A Christ who has died for sinners that do not renounce their sins and live a new life, does not exist and is not to be found.'[16]

11 M. Luther, WA *Deutsch Bibel* 8: 3f.; cf. *Die Vorlesung über den Römerbrief* (WA 56: 257). 'A Christian is a free lord over every thing, is subject to none' (WA 7: 21). 12 Cf. R. Hermann, *Zum Streit um die Überwindung des Gesetzes. Erörterungen zu Luthers Antinomerthesen*, Weimar 1958; J. Rogge, *Johannes Agricolas Lutherverständnis unter besonderer Berücksichtigung des Antinomismus*, Berlin 1960; M. Schlömann, *Natürliches und gepredigtes Gesetz bei Luther. Ein Studie zur Frage nach der Einheit der Gesetzesauffassung Luthers mit besonderer Berücksichtigung seiner Auseinandersetzung mit der Antinomern*, Berlin 1961; L. Pinomaa, *Sieg des Glaubens. Grundlinien der Theologie Luthers*, Göttingen 1964, pp. 95 ff.; B. Lohse, 'Die Auseinandersetzung mit den "Schwärmern". . . mit den Antinomern', in C. Andresen (ed.), *Handbuch der Dogmen- und Theologiegeschichte*, vol. 2, Göttingen 1980, pp. 27–33; 39–45. 13 M. Luther, *Tr. de bonis operibus* (1520: WA 6: 231). 14 Idem., *In ep. S. Pauli ad Galatas Comm.* (WA 40/1: 266). 15 Idem., *Sermon no. 8* (1539: WA 47: 672). 16 M. Luther, *Von den Konziliis und Kirche* (1539: WA 50: 599).

However, it should be noted that Luther had to some degree left himself open to the antinomian interpretation. His insistence on justification by faith, 'without works of the law' brought him to consider relevant only 'two uses of the law', one for the restraint of sin through political authority (*usus legis politicus*), the other for the disclosure of sin through accusation and exhortation (*usus legis theologicus* or *pædagogicus*, also termed *elenchticus*).[17] Later Lutheran confessional documents, such as the 1577 *Formula of Concord*, aware that this interpretation of Luther's teaching was still common and could be interpreted in an antinomistic sense, insisted on a 'third use of the law'.[18] According to this, believers were reminded of their strict obligation to observe the law, so that, unlike the *Schwärmer*, 'they will not be thrown back on their own holiness and piety and, under the pretext of the Holy Spirit's guidance, set up a self-elected service of God without his Word and command.'[19]

2.   The Church and the preached word

It was not that the *Schwärmer* denied as such the value of doing the will of God which the law expressed. The specific point they held rather was this: no created reality on earth is capable of or authorized to communicate or mediate God's commands. They spoke commonly therefore of the *verbum internum,* the word which God speaks to man in the silence of his own heart, without any need for Church or preached word. Although their teaching had a certain amount in common with the neo-Platonic mysticisms of the later Middle Ages, especially those of Tauler and Gerson, well known and appreciated by Luther',[20] the latter was quite clear that the very logic of the gratuitousness of salvation and the sinfulness of man demanded that God's saving word could only come to us from outside ourselves (*extra nos*). In particular, the 'otherness' of salvation strictly required the external preaching of the word (the *verbum externum*), in such a way that the Church itself, the community of believers, is produced and constituted by the preached word; in Luther's words, it is a *creatura Evangelii*, a 'creature of the Gospel'.[21]

Clearly, Luther's insistence on the *verbum externum* disqualifies antinomian doctrine in unequivocal terms. Subilia, for example, observes: 'Luther maintains with intransigent firmness this radical *extra nos* character of the action, the reality and the presence of the living God, over and against all attempts to transform it into

---

17 Cf. M. Luther, *Die dritte Disputation gegen die Antinomer* (1537: WA 39/1: 361); USA 61.   18 Calvin and, following him, K. Barth (*Evangelium und Gesetz*, Munich 1935) considered the law as a part of the gospel, in such a way that the law is an important part of Christian preaching. Luther is more circumspect on the matter, considering Christ as the 'end of the law' (Rom 10:4). However, as W. Joest points out (*Gesetz und Freiheit*. . . op. cit., p. 14), Luther also accords a certain validity to the *tertius usus legis*.   19 *Formula Concordiae: Solida Declaratio* 6: 20. English translation in T.G. Tappert et al., (ed.), *The Book of Concord: the Confessions of the Evangelical Lutheran Church*, Minneapolis 1988, p. 567.   20 Cf. V. Subilia, op. cit., p. 156, with bibliography. 21 Cf. M. Luther, *Resolutiones Lutherianae super propositionibus suis Lipsiae disputis* (WA 2: 430).

something that can be derived partially or totally from man or placed at his disposition for his reasoned inferences, for his institutional systematizing, for his interior experiences.'[22] And Mühlen explains that 'the purpose of the Lutheran *extra nos* is not one of a simple modification of man's interiority, but rather of understanding the latter as exteriority, as a being *extra se* . . . Luther interprets this mystical transfer of man in an upward direction, that is, outside himself, through the relationship with the word and with faith, in which the word is the preached word.'[23]

It should be noted, however, that Luther's insistence can, besides, be interpreted in an anti-ecclesial fashion, in the sense that the priority of the *verbum externum* would necessarily exclude all possible manipulation of God's word at the hands of man or of the institutional Church, thus allowing antinomism and mystical interiorism enter, as it were, by the back door.

EXTRINSIC JUSTIFICATION, MELANCHTHON AND THE 'CONFESSIO AUGUSTANA' (1530)

It should be noted that the strong antinomian reaction among some of Luther's disciples, that for example of Johannes Agricola,[24] was not occasioned directly by the former's own teaching, but more so by that of Philip Melanchthon.[25] In fact, the latter attributed a much more critical rôle to observance of the law in Christian life than did Luther, teaching not so much that works flowed from justification naturally, necessarily, almost passively, as good fruits grow on a good tree, but rather that justification provides the believer with a *new capacity* to fulfill the law.[26] In his *Instructions for Parish Visitations* (1527), for example, he insisted that the preaching of the law is at the heart of Christian instruction, and said that without the observance of the law, both repentance and faith are impossible.[27]

1.   *Melanchthon and Luther*

The fact is that Melanchthon himself was somewhat ill at ease with many facets of Luther's teachings, particularly as regards the latter's apparent insistence on man's total passivity in justification. For Luther, there is a perfect, almost mystical, continuity between faith and works; works would be the automatic (hence passive) product of the former, much in the same way as the life of faith is virtually identified

22 V. Subilia, op. cit., p. 157.   23 K.H. zur Mühlen, *Nos extra nos. Luthers Theologie zwischen Mystik und Scholastik*, Tübingen 1972, pp. 226; 200.   24 Cf. J. Rogge, *Johannes Agricolas Lutherverständnis unter besonderer Berücksichtigung des Antinomismus*, op. cit.   25 On Melanchthon, cf. for example C.L. Manschreck, *Melanchthon, the Quiet Reformer*, New York 1958; R. Stupperich, *Melanchthon*, Berlin 1960; B. Lohse, 'Grundzüge der Theologie Melanchthons', in C. Andresen (ed.), *Handbuch der Dogmen- und Theologiegeschichte* . . . , op. cit., vol. 2, pp. 69–81.   26 P. Melanchthon, 'Annotationes in Ev. Matthaei', in *Corpus Reformatorum* 14: 498–500 (on Mt 5:17). 27 Cf. P. Melanchthon, 'Articuli di quibus egerunt per visitatores in Reg. Saxoniae', in *Corpus Reformatorum* 26: 7–96, especially as regards article 1.

with the action of God's Spirit in man. When Christ 'takes over' in the *admirabile commercium*, according to Luther, man no longer acts, for Christ 'lives in him'.

Melanchthon, in the later editions of his often re-written work *Loci communes*, explains that justification must make reference to *three* contributing factors: the Word of God, the Holy Spirit and the faculty of the human will, not only the first two as Luther would have held. The latter he terms the *facultas applicandi se ad gratiam*, a way of speaking hardly to Luther's liking. In addition, his early commitment to a doctrine of predestination *ante praevisa merita* (1521) in line with Luther's, is replaced later on by that of predestination *post praevisa merita* (1535).[28] The significance the ex-humanist always attached to the tangible human factor in Christian life made it difficult for him to conceive of Christ's action and presence 'taking over' completely, as it were, in man. After his 1519–20 conversion from an ethical doctrine of justification centered on mortification of the flesh and the affections, to a strongly Lutheran position in early 1520s,[29] a certain rationalizing of the Lutheran message comes to the fore again in the late '20s and '30s.

In specific terms, Melanchthon constantly attempts to clarify and reconcile a series of elements of Luther's theology seemingly at odds with one another: (1) the central rôle of the person of Christ and our union with him;[30] (2) the forensic or extrinsicist notion of grace and justification (justice as *favor Dei*);[31] (3) the regenerative or real effectiveness of justification in the believer and his cooperation with grace.[32] Melanchthon's relevance for the theological history of Lutheranism lies not so much in having resolved the tensions between these elements, but for having formulated them clearly in the first place.

However, Melanchthon's reflection is characterized by an incapacity to hold on to the three realities at one and the same time, as Luther had done in his brilliant, living and paradoxical theologizing. Under Melanchthon's influence, the dialectical genius of Luther seems to come to pieces; his vision of grace and Christian life becomes functional, almost mechanical. He moves away from a personalist view of Christ to one centered on analyzing his *work*:[33] *hoc est Christum cognoscere, beneficia eius cognoscere.*[34] A formal distinction, not to be found in Luther, is drawn between justification, the external act by which God pronounces or declares the believer to be righteous (*Gerechtsprechung*), and regeneration, the internal process of renewal in which the believer is sanctified in collaborating with the action of the Christ's Spirit. The former becomes more and more emphasized and established as the hall-

28 Cf. A. Evard, *Étude sur les variations du dogme de la prédestination et du libre arbitre dans la théologie di Melanchthon*, Laval 1901.   29 Cf. W. Maurer, *Der junge Melanchthon zwischen Humanismus und Reformation*, vol. 2: *Die Theologe*, Göttingen 1969, pp. 361–368.   30 Cf. for example P. Melanchthon, *Annotationes in Evang. Iohannis* (1523), in *Corpus Reformatorum* 14: 1047–1220; 15: 1–440.   31 'Non aliud enim est gratia, si exactissime describenda sit, nisi Dei benevolentia erga nos' (P. Melanchthon, *Loci Communes, in Corpus Reformatorum* 21: 158).   32 Cf. E. Bizer, *Theologie der Verheißung: Studien zur theologischen Entwicklung des jungen Melanchthon 1519–1524*, Neukirchen 1964, pp. 82–85.   33 Cf. A.E. McGrath, *Iustitia Dei . . .* op. cit., vol. 2, p. 23.   34 P. Melanchthon, *Loci communes* (1521), *praefatio* (*Corpus Reformatorum* 21: 85).

mark of genuine Lutheranism.[35] Melanchthon speaks increasingly of *iustitia aliena* as something quite distinct from sanctification and renewal, in such a way that he (and not Luther!) should be considered as the most authentic representative before history of the classic notion of extrinsic (imputed or forensic) justification[36] consistently (and perhaps not unjustly) censured by Catholic theologians for its one-sidedness.

No longer is justification language vouched in terms of Luther's spousal, personalist and mysterious Christ-centered *admirabile commercium*, which harmonized the extrinsic and inner elements of justification in an impressive, closely-woven, though elusive dialectic. Melanchthon and a good part of Lutheranism of his time explained justification in terms of a juridical analogy based on Roman law. Just as in legal affairs, the transgressor is *declared* or considered free *in foro*, so also the sinner is justified, that is, declared to be righteous, *in foro divino*; hence the term 'forensic' as applied to justification. Melanchthon says: 'Justification means the remission of sins, the reconciliation or acceptance of the person for eternal life. For the Hebrews "to justify" is a forensic term; it is as if I were to say that the Roman people had justified Scipius, who had been accused by the tribunes, when the latter had, in their turn, absolved him or "declared" him just. Paul uses the term "justification", following the custom of Hebrew speech, to mean acceptance, that is, reconciliation and remission of sins.'[37]

35 H. Schmid sums up classical 'Lutheran' doctrine as follows: 'The effect of faith is justification; by which is to be understood that act of God by which He removes the sentence of condemnation, to which man is exposed in consequence of his sins, releases him from his guilt, and ascribes to him the merit of Christ . . . "Justification denotes that act by which the sinner, who is responsible for guilt and liable to punishment, but who believes in Christ, is pronounced just by God the judge". This act occurs at the instant in which the merit of Christ is appropriated by faith, and can properly be designated a forensic or judicial act, since God in it, as if in a civil court, pronounces a judgement upon man, which assigns to him an entirely different position, and entirely different rights. By justification we are, therefore, by no means to understand a moral condition existing in man, or a moral change which he has experienced, but only a judgement pronounced upon man, by which his relation to God is reversed, and indeed in such a manner, that a man can now consider himself one whose sins are blotted out, who is no longer responsible for them before God, who, on the other hand, appears before God as accepted and righteous, in whom God finds nothing more to punish, with whom He has no longer any occasion to be displeased' (H. Schmid, *The Doctrinal Theology of the Evangelical Lutheran Church*, Minneapolis n/d, pp. 424f.).   36 Karl Holl, using Kantian terminology, established a distinction between 'analytic' and 'synthetic' justification. Synthetic justification was defined as a declarative judgement of God whereby the sinner is justified solely on the basis of Christ's work, as a kind of legal fiction. According to Holl, Luther rejected this understanding; it was Melanchthon who understood and expressed the doctrine of justification in this way, and popularized it. Luther's understanding of justification, conversely, was analytic, according to Holl, insofar as God really makes the sinner righteous; were he not to have done so, he would be a liar, in treating the sinner as righteous when in fact he was not so. cf. K. Holl, 'Luther's Bedeutung für den Fortschritt der Auslegungskunst', in *Gesammelte Aufsätze zur Kirchengeschichte*, vol. 1: Luther, Tübingen 1927, pp. 544–582. The same point is made by V. Subilia, *La giustificazione per fede* . . . , op. cit., p. 163; A.E. McGrath, *Iustitia Dei* . . . , op. cit., vol. 1, p. 182; and W. Pannenberg, 'Die Rechtfertigungslehre im ökumenischen Gespräch', in *Zeitschrift für Theologie und Kirche* 88 (1991) 232–246, here p. 244. For others who speak in the

To be noted in respect of Melanchthon's way of expressing the doctrine of justification is the fact that Erasmus, in his *Novum instrumentum omne* (1516), employs the forensic concept *acceptilatio* (the purely verbal remission of a debt without payment) as an illustration of the biblical term *imputare*.[38] It would seem therefore that Melanchthon's teaching cannot be taken simply as a further expression or natural development of Luther's *extra nos*, but to some degree a return (perhaps unwittingly made) to the very categories which, as a follower of Luther, he had ostensibly abjured.

2. *Melanchthon and the* Confessio Augustana *(1530)*

The fact of course is that Melanchthon was a conciliator where Luther was not. He thought little of keeping two virtually irreconcilable doctrines ('forensic' and 'inherent' justification) in the air at the same time, when Luther's reflection would have erupted at the prospect. His spirit is one of promoting reconciliation, especially with Rome, as the following text shows: 'We have no doctrine different from the Roman Church . . . We are ready to obey the Roman Church if she can overlook or let pass certain matters that we cannot now change, even though we would wish to do so [he had in mind Masses for the dead and suchlike matters] . . . We honour the Roman Pope and the whole ecclesiastical organization, if only the Pope does not cast us off. Then we could easily come to union.'[39]

The culmination of his conciliating work is to be found in the famed *Confessio Augustana* (1530),[40] and its complement, the *Apologia* to the *Confessio Augustana*.[41]

same fashion, cf. F. Buzzi, 'La teologia dei Lutero . . .', op. cit., pp. 102ff.   37 P. Melanchthon, *Loci communes* (1535) in *Corpus Reformatorum* 21: 421. For the contrast between Luther and Melanchthon on this point, cf. R. Stupperich, 'Die Rechtfertigungslehre bei Luther und Melanchthon 1530–1536', in *Luther und Melanchthon: Referate und Berichte des Zweitens Internationalen Kongresses für Lutherforschung*, Göttingen 1961, pp. 73–88; L. Haikola, 'Melanchthons und Luthers Lehre von der Rechtfertigung', in idem., pp. 89–103; M. Greschat, *Melanchthon neben Luther: Studien zur Gestalt der Rechtfertigungslehre zwischen 1528 und 1537*, Witten 1965.   38 Cf. A.E. McGrath, op. cit., vol. 2, pp. 24; 31–32. Erasmus' 1516 translation of the New Testament from Greek changed the Vulgate version of Rom 4:5 ('Credidit Abraham deo et *reputatum* est illi ad iustitiam') to 'Credidit Abraham deo et imputatum est ei ad iustitiam'). The key word 'to impute, to repute', λογίζηται, was considered by Erasmus as equivalent to the Latin juridical term *acceptilatio*: 'Accepto fert: λογίζηται, id est, imputat sive acceptum fert. Est autem acceptum fere, debere, sive pro accepto habere, quod non acceperis, quae apud iure consultos vocatur acceptilatio' (Erasmus, *Novum instrumentum omne*, Basilea 1516, p. 429).   39 P. Melanchthon, *Epistula*, in *Corpus Reformatorum* 2: 170.   40 The text is in H. Lietzmann, H. Bornkamm, H. Volz and E. Wolf, *Die Bekenntnisschriften der evangelisch-lutherischen Kirche*, Göttingen 1967, pp. 44–137. English translation in T.G. Tappert et al., (ed.), *The Book of Concord: the Confessions of the Evangelical Lutheran Church* . . . op. cit., pp. 23–96. The following commentaries on the *Confessio Augustana*, are relevant: V. Pfnür, *Einig in der Rechtfertigungslehre?: die Rechtfertigungslehre der 'Confessio Augustana' (1530) und die Stellungnahme der katholischen Kontroverstheologie zwischen 1530 und 1535*, Wiesbaden 1970; H. Meyer, H. Schütte and H.-J. Mund, (eds), *Katholische Anerkennung des Augsburgischen Bekenntnisses?: ein Vorstoß zur Einheit zwischen katholischer und lutherischer Kirche*, Frankfurt a.

Both documents were prepared at the so-called Diet of Augsburg (*Augusta*) convoked by the Emperor Charles V with a view to resolving differences between Catholics and followers of Luther. The *Confessio Augustana*, after speaking of God, original sin and Christ, the Son of God, in the first three articles, speaks in the fourth article of justification, using clearly 'forensic' language. 'Our churches teach that humans cannot be justified before God by their own strength, merits or works', it says, 'but are freely justified for Christ's sake through faith (*propter Christum, per fidem*) when they believe that they are received into favour and that their sins are forgiven on account of Christ, who by his death made satisfaction for our sins. This faith God imputes for righteousness in his sight (Rom 3:4).'[42]

The *Confessio* did not achieve the Emperor Charles V's desired goal, the reestablishment of unity among Christians, and following attempts at reconciliation consolidated rather than resolved opposing positions of the different sides. Of special interest are the so-called *Confutatio* of the *Confessio Augustana*, prepared by theologians appointed by the Emperor, and seen to represent the Catholic position,[43] followed by the *Apologia* of the *Confessio Augustana*, drafted again by Melanchthon, in reply to the *Confutatio*, and, a decade later, the Diet of Regensburg (1541).

According to the *Confutatio*, serious divergences between Catholics and Lutherans remained unsolved in the *Confessio*, particularly in their respective understandings of concupiscence, 'faith formed by charity', and other practical issues relating to the life of the Church and the administration of the sacraments. Furthermore, it stated that the doctrine of justification by faith alone, as enunciated by the *Confessio Augustana* was 'diametrically opposed to the truth of the Gospel, which does not exclude works'.[44] In the *Apologia*, therefore, Melanchthon attempted to provide a

M. 1977; H. Meyer (ed.), *The Augsburg Confession in Ecumenical Perspective*, Stuttgart 1979; G.W. Forell and J.F. McCue, *Confessing One Faith: a joint commentary on the Augsburg Confession by Lutheran and Catholic theologians*, Minneapolis 1982; especially the contributions of W. Breuning and B. Hägglund, 'Sin and Original Sin', in ibid., pp. 94–116; G. Müller and V. Pfnür, 'Justification—Faith—Works', in ibid., pp. 117–146; H.M. Müller, 'Keine romantische Verbrüderung. Mit der "Confessio Augustana" auf dem Weg zur Einheit', in *Lutherische Monatschefte* 21 (1982) 23–26; J.F. Johnson, *Justification according to the Apology of the Augsburg Confession and the Formula of Concord*, in H.G. Anderson et al. (eds), *Justification by faith* (*Lutherans and Catholics in Dialogue*, VII), Minneapolis 1985, pp. 185–199; N. Beck, *The Doctrine of Faith: a study of the Augsburg Confession and contemporary ecumenical documents*, St Louis 1987; J.A. Burgess (ed.), *The Role of the Augsburg Confession: Catholic and Lutheran views*, Philadelphia 1991.   41 *Apologia Confessionis Augustanae*, in H. Lietzmann et al. (eds.), *Die Bekenntnisschriften der evangelisch-lutherischen Kirche* . . . , op. cit., pp. 141–404. English translation in T.G. Tappert et al. (eds.), op. cit., pp. 97–285.   42 *Confessio Augustana* IV, in T.G. Tappert et al. (eds.), op. cit., p. 30. Emphasis added. On this article, cf. the study of G. Müller and V. Pfnür, 'Justification—Faith—Works', op. cit., pp. 117–146.   43 Cf. H. Immenkötter (ed.), *Die Confutatio der Confessio Augustana vom 3. August 1530, in Corpus Catholicorum* 33, Münster 1979. English translation in J.M. Reu (ed.), *The Augsburg Confession: a Collection of Sources with an Historical Introduction*, St Louis 1966, pp. 348–383. For a comparison with the *Confessio Augustana*, cf. M. Cassese (ed.), *Augusta 1530: il dibattito Luterano-Cattolico: la confessione augustana e la confutazione pontifica*, Milano 1981.   44 *Confutatio* 6:3, in H. Immenkötter, *Die Confutatio* . . . , op. cit., 90.

more refined understanding of the doctrine of justification, too succinctly expressed in the *Confessio* by the phrase *propter Christum per fidem*.

Justification, law and Gospel in the Apologia   Melanchthon insisted on the notion of the extrinsic imputation of God's righteousness, and went as far as to exemplify it by saying that just as a man might pay the debt of a friend, so the believer may be considered just on account of the alien merit of Christ being paid for him.[45] He states: 'In this passage [Rom 5:1] "to justify" is used in a judicial way to mean "to absolve a guilty man and pronounce him righteous," and to do so on account of someone else's righteousness, namely, Christ's, which is communicated to us through faith.'[46] Man has no righteousness of his own, and so is justified on the basis of an external and alien righteousness which is not his and never becomes his, a righteousness reputed or imputed to him: *propter Christum coram Deum* [sic] *iusti reputemur.*[47]

It might seem that Melanchthon's insistence on the forensic nature of justification would take away from the regenerative side (renewal, sanctification) of justification. This is not the case. And the point is important, as the *Apologia*'s reflection on 'law and gospel' shows.

'In this controversy, the main doctrine of Christianity is involved', Melanchthon says, 'that is, the proper distinction between law and gospel grounded in Scripture.'[48] He explains that justification is the cornerstone of a theology which must properly distinguish between two ways in which God deals with the human creature: *firstly*, in the demands of the law, where God reveals human sin, and *secondly* in his gift of the gospel where he promises the righteousness of faith in Christ. Justification belongs *exclusively* to the realm of faith, not to that of the law. 'If the doctrine of faith is omitted, it is vain to say that our works are valid by virtue of the suffering of Christ . . . God pronounces righteous those who believe in him from their heart and then have good fruits, which please him because of faith and therefore are a keeping of the law.'[49]

Two rules, two domains, side by side, connected yet not integrated: one of law, of justice, of ethical endeavour, of moral renewal, of correspondence to grace, of 'inherent' justice; the other of grace, of mercy, of divine action, of total trust in God, of 'forensic' justice.

'Fides charitate formata'   Melanchthon's argumentation becomes more specific when he deals with the controversial argument on the relationship between faith and charity, centered on the interpretation of the Pauline formula 'faith made effective through

45 Cf. *Apologia* 21: 19, in T.G. Tappert et al. (eds.), op. cit., p. 213.   46 *Apologia* 4: 305, in T.G. Tappert et al. (eds.), op. cit., p. 154.   47 Cf. *Apologia* 4: 214, in T.G. Tappert et al. (eds.), op. cit., p. 136.   48 *Apologia* 4: 2-8, in T.G. Tappert et al. (eds.), op. cit., pp. 107–108.   49 *Apologia* 4: 382; 252, in T.G. Tappert et al. (eds.), op. cit., pp. 165; 143.

love' (Gal 5:6: πίστις δι ἀγάπες ἐνεργουμένε; Vulg.: *fides charitate formata*). The com-
monly-held Scholastic doctrine understood this text as meaning that faith justifies
because it is animated or 'energized' by charity, thus – as Melanchthon understood
things – situating a human reality in antecedence to faith. In fact Melanchthon
considered charity to be a 'work', indeed 'the greatest work of the law',[50] and refused to recognize it as the perfecting form of all Christian life, and even less its
priority over faith. Charity, like other works, was the necessary fruit and natural
result of faith, not the other way around. This was also Luther's position.[51]

We shall return to the critical notion of *fides charitate formata* when examining
the doctrine of the Council of Trent,[52] and in the second part of the work. Suffice it
to say for the moment that Melanchthon's insistence on the priority of faith over
charity goes to the very heart of the debate: the exact nature of the playoff between
divine justifying action and human response to grace.

For Melanchthon, it is probably fair to say that *charity does hold priority over faith*
in an important (and fully acceptable) sense: the merciful *love of God* and his unconditional promise of pardon is at the very start of justification. Yet instead of
saying that faith saves us insofar as *it is animated by charity* (that is, Charity), he
holds it does so because *it clings to its object*, which is God's promise of forgiveness of
sin on account of the death and resurrection of Jesus Christ, that is, Charity itself
made accessible or 'clingable to' in Christ. In *that* sense there is no difference between faith being *animated* (or 'energized') by *Charity* and faith *clinging to its object*.

And for Melanchthon the key point is, of course, that good works and the exercise of free will *are not 'informable' as such* by Charity, God's merciful love, because
this is extrinsic, forensic, imputed to man on the basis of Christ's alien merits. The
denial of the classical understanding of the *fides charitate formata* is therefore just
another way of expressing the doctrine of 'forensic' justification. A critical anthropological affirmation is being made: God's love and mercy *cannot* be transformatively
'poured into' the heart of the sinner and believer, bringing him to partake truly in
the love with which God loves himself and creatures, in loving God above all things.[53]

---

50 *Apologia* 4: 229, in T.G. Tappert et al. (eds.), op. cit., p. 139.   51 For Luther as well, faith is the
form of charity, and not vice-versa. 'Christian faith . . . is an assured confidence of the heart and a
firm assent, by which Christ is grasped, in such a way that Christ is the object of the faith. Or,
better, he is not the object, but rather, more correctly, Christ is present in faith itself. Faith is
therefore in a sense knowledge, or darkness, it sees nothing . . . So our formal justice is not charity,
which *formaverit* faith, but it is faith itself and a cloud in the heart (*nebula cordis*), that is, an
assurance of something we cannot see, that is, in Christ who, no matter how dense the clouds that
block our view, is nonetheless present (*fides est. . . fiducia . . . in Christum qui, ut maxime non
videatur, tamen praesens est*)' (M. Luther, *In ep. S. Pauli ad Galatas Comm.*: WA 40/1: 228 f.; cf.
ibid., p. 239). cf. also his *Zirkulardisputation de veste nuptiali, 1537*: WA 39/1: 318.   52 On Trent,
cf. pp. 70–94.   53 Later on (cf. pp. 223–226), when examining Romans 5:5 ('The love of God has
been poured into our hearts through the Holy Spirit which has been given to us'), we shall observe
the contrast between Augustine's 're-creationist' understanding of this text (by the effusion of the
Holy Spirit we are made *dilectores suos*), and Luther's dynamic and actualist one which, it would
seem, leaves the believer ontologically untouched.

3. *The Diet of Regensburg (1541)*

In spite of a gradual hardening in the respective positions of Luther and Melanchthon, many Catholics and Lutherans persevered in their efforts at theological reconciliation. A high point was undoubtedly the *Diet of Regensburg* (or Ratisbon), held in 1541 under the auspices of the Emperor Charles V. Notable among the Catholic participants were J. Gropper,[54] Pighius,[55] and G. Contarini.[56] However, despite the best efforts of both sides, the consensus statement, recorded in the so-called *Liber Ratisbonensis*,[57] seems to have been fatally conditioned by previous discussions and entrenched positions, and was not a success.

This can be seen particularly in the 'double-justice' (*duplex iustitia*) formula coined by the authors of the *Liber Ratisbonensis*, intending as they did to distinguish formally between 'inherent righteousness' (*iustitia inhaerens*), that is, the infusion of charity by which the will is healed (the point emphasized particularly by Catholic participants at the Diet), and an 'imputed righteousness' (*iustitia imputata*) which is given only on account of Christ's merits (the understanding Lutherans leaned towards). Only in the latter can assurance of grace be found, the document added.

Aside from the fact that agreement had not been reached on critical issues such as Eucharistic transubstantiation, confession, Church authority, etc., the document was not approved either by Rome or by Luther, and, strange though it may seem, for reasons more or less of a kind. For the former, the notion of 'double justice' was

---

54 Cf. J. Gropper, *Enchiridion Christianae Institutiones*, Köln 1536. On his teaching, cf. A.E. McGrath, *Iustitia Dei . . .* op. cit., vol. 2, pp. 57–60; S. Ehses, 'Johannes Groppers Rechtfertigungslehre auf dem Konzil von Trient', in *Römische Quartalschrift* 20 (1906) 175–188; W. Lipgens, *Kardinal Johannes Gropper (1503–1559) und die Anfänge der katholischen Reform in Deutschland*, Münster 1951; R. Braunisch, *Die Theologie der Rechtfertigung im 'Enchiridion' (1538) des Johannes Gropper: Sein kritischer Dialog mit Philipp Melanchthon*, Münster 1974. 55 On Pighius, cf. H. Jedin, *Studien über die Schriftstellertätigkeit Albert Pigges*, Münster 1931. 56 Cf. G. Contarini, 'Epistola de iustificatione' (1541), in *Corpus Catholicorum*, vol. 7. cf. also F. Hünermann, 'Die Rechtfertigungslehre des Kard. Kaspar Contarini', in *Theologische Quartalschrift* 102 (1921) 1–22; H. Rückert, *Die theologische Entwicklung Gasparo Contarinis*, Bonn 1926; H. Jedin, *Kardinal Contarini als Kontroverstheologe*, Münster 1949; O. Ferrara, *Gasparo Contarini et ses missions*, Paris 1956; H. Mackenson, 'Contarini's Theological Role at Ratisbon in 1541', in *Archiv für Reformationsgeschichte* 51 (1960) 36–57; P. Matheson, *Cardinal Contarini at Regensburg*, Oxford 1972; G. Fragnito, *Gasparo Contarini: un magistrato veneziano al servizio della cristianità*, Firenze 1988. 57 The document produced, the *Liber Ratisbonensis*, is to be found in *Corpus Reformatorum* 4:190–238. On the history of the Regensburg agreement, cf. R. Stupperich, *Der Humanismus und die Wiedervereinigung der Konfessionen*, Leipzig 1936; idem., 'Der Ursprung des Regensburger Buches von 1541 und seine Rechtfertigungslehre', in *Archiv für Reformationsgeschichte* 36 (1939) 88–116; W. von Löwenich, *Duplex iustitia: Luthers Stellung zu einer Unionsformel des 16. Jahrhunderts*, Wiesbaden 1972; W.H. Neuser, *Die Vorbereitung der Religionsgespräche von Worms und Regensburg 1540/41*, Neukirchen 1974; V. Pfnür, *Die Einigung bei den Religionsgesprächen von Worms und Regensburg 1540/41: Eine Täuschung?*, Gütersloh 1980; H.M. Barth (ed.), *Das Regensburger Religionsgespräch im Jahr 1541*, Regensburg 1992.

confusing for the faithful.[58] As the Council of Trent would make clear some years later, in explicitly rejecting the double-justification formula put forward by authors (such as Seripando) influenced by Gropper, Contarini etc., justice has only one *'formal' cause*.[59] We will look at the issue in greater detail in the next chapter.

Interestingly enough, Luther had mooted a doctrine of 'double justice' in embryonic form as far back as 1519 in his sermon *De duplici iustitia*,[60] and made reference again to the idea in 1536.[61] However, apart from the concept of free will, as contained in the Regensburg document, being unacceptable to him, apart from his suspicions that the participants at the Diet were not truly seeking 'peace with God',[62] Luther was particularly uneasy with what he saw as the artificial pasting together (*zusammenleimen*) of biblical justification and the scholastic doctrine of *fides charitate formata*.[63] The key question, of course, was and remains the following: were the delegates at Regensburg attempting to paste together what *Luther*, or what *Melanchthon* had put apart?

INCHOATE JUSTIFICATION, OSIANDER, THE GNESIO-LUTHERANS AND THE 'FORMULA CONCORDIAE' (1577)

Understandably, Melanchthon's unilateral emphasis on forensic justification did not go unchallenged among Luther's disciples. For Andreas Osiander,[64] leader of the Evangelicals or Gnesio-Lutherans at Nuremberg, Melanchthon's concept of justification as *Gerechtsprechung* was not only unacceptable, but considered a betrayal of Luther's genuine thought. Bringing to bear a series of Johannine texts related to the doctrine of justification, Osiander, resolutely rejecting the conception of extrinsic justification found in the *Apologia*, taught that saving righteousness, infused into the soul, was none other than the essential indwelling (*Einwohnung*) of Christ according to his divinity.[65]

Osiander in his turn was opposed on several fronts. Francesco Stancari (d.1574), looking to Melanchthon for support, opposed Osiander decisively on the latter point, stating that Christ's *humanity*, and especially his sufferings and death on the Cross,

---

58 Cf. H. Jedin, *A History of the Council of Trent*, Edinburgh 1961, vol. 1, p. 382.   59 Cf. DH 1529.   60 Cf. WA 2: 143–152. cf. D. Olivier, 'Les deux sermons sur la double et la triple justice', in *Ôcumenica vol. 3*, Minneapolis/Gütersloh 1968, pp. 39–69.   61 Cf. WA 39/1: 19.   62 Cf. WA *Briefwechsel* 9: 350 (1541).   63 M. Luther, *Letter to J. Frederick* (1541): WA *Briefwechsel* 9: 406. K. Holl has confirmed that Luther at no stage accepted a doctrine of 'double-justification' ('Die Rechtfertigungslehre in Luthers Vorlesung über den Römerbrief mit besonderer Rücksicht auf die Frage der Heilsgewißheit', in *Gesammelte Aufsätze . . .*, op. cit., vol. 1, pp. 111–154, here p. 117).   64 On Osiander's doctrine on justification and related matters, cf. F.C. Baur, *Brevis disquisitio in Andreae Osiandi de iustificatione doctrinam*, Berlin 1831; A. Ritschl, 'Die Rechtfertigungslehre des Andreas Osiander', in *Jahrbücher für deutsche Theologie* 2 (1857) 785–829; E. Hirsch, *Die Theologie des Andreas Osiander und ihre geschichtliche Voraussetzung*, Göttingen 1919; W. Niesel, 'Calvin wider Osianders Rechtfertigungslehre', in *Zeitschrift für Kirchengeschichte* 46 (1982) 410–430; A.E. McGrath, *Iustitia Dei . . .* op. cit., vol. 2, pp. 36f.   65 Cf. A. Osiander, *Von dem einigen Mittler*, E iib.

and not his divinity, is the objective basis of justification.[66] More relevant from many standpoints was Calvin's opposition to Osiander. Calvin, though he retained the deeply personal quality of the Christian's relationship to God in Christ[67] which Melanchthon had clearly neglected, was at one with the latter in maintaining the predominantly forensic understanding of justification:[68] *justificatio [interpretatur]* ... *acceptionem qua nos Deus in gratiam receptos pro iustos habet.*[69] For Calvin, justification involves the 'remission of sins and imputation of Christ's justice'.[70] Man's righteousness is *extra seipsum ... non in nobis sed in Christo.*[71] And against Osiander who advocated what Calvin termed a *crassa mixtura Christi cum fidelibus*,[72] he spoke of a spiritual union with Christ, an *incorporatio*, or *insitio*,[73] a new life in Christ with two sides to it, justification and sanctification.

In any case, two parties clearly emerged, Osiander's ardently defending the position of 'total inhabitation', retaining likewise Luther's doctrine of *servum arbitrium* and excluding any kind of natural human goodness, Melanchthon's attempting to retain side by side the doctrine of the collaboration of human free will, alongside 'forensic' justification.[74] After several unsuccessful attempts at reconciliation (for example, the *Augsburg Interim* of 1548, the Peace of Augsburg of 1555, the Weimar Colloquy of 1560) the conflict concerning the right meaning of Luther's principal article came to a head and was given a would-be definitive solution in the 1577 *Formula of Concord*.[75] The following points of agreement were made, among others.[76]

1. The *antinomian error* (specifically that of George Major) was put aside by insisting that good works are obligatory, not only insofar as they are an appropriate and natural expression of faith and gratitude to God, but also because God commands them to be done.[77] This is what the so-called *tertius usus legis* expresses. Clarity is

---

66 On Stancari, cf. C.A. Selig, *Vollständige Historie der Augsburger Confession*, Halle 1730, vol. 2, pp. 714–947; cf. L. Cristiani, 'Stancaro', in *Dictionnaire de Théologie Catholique* 14, col. 2558–2561. This author, later expelled from the Protestant communion, was generally considered Nestorian, and his teaching paved the way, as we shall see, for some aspects of the *Aufklärung* theologies of justification.   67 Which he termed an *incorporatio*, or *induitio* (cf. J. Calvin, *Institutiones christianae III*, 11: 10).   68 See bibliography on Calvin's doctrine of justification in note 10 above. Calvin's theological and cultural dependencies seem not to have been unlike Melanchthon's: cf. A.E. McGrath, 'John Calvin and Late Medieval Thought: A Study in Late Medieval Influences upon Calvin's Theological Thought', in *Archiv für Reformationsgeschichte 77* (1986) 58–78.   69 J. Calvin, *Institutiones christianae III*, 11: 2 (1559).   70 Ibid.   71 Ibid., 23.   72 Ibid., 10.   73 Ibid. cf. W. Niesel, 'Calvin wider Osianders Rechtfertigungslehre', op. cit.   74 Cf. A.E. McGrath, op. cit., vol. 2, pp. 28–30.   75 *Formula Concordiae*, in H. Lietzmann et al. (eds.), *Die Bekenntnisschriften der evangelisch-lutherischen Kirche* ... op. cit., pp. 735–1100. English translation in T.G. Tappert et al., (ed.), The *Book of Concord: the Confessions of the Evangelical Lutheran Church* ..., op. cit., pp. 463–636.   76 On the areas of conflict between Protestants present at the preparation of the document, cf. B. Lohse, 'Innerprotestantische Lehrstreitigkeiten', in C. Andresen (ed.), *Handbuch der Dogmen- und Theologiegeschichte* ..., op. cit., vol. 2, pp. 102–138, and on the *Formula Concordiae*, cf. 'Das Konkordienbuch', in ibid., pp. 138–164.   77 *Formula Concordiae, Epitome*, 4: 6; 18, in T.G. Tappert et al. (eds.), op. cit., pp. 476f.

lost somewhat, however, when the *Formula* adds that works are not mandatory or necessary *for salvation*.[78]

2. The *synergist error* of Melanchthon and others, which held that man more or less cooperated with God in his salvation, was likewise rejected. Melanchthon's optimistic interpretation of John 6:44 ('No one can come to me unless drawn by the Father who sent me'), according to which God draws to himself *only those who wish to be drawn*, was put aside, and it was made clear that free will is impotent before God and remains completely under the sway on grace.[79] Of the three concurrent 'causes' of justification suggested by Melanchthon in 1535 (the Word, the Holy Spirit, man's will), the *Formula* retains only the second.[80] One of Melanchthon's disciples, V. Strigel,[81] had defended an Augustinian understanding of free will at the Weimar Colloquy in 1560. He held that sin acts on free will as garlic does on a magnet, temporarily removing its power of attraction; he added however that once the garlic is removed, the magnet recovers its own power, as does the human will once sin is forgiven. This theory was explicitly rejected by the *Formula of Concord*.[82]

3. In spite of all that, the document turned out substantially as a revindication of Melanchthon's fundamental position, insisting on a predominantly forensic understanding of justification as a divine reckoning, which must be distinguished from any intrinsic human righteousness.[83] 'The term *justification* in this matter means', the *Formula* says, 'to declare righteous and free from sins and from the eternal punishment of these sins on account of the righteousness of Christ which God reckons to faith.'[84]

A clear distinction was made between the 'imputed righteousness of faith', and the 'inchoate righteousness of the new obedience of faith' linked with works. Only the former counts before God; the latter, closely linked to fulfillment of the law, which is obligatory (the document speaks of the *tertius usus legis*), is impure and cannot stand before God. An unambiguous position was taken against Osiander and Stancari in favour of justification by the righteousness of Christ who is mediator as *both* God and man.[85]

Melanchthon's interpretation of Luther had clearly won out. But would it hold? 'Classical' Lutheran doctrines such as the presence of Christ in the believer, double predestination and the concept of *servum arbitrium*, tended to slip into the back-

---

78 Ibid., 4: 16, in T.G. Tappert et al. (eds.), op. cit., p. 477.   79 P. Melanchthon, *Annotationes in Ev. Io.*, in *Corpus Reformatorum* 15: 146: 'Deus . . . trahat autem volentem'.   80 *Formula Concordiae, Epitome*, 2: 5–6, in T.G. Tappert et al. (eds.), op. cit., p. 470.   81 Cf. V. Strigel, *Loci theologici*, ed., Petzel (4 vols, Neustadt 1581–1584). cf. H. Merz, *Historia vitae et controversiae V. Strigelii*, Tübingen 1732.   82 *Formula Concordiae, Epitome* 1: 15, in T.G. Tappert et al. (eds.), op. cit., p. 468.   83 Cf. USA 59.   84 *Formula Concordiae, Solida Declaratio* 3: 17, in T.G. Tappert et al. (eds.), op. cit., pp. 541f.   85 Ibid., 3: 4; 12; 56; 60, in T.G. Tappert et al. (eds.), op. cit., pp. 540f.; 549f.

ground. And the question remained: could a strictly forensic view of justification couple successfully with a relatively optimistic view of human freedom and its capacity to collaborate with the Holy Spirit, and avoid provoking an untenable or even explosive form of synergism not unlike the 'double justice' rejected by Rome and Luther after the Diet of Regensburg?

The authors of the *Formula of Concord* were clearly aware of this tension, and insisted that Christians above all should draw comfort and strength from Luther's injunction to distinguish between law and gospel.[86] At the level of everyday Christian life and commitment, such an overriding attitude might be sufficient, but it is quite clear that systematic theological reflection on the doctrine of justification in the following centuries, in attempting to resolve the tension existing between extrinsic divine action (mysterious and even unintelligible) and tangible human response (objective and accessible), would incline more and more towards a secularization of the Christian message and a predominance of a phenomenological and psychological (certainly non-theological) approach to anthropology.

THE ENLIGHTENMENT CRITIQUE OF ORTHODOX JUSTIFICATION DOCTRINE

Orthodox Lutheranism of the seventeenth century reflected extensively on the *Formula of Concord*, attempting to systematize the relationship between justification as an objective forensic act of God, and the dynamics of man's personal and conscious response to this gift. Understandably, an ever-growing interest was taken in the latter, what might be termed the psychology of grace and its subjective appropriation by the believer. Melanchthon had given expression to three aspects of Christian faith, *notitia*, *assensus* and *fiducia* (knowledge of objective truth, assent to the truth, heartfelt trust),[87] where Luther had paid attention principally to the last of the three, trust, wanting to avoid separating the objective means of salvation coming from God, from the subjective means of appropriation on the part of the believer.[88] More and more theologians turned their attention to the 'workings' of grace: Gospel call, illumination, conversion, regeneration, renewal, mystical union, sanctification, good works, perseverance, etc. At a confessional level, the immediate effect of this emphasis was an even greater sharpening of the distinction between justification and sanctification, and the practical outcome was the growth of the Lutheran pietistic movement, not unlinked with evangelicalism and interested chiefly in the experiential impact of God's grace. At an intellectual level, theological reflection on

---

86 *Formula Concordiae, Solida Declaratio* 5: 27, in T.G. Tappert et al. (eds.), op. cit., p. 563.   87 Melanchthon understood theology in terms of a progression from knowledge of the objective fact, to assent, and finally to trust. cf. USA 65.   88 Cf. J. Pelikan, 'The Origins of the Subject-Object Antithesis in Lutheran Theology', in *Concordia Theological Monthly* 21 (1950) 94–104.

justification had, at least indirectly, a decisive and lasting influence on the moralism of the *Aufklärung* or Enlightenment movement.[89]

Many illustrative episodes could be fruitfully considered. Three of them will be briefly examined: (1) Justification and Pietism; (2) Justification and the Enlightenment critique; (3) Justification, Kant, Schleiermacher and Ritschl. Whatever of the individual merits of these authors and currents of thought, it is generally held that 'almost all evangelical theologians of the age of the Enlightenment developed and propounded a new doctrine of justification which had hardly anything in common with the Augsburg Confession'.[90]

1. *Justification and Pietism*

Although Lutherans insisted consistently on the notion of forensic justification, scholarly attention came to be paid increasingly to the practical and experiential aspects of grace, conversion and Christian life. This occasioned a important rift between the stance of orthodox Lutherans and that of the Pietists, whose views were propagated and consolidated principally at the University of Halle.[91] One of the movement's best known exponents, Philipp Spener, put aside the forensic character of justification completely, and insisted on the active nature of faith and the transformational character of grace.[92] Similar notions are to be found in the writings of Jakob Böhme,[93] and in England in those of the Quaker Robert Barclay[94] and the Methodist John Wesley.[95]

---

89 The term *Aufklärung* was probably coined by Christian Wolff. On this period, cf. F. Copleston, *History of Philosophy*, vols 6 and 7, London 1947; H. Berkhof, *200 Jahre Theologie. Ein Reisebericht*, Neukirchen 1985; P. Hazard, *La crise de la conscience européenne* (1680–1715), 3 vols, Paris 1935; D. Innerarity, *Dialéctica de la modernidad*, Madrid 1990.   90 G. Müller and V. Pfnür, 'Justification—Faith—Works', in G.W. Forrell and J.F. McCue, *Confessing One Faith* . . . op. cit., pp. 117–146 (here, p. 140). On this question, cf. also G. Müller, *Die Rechtfertigungslehre: Geschichte und Probleme*, Gütersloh 1977, pp. 83ff.   91 Cf. A.B. Ritschl, *Geschichte des Pietismus*, 3 vols, Bonn 1880–1886; M. Schian, *Orthodoxie und Pietismus in Kampf um die Predigt*, Giessen 1912; R. Knox, *Enthusiasm: a Chapter in the History of Religion*, Oxford 1950; M. Schmidt, *Wiedergeburt und neuer Mensch: Gesammelte Studien zur Geschichte des Pietismus*, Witten 1969; G. Hornig, 'Der Pietismus', in C. Andresen (ed.), *Handbuch der Dogmen- und Theologiegeschichte*, vol. 3, Göttingen 1984, pp. 97–115; A.E. McGrath, *Iustitia Dei* . . . , op. cit., vol. 2, pp. 51–53.   92 Cf. A.J. Beachy, *The concept of Grace in the Radical Reformers*, Nieuwkoop 1977, on the presence of transformational motifs and their link-up with 'deification'.   93 Cf. J. Böhme, *The Way to Christ*, New York 1978. cf. G.A. Benrath, 'Jakob Böhme', in C. Andresen (ed.), *Handbuch der Dogmen- und Theologiegeschichte* . . . , op. cit., vol. 2, pp. 603–607.   94 Cf. R. Barclay, *An Apologie for the True Christian Divinity*, Manchester 1869, for whom the formal cause of justification is 'the revelation of God in the soul, changing, altering and renewing the mind' (ibid., p. 136), and that, because man is truly made righteous (cf. ibid., p. 131).   95 Cf. M. Piette, *John Wesley in the Evolution of Protestantism*, New York 1937; D. Lerch, *Heil und Heiligung bei John Wesley*, Zürich 1941; R. Knox, *Enthusiasm* . . . , op. cit., pp. 422–548; H. Lindström, *Wesley and Sanctification: A Study in the Doctrine of Salvation*, London 1956; A.C. Outler (ed.), *John Wesley*, New York 1964; G.H. Tavard, *Justification* . . . , op. cit., pp. 84–94.

Much of the Pietists' reflection constituted an attempt to return to Luther's doctrine of the direct 'mystical' presence of Christ in the believer, and was closely related to St Peter's concept of 'partaking in the divine nature' (cf. 2 Pet 1:4). In brief terms, Pietist authors held that if faith means to lay hold of Christ, it must constitute something active in the believer, linked to and nourished by a deep personal piety tending towards Christian perfection; Wesley's teaching of 'total sanctification' is a case in point.

Understandably Pietism manifests distinct hostility towards the *als-ob-Theologie* of forensic justification.[96] Pietists did not consider Christ as 'our (alien) justice', and simply avoid the notion of his 'vicarious satisfaction'. If Christ had in some way fulfilled the law *for us*, we would no longer be obliged to follow it. This sheer alternative comes to the fore clearly in Wesley's sermon *Justification by faith*: 'Least of all does justification imply that God is deceived in those whom he justifies; that he thinks them to be what, in fact, they are not; that he accounts them to be otherwise than they are. It does by no means imply that God judges concerning us contrary to the real nature of things; that he esteems us better than we really are, or believes us righteous when we are unrighteous . . . or judges that I am righteous, because another is so.'[97]

Still, there is no getting away from the fact that Pietism, despite its interest in renewing the practice of Christian piety threatened by the starkness and lopsidedness of forensic justification, tended in spite of its best intentions to gradually *displace faith* and confidence in God by a concentration on the practice of piety and ethical integrity. A virtuous *imitatio Christi* became not only the result and demonstration of justification, but in a sense its cause, in practice if not in theory. And the step to the unilateral moralism of the Enlightenment movement would be but a small one.

2. *Justification, Deism and the Enlightenment critique*

Christians had always considered the saving work of Christ on two distinct though complementary planes: (1) as a work of saving: redemption, reconciliation, being snatched from Satan and the clutches of sin; (2) as a work of teaching, through the preached word, deed and example. The first aspect stresses divine initiative, the work of grace, and man's sinful, alienated state. The second highlights the rôle of the Church, personal assimilation by the believer and intelligent response to grace.

---

96 Cf. J. Baur, *Salus Christiana: die Rechtfertigungslehre in der Geschichte des christlichen Heilsverständnisses*, Gütersloh 1968, pp. 91–95; J. Buchanan, *The Doctrine of Justification. An outline of its history in the Church and of its exposition from Scripture*, London 1867 (reprinted 1961), pp. 193–194. 97 J. Wesley, *Standard Sermons*, London 1920, vol. 1, p. 120. cf. W.R. Cannon, *The Theology of John Wesley, with Special Reference to the Doctrine of Justification*, New York 1946. G. Tavard, (*Justification* . . . , op. cit., p. 85) holds that Wesley's position in real terms is close to that of Luther's.

The two elements are inseparable in practice in the life of the Church and of each Christian.

From what we have seen, the Reformation, in drawing attention away from the relevance of human cooperation and personal involvement in the work of salvation, had to some degree placed a wedge between the two stages: salvation (God's action) and sanctification (man's work) move on different though not unconnected planes. The key element that facilitated the rise of the unilateral moralism characteristic of the Enlightenment period, centered on man's action, was an optimistic *denial of the unsaved state of man*. The doctrine of original sin, understood in terms of an inborn alienation from God within the creaturely condition, latent in historical human nature, commonly accepted though differently understood by Catholics and Lutherans alike, was put aside.[98] Hence Christ's work (and derivatively, therefore, the Church's) was seen to consist above all in *teaching humans how to behave well*, how to live properly, how to use their talents and qualities to the maximum benefit. This doctrine developed on two fronts, that of Deism in England, that of the *Aufklärung* (or Enlightenment) in Germany.

Deism[99] The moralistic version of Christianity that characterizes this period is clearly to be found in the work of Edward Herbert (Lord Cherbury), *De veritate religionis* (1624).[100] Herbert's ethical construct is naturalistic and static, Stoic and centered on the concept of self-determination of the individual will. Yet, insofar as man obtains his end in praising God, he must, besides, seek pardon upon sinning, and hope confidently for an eternal reward after this life. A clear about-turn can be detected in respect of orthodox Lutheranism: the real aim of religion is the promotion of morality; forgiveness is obtained not *per fidem, propter Christum*, as the *Confessio Augustana* would have it, but *propter poenitentiam*, in the measure that man turns back to God. God's action and initiative in Christ is simply excluded as irrelevant.

In the same direction, the philosopher John Locke concedes that, though the doctrine of original sin as such is unworthy of God,[101] man is beset from the beginning of his existence by a kind of congenital weakness. To be freed from this state, therefore, he must believe; to believe that, since the 'law of works makes no allowance for failing on any occasion . . . faith supplies the defect of full obedience'.[102] Therefore, 'these two, faith and repentance, i.e. believing Jesus to be the Messiah, *and a good life*, are the indispensable conditions of the new covenant, to be performed by all those who would obtain eternal life.'[103] And this is so, he explains, because the perfect obedience required of the Christian has become *more difficult*

98 Cf. A.E. McGrath, *Iustitia Dei . . .* , op. cit., vol. 2, pp. 135–148.   99 Cf. J. Forget, 'Déisme', in *Dictionnaire de Théologie Catholique* 4, col. 232–243; G. Hornig, 'Der englische Deismus', in C. Andresen (ed.), *Handbuch der Dogmen- und Theologiegeschichte . . .* , op. cit., vol. 3, pp. 115–125.   100 Cf. E.D. Hill, *Edward, Lord Herbert of Cherbury*, Boston 1987.   101 Cf. J. Locke, 'The Reasonableness of Christianity', in *The Works of John Locke*, Aalen 1963, vol. 7, pp. 6; 112.   102 Ibid., p. 14.   103 Ibid., p. 105. His notion is not unconnected with the theory of 'double justice'; cf. pp. 80–83 below.

after the fall.[104] The saving work of Christ consists above all, therefore, in the 'great encouragement he brought to a virtuous and pious life'.[105]

The idea of Locke would stick. Not only did Deism involve an eclipsing of the dogma of original sin and a renewed emphasis on the ethical or moralistic character of Christianity, especially on the idea of Christ as a great moral master, but in doing so, it relegated Christ's life and teaching to a *mere supplementary rôle*, making his divinity, and therefore his divine authority (communicated by the Church) at best optional, at worst superfluous. The law of Christ amounts to a slightly improved version of the eternal law of nature, a concession to weakness, a supplement to ineptitude. The title of Matthew Tindal's work *Christianity as Old as the Creation*[106] makes this quite clear.[107]

Thomas Chubb, in his work *The True Gospel of Jesus Christ* (1738), quite clearly affirmed the identity of the law of Christ with that of reason and nature, which had always existed.[108] Christ's rôle is one of establishing the laws man must live according to, encouraging and facilitating their observance, but always in the context that man is capable of discovering these laws for himself with unaided reason. Significantly, Chubb remarked that '*Christ preached his own life*, if I may so speak, and *lived his own doctrine*'.[109] At best Christ is considered as the guarantor of the moral law.

For Chubb, doctrines such as imputed righteousness and the vicarious value of the death of Christ, have complicated things unnecessarily and compromised Christian simplicity. Christ 'saves' us by moving us towards repentance and conversion.[110] Paul's affirmation that the 'blood of Christ takes away sin' (Eph 2:13) means simply this: that the courageous example of the Lord's death on Calvary moves the sinner to repentance, and he in turn makes *himself* worthy of receiving pardon.[111] Christ no longer mediates salvation as such, but only *confirms* the validity of the eternal law of nature, and facilitates our union with God by his inspiring example.

The Aufklärung   The pietistic re-awakening that took place in England under Wesley and Methodism certainly stemmed the tide of unilaterally rationalistic interpretations of Christianity rampant during the first half of the eighteenth century. As we saw, however, likenesses between the two 'spiritualities' are not superficial or casual, among other reasons because in both cases the rôle of man's freedom and action is made positively determinative.

In England, Pietism came in the wake of rationalistic Deism. In Germany, things

---

104 Cf. J. Locke, op. cit., pp. 3–15.   105 Ibid., p. 148.   106 Cf. M. Tindal, *Christianity as old as the creation* (G. Gawlick, ed.), Stuttgart-Bad Cannstatt 1967.   107 The notion that Christianity represents simply the best rendering of the law of nature becomes very common; cf. for example, T. Morgan, *The Moral Philosopher*, vol. 1, London 1738, p. 439, who notes that Christ was simply a 'superior' moral legislator to Moses, Zarathustra, Confucius or Mohammed (cf. ibid., pp. 411–412).   108 Cf. T. Chubb, 'The True Gospel of Jesus Christ', in *Posthumous Works*, vol. 2, London 1748, p. 20.   109 Ibid., p. 55. Emphasis added.   110 Cf. ibid., pp. 32; 43–49; 112–120; 164.   111 Cf. ibid., pp. 115–116.

moved in the opposite direction, for the *Aufklärung* (or Enlightenment) movement followed and consolidated that of Pietism. The seventeenth-century pietistic critique of orthodox Lutheran doctrines of justification, emphasizing the moral dimension of the latter, inevitably ended up by concentrating principally on the changeabout that takes place in man at justification. How this happens or who effects it and why, is of secondary interest. Lip service is still paid to the forensic or declaratory side of justification. And the point is that the latter is considered *possible and meaningful* only *because* of the reality of inherent justice in man. In other words, justification 'by faith alone' is no longer the *articulus stantis et cadentis ecclesiae*. In fact, many of these authors see no difficulty in holding on to a forensic or declaratory understanding of justification on God's part, and, at the same time, an autonomous inherent justification (*mutatio moralis*) on man's.[112] In simple terms, justification means that God endorses or seals *a posteriori* what has already taken place *a priori* in man's own life.[113]

The re-evaluation of the regenerative side of justification was unquestionably among the principal merits of the *Aufklärung* movement in Germany. Unfortunately, as later developments were to show, the movement would produce a radical about-face in Christians' understanding both of the relationship between God and man, and of the person and work of Jesus Christ. Three authors are particularly representative of this period: J.K. Dippel,[114] J.G. Töllner,[115] and G.S. Steinbart.[116]

Dippel, taking his cue from the theologically-based political philosophy of Thomas Hobbes[117] expressed his understanding of sin and redemption in the context of a parallel between God and the State. The function of both is that of man's well-being. Yet neither can be said, strictly speaking, to be *offended* as such by the transgressions of its subjects, and so the only purpose of punishment is the deterrence of man from sin and his correction in case of transgression. In other words, the only one damaged or affected by sin is man himself. God is 'affected' only insofar as his divine plan of creation and providence is temporarily disturbed. But insofar as there

---

112 L. von Mosheim, for example, in his *Elementa theologiae dogmaticae*, Nuremberg 1758, pp. 713; 822, says that justification is a divine action which imputes the justice of Christ, absolves from guilt and punishment and accords the right to grace and glory. However all three aspects are dependent on the previous conversion, faith and regeneration of the believer. God, it would seem, simply 'rubber stamps' what has already been established and consolidated. For the influence of this theology on preaching, cf. R. Krause, *Die Predigt der späten deutschen Aufklärung*, Stuttgart 1965.   113 Cf. A.E. McGrath, *Iustitia Dei . . .*, op. cit., vol. 2, pp. 142–148.   114 On Dippel, cf. A.B. Ritschl, *Die christliche Lehre von der Rechtfertigung und Versöhnung*, vol. 3, Bonn 1888 (English translation, *The Christian Doctrine of Justification and Reconciliation*, Edinburgh 1871, pp. 337–341).   115 Cf. especially J.G. Töllner, *Der thätige Gehorsam Christi untersucht*, Breslau 1768; cf. A.B. Ritschl, *The Christian Doctrine of Justification and Reconciliation*, op. cit., pp. 346–355; J. Baur, *Salus Christiana*, op. cit., pp. 132–144.   116 Cf. especially G.S. Steinbart, *System der reinen Philosophie oder Glückseligkeitslehre des Christentums*, Züllichau 1778.   117 Cf. T. Hobbes, *Leviathan*, London 1651. On Hobbes, cf. for example G. Schedler, 'Hobbes on the Basis of Political Obligation', in *Journal of the History of Philosophy* 15 (1977)165–170; P.E. Moreau, 'Loi divine et loi naturelle selon Hobbes', in *Revue Internationale de Philosophie* 33 (1979) 443–451.

is nothing 'personal' involved, there is no place for 'vindictive' or 'retributive' justice, divine wrath and suchlike. As a result, the whole understanding of the soteriological rôle of Christ is changed. Christ is no longer required to appease God or make satisfaction to him by dying on the Cross. The passion and death of Jesus, in all its nobility, virtue and pathos, offers simply an inspiring model and encouragement for man.

Dippel's views were extended and deepened by *J.G. Töllner's* devastating criticism of the doctrine of the satisfying value of Christ's 'active' obedience on the Cross.[118] He takes Christ exclusively 'according to his humanity' and argues that, insofar as he was under the same obligation as anybody else to obey the law (he was not *ex lex* as the Lutherans held), his obedience was of value for himself but for nobody else. Töllner was not prepared to accept common Reformation teaching of Christ as *caput et sponsor electorum*, since he found it impossible to consider Christ either as an authorized representative of humanity, on whose behalf he would suffer and make amends, or as one whose obedience would be accepted by God as if it was performed by those who did not and could not perform it.

Hence, for Töllner, it is the renewal (*Heiligung*) of man rather than the satisfaction of Christ that leads to the bestowal of grace (*Begnadigung*). Christ's obedience is a supreme moral quality that inspires a generous response in man insofar as it assures humanity of God's graciousness towards it, and confirms the reliability of the divine promise of grace. In other words, Christ represents God to man, but not the other way round.

Again, *G.S. Steinbart's* reflection is centered on Christ as the supreme personification of perfect and complete human morality. Christ's simple revolutionary message has been obscured, he claimed, by the accumulation, throughout the history of Christianity, of a series of theological accretions such as original sin, predestination (Augustine), Christ's satisfaction (Anselm), imputation of the righteousness of Christ (Luther). He sees in them all the reflection of an unresolved Manichaean tension between God and man which must be eliminated. Christ's saving work consisted above all, according to Steinbart, of freeing us from *false conceptions of God* (for example, as a wrathful tyrant or jail-keeper), thus restoring the right order between man and his creator that had been damaged by the former's transgressions. It is made quite clear that man is not *naturally* alienated from God as Lutherans held. Man may turn away from God, but can be reconciled by simply turning back again, and is *inspired* to do so in fact by the life, death and outstanding moral character of Jesus Christ. If Christ is said to *redeem* man from sin, all this means is that he has redeemed man from a *false* idea of God, of Satan, etc.

118 Cf. J.G. Töllner, *Der thätige Gehorsam Christi untersucht . . .* , op. cit.

3. *Justification, Kant, Schleiermacher and Ritschl*

Aufklärung soteriology had, to all appearances, dealt a definitive death blow to the classical Lutheran understanding of justification *propter Christum per fidem*. The reasonableness of the criticisms made to the seemingly immoderate claims of Lutheran divines was evident. How could Christ 'take our place'? How, therefore, could God consider and make us just through *his* Incarnation, life, death and resurrection? Was it not sufficient to say that his life offered us a noble, inspiring example of courage and solidarity which we should strive to emulate?

The last word, however, had not been said. In this countering of *Aufklärung* soteriology and anthropology, the contributions of Kant, Schleiermacher and Ritschl must be given careful attention.

Kant, the categorical imperative and reconciliation   The influence of Kant on modern thought forms, particularly in the area of epistemology and ethics, is unquestioned. His insistence on the inalienable subjectivity of human judgement, on the existence of synthetic *a priori* judgements, has left a deep mark on western thought and even on Christian theology. However, as regards the justification debate and in particular the difficulties brought to the fore by German *Aufklärung* thinkers, the key issue for Kant lies in the area of ethics, specifically that of the *absolute autonomy of moral life*, which calls into serious question the value of pure *moral exemplarism*, essential to *Aufklärung* soteriology. Apart of course from the *Critique of Practical Reason*, his 1793 work *Religion within the limits of mere reason* is particularly relevant for the theme we are now considering.[119]

Reflection on ethical life for Kant is focussed not so much on the significance of particular precepts (*casuistry*), but rather on the *unconditional authority* of the moral law in general (*das Sollen*, the 'must', what has to be done). Compliance to the law, and with it a human 'sense of duty', is not a means to an end (fulfillment or happiness, as the *Aufklärer* would have held), but is the *end* itself, man's highest achievement. Man's sense of moral obligation (the 'categorical imperative' of the autonomous free will), in other words, is prior to the tangible usefulness, effectiveness or productivity of particular moral acts. His moral action therefore is not conditioned even by the existence or commanding will of a Supreme Being, God, whom Kant accepts at best as the exterior guarantor of the moral law.

119 Cf. I. Kant, 'Religion innerhalb der Grenzen der bloßen Vernunft', in *Kants gesammelte Schriften*, vol. 6, Berlin 1969 (English tr., *Religion within the Limits of Reason Alone*, New York 1960). On this work, cf. A. Schweitzer's study *Die Religionsphilosophie Kants in der Kritik der reinen Vernunft bis Religion innerhalb der Grenzen der bloßen Vernunft*, Freiburg i. Br. 1899; G. di Giovanni, 'Free Choice and Radical Evil. The Irrationalism of Kant's Moral Theory', in G. Funke—T.M. Seebohm (eds), *Proceedings of the Sixth International Kant Congress II/2*, Washington 1989, pp. 311–325; G.E. Michaelson, *Fallen Freedom. Kant on radical Evil and moral Regeneration*, Cambridge 1990; J.M. Odero, *La fe en Kant*, Pamplona 1992, pp. 99–109.

The reason why *das Sollen*, or moral obligation, can exist in man and constitutes the very core of his human dignity, lies in the fact that man retains the factual possibility of achieving moral perfection, a possibility, however, which inevitably involves the possibility of *failing* to achieve such perfection, when man subordinates the demands of *das Sollen* to those of sensitive nature. Sin or transgression, therefore, strikes to the very core of man's moral being, not only nor principally insofar as he is capable of acting in ways not conducive to perfection or happiness, but because when 'the must' is thwarted, the very moral substance of man's being is affected, and he *becomes* 'evil'. Sinful transgression therefore, bringing man to irresponsibility and neglect of duty, has ontological weight; it goes to the core of the human being and 'makes' him evil.

Now the question arises: how is it that man does in fact choose in this mistaken way? If there is no evil within man unless he himself brings it about, how does the will come to be corrupted? How can the fundamental ambivalence of the human will be accounted for? Kant, avoiding the theme of original sin as such, speaks however of a kind of 'radical evil' within the human condition which accounts for the factual distance that lies between man's actual state and the unattainable perfection (*Urbild*) he aspires to and must (*sollen*) attain. Unable to procure the perfection he strives after in a single move, man must be satisfied with retaining and reinforcing a firm disposition or intention (*Gesinnung*) towards obtaining perfection.

From the point of view of the question we have in hand, Kant's contribution comes in at this point. God treats man in possession of this upright disposition or intention of working towards moral perfection as if he were already in *full* possession of such perfection. In brief terms, by grace (*aus Gnaden*) God transforms the *Gesinnung* into the *Urbild*.[120] The *als-ob-Theologie*, characteristic of orthodox Lutheran forensic justification doctrine, crops up once more. For the *Aufklärer*, conversely, moral improvement (*Verbesserung*) actually paves the way for being graced (*Begnadigung*). But for Kant, things work the other way around. Man is made 'pleasing to God' on the basis of God's gratuitous act of overlooking his present deficiencies. Referring doubtlessly to a phrase which lies at the very heart of the justification debate, Kant says that whoever strives to be pleasing to God 'in so far as it lies within his ability', may rely on God to supplement his deficiencies.[121] In this sense Kant's understanding, taken from different angles, is not distant either from the *facienti quod est in se* of the *via moderna*, or from the 'rubber-stamp' rendering of forensic justification not uncommon in the *Aufklärung* period, interpretations hardly acceptable to orthodox Lutheranism.

But Kant's contribution to the topic of justification does not end there. In principle he would be in complete agreement with the *Aufklärer* in denying the notion of vicarious satisfaction, because the very notion of moral autonomy and his insist-

120 Cf. I. Kant, 'Religion innerhalb der Grenzen der bloßen Vernunft', op. cit., pp. 75f. 121 Cf. ibid., pp. 117; 120.

ence on personal responsibility could never envisage a single (outstanding) individual compensating for or removing the guilt of one destitute of moral qualities. However, what could be said of the person who repents deeply of his past life, radically altering his evil disposition, yet carrying the guilt of previous transgressions?[122] In being reconciled, what 'happens' to his past life, to his sinful identity, deeply inscribed into his very being? Surprisingly, Kant comes quite close here to the notion of vicarious substitution, though from another perspective, in saying that such an individual becomes *moralisch ein anderer*, 'morally speaking a different person'.[123] The new *Gesinnung* or disposition takes the place of (*vertitt*) the old, and man, whose former guilt is abolished (*abgetan*), is now justified by God: this is what *reconciliation* means.[124]

In many ways the analysis of Kant is not completely satisfactory, at heart because he attempts to reflect in an exclusively philosophical way on a deeply theological question in an idealistic and anthropocentric framework. For him, the necessity of grace is as much a postulate of practical reason as is the existence of God. Yet, in facing up to the notion of 'radical evil', in questioning the value of pure moral exemplarism, and in clarifying the complexity of the relationship between justification and moral renewal, he did have the merit of significantly countering the superficial optimism and anthropological individualism promoted by the *Aufklärer*.

Schleiermacher and religious experience   Friedrich Schleiermacher, though not normally considered as a Romantic himself, reacted, much as the Romantics did, against both the moralistic shallowness of the *Aufklärer* and the 'bloodless ballet of Kantian categories' (Bradley). In his principal work *The Christian faith* (first edition, 1821–22),[125] centre stage is now taken by the individual's religious faith and piety (*Frömmigkeit*), and no longer by the quality of his moral action. Concrete and personal religious life is the fundamental reality (*Grundtatsache*) Christian life must be centered on, and theology must account for. According to Schleiermacher the *starting point* for theology is piety or religious experience,[126] the essence of which is identified with feeling (*Gefühl*), or immediate self-consciousness.[127] Christian doctrines, practically speaking, are simply individual accounts of Christian religious experience.[128]

The peculiar character of Christian self-consciousness, completely tied in with the dynamics of sin and redemption, is 'a feeling of absolute dependence', which faith presents to us as a consciousness of *God*,[129] our Creator and Lord. This sense of dependency on God, at the origin of piety, is the result of the action of Christ on the collective consciousness of the Christian community. Neither moralism nor in-

---

122 Cf. ibid., pp. 66–78.   123 Ibid., p. 74.   124 Cf. ibid., p. 183–184.   125 Cf. F.D.E. Schleiermacher, *The Christian Faith*, Edinburgh 1989 (orig., *Der christliche Glaube*, 2 vols, Berlin 1960, corresponding to Schleiermacher's fourth edition, 1842).   126 Cf. ibid., no. 33, 3 (*The Christian Faith* . . . , op. cit., pp. 136f.).   127 Cf. ibid., no. 3, 2–4 (pp. 6–11).   128 Cf. ibid., no. 15, 1 (pp. 76 f.).   129 Cf. ibid., no. 4, 4 (p. 17).

tellectualism have any place; this is 'pure' religion. Christ's action consists of a stimulation, elevation and renewal of the feeble and repressed God-consciousness present in 'fallen' human nature, by the communication of the uninterrupted 'absolutely powerful God-consciousness' present in Christ himself.[130]

In this Schleiermacher goes beyond the teaching of the *Aufklärer*, for whom Christ is considered as a mere teacher of abstract moral principles which in principle should effect an ever-increasing perfection in us.[131] Besides, the *first stage* of redemption for him is the consciousness of sin, understood as the first presentiment of the possibility of both redemption[132] and punishment[133] from without. The *Aufklärer*, conversely, only accepted the notion of punishment in the context of a natural self-inflicted consequence of moral transgression.

Like the *Aufklärer*, however, justification for Schleiermacher is contingent upon and posterior to a real change in man. The difference between the two approaches lies in the nature of this change. For the former, a moral change is required, and strict proportion is observed between human good and divine reward. For the latter, there is no strict correlation between human good and divine reward,[134] for the change consists of 'laying hold of Christ in a believing manner' (*Christum gläubig ergreifen*).[135] This is a result not of man's previous action (in man there is an inherent disposition towards sin, a 'total incapacity for the good'[136]), but of being assumed into fellowship with Christ.[137] Against the Pelagians, he insists that *man needs to be saved* (from outside, as it were); against the Manichaeans that *he must be savable*.[138]

Schleiermacher likewise criticizes the orthodox Lutheran understanding of justification by Christ's alien merit seeing in it an untenable, purely objective external transaction, and considering it 'magical' and Docetical.[139] Such a salvation, he hold, since it is 'not mediated by anything natural', exerts no real influence on man's situation; the historical figure of Jesus of Nazareth is thus made superfluous.[140]

Ritschl and the triumph of the Aufklärung   Schleiermacher's 'theological' successor was undoubtedly Albrecht Ritschl. In his work major work on the history of the doctrine of justification, *Justification and Reconciliation* (1870),[141] he insists, like his master, that Christianity is essentially soteriological in character, in that there is no true knowledge of God and his action outside the sphere of the redemptive activity

---

130 Cf. ibid., no. 94 (pp. 385–389); no. 106, 1 (pp. 476 f.).   131 Cf. ibid., no. 100, 3 (pp. 428–431).   132 Cf. ibid., no. 109, 4 (pp. 503ff.).   133 Cf. ibid., no. 84, 3 (pp. 349f.).   134 Cf. ibid., no. 84, 1 (pp. 345–347).   135 Ibid., no. 109, 4 (p. 503).   136 Ibid., no. 70, 2 (p. 283).   137 Cf. ibid., no. 107, 1 (p. 478f.).   138 Cf. ibid., no. 22, 2 (pp. 98–99).   139 Cf. ibid., no. 22, 2 (p. 99); no. 104, 4–5 (pp. 457ff.), where he criticizes the doctrine of 'vicarious satisfaction'.   140 Cf. ibid., no. 22, 2 (pp. 98f.).   141 Cf. A.B. Ritschl, *Die christliche Lehre von der Rechtfertigung und Versöhnung*, 3 vols, especially the last: *Die positive Entwicklung der Lehre*, Bonn 1888 (English translation, *The Christian Doctrine of Justification and Reconciliation*, Edinburgh 1871). On Ritschl, cf. K. Barth, *Die protestantische Theologie im 19. Jahrhundert*, Zurich 1947, pp. 601ff.; A.E. McGrath, *Iustitia Dei . . .*, op. cit., vol. 2, pp. 159–170.

of Christ. Hence his intense suspicion towards the rôle played by Hellenic thought and metaphysics in theological reflection, and, by implication, of the rationalizing and conciliating efforts of the *Aufklärer*. On the question of justification, Ritschl insists principally on its objective side, that is, on the effective remission of sin.[142] This objective dimension is prior to, though inseparable from the subjective awareness of forgiveness[143] (in this he leans on Schleiermacher), and a real renewal of one's life.[144] Reconciliation (*Versöhnung*) is, therefore, the direct consequence and, as it were, the 'ethical complement' of justification.

Ritschl's clearest break with the *Aufklärung* moralistic soteriologies lies in the fact that he considers justification as a synthetic judgement on God's part, and not as an analytic one. The *Aufklärer* contended that God 'analyses' or reflects upon the righteousness *already* present in man, and, on the basis of such an analysis, pronounces man to be justified, that is, proclaims the verdict of justification. Ritschl, conversely, insists that justification on God's part is a synthetic or creative action, in such a way that God concedes a 'new predicate' to the sinner.[145] In other words, God *effects* rather than *endorses* the righteousness of man.

Thus, as regards the priority of divine action over the life and action of the sinner, Ritschl sides clearly with orthodox Lutheranism. Insisting, however, that God's work does leave its reconciling mark on the sinner, his affinity to the *Aufklärer* in the area of Christology is closer than he might be prepared to admit.[146] McGrath summarizes Ritschl's position as follows: 'Christ is *the revealer of certain significant . . . insights* concerning *an unchangeable situation* between God and man, rather than the founder of a new relation between God and man.'[147] Salvation in Jesus Christ, in other words, is dehistoricized. God acts, certainly, justifying and reconciling; but the Gospel of the Kingdom simply *proclaims what God has effected*; God offers grace, of which Christ's historic life and work is but a symbol and an *a posteriori* confirmation, but not an effective mediation. The individual's appropriation of such a gift, faith, is directed elsewhere than to Christ.

As a result of Ritschl's reflection, scholarly research tended to turn its attention more and more to the life of Christ, that is, to his *typological* 'religious personality and cosmic significance', and not so much to his *personal* mediating and saving work. The *Aufklärer* had made their point and left their mark.[148] A silent though complete turn-about had taken place regarding the central dogma of Christian faith, that is, the saving Incarnation of God's Word, the supreme and definitive divine gesture that *reveals* sinfulness and human dignity, and at the same time *effects* salvation.

---

142 Ritschl does not hide his admiration for Osiander (cf. his study 'Die Rechtfertigungslehre des Andreas Osiander', in *Jahrbücher für deutsche Theologie* 2 (1857) 785–829).   143 Cf. A.B. Ritschl, *Die christliche Lehre von der Rechtfertigung und Versöhnung*, op. cit., no. 31.   144 Cf. ibid., no. 15.   145 Cf. ibid., no. 16.   146 As M. Kähler points out (*Zur Lehre von der Versöhnung*, Leipzig 1898).   147 A.E. McGrath, *Iustitia Dei . . .* , op. cit., vol. 2, p. 169. Emphasis added. cf. idem., *The Making of Modern German Christology: From the Enlightenment to Pannenberg*, Oxford 1986, pp. 53–68 (on the Christology of Ritschl and Harnack).   148 The theologies of Rénan, Réville, Sabatier, Harnack, are all seem based on a narrative or inspirational Christology.

Reactions to Christologies of this kind, unrecognizable for the great majority of Christians, did not take long to appear, among Catholics and Protestants, most of them attempting to resolve the tensions between what has come to be denominated as the 'Jesus of history' and the 'Christ of faith'. Theologies of authors particularly relevant in this area, such as A. Harnack, A. Schweitzer, K. Barth, R. Bultmann, E. Käsemann etc., will be taken into account in the second part of this work. And, as we shall see, several of them will be seen to have been responsible for putting the doctrine of justification once more in the limelight.

CHAPTER THREE

Justification at the Council of Trent (1547)

One of the most striking features of the theology that developed in the wake of the establishment of Lutheranism, examined in chapter two, was that the theological, social and spiritual reality of Catholicism simply slipped into the background. Catholic and Lutheran attempts at public reconciliation through doctrinal clarification and reform remain a constant feature of the life of Christendom during first half of the sixteenth century, but after that, both sides seem to go their own way. Superficial or simply inaccurate renderings of Catholic doctrine and spirituality abound in the centuries we have just been examining,[1] as do imprecise presentations of Lutheran doctrines among Catholics.[2]

However, though explicit dialogue simply died out between the two sides in the centuries following the break, the same fundamental issues keep on being discussed, particularly in the area of the relationship between grace and freedom (Jansenism, Quietism, the controversy *de auxiliis*), and the linkup between forensic justification, moralistic reconciliation and sanctification, already examined.

In any case, of particular interest in obtaining a better understanding both of the impact of Luther's theology on his contemporaries, and of the justification theologies of the period preceding the sixteenth century, is the decree on justification emanated by the sixth session of the Council of Trent (1547),[3] four hundred and fifty years ago.

1 Cf. for example the comments of Ritschl on Catholic 'moralism' which he more or less confuses with the *Aufklärung*, and particularly his misunderstanding of the notion of *gratia gratum faciens*: cf. A.B. Ritschl, *Die christliche Lehre von der Rechtfertigung und Versöhnung*, op. cit., no. 16. 2 Cf. especially M. Bogdahn, *Die Rechtfertigungslehre Luthers im Urteil der neueren katholischen Theologie: Möglichkeiten und Tendenzen der katholischen Lutherdeutung in evangelischer Sicht*, Göttingen, 1971; H.G. Pöhlmann, *Rechtfertigung: die gegenwaertige kontroverstheologische Problematik der Rechtfertigungslehre zwischen der evangelisch-lutherischen und der römisch-katholischen Kirche*, Gütersloh 1971. 3 The bibliography on this session of the Council is vast. cf. especially H. Jedin, *A History of the Council of Trent*, Edinburgh 1961, vol. 2, pp. 166–196; 239–316 and also J. Hefner, *Die Entstehungsgeschichte der Trienter Rechtfertigungsdekretes: ein Beitrag zur Geschichte des Reformationszeitalters*, Paderborn 1909; J. Rivière, 'Justification: le Concile de Trente', in *Dictionnaire de Théologie Catholique* 8/2 (1925) 1964–1992. Besides, in roughly chronological order, cf. H. Rückert, *Die Rechtfertigungslehre auf dem Tridentinischen Konzil*, Bonn 1925; idem., 'Promereri: Eine Studie zum tridentinischen Rechtfertigungsdekret als Antwort an H.A. Oberman', in *Zeitschrift für Theologie und Kirche* 68 (1971) 162–194; H. Huthmacher, 'La Certitude de la grâce au Concile de Trente', in *Nouvelle Revue Théologique* 65 (1933) 213–226; E. Stakemeier, 'Die theologischen Schulen auf dem Trienter Konzil während der Rechtfertigungsverhandlung', in *Theologisches Quartalschrift* 117 (1936) 188–207; 322–350; 446–504; idem., *Glaube und Rechtfertigung. Das Mysterium der christlichen Rechtfertigung aus dem Glauben dargestellt nach den Verhandlungen und Lehrbestimmungen des Konzils von Trient*, Freiburg i. Br. 1937; V. Heynck, 'Untersuchungen über

70

HISTORY OF THE DECREE ON JUSTIFICATION[4]

In justice it should be said that the Council Fathers gathered at Trent were keenly aware of the centrality of the doctrine of justification. Luther had made his point,

die Reuelehre der tridentinischen Zeit', in *Franziskanische Studien* 29 (1942) 25–44; 120–150; 30 (1943) 53–73; idem., 'A Controversy at the Council of Trent concerning the Doctrine of Duns Scotus', in *Franciscan Studies* 9 (1949) 181–258; idem., 'Der Anteil des Konzilstheologen Andreas de Vega O.F.M. an dem ersten amtlichen Entwurf des Trienter Rechtfertigungsdekretes', in *Franziskanische Studien* 33 (1951) 49–81; idem., 'Zur Kontroverse über die Gnadengewißheit auf dem Konzil von Trient', in *Franziskanische Studien* 37 (1955) 1–17; 161–188; idem., 'Die Bedeutung von "mereri" und "promereri" bei dem Konzilstheologen Andreas de Vega', in *Franziskanische Studien* 50 (1968) 224–238; F. Cavallera, 'La session VI du concile de Trente', in *Bulletin de littérature écclésiastique* 44 (1943) 229–238; 45 (1944) 220–231; 46 (1945) 54–56; 47 (1946) 103–112; idem., 'Le Décret du concile de Trente sur la justification', in ibid. 49 (1948) 21–31; 51 (1950) 65–76; 146–168; idem., 'La Session VI du concile de Trente. Foi et justification', in ibid., 53 (1952) 99–108; G. Gutiérrez, 'Un capítulo de teología pretridentino: el problema de la justificación', in *Miscelánea Comillas* 4 (1945) 7–31; A. de Villalmonte, 'Andrés de Vega y el proceso de la justificación según el Concilio Tridentino', in *Revista Española de Teología* 5 (1945) 311–374; B. Xiberta, 'La causa meritoria de la justificación en las controversias pretridentinas', in *Revista Española de Teología* 5 (1945) 87–106; J. Sagués, 'Un libro pretridentino de Andrés de Vega sobre la justificación', in *Estudios Eclesiásticos* 20 (1946) 175–209; S. Gonzáles Rivas, 'Los teólogos salmantinos y el decreto de la justificación', in *Estudios Eclesiásticos* 21 (1947) 147–170; A. Stakemeier, *Das Konzil von Trient über die Heilsgewißheit*, Heidelberg 1949; G. Schreiber (ed.), *Das Weltkonzil von Trient: Sein Werden und Wirken*, 2 vols, Freiburg i. Br. 1951, particularly the studies of F. Buuck, V. Heynck, and F.J. Schierse; A. Walz, 'La giustificazione tridentina. Nota sul dibattito e sul decreto conciliare', in *Angelicum* 28 (1951) 97–138; P. Pas, 'La doctrine de la double justice au Concile de Trente', in *Ephemerides Theologiae Lovanensis* 30 (1954) 5–53; J. Olzarán, *Documentos inéditos tridentinos sobre la justificación*, Madrid 1957; H. Jedin, 'Le Concile de Trente fut-il un obstacle a la réunion des chrétiens?', in Various authors, *Union et désunion des chrétiens*, Paris 1963, pp. 79–94; W. Joest, 'Die tridentinische Rechtfertigungslehre', in *Kerygma und Dogma* 9 (1963) 41-59; P. Brunner, 'Die Rechtfertigungslehre des Konzils von Trient', in E. Schlink and H. Volk (eds.), *Pro veritate: Ein theologischer Dialog*, Münster 1963, pp. 59–69; M. Flick and Z. Alszeghy, *Il vangelo della grazia*, Firenze 1964, pp. 428–433; H.A. Oberman, 'Das tridentinische Rechtfertigungsdekret im Lichte spätmittelalterlicher Theologie', in *Zeitschrift für Theologie und Kirche* 61 (1964) 251–282; idem., ' "Iustitia Christi" and "Iustitia Dei": Luther and the Scholastic Doctrines of Justification', in *Harvard Theological Review* 59 (1966) 1–26; K.J. Becker, *Die Rechtfertigungslehre nach Domingo de Soto: Das Denken eines Konzilsteilnehmers vor, in und nach Trient*, Rome 1967; G. Bavaud, 'La doctrine de la justification d'après Calvin et le Concile de Trent', in *Verbum Caro* 22 (1968) 83–92; G. Philips, 'La justification luthéreienne et la Concile de Trente', in *Ephemerides Theologiae Lovanensis* 47 (1971) 340–358; idem., *L'union personnelle avec le Dieu vivant. Essai sur l'origine et le sens de la grâce créée*, Leuven 1974, pp. 201–208; V. Pfnür, 'Zur Verurteilung der reformatorischen Rechtfertigungslehre auf dem Konzil von Trient', in *Annuarium Historiae Conciliorum* 8 (1976) 407–428; J. Alfaro, 'Certitude de l'espérance et certitude de la grâce', in *Nouvelle Revue Théologique* 94 (1972) 3–42, especially pp. 10–35; J.M. Rovira Belloso, *Trento. Una interpretación teológica*, Barcelona 1979, pp. 153–244; W. Dantine, 'Das Dogma im tridentinischen Katholizismus: Die Lehre von der Rechtfertigung', in C. Andresen (ed.), *Handbuch der Dogmen- und Theologiegeschichte . . .*, op. cit., vol. 2, pp. 453–464; G.H. Tavard, *Justification . . .*, op. cit., pp. 70–80; A.E. McGrath, *Iustitia Dei . . .*, op. cit., vol. 2, pp. 80–97; J.-M. Capdevila i Montaner, *Liberación y divinización del hombre*, vol. 2: *Estudio sistemático*, Salamanca 1994, pp. 137–157; F. Buzzi, *Il Concilio di Trento (1545–1563). Breve introduzione ad alcuni temi teologici principali*, Milan 1995, pp. 71–119.   4 Cf. especially the works of J. Hefner, *Die Entstehungs geschichte des Trienter Rechtfertigungsdekretes . . .*,

and a satisfactory reply had to be supplied.[5] Indeed, although the decree on justification was not the first nor perhaps even the most directly influential of the council decrees, it was, theologically speaking, the most important one, acting as a point of reference for all the others, and indeed for the development of Catholic spirituality and theology of grace over the centuries that followed. The promulgation of the decree marked perhaps the first time for an ecumenical council to treat a particular dogmatic issue at such length in a positive and expository fashion *before* the reproving canons are listed.[6] Adolph Harnack would not be the only one to suggest that, if this decree had been emitted some thirty years earlier, for example at the Fifth Lateran Council, the Lutheran schism might never have happened in the first place.[7]

In many ways, the scene for the decree on justification (the sixth session of Trent) was set by the previous session, the fifth, on original sin, indicating as it did, for both Catholics and Lutherans, the *terminus a quo* for justification. The five canons of the fifth session offered a brief though adequate summary of Church teaching on the matter, although the first four are virtual repetitions of previous Councils (Carthage XV, 418, and Orange II, 529, connected respectively to the Pelagian and Semipelagian controversies), and only the last (on the nature of concupiscence, or the sinfulness that remains after Baptism) is related to Lutheranism. On the area of justification, however, no previous magisterial declarations were available: very little had been said on the saving work of Christ, on the nature of faith, or even on grace itself in a soteriological context. So the significance of the decree for the life of the Church and for the counter-Reformation can hardly be sufficiently appreciated.

1. *Schools of thought at Trent* [8]

It is sometimes said that three theological schools or tendencies were represented and active during the Council sessions which dealt with justification: the Augustinian, the Scotist and the Thomistic.[9] In reality, only the second two were clearly identifiable.

Franciscan theologians, for the most part followers of Scotus, were numerous at Trent. Most prominent among them was Andrés de Vega.[10] Perhaps the most salient feature of the Scotist position in respect of justification was that it considered both faith and repentance as a true *preparation* for justification.[11] Their position

op. cit.; A. Walz, 'La giustificazione tridentina', op. cit.; H. Jedin op. cit.; F. Buzzi, *Il Concilio di Trento* (1545–1563), op. cit., pp. 75–85.   5 Cf. H. Jedin, *A History of the Council of Trent . . .* , op. cit., vol. 2, p. 171.   6 Cf. A.E. McGrath, *Iustitia Dei . . .* , op. cit., vol. 2, pp. 8of.   7 Cf. A. Harnack, *Dogmengeschichte III* (5 ed.), Tübingen 1931, p. 711. Authors such as V. Subilia (*La giustificazione per fede . . .* op. cit., p. 84) do not share Harnack's optimism.   8 Cf. A.E. McGrath, op. cit., vol. 2, pp. 63–68.   9 This is the classical position of A. Stakemeier, 'Die theologischen Schulen . . .', op. cit.   10 Cf. the studies of V. Heynck, cited above, of A. de Villalmonte, 'Andrés de Vega y el proceso de la justificación según el Concilio Tridentino', op. cit. and of A.E. McGrath, *Iustitia Dei . . .* , op. cit., vol. 1, pp. 160–172.   11 This can be seen in de Vega's *Opusculum de iustificatione*, Venice 1546, published shortly before Trent, and extensively used by Council Fa-

was, at least ostensibly, at loggerheads with Lutheranism, which in many ways can be said to have developed and consolidated in the context of opposition to Scotist teachings. In evaluating their view, however, it should be taken into account that Scotists were particularly conscious of the psychological and experiential repercussions of the process of justification, and not so much of its ontological implications. Their priority, in other words, was the integrity and authenticity of human reality and response to grace. In fact for Scotus, justification *on God's side* is a free and merciful *acceptatio* of the sinner which involves the ontological renewal of the person at the level of an *a posteriori* effect.[12] Though Scotus himself, like Thomas Aquinas, did not hold to the possibility of enjoying certainty of the presence of God's grace,[13] many of the Scotists at Trent held him to be a firm defender of such certainty.[14] God's action and human response, in other words, remain somewhat disconnected, in such a way that special interest in the human integrity of justification does not take away from the real priority of God's grace.

Conversely, the Thomistic school, consolidated in the previous century under John Capreolus, and centered on Aquinas' *Summa Theologiae* rather than his *Commentary on the Sentences*, insisted that faith and repentance of sins are solely the *effects* of infused, justifying grace, a position in principle more in keeping with the Lutheran view. Man on no account can merit justification.[15] Primacy is accorded to the transcendence of God's action and of divine grace.[16] It might be noted that Aquinas was, after Augustine, cited more than any other theologian at Trent.[17] Besides, the imperial theologian, by appointment of the Emperor Charles V, was the Thomist Domingo de Soto.

thers. 'In this work, Vega defends the notion of the necessity of a human disposition towards justification which is meritorious *de congruo*. The extreme opinions on this question, according to Vega, are the Pelagian concept of justification *ex meritis*, and the Thomist denial of all merit prior to justification. Vega argues for the *via media*: the denial of merit de condigno and recognition of merit *de congruo* prior to grace—a doctrine which he associates with Duns Scotus and Gabriel Biel' (McGrath, op. cit., vol. 2, p. 65). Cf. specifically Duns Scotus' own *Op. oxon. in IV Sent.*, D. 4, a. 5, no. 2.   12 Cf. A.E. McGrath, *Iustitia Dei . . .* op. cit., vol. 1, pp. 145–154 and passim.   13 Cf. J. Auer, 'Die "skotistische" Lehre von der Heilsgewißheit. Walter von Chatton, der erst "Skotist" ', in *Wissenschaft und Weisheit* 16 (1953) 1–19.   14 Cf. V. Heynck, 'Zur Kontroverse über die Gnadengewißheit . . .', op. cit., pp. 178–188.   15 Cf. B. Xiberta, 'La causa meritoria de la justificación', op. cit. Reformed rejection of the doctrine of merit was directed at an idea of merit 'which considered human works as a preparation for receiving grace', and not at the Augustinian and Thomistic concept of merit 'founded on the absolute preliminary condition of grace in Jesus Christ' (V. Vajta, 'Sine Meritis. Zur kritischen Funktion der Rechtfertigunglehre', in *Ōcumenica*, Neuchâtel/Augsburg 1968, pp. 193f.).   16 According to McGrath (*Iustitia Dei . . .*, op. cit., vol. 1, pp. 145ff.), the contrast between Scotist and Thomistic positions lies in that the former consider 'divine acceptation' to be prior to ontological renewal which results from the infusion of supernatural habits, and the latter that such acceptation is posterior to ontological renewal. 'Is the infusion of supernatural habits theologically prior or posterior to divine acceptation? It is this question which lay at the heart of the fourteenth-century debate on the rôle of supernatural habits in justification' (ibid., p. 145).   17 Cf. the *Index nominum et rerum* in CT 5:1053–72.

It is probably fair to say, however, that there was no distinctively 'Augustinian' school at the council, in the sense *all* participants, declared anti-Pelagians, considered themselves 'Augustinians' in one way or another, as did Luther himself for that matter. As we shall see, the only school which might have been considered 'Augustinian' was the one led by Seripando, master-general of the Augustinian order.[18] This school, which turned out to be less consistent theologically than had originally appeared, advanced a conciliatory doctrine of 'double justice', already proposed at the Diet of Regensburg, which was eventually rejected by the Council.[19]

2. *Council discussions*

Session six, under the presidency of Cardinal Cervini (later, for a brief period, Pope Marcellus II), began half way through the year 1546. It took as its starting point the basic notion of justification as a process, that is, as a *transfer from the state of sin to the state of grace*, remission of sin by the infusion of grace, presence in the soul of the state of justice.[20] The idea was accepted widely at the Council; the notion of an unilaterally 'extrinsic' justification was considered unthinkable. The principal controversial issues, that turned out to be of critical importance during the Council and afterwards, were two: the question of the certitude (or otherwise) of being in God's grace; and that of 'double justice' (one forensic, the other inherent) in the justified. Three principal projects, containing several other sub-projects and drafts, were submitted before the final document could be presented and voted on.

The *first draft* (or July project) was unclear on a variety of points, and was not accepted by the Fathers.[21] The *second draft* (the September project) prepared by Seripando and presented in a positive and expository form,[22] was considered much richer and more promising for future work. Indeed it eventually served as the basis for the final project. Cervini and other theologians (Soto, Jean de Conseil, Laínez, Salmerón), upon receiving the draft from Seripando, modified it significantly before presenting it to the Council fathers. The modifications made insisted above all on two points which turned out to be very central in the debate with Lutheranism: a more positive evaluation of the rôle of human cooperation in justification, and the notion of grace as an 'inherent form' in man, against Seripando's notion of 'double justice'.

18 Cf. H. Jedin, *Girolamo Seripando. Sein Leben und Denken im Geisteskampf des 16. Jahrhunderts,* Würzburg 1937; D. Gutiérrez Miras, 'Hieronymi Seripandi scripti', in *Latinitas* 12 (1964) 142–152. On Seripandus' understanding of justification, cf. J. Henninger, *S. Augustinus et doctrina de duplici iustitia. Inquisitio historico-critica in opinionem Hieronymi Seripandi (1493–1563) de justificatione ejusque habitudinem ad doctrinam S. Augustini,* Rome 1935; V. Grossi, 'La giustificazione secondo Girolamo Seripando nel contesto dei dibattiti tridentini', in *Analecta Augustiniana* 41 (1978) 6–24. 19 In spite of Seripando's assertions, this doctrine can hardly be considered fully Augustinian (cf. McGrath, op. cit., vol. 2, p. 67). 20 Cf. CT 5: 337ff. 21 Cf. CT 5: 384–391; McGrath, op. cit., vol. 2, pp. 71–73. 22 In fact, he prepared two separate drafts: CT 5:821–833.

Seripando defended his doctrine of 'double justice'[23] as a *via media* between Catholic and Lutheran doctrines, on the basis that the violence of sinful concupiscence is such and the sinfulness and inadequacy of man so real, that in order to appear before God and be glorified, the Christian is in need of an exterior supplement of the justice of Christ.[24] We shall return to the discussion in the next section of this chapter, dealing with the content of the decree.

In the meantime, it transpired that Scotists were generally unhappy about the way in which the idea of the 'certitude of being in grace' was being presented,[25] opining that the Thomistic position, excluding any kind of certitude on grace, was holding excessive sway. After protracted discussions on the matter,[26] the final draft left things more or less as they stood in the second one, though Council fathers did avoid condemning the Scotist doctrine.[27]

3. *Final stages: the nature of faith; the causes of justification*

In spite of previous controversies, Cervini also gave Seripando the task of preparing the *final draft* (or November project), requesting him to take into account the suggestions made. However, two other important issues arose and had to be dealt with before things could be finalized.

1. The first one was a central issue in Pauline exegesis, at the very heart of Luther's doctrine of *sola fides*: what exactly did it mean to be 'justified by faith'?[28] Some

---

23 As we saw when studying the *Diet of Regensburg*, this view was also held by the doctors of the 'school of Köln', particularly Gropper, Contarini and Pighius. On the pre-Regensburg and pre-Tridentine history of the concept, cf. P. Pas, 'La doctrine de la double justice', op. cit.; G. Philips, *L'union personnelle* . . . op. cit., pp. 204–207; A.E. McGrath, op. cit., vol. 2, pp. 57–61. 24 It should be noted that not all authors are convinced that Seripando propounded the *duplex iustitia* thesis as seriously as did Gropper, Contarini and Pighius (cf. H. Rückert, *Die Rechtfertigungslehre* . . . , op. cit., pp. 217ff.; J. Henninger, *S. Augustinus et doctrina de duplici iustitia* . . . , op. cit., pp. 31–33; P. Pas, 'La double justice . . .', op. cit., p. 11). Others hold that Seripando's view of the matter is quite in line with Gropper's and the others (cf. H. Jedin, *Seripando* . . . , op. cit., vol. 1, pp. 102–132; V. Grossi, 'La giustificazione secondo Gerolamo Seripando . . .', op. cit., pp. 6–24). 25 On historical questions associated with the assurance or certitude of being in God's grace, cf. (for Luther) H.J. Iwand, *Nachgelassene Werke, vol. 5: Luthers Theologie*, München 1974, pp. 64–104. cf. also: V. Heynck, 'Zur Kontroverse über die Gnadengewißheit auf dem Konzil von Trient', op. cit.; M.L. Guérard des Lauriers, 'Saint Augustin et la question de la certitude de la grâce au Concile de Trente', in Various authors, *Augustinus Magister*, Paris 1954, vol. 2, pp. 1057–1067; F.J. Schierse, 'Das Trienter Konzil und die Frage nach der christlichen Gewißheit', in G. Schreiber (ed.), *Das Weltkonzil von Trient: Sein Werden und Wirken*, op. cit., pp. 145–167. 26 Both Thomists and Scotists agreed (1) that grace cannot be experienced physically or with empirical certitude; (2) that God can, in certain cases, give the believer certitude of the state of his soul. Yet whereas Thomists admit only moral certitude at an experimental level (good conscience, etc.), Scotists insisted that a real certitude of faith can be deduced from the proper reception of the sacraments of Baptism and Penance insofar as they produce grace necessarily in those who place no obstacles. cf. H. Jedin, *A History* . . . , op. cit., p. 252. 27 Cf. ibid., p. 288. 28 The text of particular relevance is from Romans 3:28: 'man is justified by faith and not by doing what the Law tells him to do'.

faith → justification

faith in justifying act of God

Council fathers suggested that Paul's doctrine is related to the *act* of faith as a *first disposition* for salvation, and is linked accidentally with justification in that it belongs to the preparatory stage. Others took it that Paul was thinking about the *virtue* of faith which is given in the very moment of justification, and is therefore inextricably *united to charity*.[29] Cervini, wishing to give the fullest possible weight to the doctrine of 'justification by faith', insisted that the latter is 'the principle of all human salvation, the foundation and root of justification' (in the very instant of justification, and *in every single stage* of its preparation and growth), following a line more in keeping with some Fathers of the Church[30] than with Thomas Aquinas.

2. The second question turned out to be closely linked to the first, and centered on the chapter on the *causes* of justification. Cervini asked whether or not faith was, as such, a cause of justification? The Scotists, as we saw, wished to relegate it to a mere preparatory phase of justification, linked accidentally to it, whereas several Thomists held it should be considered as an instrumental cause of justification.[31] Cervini,[32] it would seem, and Soto[33] inclined towards the latter position.

Eventually, although the founding quality of the faith for justification came to be unequivocally affirmed, faith was designated neither as instrumental nor formal cause of justification by the Council.

CONTENT OF THE DECREE ON JUSTIFICATION

The decree was approved on 13 January 1547, was then, and is still considered to be one of the most beautiful and enduring pages of Church magisterium.

De iustificatione did not concern itself with the justification of infants, who receive the grace of justification by Baptism without their personal involvement (infant Baptism was not an issue with Lutherans),[34] but exclusively with that of adults. It consists of a forward, sixteen chapters and thirty-three canons,[35] and is structured on the basis of a triple-stage justification: the moment when it is first attained (including preparation); the preservation and increase of justification; its recovery when lost through sin.

29 Cf. CT 5: 696–700; 724–735. **30** Cf. CT 5: 729; 731; 734. Reference is made especially to Origen, *Epist. ad Rom.* 3,9 (PG 14:953) and John Chrysostom, *Hom.* 7, c.5 in *Epist. ad Rom.* 3,28 (PG 60:446). **31** Following the Thomistic line, the Bishops of Bitonto and Oporto suggested faith should be considered as the *formal cause* of justification, a position not unlike that of Lutherans (cf. CT 5:740). **32** Cf. CT 5:742. **33** 'Sancta debet esse Catholicis confessio haec, quod nostra justitia est fides quae per charitatem operatur, ut de verbis istis inter nos et Lutheranos nulla sit discordia' (Domingo de Soto, *De Natura et Gratia II*, 12, ed. Paris, 1549). **34** Session V of Trent on original sin dealt with the question of infant baptism, in the context of the Anabaptist heresy (cf. its canon 4: DH 1514). The fact that the question of infant justification does not come up in session VI only goes to confirm that the latter's principal object is rejection of Lutheran doctrine. **35** Cf. DH 1520–1583. In the main I have followed the English translations of Church documents of J. Neuner and J. Dupuis, *The Christian Faith in the Doctrinal Documents of the Catholic Church*, London 1982, nos. 1924–83 with occasional slight modifications.

The forward makes it clear that the object of the decree is 'a certain erroneous doctrine about justification', in all likelihood Lutheranism, which is causing 'serious damage to Church unity'; the decree forbids Christians 'to believe, preach or teach anything contrary' to what it teaches.[36]

1. Chapters 1–3: God's plan of salvation

In brief terms, the content of the first three chapters make the following assertions: man is unable to justify himself (chapter 1), but, thanks to the free and merciful divine dispensation manifested in Christ (chapter 2), attains justification through him (chapter 3).

Chapter one links up with the doctrine on original sin, and insists that 'so completely were they [all men] slaves of sin . . . and under the power of the devil and of death, that not only the Gentiles by means of the power of nature but even the Jews by means of the letter of the Law of Moses were unable to liberate themselves and to rise from that state.'[37] However, against Luther's understanding of freedom as a *res de solo titulo*, it adds that 'their free will, weakened and distorted as it was, was in no way extinct'.[38]

Chapter two, in terms quite acceptable to Lutherans, speaks of God's merciful initiative in sending his Son to save mankind from sin: 'He was sent that the Jews, who were under the Law, might be redeemed, and that the Gentiles "who were not pursuing righteousness" (Rom 9:30) might attain it, and that all "might receive adoption as sons" (Gal 4:5). God has "put Him forward as an expiation by His blood, to be received by faith" (Rom 3:25), for our sins and "not for our sins only, but also for the sins of the whole world" (1 Jn 2:2).'[39]

Chapter three, however, clarifies that not all necessarily benefit from the death of Christ, 'but only those to whom the merit of his passion is imparted . . . they would never be justified if they were not reborn in Christ, for it is this rebirth that bestows on them, through the merit of his passion, the grace by which they become just.'[40] Justification, in other words, is not a mere extrinsic favour, but involves, and even requires man's rebirth through grace.

2. Chapters 4–9: first justification

Chapters four to nine describe what justification is, what preparation for it consists of, its causes, the rôle of faith in justification, and the question of the certainty or assurance of God's grace. All the critical issues of the decree are contained, at least germinally, in this part. Justification is described throughout these chapters as a process, that is, from man's standpoint, 'a transition from the state in which man is

36 DH 1520.   37 DH 1521. This point is corroborated by canon 1 (DH 1551).   38 DH 1521. Canon 5 (DH 1555) says the same thing, employing Luther's expression *liberum arbitrium . . . res est de solo titulo*.   39 DH 1522.   40 DH 1523.

born a son of the first Adam, to the state of grace and adoption as sons of God (cf. Rom 8:15) through the second Adam, Christ our Saviour.'[41] It adds that, once the Gospel has been promulgated, this process cannot take place without the sacrament of Baptism.[42]

Preparation for justification and the need for God's grace   Chapter five speaks of the absolute need for God's grace in preparing for justification, in the following terms. 'In adults the beginning of justification must be attributed to God's prevenient grace through Jesus Christ, that is, to his call addressed to them without any previous merits of theirs. Thus, those who through their sins were turned away from God, awakened and assisted by his grace, are disposed to turn to their own justification by freely assenting to and cooperating with that grace. In this way, God touches the heart of man with the illumination of the Holy Spirit, but man himself is not inactive while receiving that inspiration, since he can reject it; and yet, without God's grace, he cannot by his own free will take one step towards justice in God's sight.'[43]

God's prevenient grace which illumines, disposes and touches the heart, is what prepares man for justification, and brings him to freely assent to and cooperate with grace. Man, the decree says, 'is not inactive while receiving that inspiration', because he can reject it, but without grace, not a single step can be made.[44]

Chapter six explains *in four stages* the way in which the grace of God is experienced by man in preparation for justification: (1) the conception of faith, (2) repentance of sin or unwavering confidence in God's mercy, (3) loving God as the source of justice and thus hating sin, and finally (4) the determination to receive Baptism and live a Christian life. The text says:

> Adults are disposed for that justice *when*, awakened and assisted by divine grace, they conceive faith from hearing (cf. Rom 10:17) and are freely led to God, believing to be true what has been divinely revealed and promised, especially that the sinner is justified by God's grace 'through the redemption which is in Christ Jesus' (Rom 3:24); *when*, understanding that they are sinners and turning from the fear of divine justice – which gives them a salutary shock—to the consideration of divine mercy, they are aroused to the confident hope that God will be propitious to them because of Christ (*propter Christum*); when they begin to love God as the source of all justice and are thereby moved by a certain hatred and detestation of sin, that is, by that repentance that must be practiced before baptism; *when*, finally, they determine to receive baptism, to begin a new life and to keep the divine commandments.[45]

---

41 DH 1524.   42 Cf. ibid.; also cf. *sessio VII de Baptismo*, canon 5 (DH 1618).   43 DH 1525. Emphasis added. cf. can. 3 (DH 1553).   44 Canon 4 (DH 1554) reiterate the content of this chapter, repeating the term *cooperatio*, and adds that human free will cannot be considered as a 'lifeless object, doing nothing at all and is merely passive'.   45 DH 1526. This chapter also offers

Notice that faith is considered as the first fruit in this 'process' of justifying grace, but is not 'left on its own' as it were: faith gives rise to repentance of sin and unwavering confidence in God's mercy; this in its turn brings man to love God as the source of all justice and therefore turns him against sin. A clear echo is to be found of Aquinas' double *motus* of the free will in justification, the *motus liberi arbitrii in Deum per fidem*, followed by the *motus liberi arbitrii in peccatum*, both of which he considers to be the result of *gratiae infusio*.[46] Through faith, in other words, man *first* discovers divine mercy in Christ, and *then* the hatefulness of sin, from which there springs a determination to receive Baptism and lead a Christian life. The priority of grace is unequivocally stated, though not its exclusiveness.

Finally, the point is made that preparation for justification and justification itself are not the same thing: the former is distinct from and followed by the latter. For justification 'is not the remission of sins alone, but the sanctification and renewal of the interior man through the voluntary reception of grace (*sanctificatio et renovatio interioris hominis per voluntariam susceptionem gratiae et donorum*), whereby from unjust man becomes just, and from enemy a friend, that he may be "an heir in hope of eternal life" (Tit 3:7)'.[47]

The causes of justification (chapter 7); the 'unica causa formalis' The decree goes on to list the five 'causes' of justification, making use the Aristotelic-Scholastic terminology of causality.[48] In many respects, this is the central chapter of the decree.

> The causes of justification are the following: the final cause is the glory of God and of Christ, and life everlasting. The *efficient cause* is the merciful God who gratuitously washes and sanctifies (cf. 1 Cor 6:11), sealing and anointing 'with the promised Holy Spirit, who is the guarantee of our inheritance' (Eph 1:13). The *meritorious cause* is the beloved only-begotten Son of God, our Lord Jesus Christ, who, 'while we were still sinners' (Rom 5:10), 'out of the great love by which he loved us' (Eph 2:4) merited for us justification by his most holy passion on the wood of the Cross and made satisfaction to the Father. The *instrumental cause* is the sacrament of baptism which is the 'sacrament of faith', without which [*sine qua*, referring to faith] no one has ever been justified. Finally, the *only formal cause* is 'the justice of God, not

---

a list of Scriptural texts to justify the notion of preparation for justification: DH 1527, quoting Heb 11:6; Mt 9:2; Sir 1:27 (Vulg.); Acts 2:38; Mt 28:19; 1 Sam 7:3. Canon 7 explains that good works performed before justification may not be considered 'as truly sins or deserving of God's hatred, or that the more earnestly one tries to dispose himself for grace, the more grievously he sins' (DH 1557). 46 Cf. Thomas Aquinas, *Summa Theologiae I-II*, q. 113, a. 6. 47 DH 1528. 48 Obviously this does not imply a pure and simple acceptance of Aristotle's metaphysics or categories of thought. cf. G. Philips, op. cit., pp. 202f. Lutheran theologians such as Melanchthon and Johann Gerhard (*Loci theologici XXII*, 5, 37, 40) had few scruples in using terminology of an Aristotelic kind.

FINAL CAUSE = GLORY OF GOD AND XT & ETERNAL LIFE

FORMAL CAUSE = JUSTICE OF GOD

INSTRUMENTAL CAUSE = BAPTISM.
MERITORIOUS " = CROSS OF XT
EFFICIENT CAUSE = MERCIFUL GOD. WHO CLEANSES ...

that by which he himself is just, but that by which he makes us just [*qua nos iustos fecit*]', namely the justice which we have as a gift from him and by which we are spiritually renewed. Thus, not only are we considered just, but we are truly called just and we are just, each receiving within himself his own justice, according to the measure which 'the Holy Spirit apportions to each one individually as he wills' (1 Cor 12:11), and according to each one's personal disposition and cooperation.[49]

The first two causes present little difficulty: Lutherans and Catholics have no bones of contention in respect of the origin and purpose of justification.

As regards the third, the 'meritorious cause', the text makes it clear that on no account do we merit our own justification; only Christ does. Nothing other than the life, death and resurrection of the divine Son can move God, as it were, to save mankind. In respect of the theology of grace and its associated terminology common in previous centuries, recuperation of the Christological dimension of justification is to be welcomed. But the decree also adds that, though Christ and he alone merited justification for us, his justice does not become *ours*,[50] as an improper rendering of the *admirabile commercium* motif might suggest; for if it did, we would seen to merit our own justification, which is absurd.[51] The text of the decree continues: 'for although no one can be just unless the merits of the passion of our Lord are imparted to him, still this communication takes place in the justification of the sinner, when by the merit of the same most holy passion, "God's love is poured through the Holy Spirit into the hearts" (Rom 5:5) of those who are being justified and inheres in them. Hence, in the very act of justification, together with the remission of sins, man receives through Jesus Christ, into whom he is inserted, the gifts of faith, hope and charity, all infused at the same time.'[52]

The discussion on the 'only formal cause' of justification moves in the same direction: the reality of justification in the baptized, its formal cause, is indeed the justice of God, but not God's *own* justice imputed to us, but rather the justice 'by which he makes us just' (this phrase is taken directly from St Augustine),[53] the justice 'we have as a gift from him', the justice by which 'we are *called* just and *are* just', according to the gift of the Spirit and the cooperation of each one.

Insistence on a 'single formal cause' in justification is linked directly to Trent's

---

49 DH 1529.   50 Canon 10 leaves no doubt on the matter: 'If anyone says that men are justified without the justice of Christ, by which he merited for us, or that they are formally just by his own justice (*homines per Christi iustitiam formaliter iustos esse*), *anathema sit*' (DH 1560).   51 Thomists at Trent spoke of Christ not only as meritorious cause of justification, but also as the very content of the justified state. 'Non Christus solum est iustitia nostra, quia (ut dictum est) eius est causa efficiens et conservans, sed quia est obiectum nostrae iustitiae et in nobis per fidem, spem et caritatem est, sicut cognitum in cognoscente et amatum in amante' (CT 5:668), referring to Aquinas' *Summa Theologiae* I, q. 43, a. 3, c. But the Council did not incorporate this Thomistic way of speaking into the text.   52 DH 1530.   53 Cf. Augustine, *De Trinitate XIV*, 12: 15; cf. also his *De spiritu et littera* 9: 15; 11: 18; 18:31; 32: 56. On this text, cf. A. Trapè, *S. Agostino. Introduzione alla dottrina della grazia*, vol. 1: *Natura e grazia*, Roma 1987, p. 228.

discussion of the doctrine of 'double justice', a hand-over from the Regensburg discussions, which had been defended tenaciously during Council sessions by the Master General of the Augustinians, Seripando, as a theological *via media* between Catholics and Lutherans. On the basis that the violence of sinful concupiscence is so great, and man's sinfulness and inadequacy so real, Seripando held that, besides 'inhering justice', man is in need of a supplement of the justice of Christ for him to appear before God and be glorified.[54]

As things turned out, the doctrine of 'double justice' was rejected by the vast majority of the fathers at Trent, on the basis that grace that does not regenerate man and thus lead to him glory, is not grace in the true sense of the word. Sanctifying grace, bringing about in man a true *iustitia inhaerens*, gives rise to a real union with Christ. In this union, fruit of grace, man *becomes pleasing to God*, and thus deserves favourable judgement, standing in no need of a supplement of 'extra' imputed justice.

Laínez, one of the Council fathers who most consistently opposed Seripando, argued that although the life of the justified is *imperfect*, no *guilt* attaches to such imperfection because it is 'inevitable'.[55] Besides, any admission of supplementary imputed righteousness overthrows the notion of a heavenly reward appropriate to the different levels of sanctity, making the Johannine doctrine of 'many mansions' (Jn 14:2) pointless, and putting into question the doctrine of purgatory.

In fact it can be observed that the doctrine of the 'single formal cause' of justification is an direct corollary of Trent's previously defined doctrine on the nature of 'concupiscence' remaining in the baptized. Such concupiscence, or sinful inclination, according to Trent, though 'coming from sin and inclining to sin', no matter how violent it may be, is *not* sin.[56] A clear line – of considerable significance for

---

54 Seripando said: 'Totius huius quaestionis hunc esse statum aiunt, utrum nos qui iustificati sumus et consequenter glorificandi sumus, iuxta illud "Quos iustificavit hos et glorificavit", apud divinum tribunal iudicandi simus ex una tantum iustitia, iustitia inquam operum nostrorum procedentium ex gratia Dei, quae in nobis est, aut ex duplici iustitia, nostra sc., quam modo dixi, et iustitia Christi, passione sc., merito et satisfactione Christi supplente imperfectionem iustitiae nostrae' (CT 5:486). Other defenders of the doctrine of 'double justice' at Trent were not so clear-cut in their affirmations (cf. McGrath, op. cit., vol. 2, pp. 75 f.); in general they seemed to draw on J. Gropper's *Enchiridion Christianae Institutiones*, Köln 1536.   55 Cf. the decisive texts of Laínez in CT 5:612–629. On the different aspects of the critique of Seripando, cf. P. Pas, op. cit., pp. 31–43.   56 Session V *de peccato originale*, canon 5 states: 'If anyone... asserts that all that is sin in the true and proper sense of the word is not taken away but only brushed over or not imputed, *anathema sit*. For, *in those who are reborn God hates nothing*, because there is no condemnation for those who are buried with Christ through Baptism unto death . . . so that nothing henceforward holds them back from entering into heaven . . . The holy Council, however, professes and considers that concupiscence or the inclination to sin remains in the baptized. Since it is left for us to wrestle with, it cannot harm those who do not consent but manfully resist it by the grace of Jesus Christ . . . Of this concupiscence which the apostle occasionally calls "sin" (cf. Rom 6:12 ff.; 7:7,14–20) the holy Council declares: The Catholic Church has never understood that it is called sin because it would be sin in the true and proper sense in those who have been reborn, but because it comes from sin and inclines to sin' (DH 1515). Emphasis added.

theology and spirituality – is thus drawn between *sin*, as a wilful transgression of the law of God, and *limitation* or imperfection, even when this can result from sin and incline towards it. Such a distinction is not easy to find in Luther's theology. Cardinal Bellarmine was later to say that 'the whole controversy between Catholics and Lutherans is on this point: whether or not the corruption of nature and especially concupiscence as such, as it is found in the baptized, is to be identified with original sin.'[57]

It is interesting, though not surprising, to observe that during the previous session of Trent, on original sin, the issue had already cropped up. Seripando[58] and others,[59] uncomfortable with the phrase *in renatis nihil odit Deus*,[60] had attempted to include in the text describing 'concupiscence' some reference to strongly anti-Pelagian texts of Augustine,[61] used by Luther, which defended the true and proper sinfulness of concupiscence.[62]

In any case, Seripando's 'double justice' theory, though not eventually condemned in an explicit fashion, was unequivocally excluded; no ulterior justice need be added to those justified by Baptism to supplement their lack of justice in God's sight.[63] At the same time, however, by opting for the Augustinian concept of *iustitia Dei qua nos iustos facit*, the Council avoided taking sides on the medieval dispute regarding the precise nature of the formal cause of justification, which oscillated between the notion of an intrinsic created *habitus*, and one of an extrinsic denomination of the divine acceptance.[64]

Of course, the tension between the Tridentine declaration and the perceived Lutheran position is obvious on this point: justification, according to Trent, brings about the regeneration, the interior or inherent renewal of the sinner. Canon eleven, a truly critical one in the decree, insists unequivocally on the matter, rejecting the notion 'that men are justified either by the imputation of Christ's justice alone, or by the remission of sins alone, excluding grace and charity which is poured into their hearts by the Holy Spirit and inheres in them, or also that the grace which justifies us is only the favour of God'.[65]

Undoubtedly the 'double justice' theory was rejected by Trent insofar as it detracted from the 'inherent' side of the justified state, from the efficacy of God's grace on the sinner. But paradoxically, and in spite of Seripando's best intentions, 'double justice' had also to be put aside insofar as it could be seen to advocate, in real

57 R. Bellarmino, *De amissione gratiae et statu peccati V*, 5, in *Opera Omnia V*, 401.   58 Cf. CT 5: 194 f.; 541–553.   59 Such as Reginald Pole (cf. CT 1:75; 5:220). On Pole's theology of justification, cf. F.W. Bruskewitz, *The Theology of Justification of Reginald Cardinal Pole*, Rome 1969.   60 DH 1515.   61 Such as Augustine, *Tr. in Io.*, tr. 5: 1 (on Jn 1:33).   62 Seripando suggested the following syllogism: 'Ex concupiscentia oritur peccatum; peccatum odit Deus, ergo et concupiscentiam a qua peccatum ascendit; ergo aliquid remanet in baptizatis quod odit Deus' (CT 5: 203).   63 On Seripando's later works, for example his debate on 'Justice and freedom of the Christian', cf. A. Marranzini, *Dibattito Lutero-Seripando*, Brescia 1981.   64 Cf. G. Philips, op. cit., p. 202f.   65 DH 1561.

terms, a strong, almost Pelagian, theology of human cooperation, very far from both Lutheran and Catholic theology. Canon two makes it clear that such a possibility exists: 'If anyone says that divine grace is given through Jesus Christ only in order that man *may more easily live justly* and merit eternal life, as if by his free will without grace he could do both, although with great difficulty, *anathema sit*.'[66]

The point being made is, I believe, of considerable significance to Christian theology and spirituality. Divine grace does not as such 'facilitate' upright human action, supplementing, as need would have it, the greater or lesser energies of created nature, in order to produce the desired effect. A 'good work' in the Christian sense is not *half* the work of grace, *half* that of the human will, in other words, an aggregate of imputed and inherent justice. Rather it *fully* involves *both* the action of grace and human correspondence.

In sum, the disadvantages of the doctrine of 'double justice' far outweigh its apparent, conciliating, advantages, because it splits the simple, lineal reality of justification down the middle, making imputation and renewal irreconcilable, separating the forensic and the inherent. And in doing so, the theory is as far from Trent as it is from Luther. Not surprisingly one author, commenting on Trent's *unica causa formalis*, has it that 'it differs somewhat in words, but not truly in substance, from Luther's understanding of justification as making the sinner just'.[67]

Justification, faith and charity   The *instrumental cause* of justification is clearly stated to be the sacrament of Baptism. As we saw above, some Council fathers, taking a more Thomistic line and wishing to do full justice to the Lutheran *sola fides*, suggested that faith be declared as the instrumental or formal cause of justification. Robert Bellarmine in his work on justification written after the Council taught that for Catholic thought faith is, at one and the same time, the beginning of all justice and, as he called it, the 'inchoate formal cause of justification'.[68]

Understandably the Council fathers wished to avoid directly supporting the Lutheran position, according to which justification is effected by *faith alone* and nothing else. Rather they insisted on the *ecclesial side of justification* by mentioning the rôle of Baptism. But Baptism is, the decree adds, the 'sacrament of faith', and without faith 'no one has ever been justified'.[69] Thus it is made clear that faith is inseparable from Baptism, and therefore from the Church. And, as we have seen above, when Lutherans speak of *sola fides*, on no account do they mean faith was incompatible with or unrelated to Church and sacraments.

66 Canon 2, DH 1552. Emphasis added.   67 G.H. Tavard, *Justification* . . . op. cit., p. 76; cf. ibid., p. 94.   68 Cf. R. Bellarmino, *De Justificatione Impii I*, 17, in *Opera Omnia VI*, p. 188. Elsewhere he makes it clear that faith alone is not the formal cause of our justification (cf. ibid., II, 4, in *Opera Omnia VI*, p. 217).   69 'Sacramentum baptismati, quod est "sacramentum fidei", sine *qua* [referring to "faith"] nulli umquam contigit iustificatio' (DH 1529). The notion of the 'sacrament of faith' is taken here from Ambrose, *De Spiritu Sancto I*, 3, no. 42; Augustine, *Ep. 98 ad Bonifat. episc.*, 9ff. cf. T. Camelot, 'Sacramentum fidei', in Various authors, *Augustinus Magister*, Paris 1954, vol. 2, pp. 891–896.

However, the real point of the discussion comes up straight away, when the Council insisted not only that justifying faith is linked with Baptism, but above all that it is tied in with the theological virtues of hope and charity. This is where the traditional *punctum dolens* of the controversy between Catholics and Lutherans lies.

> In the very act of justification, together with the remission of sins, man receives through Jesus Christ, into whom he is inserted, the gifts of faith, hope and charity, all infused at the same time . . . For *faith without hope and charity neither unites a man perfectly with Christ*, nor makes him a living member of his body. Therefore it is rightly said that 'faith by itself, if it has no works, is dead' (Jas 2:17) and unprofitable, and that 'in Christ Jesus neither circumcision or uncircumcision is of any avail, but faith working through love' (*fidem quae per caritatem operatur*: Gal 5:6; 6:15).[70]

Catholics understood that when Luther spoke of *sola fides* he meant above all 'faith without works', faith lived *as if* works did not matter. The Council authoritatively cites the Epistle of James to teach that works *do* matter, knowing that Luther considered it 'a letter of straw'.[71] However, as we have seen, Luther, with growing insistence in his later writings against the antinomists, could not envisage the possibility of an authentic faith *not* producing works. The theological issue addressed by Trent is more in the area of the nature of these works, and of their essential link-up with faith: the expression used is 'faith [that] works through charity'. And charity is not understood by Trent only as God's prevenient loving, merciful action on the sinner, which produces in man works pleasing to the divinity, pleasing to him, that is, as works of his, reflecting his eternal splendour. Rather it is taken as the *infused virtue of charity*, which renews man's heart and animates Christian life and action from within. Charity in this sense, as *the love of man for God resulting from the infusion of grace*, was considered, certainly by Melanchthon, a 'work', and therefore totally subordinate to faith.

The gratuitousness of justification (chapter 8)   The Council teaches clearly that 'we are said to be justified gratuitously because nothing that precedes justification, neither faith nor works, merits (*promeretur*) the grace of justification.'[72] At first sight

---

70 DH 1530–1531. The text continues, explaining the importance of works to show up faith. 'This is the faith which, in keeping with apostolic tradition, the catechumens ask of the Church before the reception of baptism when they ask for "the faith that gives eternal life" (Roman Ritual, *Order of Baptism*, 1), a life which faith without hope or charity cannot give. Hence they immediately hear Christ's words: "If you would enter life, keep the commandments" (Mt 19:17). Accordingly, while they receive the true Christian justice, as soon as they have been reborn, they are commanded to keep it resplendent and spotless, like their "best robe" (Lk 15:22) given to them through Jesus Christ in place of the one Adam lost for himself and for us by his disobedience, so that they may wear it before the tribunal of our Lord Jesus Christ and have eternal life' (DH 1531).   71 For example cf. M. Luther, WA *Tischreden* 3: 382 (1537).   72 DH 1532.

the text presents no special difficulty, and would seem to be acceptable by Catholics and Lutherans alike, insisting on what was said in the introductory chapters of the decree.

Some authors, however, saw in the use of the term *promereri* (as distinct from the usual term *mereri*) a concession to the doctrine of *de congruo* pre-justification merit espoused by many Scotists present at the Council.[73] A doctrine of this kind was held, quite possibly, by the Franciscan Andrés de Vega.[74] In fact, many Scotists at Trent held that good works preceding justification can merit the grace of justification, not indeed *de condigno* (meriting or deserving in the strict sense of the term), but *de congruo*, that is, *ex convenientia*, out of propriety. It was suggested that *promereri* in Trent, though not often used in the decree,[75] should be taken as making reference to *de condigno* merit, and *mereri* to *de condigno* merit. The end result would be that, by denying that the grace of first justification could be merited strictly, *de condigno*, the possibility was at least left open for such merit in the general sense of the term, that is, *de congruo*. This, of course, would be unacceptable for Lutherans.

Such a distinction between the two terms *mereri* and *promereri* has since come to be discarded by other authors, who have pointed out their equivalence.[76] In fact Trent wanted to avoid using the technical terms *de congruo* and *de condigno*, and expressed the latter employing commonly used terms like *proprie et vere mereri* or *mereri ex debitum*. Catholic theology of justification subsequent to the Council demonstrates the fact.[77] Though avoiding special terminology which would link its decrees to particular schools of thought, it would seem that Trent does not admit of merit, even in the most ample sense of the term, prior to justification.

Certainty and assurance of saving grace (chapter 9) The Council then turned its attention to the question of the possibility of the Christian attaining existential certainty or assurance of being in God's grace.[78] This topic was another important cause of contention during council discussions. Probably making reference to the Lutheran doctrine of assurance of salvation, chapter nine reads as follows. 'It is necessary to believe that sins are not forgiven and have never been forgiven except

73 This position was defended especially by H.A. Oberman, 'Das tridentinische Rechtfertigungsdekret . . . ', op. cit. (1964). cf. A.E. McGrath, op. cit., vol. 2, pp. 87–89.   74 Cf. the studies of V. Heynck, cited above, and of A. de Villalmonte, 'Andrés de Vega y el proceso de la justificación según el Concilio Tridentino', op. cit.   75 The term *promereri* is also used in canon 2 (DH 1552) and chapter 16 (DH 1546). In canon 2 it seems to refer to 'first justification', in the text in chapter 16, to the fact that the justified deserve or merit eternal life (eternal life may be merited *de condigno* according to the Scholastic tradition). However, in the latter the term *vere promereri* is employed.   76 Cf. H. Rückert, 'Promereri: Eine Studie zum tridentinischen Rechtfertigungsdekret als Antwort an H.A. Oberman', op. cit. (1971); V. Heynck, 'Die Bedeutung von "mereri" und "promereri" bei dem Konzilstheologen Andreas de Vega', op. cit. (1968).   77 Cf. A.E. McGrath, op. cit., vol. 2, pp. 88f., referring mainly to the differing interpretations of Trent by Domingo Soto and Andrés de Vega.   78 Cf. J. Alfaro, 'Certitude de l'espérance et certitude de la grâce', op. cit., especially pp. 10–35; H. Huthmacher, 'La Certitude de la grâce au Concile de Trente', op. cit.

gratuitously by the divine mercy on account of Christ (*nisi gratis divina misericordia propter Christum*). And yet it must not be said that sins are forgiven or have been forgiven to anyone who boasts of his confidence and certainty that his sins are forgiven (*fiduciam et certitudinem remissionis peccatorum suorum iactanti*) and who relies upon this confidence alone.'[79]

The text goes on: 'moreover it must not be asserted that those who are truly justified should unhesitatingly determine within themselves that they are justified, and that no one is absolved from his sins and justified unless he believes with certainty that he is absolved and justified, and that absolution and justification are brought about by this faith alone, as if whoever lacks this faith were doubting God's promises and the efficacy of Christ's death and resurrection. For just as no devout man should doubt God's mercy, Christ's merit and the power and efficacy of the sacraments, so also, whoever considers himself, his personal weakness and his lack of disposition, may fear and tremble about his own grace, since no one can know with a certitude of faith which cannot be subject to error, that he has obtained God's grace (*nullus scire valet certitudine fidei, cui non potest subesse falsum, se gratiam Dei esse consecutum*).'[80]

The Council thus made a clear distinction between the *certainty of faith* (that God pardons) and the *certainty of personal salvation* (that God has in fact pardoned me), the first corresponding, one might say, to 'ecclesial faith' and its content, the second to personal faith and hope. Whereas a Christian may not doubt God's goodness and merciful will to pardon humanity in general, he cannot apply that faith infallibly to his own person with the same degree of certainty. Insofar as God's unconditional gift of mercy needs to be personally accepted and interiorized, the believer may not in fact be sure of being in God's grace, not because of God, but because of the possible imperfection of his own response.[81] The point of tension between Lutherans and Catholics is related to that of the rôle of personal human freedom and cooperation to divine grace.

Not excluded by the text, of course, is the possibility that the Christian may well have a *moral certainty* of having obtained grace.

3.   *Chapters 10–13: 'second justification', growth and preservation in grace*

These four chapters draw the logical consequences from Trent's teaching to the effect that the reception of justifying grace involves a true regeneration or graced renewal of the sinner, especially insofar as this relates to of the rôle of *good works*.

---

79 DH 1533. Canon 12 states: 'If anyone says that justifying faith is nothing else than confidence in the divine mercy that remits sins on account of Christ, or that it is this confidence alone that justifies, *anathema sit*' (DH 1562).   80 DH 1534.   81 This position is quite in keeping with the teaching of Thomas Aquinas. Cf. M. Basse, *Certitudo Spei. Thomas von Aquins Begründung der Hoffnungsgewißheit und ihre Rezeption bis zum Konzil von Trient*, Göttingen 1993.

Man can, the Council teaches, either adversely condition or generously accept God's efficacious will to justify him, and in that sense to a significant though not decisive degree condition the reality and depth of divine life in himself.

'The justified become both "friends of God" and "members of his household" (Jn 15:15; Eph 2:19)', chapter ten reads. "They go from strength to strength" (Ps 84:7), "renewed (as the Apostle says) every day" (2 Cor 4:16), that is "by putting to the death the members of their flesh" (Col 3:5, Vulg.) and using them "as instruments of righteousness" (Rom 6:13.19) unto sanctification by observing the commandments of God and of the Church.'[82]

The points made in these chapters are four: (1) grace can grow in the believer; (2) the commandments of God and the Church *can and must be* observed; (3) insofar as man can sin, he can never be sure of being in God's grace; (4) to persevere to the end, the grace of God is required.

The growth of grace God's justifying will, as such, is unchangeable. So Scripture would seem to teach. It would only make sense to speak of an 'increase' in grace therefore if the latter is understood in the ambit of the receiving justified subject. 'When "faith is active along with works" (Jas 2:22), they increase in the very justice they have received through the grace of Christ, and are further justified, as it is written: "Let the holy still be holy" (Rev 22:11); and again: "Fear not to be justified until you die" (Sir 18:22, Vulg.); and again: "You see that a man is justified by works and not by faith alone" (Jas 2:24). It is this increase in faith that the holy Church asks for when she prays: "Give us, O Lord, an increase of faith, hope and charity" '.[83]

The corresponding canon makes it quite clear that man's cooperation in his justification is critical. It condemns 'anyone who says that the justice received is not preserved and even increased before God through good works, but that such good works are merely the fruits and the signs of the justification, and not also the cause of its increase (*ipsius augendae causam*)'.[84]

Observing the commandments and the meaning of 'faith alone' Against the optimistic antinomian version of Lutheranism, the Council makes it quite clear that the reception of justification exempts nobody from observing the law, whether divine or ecclesiastical. At the same time, it teaches that the observance of the law is possible, for the power of grace renews man in his heart. 'No one, however much he is justified, should consider himself exempt from the observance of the commandments; and no one should say that the observation of God's commandments is impossible for the man justified . . . "For God does not command the impossible, but when He

---

82 DH 1535.   83 Ibid. The last citation is from the *Roman Missal*.   84 Canon 24, DH 1574; cf. canon 32, DH 1582. On this canon, cf. H. Chadwick, 'Justification by Faith: a Perspective', in *One in Christ* 20 (1984) 191–225, here, pp. 207f. This doctrine is directly taken up and opposed by the *Formula of Concord, Solida Declaratio* 4: 35.

commands He admonishes you to do what you can and to pray for what you cannot do", and He helps you to be able to do it. "His commandments are not burdensome" (1 Jn 5:3); His "yoke is easy and His burden light" (Mt 11:30).'[85]

Insisting that we should not trust in our own powers, the Council goes on to teach that by 'faith alone' man cannot be saved, in the sense that he must fight valiantly to persevere in the love of God. 'Nobody should flatter himself with faith alone, thinking that by faith alone he is made an heir and will obtain the inheritance, even if he does not "suffer with Christ in order that he may also be glorified with Him" (Rom 8:17) . . .'[86]

It is interesting to note that the Council understands the phrase 'faith alone', just mentioned, as that faith which would *exclude* fulfillment of the commandments and the virtue of charity, or be understood in independence of them. It seems probable, from what we have seen in the last chapter, that this particular understanding of 'faith alone' does not correspond *tout-court* with the Lutheran notion of 'faith alone', held during the first half of the sixteenth century and later. Several canons go on to clarify how Trent understood 'faith alone', condemning those who say that

> . . . The sinner is justified by faith alone in the sense that *nothing else is required by way of cooperation in* order to obtain the grace of justification, and that it is not at all necessary that he should be prepared and disposed by the movement of his will';[87] '. . . nothing is commanded in the Gospel except faith, *and that everything else is indifferent, neither prescribed nor prohibited, but free*; or that the ten commandments in no way concern Christians';[88] '. . . a justified man, however perfect he may be, is not bound to observe the commandments of God and of the Church, but is bound only to believe, *as if the Gospel were merely an absolute promise of eternal life* without the condition that the commandments be observed.[89]

Few Lutherans would consider themselves affected by the condemnations referred to in the second canon. More would consider themselves under scrutiny in the first, although it would still have to be seen what 'cooperation', 'movement of the will', etc. really mean in their context. We shall attempt to clarify the matter further in the final chapter of this work.[90]

The chapter, taking occasion of a series of Luther's own texts, ends by making it clear that good works and ascetical struggle are not, as such, sinful. 'It is clear that those are opposed to the orthodox doctrine of religion who maintain that the *just man sins at least venially in every good work*, or . . . that he merits eternal punishment.

85 DH 1536. The long quotation is from Augustine, *De natura et gratia*, 43: 50.   86 DH 1538. The text continues speaking of Christ himself who 'learned obedience through what he suffered' (Heb 5:8 f.), of Paul who pummeled his body and subdued it (cf. 1 Cor 9:24–27), etc.   87 Canon 9, DH 1559. Emphasis added.   88 Canon 19, DH 1569. Emphasis added.   89 Canon 20, DH 1570. Emphasis added.   90 Cf.210–214 *infra*.

They too are opposed to it who assert that the just sin in all their works if in those works, while overcoming their sloth and encouraging themselves to run the race, they look for an eternal reward in addition to their primary intention of glorifying God.'[91]

So, according to Trent, there is no necessary opposition between glorifying God and desiring the joys of eternal salvation. 'If anyone says that for the good works performed in God the just *ought not to expect and hope for an eternal reward from God* through His mercy and the merits of Jesus Christ, if they persevere to the end in doing good and in keeping the divine commandments, *anathema sit.*'[92]

Man cannot be sure of being predestined 'Certainty of faith' was sometimes confused by Protestants (Calvinists more than Lutherans) with certainty of personal *predestination* to glory. Not only can and should the Christian be sure of being in God's grace, they say, but also that they will *persevere* in such grace, that is, they are predestined to glory. The Council had it to say that 'no one, so long as he live in this mortal condition, ought to be so presumptuous about the deep mystery of divine predestination as to determine with certainty that he is definitely among the number of the predestined, as if it were true either that the one justified cannot sin anymore or that, if he sins, he should promise himself an assured repentance. For without special revelation it is impossible to know whom God has chosen for Himself.'[93]

The doctrine is confirmed in several canons. The position of those who say 'that a man who has been reborn and justified is bound by faith to believe that he is certainly (*teneri ex fide ad credendum se certo esse*) among the number of the predestined'[94] is rejected. As is that of those who hold 'that a man once justified cannot sin again and cannot lose grace and that therefore the man who falls an sins was never truly justified; or, on the contrary, says that a man once justified can avoid all sins, even venial ones throughout his entire life, unless it be by a special privilege of God as the Church holds of the Blessed Virgin Mary'.[95]

The grace of perseverance Just as the Christian can never be sure of being predestined, or saved, neither can he be sure of persevering in grace until the end of his life. In fact he is in need of God's special gift to ensure such perseverance. '. . . This gift [of final perseverance] can be had only from Him who has the power to uphold him who stands . . . and who can lift him who falls. Let no one promise himself any security about this gift with absolute certitude, although all should place their firmest hope in God's help. For, unless they themselves are unfaithful to His grace, God, who began the good work, will bring it to completion (cf. Phil 2:13). Yet "let anyone who thinks that he stands take heed lest he fall" (1 Cor 10:12) and let him

---

91 DH 1539. Emphasis added. cf. canons 25, 26 and 31.   92 Canon 26, DH 1576. Emphasis added.   93 DH 1540.   94 Canon 15, DH 1565; cf. also canon 16.   95 Canon 23, DH 1573.

"work out his salvation with fear and trembling" (Phil 2:12), in labours, in vigils, in almsgiving, in prayers and in offerings, in fastings and chastity (cf. 2 Cor 6:3ff.).'[96]

4.   Chapters 14-15: loss and recovery of justification

From the standpoint of God's will and action, justification as such (in the extrinsic sense) cannot be lost. But justice from man's side, from the point of view of inherent justice, the life of grace that abides in man due to God's justifying, recreating action, can indeed be forfeited through sin, though regained through the sacrament of Penance. And the Council says so clearly. 'Those who through sin have forfeited the grace of justification they had received, can be justified again (*rursus iustificari possunt*) when, awakened by God, they make the effort to regain through the sacrament of penance and by the merits of Christ the grace they have lost. This manner of justification is the restoration of the sinner (*lapsi reparatio*) which the holy Fathers aptly called "the second plank after the shipwreck of the loss of grace".'[97]

The Council, making it quite clear that such a form of justification is clearly distinct from 'first justification', that of Baptism,[98] goes on to explain what is required for proper reception of the Sacrament of Penance.[99]

Finally it clarifies that whereas grace and charity are lost through mortal sin, 'faith' as such is not. 'The grace of justification, once received, is lost not only by unbelief which causes the loss of faith itself, but also by any other mortal sin, even though faith is not lost. Thus is defended the teaching of divine law that excludes from the kingdom of God not only unbelievers, but also the faithful who . . . commit mortal sins which they can avoid with the help of divine grace and which separate them from the grace of God.'[100]

Two points are being made here. *Firstly*, not only does the sin of unbelief destroy the justified state; sins against virtues other than faith also involve the loss of grace, although all virtues necessarily retain some relationship with faith. *Secondly*, sins directly against faith have a special gravity; other mortal sins leave faith intact, though such faith remaining is 'dead', or useless for salvation. In fact canon 28 rejects the position of those who say that 'with the loss of grace through sin faith is also always lost, or that the faith which remains is not true faith, granted that it is not a living faith (*fides non viva*); or that the man who has faith without charity is not a Christian'.[101]

The issue involved is, as we saw above, that of the distinction between *fides* and *fides charitate formata*. The Council makes it clear that sins not directly against faith destroy charity but not faith.

96 DH 1541. Canon 22 insists: 'If anyone says that without God's special help a justified man can persevere in the justice he has received, or that with it he cannot persevere, *anathema sit*' (DH 1572). cf. also canon 16, DH 1566.   97 DH 1542.   98 Cf. DH 1543.   99 Cf. Conc. Trid., *sessio XIV de sacramento Paenitentiae* (DH 1667-1693).   100 DH 1544. cf. canons 27; 28.   101 Canon 28, DH 1578. The terminology relating to *fides informis* comes from P. Lombard, *III Sent.* D. 23, q. 5.

5. *Chapter 16: justification, good works and merit*

The final chapter of the decree on justification goes back again to the doctrine of good works and their relationship to justifying grace. This is commonly considered one of the most balanced and successful chapters of the decree. Specifically it refers to the justified Christian who acts properly in God's sight and is promised a divine reward as a result. This is the doctrine of 'merit', the most divisive issue, certainly at an overt level, between Catholics and Protestants in general.[102] Three areas are dealt with: the importance and value of good works; the *ratio meriti*, that is, what exactly makes it possible for the justified to merit; and the importance of reliance on God and confidence in him.

Firstly the Council, in strongly Scriptural terms, unequivocally exhorts Christians to abound in good works, attentive to the reward of eternal life that awaits them.[103] It continues as follows. 'Eternal life should be set before those who persevere in good works "to the end" (Mt 10:22) and who hope in God, both as a grace mercifully promised to the sons of God through Jesus Christ, and "as a reward" which according to the promise of God Himself, will faithfully be given them for the good works and merits.'[104]

Secondly, it deals with the question of the *ratio meriti* (how good works obtain their value from God's grace) in Christological terms. 'For Jesus Christ Himself continuously infuses strength into the justified (*in ipsos iustificatos iugiter virtutem influat*), as head into the members (cf. Eph 4:15) and the vine into the branches (cf. Jn 15:5); this strength always precedes, accompanies and follows their good works which, without it, could in no way be pleasing to God and meritorious . . . They can be regarded as having truly merited eternal life, which they will obtain in due time, provided they die in the state of grace, since Christ our Saviour says: "Whoever drinks of the water that I shall give him will never thirst; the water that I shall give him will become in him a spring of water welling up to eternal life" (Jn 4:14).'[105]

In other words, the possibility of our works being meritorious in God's sight is due exclusively to our 'belonging to Christ', and is rooted specifically to *the inherence of Christ's regenerating grace* in the justified.[106] In real terms, therefore, 'our' merit is not really ours, as our justice is not our own; it partakes of the merit of Christ, as our justice partakes in that of God. The following phrase is illustrative. 'Neither is our justice considered as coming from us, nor is God's justice disregarded or denied; for the justice which is said to be ours because we become just by its inherence in us is that of God himself (*iustitia nostra dicitur, quia per eam nobis*

---

102 According to the *Realenzyklopädie für Protestant Theologie XX*, Leipzig, 1908 (3rd ed.), p. 506, 'the Reformation was in the main a struggle against the doctrine of merit'.   103 Cf. DH 1545, cf. also canon 26, DH 1576.   104 DH 1545.   105 DH 1546. One of the reasons Thomas Aquinas gives for Christ being the head of the Church is that 'virtutem habuit influendi gratiam in omnia membra Ecclesiae' (*Summa Theologiae III*, q. 8, a. 1, c.).   106 Cf. also canons 10; 11, DH 1560f.

inhaerentem iustificamur, illa eadem Dei est), since it is infused in us by God through the merit of Christ.'[107]

Canon 32 goes on to specify the object of merit, rejecting the position of those who say 'that the good works of the justified are the gifts of God in such a way that they are not also the good merits of the justified himself; or that by the good works he performs through the grace of God and the merits of Jesus Christ (of whom he is a living member), the justified does not truly merit an increase in grace, eternal life and, provided he dies in the state of grace, the attainment of this eternal life, as well as an increase in glory'.[108] Note that the Council does not accept that 'good works' be identified purely and simply with the fruits of God's grace working in the justified.

Thirdly, the decree reminds Christians in carrying out good works never to rely exclusively on themselves. 'A Christian should never rely on himself or glory in himself instead of in the Lord (cf. 1 Cor 1:31; 2 Cor 10:17), whose goodness towards all men is such that He wants His own gifts to be their merits.'[109]

And as a result we should not remember only God's mercy, but also his judgement. 'Neither should anyone pass judgement on himself, even if he is conscious of no wrong, because the entire life of man should be examined and judged, not by human judgement but by the judgement of God . . .'.[110]

INTERPRETATION OF TRENT'S DECREE ON JUSTIFICATION

Speaking of the 450th anniversary of the opening of the Council of Trent, 30 April 1545, Pope John Paul II said: 'The dogmatic affirmations of the Council of Trent retain of course all their value. Yet a serene study of revealed truth, in obedience to God's Spirit and in an attitude of mutual attentiveness, will bring us close together, making the very misunderstandings of the past occasions for growth in faith and love.'[111]

The theological and magisterial value of the decree on justification of the Council of Trent is evident. Certainly it is the most significant statement on the topic of grace and justification ever to be made by the Church. Alongside previous magisterial declarations on related topics, the decree is extensive, positive, and, at least intentionally, exhaustive. It is a significant point of arrival and of departure for understanding the doctrine of justification. A few comments on its correct interpretation, therefore, are not out of place.

The first point to be made is that Trent generally avoided taking position on theological opinions commonly held and often vigorously defended throughout the Middle Ages. Hubert Jedin had the following to say: 'since the Council's intention was to draw a line of demarcation between Catholic dogma and Protestant teaching

107 DH 1547. Emphasis added.   108 Canon 32, DH 1582.   109 DH 1548.   110 DH 1549.   111 John Paul II, in *Osservatore Romano*, 2–3 May, 1995.

– not to settle controverted opinions in the Catholic schools of theology – it follows that in all doubtful cases, previously professed theological opinions may continue to be held'.[112] In McGrath's words, 'Trent may be regarded as endorsing the medieval Catholic heritage on justification, while eliminating much of its technical vocabulary, substituting biblical or Augustinian phrases in its place . . . It marks the deliberate and systematic rejection of much of the *terminology* of medieval schools, while retaining the *theology* which it expressed.'[113]

If pressed to the point, it may well be argued, however, that some kind of Thomistic Augustinianism prevailed at Trent.[114] In many ways, of course, this is a purely academic issue which has little hope of ever being satisfactorily resolved. But an important point can be made: there is no such thing, strictly speaking, as a simple and unique 'Tridentine' doctrine on justification.[115] Trent was interested, in the main, in presenting a complete widely acceptable doctrine on justification for Catholics.

The second area of interest relates to the degree of accuracy with which the Council's decree and especially its condemnations of 'Lutheran' doctrine on justification, actually addressed Luther's own teaching, early Lutheran confessional documents (such as the *Confessio Augustana*) and subsequent Lutheranism.[116] Two preliminary points can be made without misgivings. Firstly, the fundamental lines of the decree on justification have in fact a great deal in common with the main thrust of Luther's doctrine, especially in respect of his revindication of the absolute priority of God's grace in justification. Secondly, unlike the previous Tridentine decree (session five) which was directed towards a host of erroneous and even opposing understandings of the doctrine of original sin, the decree on justification explicitly targeted Luther and Lutheranism. The question that arises spontaneously is the following: did Trent correctly interpret the content and import of Luther's and Lutheran teaching?

Of course if Trent had got things completely right as regards Luther and Lutheranism on every single point, dialogue between Lutherans and Catholics would have to be excluded from that moment on, at least from the Catholic side. But this I believe is not the case, and the reason is simple: 'authentic' interpretations of Luther's teaching were, even in the sixteenth century, many, varied and even op-

112 H. Jedin, *A History of the Council of Trent* . . . op. cit., vol. 2, p. 309.   113 A.E. McGrath, op. cit., vol. 2, p. 86. G. Philips, op. cit., pp. 207f. is of the same mind.   114 Cf. H. Rückert, *Die Rechtfertigungslehre auf dem Tridentinischen Konzil*, Bonn 1925, p. 185. Rückert's position, understandably, is not accepted by all (cf. A.E. McGrath, op. cit., vol. 2, p. 86).   115 Proof of the matter may be found in the diversity of commentaries made on session VI, shortly after promulgation of the decree, of the Dominican Domingo Soto and the Franciscan Andrés de Vega. 'The Council's decision on justification . . . came to receive a wide variety of exegesis from its defenders' (H. Chadwick, 'Justification by Faith: a Perspective', op. cit., p. 209).   116 On the situation of Catholic theology in relation to justification over this period, H. Laemmer's work, *Die Vortridentinisch-katholische Theologie des Reformations-Zeitalters aus den Quellen dargestellt*, Berlin 1858, is still useful.

posing. Luther's own doctrine is not easy to map out and pin down. Melanchthon, the *Confessio Augustana* and the *Apologia* have their own priorities. George Major and the antinomists took their own line. Trent, it might be said, rejected certain facets of Lutheranism, or, perhaps better, a popular school of Lutheranism (in certain points close to that of the antinomists, in others to that of Melanchthon) spawned, inevitably perhaps, by the explosive, paradoxical quality of Luther's own reflection and tormented spirituality.[117]

This does not take away in the slightest from the magisterial authority of the decree on justification. Quite the contrary. The Council in fact did not condemn persons, theologies, or movements, but particular, popular though influential theological positions, which were in fact threatening fundamental points of Christian doctrine and spirituality. The principal point rejected was the purely *forensic or exterior view of justification* which the Council saw as amounting to a denial of the reality and efficacy of saving grace, and by implication, a toning down of the solid realism of human response to God's gifts. Against this, it clearly and unequivocally stated the inherent or infused nature of justification, the realism of incarnate redemption and the meaningfulness of human 'cooperation'. Other issues in the decree are either directly related to this one, or of lesser importance.

The question that remains, of course, is whether or not Trent's vision is at heart compatible with the theology of Luther and with contemporary Lutheranism. This is one of the underlying issues commonly dealt with in the many ecumenical dialogue statements on justification that have be published over the last thirty years. We shall examine them in the coming chapter.

117 Though some authors (such as E. Stakemeier, *Glaube und Rechtfertigung* . . . , op. cit., p. 156) hold that the Council Fathers had an accurate knowledge of the writings of the reformers, others (such as V. Pfnür, 'Zur Verurteilung der reformatorischen Rechtfertigungslehre auf dem Konzil von Trient', op. cit.) take it that their knowledge came through the works of Catholic controversialists such as J. Dietenberger, J. Fabri, J. Eck and J. Cochlaeus.

CHAPTER FOUR

Justification in recent ecumenical documents

We have examined three particularly significant episodes or periods in which the doctrine on justification came to the fore: that of Luther, that of history of Lutheranism, that of the Council of Trent. As was mentioned earlier, many other understandings of the doctrine of justification could have been profitably reflected upon, those of Augustine, Aquinas, Catholic scholarship in the wake of Trent. On the Protestant side, Ritschl by no means had the last word. But he did represent the culmination of a process of rationalization and distortion of the orthodox doctrine of justification that stood in need of another 'Lutheran' revolution. Although such a revolution was initiated by certain evangelical theologians this century, and indirectly at least by Karl Barth, the fact is that the original doctrine of justification with all its explosive power had become, as the centuries passed, simply unrecognizable, and in many cases theologically and pastorally irrelevant. In fact the very term 'justification' has become incomprehensible to vast numbers of Christians, whether Catholic or Protestant. The reasons for this evolution are many and varied, and we shall reflect on them in the second part of this work, especially in chapter five.[1]

Yet the fact remains that the doctrine on justification, despite its persisting apparent irrelevance, has come strongly to the fore in bilateral ecumenical dialogues over the last thirty or thirty-five years, particularly those between Catholics and Lutherans. The object of this chapter is to provide a brief overview of these documents up to the present date.

The value of ecumenical agreed statements

Many ecumenical agreements between Catholics and Protestants, especially those which were produced in the immediate wake of Vatican Council II, tended to be – if the generalization is permissible – practical in nature, mainly interested in the analysis and promotion of intercommunion between Christians of different denominations in sacramental and ecclesial life. However, the assumption that ecumenical endeavour consists principally in resolving practical problems of a sacramental, ecclesial and ministerial kind, can take it for granted that fundamental theological differences are non-existent or of slight importance, the fruit of consolidated, yet unfortunate and dated misunderstandings.

The doctrine of justification would be a case in point. The action of divine grace on the soul of the Christian is, at heart, God's own affair. If on top of that, human

1 Cf. pp. 145–208 below.

response to justifying grace is considered to be of a predominantly passive or 'non-contributory' kind, then at best the whole question of justification, originally at the very core of the confessional divide, should, by right, be relegated to the sphere of the individual, of conscience, of interiority. Pressing issues of a practical, exterior kind, such as the visible union among Christians, common ethical approaches to the challenges of a de-Christianized world, easily move into the foreground. Christians simply cannot afford, it would seem, to dedicate their attention and effort to so many academic niceties.

Unfortunately, this predominantly 'practical' approach has not, over recent decades, provided the results many had hoped it would. In spite of all that has been said and done, in spite of notable progress on many fronts, positions have remained firmly entrenched, and ecumenical endeavour tends to remain a side issue in Christian churches, substantially on the margin of serious theological reflection. However, in more recent times, the mature fruits of ecumenical dialogue have borne witness to a valiant attempt to go back to the theological roots of the questions that have traditionally divided Christians.[2] One of the results of this growing awareness of a somewhat unilaterally 'practical' approach is the production, over recent decades, though especially in the last twelve or fourteen years, of several extensive, carefully elaborated and theologically profound consensus statements on the nature of justification.

'Practical' issues of course have not been neglected. Strange though it may seem, renewed reflection on the doctrine of justification, commonly considered as belonging to the sphere of the individual and his or her personal relationship with God, has brought to the fore a series of questions that are *ecclesiological* in nature. This has made it possible to deal with practical, exterior, social and ethical aspects of ecumenism at a more profound level than was possible before.

In this chapter we shall look briefly at the documents in question.[3] Firstly, we shall make a brief examination some earlier documents which, while not dealing with the topic of justification at length, broached the fundamental issues and inspired following ecumenical dialogue. Then we shall look at a series of minor documents taken mainly from dialogue statements in which either Lutherans or Catholics were not involved. Finally we shall examine the three principal documents which

2 Cf. G.H. Tavard, *Justification* . . . , op. cit., p. 1.   3 I have drawn principally on the work of H. Meyer and G. Gaβmann (eds), *Rechtfertigung im ökumenischen Dialog; Dokumente und Einführung*, Frankfurt a. M. 1987. Cf. also the comments on the documents of H. Meyer, 'The doctrine of Justification in the Lutheran Dialogue with Other Churches', in *One in Christ* 17 (1981) 86–116; G.H. Tavard, 'Justification in Dialogue', in *One in Christ* 25 (1989) 299–310; C.E. Braaten, 'An Examination of the United States Lutheran Ecumenical Dialogues on Justification by Faith', in *Justification: the Article by which the Church Stands or Falls*, Minneapolis 1990, pp. 103–126; L. Sartori, 'Chiesa e giustificazione', in *Protestantesimo* 51 (1996) 137–144; A. Maffeis, 'La giustificazione nel dialogo ecumenico. Chiarificazioni e nodi irrisolti', in *Rassegna di Teologia* 37 (1996) 623–645; M.E. Brinkman, *Justification in Ecumenical Debate. Central Aspects of Christian Soteriology in Debate*, Utrecht 1996.

have been issued on the question of justification between Catholics and Lutherans/ Evangelicals. The three are:

— *Justification by faith* (1984), jointly prepared by committees appointed by the Roman Catholic Bishops' Committee for Ecumenical and Interreligious Affairs in the United States, and the Lutheran World Federation, seventh in a line of documents published in the series *Lutherans and Catholics in Dialogue*.

— *Justification of the sinner* (1986), a chapter in the volume prepared by the work-group of evangelical and Catholic theologians in Germany with a view to possibly revising the condemnations of the time of the Reformation, under the presidency of the theologians K. Lehmann and W. Pannenberg.

— *Church and Justification* (1993), prepared jointly by the Lutheran World Federation and the Pontifical Council for Promoting Christian Unity, on the relationships between ecclesiology and justification.

EARLY DOCUMENTS RELATED TO JUSTIFICATION

As far back as 1956 a dialogue group of French-speaking Lutherans (and Reformed) and Catholics, called the Groupe des Dombes, dealt with the theological question of original sin, and included besides a significant reference to the doctrine of justification with which original sin is deeply linked.[4]

Perhaps the most significant document in question – the first which seriously broaches the question of justification in ecumenical dialogue between Catholics and Protestants – belongs to the wide-ranging Lutheran-Catholic 'Malta Report', entitled *The Gospel and the Church* (1972).[5] It makes reference to most of the fundamental issues at the heart of the justification debate. Speaking of the 'nucleus of the Gospel' the document states that 'today, *a far-reaching consensus is developing in the interpretation of justification*. Catholic theologians also emphasize in reference to justification that God's gift of salvation for the believer is unconditional as far as human accomplishments are concerned. Lutheran theologians emphasize that the event of justification is not limited to individual forgiveness of sins, and they do not see it

---

4 A. Blancy and M. Jourjon (eds.), *Pour la Communion des Églises. L'apport du Groupe des Dombes, 1937–1987*, Paris 1988, pp. 11–13. The last of the ten theses of this document reads: 'Under the action of the Holy Spirit and in dependence on him, man himself responds to the initiative of God who justifies him in Jesus Christ, and accomplishes the works by which God "gives the will and the power to act" (Phil 2:13)' (ibid., p. 13). cf. G.H. Tavard, 'Justification in Dialogue', op. cit., p. 299. 5 Gemeinsame Römisch-katholische/ Evangelisch-lutherische Kommission, 'Das Evangelium und die Kirche' (Malta 1972), in *Lutherische Rundschau* 22 (1972) 344–362. English translation in H. Meyer and L. Vischer (eds.), *Growth in Agreement. Reports and Agreed Statements of Ecumenical Conversations on a World Level*, New York/Geneva 1984, pp. 168–189. Justification is dealt with in nos. 26–30. Italian translation in EO 1:1127–1206. On this document, cf. H. Meyer, 'Le dialogue entre l'Église catholique romaine et la fédération luthérienne mondiale', in *Positions luthériennes* 20 (1972) 179–193. The optimistic tone of the document is contested somewhat by V. Subilia, *La giustificazione per fede*, op. cit., pp. 114f.; cf. also L. Sartori, 'Chiesa e giustificazione', op. cit., p. 133.

in a purely external declaration of the justification of the sinner. Rather the right-eousness of God actualized in the Christ event is conveyed to the sinner through the message of justification as an encompassing reality (*dem Sünder als eine ihn umfassende Wirklichkeit übereignet*), founding the new life of the believer.'[6]

The *Malta Report* points out that Paul's doctrine on justification must be read in the light of the dispute with Jewish legalism. Still, it says, the doctrine of justifica-tion, though it can be expressed in other New Testament representations, is at the very heart centre of the Gospel message, since it founds human freedom against legalism.[7]

As a result, and this is certainly true for Lutherans, the doctrine of justification must also be understood as a criteriological or interpretative principle for the life of the Church:

> According to Lutheran understanding . . . all traditions and institutions of the Church are subject to the criterion which asks whether they are *enablers of the proper proclamation of the Gospel* and do not *obscure the unconditional character of the gift of salvation*. It follows that *rites and orders of the Church are not to be imposed as conditions for salvation*, but are valid only as free unfolding of the obedience of faith.[8]

The document goes on to state that the Gospel and the message of justification is the foundation of Christian freedom in every sense. Yet, it concludes, 'since *Chris-tian freedom is linked to the witness of the Gospel*, it needs *institutional forms for its* mediation.'[9] Therefore 'the Church must understand and actualize itself as an insti-tution of freedom. Structures which violate this freedom cannot be legitimate in the Church of Christ.'[10]

DOCUMENTS ON JUSTIFICATION OUTSIDE LUTHERAN-REFORMED/CATHOLIC DIALOGUE

The nineteen principal documents I have found dealing directly with justification outside dialogue statements between Catholics and Lutherans/Evangelicals fall under nine categories.

1. *Lutheran/Reformed dialogue*

Apart from some minor unofficial papers,[11] three documents are worth noting. Firstly a brief section entitled 'Creation and Redemption, Law and Gospel, Justification

---

6 'The Gospel and the Church', no. 26, in H. Meyer and L. Vischer, op. cit., p. 174. cf. also no. 28. cf. W. Pannenberg, 'Die Rechtfertigungslehre im ökumenischen Gespräch', op. cit., p. 232f.   7 Cf. 'The Gospel and the Church', no. 27.   8 Ibid., no. 29. Emphasis added. Reference is made to the *Confessio Augustana* 7.   9 Ibid., no. 30.   10 Ibid.   11 For example that of the 1983 Lutheran-

and Salvation' from the 1966 USA document *Marburg Revisited*.[12] The city of Marburg of course was where Luther and Melanchthon met Zwingli and Œcolampadius in 1529 in an attempt to reconcile their differences, especially in respect of the nature of Christ's presence in the Eucharist, but not, interestingly, in respect of justification.

The following texts of *Marburg Revisited*, though hardly very committal, are worth citing, particularly for what is said of the relationship between creation and redemption. 'The God who creates also redeems and for this reason creation must be understood in the light of redemption and redemption in the context of creation . . . Some in our traditions tend to relate redemption too narrowly to man as sinner. We, however, are agreed that we should also bear adequate witness to the significance of redemption to the whole created order, inasmuch as creation and redemption have an eschatological dimension pointing to a new heaven and a new earth.'[13] 'We are agreed that each tradition has sought to preserve the wholeness of the gospel as including the forgiveness of sins and the renewal of life. Our discussions have revealed that justification and sanctification have been distinguished from each other and related to each other in rather different ways in our traditions.'[14]

Secondly, several points of the 1973 so-called 'Leuenberg Agreement' coming under the heading of 'A common understanding of the Gospel'[15] are of interest. It is known of course that the primary intention of the Leuenberg Agreement was one of

---

Conservative Evangelical Dialogue, in J.A. Burgess and F.B. Nelson (eds.), 'Lutheran-Conservative/Evangelical Dialogue', in the *Covenant Quarterly* 41 (1983) 1–99. It affirms: 'We acknowledge that salvation is by faith alone, through faith alone, and that those things which Christians believe are ultimately to be determined and tested by the standard of Scripture alone'. Note how the text is centered on 'salvation' and 'Scripture alone' rather than on 'justification'. Cf. C.E. Braaten, *Justification* . . . , op. cit., pp. 112f., who points out that a critical difference between Lutherans and Conservative Evangelicals lies in the question of infant baptism, which is not practiced by the latter. Also, cf. the 1989 Lutheran-Reformed Joint Commission, *Towards Christian Fellowship*, LWF-WARC, Geneva 1989, pp. 5–30; on justification, no. 21. Italian translation in EO 3:2528–2627; on justification, ibid., no. 2551.   12 Original: P.C. Empie and J.I. McCord, *Marburg Revisited: A Reexamination of Lutheran and Reformed Traditions*, Minneapolis 1966, pp. 151–152. Italian translation of the entire document in EO 2: 3293–3345. Cf. the essays of C. Bergendorff, 'Justification and Sanctification: Liturgy and Ethics', in P.C. Empie and J.I. McCord, *Marburg Revisited* . . . , op. cit., pp. 118–127; G.W. Forell, 'Law and Gospel', in idem., pp. 128–140; J.H. Leith, 'Creation and Redemption; Law and Gospel in the Theology of John Calvin', in idem., pp. 141–151. Also: J.B. Torrance, 'Marburg revisited—an evaluation', in *Lutheran World* 14/3 (1967) 67–70; C.E. Braaten, *Justification* . . . , op. cit., pp. 107–109.   13 P.C. Empie and J.I. McCord, *Marburg Revisited* . . . , op. cit., nos. 2–3.   14 Ibid., nos. 7–8.   15 Original: 'Leuenberger Konkordie', in W. Lohff, *Die Konkordie reformatorischer Kirchen in Europa*, Frankfurt a. M. 1985, pp. 15ff. English translation: 'The Leuenberg Agreement', in W.G. Rusch and D.F. Martensen, *The Leuenberg Agreement and Lutheran-Reformed Relationships. Evaluation by North American Theologians*, Minneapolis 1989, pp. 139–154; on justification, etc., cf. nos. 6–12 (pp. 146f.). Cf. also the commentaries appended to this work by W.G. Rusch, M. Lienhard, A. Birmelé, H. Meyer, P. Fries, R. Jenson and others; cf. also: M. Geiger, 'The Leuenberg agreement – A step forward and a beginning', in *Reformed World* 33 (1974) 160–166; E. Martikainen, 'Die Leuenberger Lehrgespräche in ökumenischer Perspektive', in *Kerygma und Dogma* 33 (1987) 23–31.

establishing ecclesial communion between Lutherans and the Reformed Churches, not so much one of reaching theological consensus on justification. Some excerpts are of special interest.

'The true understanding of the gospel was expressed by the fathers of the Reformation in the doctrine of justification . . . In this message, Jesus Christ is acknowledged as the one in whom God became man and bound himself to man; as the crucified and risen one who took God's judgement upon himself and, in so doing, demonstrated God's love for sinners; and as the coming one who, as Judge and Saviour, leads the world to its consummation.'[16] 'This message *sets Christians free for responsible service in the world and makes them ready to suffer in this service* . . . In this understanding of the gospel, we take our stand on the basis of the ancient creeds of the Church, and reaffirm the common conviction of the Reformation confessions that *the unique mediation of Jesus Christ in salvation is the heart of the Scriptures, and the message of justification as the message of God's free grace is the measure of all the Church's preaching.'[17]

Thirdly, the 1983 USA document 'An Invitation to Action' makes a forthright seven-point common declaration on justification,[18] and concludes that 'there are no substantive matters concerning justification that divide us'. Among other things, it notes that the doctrine of justification is fundamentally Christocentric in character, and that it constitutes a message of hope for the world.

'The gospel is the good news that for us and for our salvation God's Son became human in Jesus the Christ, was crucified and raised from the dead. By his life, death and resurrection he took upon himself God's judgement on human sin and proved God's love for sinners reconciling the entire world to God . . . For Christ's sake we sinners have been reconciled to God, not because we earned God's acceptance but by an act of God's sheer mercy . . . Both the Lutheran and Reformed traditions confess this gospel in the language of justification by grace through faith alone. This doctrine of justification was the central theological rediscovery of the Reformation; it was proclaimed by Martin Luther and John Calvin and their respective followers.'[19]

'This doctrine of justification continues to be *a message of hope and of new life* to persons alienated from our gracious God and from one another. Even though Christians who live by faith continue to sin, still in Christ our bondage to sin and death has been broken. By faith we already begin to participate in Christ's victory over evil, the Holy Spirit actively working to direct our lives . . . The gospel sets Christians free for good works and responsible service to the whole world. In daily repentance and renewal we praise God and serve others. As grateful servants of God

16 W.G. Rusch and D.F. Martensen, *The Leuenberg Agreement* . . . , op. cit., nos. 8–9 (p. 147). 17 Ibid., nos. 11–12. Emphasis added. 18 Cf. 'An Invitation to Action', in J.E. Andrews and J.A. Burgess (eds.), *The Lutheran Reformed Dialogue*, vol. 3: Philadelphia 1984, pp. 9–13. Italian translation: EO 2:3369–3375. 19 Ibid., nos. 2–4. Convergence between the positions of Luther and Calvin is demonstrated in a long footnote, in idem., pp. 10–12.

we are enabled to do all those good works that God commands, yet without placing our trust in them . . .'[20]

2. Lutheran / Anglican dialogue

There are two relevant documents. First of all, the brief 'Common declaration on Justification' from the 1980 second report of the United States Lutheran/Episcopalian dialogue (LED-II).[21] It is more or less taken for granted that agreement has already been achieved on the doctrine of justification. Several points are worth noting.

'*At the time of the Reformation, Anglicans and Lutherans shared a common confession and understanding of God's justifying grace*, i.e. that we are accounted righteous before God only for the merit of our Lord and Saviour Jesus Christ, by faith, and not for our own works or deservings . . . In the western cultural setting in which our communions, Episcopal and Lutheran, find themselves, the gospel of justification continues to address the needs of human beings alienated from a holy and gracious God . . . In both communions the understanding of the term "salvation" has had different emphases. Among Lutherans, salvation has commonly been synonymous with the forgiveness of sins; among Episcopalians, salvation has commonly included not only the forgiveness of sins but also the call to and promise of sanctification . . .'[22]

Secondly, there is the 1982 statement of the Anglican-Lutheran European Regional Commission,[23] followed closely by a 1986 statement from the Canadian Lutheran-Anglican Dialogue,[24] and by the 1988 Anglican-Lutheran statement in Germany *On the Way to Visible Unity*.[25] The Anglican-Lutheran European Regional Commission statement clearly takes its cue from the LED-II statement mentioned above, and speaks of the present-day relevance of the doctrine of justification, of general agreement among Christians on the matter, and, most notably, of the ecclesial significance of the doctrine of justification.

'It is in view of our common situation that the doctrine of justification takes on a fresh relevance. Today, as at all times, there are people who are burdened by their awareness of personal guilt or their sense of estrangement from God. Their troubled conscience leads them to ask whether there is a merciful God. But in addition there are now many people in our societies who suffer in a different way under a

---

20 Ibid., nos. 5–6. 21 Original: Various authors, *The Report of the Lutheran-Episcopal Dialogue*, second series: 1976–80, Cincinnati 1981, pp. 22–24. Italian translation of the entire document: EO 2:2289–2368; of the declaration on justification, no. 2302. cf. the comments of C.E. Braaten, *Justification* . . . , op. cit., pp. 114f. 22 Various authors, *The Report of the Lutheran/Episcopal Dialogue* . . . , op. cit., B-D (p. 23). 23 Original: J. Gibbs and G. Gaßmann (eds.), *Anglican-Lutheran Dialogue: The Report of the Anglican-Lutheran European Regional Commission*, Helsinki 1982, London 1983, nos. 17–21 (pp. 8–10). Italian translation of the entire document: EO 2:249–318; on justification, nos. 267–271. 24 Canadian Lutheran-Anglican Dialogue, *Report and Recommendations – April 1986*, Toronto-Winnipeg 1986. Italian translation of the entire document: EO 4:152–229; on justification, nos. 160–162; cf. no. 188. 25 Church of England—Evangelical Lutheran

burden of fear, frustration and alienation . . . When applied to this human situation, the Gospel of God's free and gracious initiative and acceptance is a power which liberates human beings from their burdens and sets them free to be God's co-workers in serving and preserving our world – his creation.'[26]

'. . . Today we [Anglicans and Lutherans] . . . share a common understanding of its [the doctrine of justification] fundamental thrust and also note with gratitude an increasing agreement with Roman Catholic theologians in the understanding of this doctrine . . . We therefore share a common understanding of God's justifying grace, i.e. *that we are accounted righteous and are made righteous before God* only by grace through faith because of the merits of our Lord and Saviour Jesus Christ, and not on account of our works and merits . . . Both our traditions affirm that justification leads and must lead to "good works"; authentic faith issues in love. We understand sanctification in relation to justification not only as an expression of the continuity of justification, the daily forgiveness of sins and acceptance by God, but also as growth in faith and love both as individuals and as members of the Christian community.'[27]

The explanation given of the rôle of the Church in justification is particularly well put. 'It is the individual person who is called to believe that he or she is accepted by God. There can be no substitute for this direct, personal relationship between a human being and God. Yet both our communions also agree that justification of the individual believer cannot be isolated from the corporate life of the community of faith. This double dimension – individual and corporate – is already rooted in Baptism. *It is in the Church that God's justifying grace is proclaimed and received through the proclamation of the word and the celebration of the Sacraments*, and that the fruits of justification are manifested in acts of love and service. *The Church is, indeed, the community of justified sinners*, empowered by the Holy Spirit to lead a life of service to all human beings and of praise to God, the Father, the Son and the Holy Spirit.'[28]

3. *Lutheran/Methodist dialogue*

Three documents from the Lutheran/Methodist dialogue, one in the United States, two in German ambit,[29] are worth mentioning. A clear tension may be perceived between the Lutheran emphasis on forensic justification and Methodist preference for inner sanctification.

Church in Germany – Federation of Evangelical Churches in the German Democratic Republic, 'On the Way to Visible Unity; Meissen 1988', in *Mid-Stream* 29 (1990) 153–165; on justification, ibid., no. 15, vi.   26 J. Gibbs and G. Gaβmann (eds.), Anglican-Lutheran Dialogue . . . , op. cit., no. 17.   27 Ibid., nos. 18–19.   28 Ibid., no. 21. Emphasis added.   29 Cf. introductory notes on Lutheran-Methodist dialogue in H. Meyer and G. Gaβmann, *Rechtfertigung im Ökumenischen Dialog* . . . , op. cit., p. 94.

Firstly, the 1979 Lutheran-United Methodist bilateral consultation on Baptism[30] made the following terse statement on justification. 'We also share the biblical Reformation doctrine of justification by grace through faith. We are agreed that we are justified by the grace of God for Christ's sake, through faith alone and not by the works demanded of us by God's law. We also recognize the common emphasis on sanctification as a divinely promised consequence of justification.'[31]

Secondly, the 1982 document prepared by a joint commission of the German Evangelical-Methodist and German Evangelical-Lutheran churches.[32] The following points in reference to justification are of interest. 'God calls all men, through his action in the Holy Spirit, to conversion and faith, and attributes to the sinner, who believes, his justice in Jesus Christ. Whoever trusts in the Gospel is by the will of Christ justified before God, freed from the accusation and power of the law and enabled to live a life of faith, hope and love . . . Salvation is understood by both Churches as generation in the holiness of Christ (*gift*) and also as the effect of justification, which finds expression in the life of the believer (*task*) . . . While Lutherans understand salvation as the gift of God in the event of justification, Methodists put particular weight in their understanding of salvation the life-transforming experience of the grace of God, and growth in love . . .'[33]

Thirdly, a section entitled 'Salvation by grace through faith' in the 1984 statement *The Church: Community of Grace*.[34] The conclusion of the document would seem to be the following: on the whole, Methodists emphasize to a greater degree than do Lutherans the radical transformational effect of justification on the sinner, the importance of 'prevenient' grace, and the unity and continuity of God's action in the world.

'We agree that, in accordance with the Scriptures, justification is the work of God in Christ and comes through faith alone . . . [faith] comprises both assent and trust . . . Wesleyans stress the prevenient grace of God which prepares humans for acknowledgment of justifying grace. They also affirm justification as the foundation for full redemption in Christ. Thus Methodists tend to understand justification by faith in Jesus Christ as initiating and, as such, determining the whole of Christian life through God's action and personal appropriation. Lutherans believe that in

---

30 Lutheran-United Methodist Bilateral Consultation, 'A Lutheran-United Methodist Statement on Baptism', in *Perkins Journal* 34 (1981) 2–6. The statement is followed by commentaries by several authors. cf. especially K. Penzel, 'How to transcend the two classical positions of Lutheranism and Methodism', in ibid., pp. 35–42. 31 Ibid., no. 2, (p. 3). 32 Original: 'Bericht über das Lehrgespräch zwischen Evangelisch-methodistischer Kirche in der Bundesrepublik Deutschland und West-Berlin (EmK) und der Vereinigten Evangelisch-Lutherischen Kirche Deutschlands (VELKD)', photocopied version, 1982, published in H. Meyer and G. Gaßmann, *Rechtfertigung im ökumenischen Dialog . . .* , op. cit., p. 95. Italian translation in EO 4:1580–1583. 33 Ibid., nos. 2.2; 3.1; 3.2. 34 Original: Joint Lutheran-Methodist Commission, *The Church, Community of grace, Lutheran World Federation*, Geneva 1984, nos. 23–27 (pp. 12–13). Italian translation of the entire document: EO 1:2438–2533. Cf. the commentary of M. Marquardt, 'Evangelische Kirchengemeinschaft. Inhalt und Ergebnisse der lutherisch-methodistischen Lehrgespräche', in *Ökumenische Rundschau* 35 (1986) 401–415.

justification, at once and constantly, God gives forgiveness, righteousness, and eternal life. Christians therefore are in every moment dependent on God's justifying grace and never move beyond or above the position of justified sinners . . .'[35]

'Reflection upon justification leads to a consideration of sanctification . . . Lutherans stress that in Christ people are justified and sanctified while at the same time they remain sinners before God (*simul justus et peccator*). Methodists speak of this drastic change as a new birth in consequence of which the regenerated Christian lives in ever deepening and more fruitful love of God and neighbour . . . There is common agreement that God's creating and sustaining grace is continuously present in the world and in human life. Lutherans maintain that in creation God gives human beings material goods necessary for our living, and . . . fights against forces that would destroy creation. In this saving action, however, God gives to people the fruits of Christ's saving work, such as forgiveness of sins and eternal life. Methodists also stress God as creator and moral governor of the world. The presence of God in the world is centered on Christ's redeeming work . . . The original significance of this prevenient grace for human beings is the development of a sense of right and wrong, the recognition of fallen life as under the wrath of God, and the drawing of people to the saving grace given to us through Word and sacrament and received by faith.'[36]

4. *Lutheran/Baptist dialogue*

Lutheran-Baptist conversations in the USA from 1979 to 1981 on the areas of grace, Baptism and ministry,[37] produced clarifying statements directly related to justification, especially in the first section of the *Lutheran-Baptist Dialogue* entitled 'Divine Initiative and Human Response'.

'Lutherans and Baptists alike describe faith as being both a divine gift and a human response. Faith is made possible only by divine initiative, yet it is realized only through human response. In this human response it is recognized that the act of the human will in believing in itself is regarded as a work of God. It is the Father's drawing the sinner to himself; it is the work of the Holy Spirit in the life of the believer . . . No one is able to believe without the prior work of God who frees a person from the bondage of sin and enables an unwilling person to do the will of Christ . . . True righteousness in us is accomplished by God's righteousness in Jesus Christ and is bestowed freely through faith in Christ.'[38]

Differences between Lutherans and Baptists, the document clarifies, lie principally in the nature of the playoff between divine initiative and human response.

---

35 Joint Lutheran-Methodist Commission, *The Church, Community of grace* . . . , op. cit., nos. 23–24.   36 Ibid., nos. 25–26.   37 Cf. J.A. Burgess and G.A. Inglehart (eds.), 'Lutheran-Baptist Dialogue', in *American Baptist Quarterly* 1 (1982) 103–112; cf. also ibid., pp. 97–271, for commentaries and papers. Italian translation of the complete document in EO 2:2395–2420.   38 Ibid., no. 1 (p. 103).

'While it is true that as sinners we cannot believe without the work of God's Spirit which imparts new life, it is equally true that God does not believe for us nor cause us to believe without the exercise of our wills. The divine act of bestowal and the human act of believing are in the closest union.'[39]

Where Lutherans insist primordially on divine initiative in salvation, Baptists, not practicing infant Baptism, give greater importance to the subjective rôle of faith. 'The Lutheran concern for giving glory to God and comfort to repentant sinners led to an emphasis on the action of God in justification. The Baptist concern for repentance and conversion led to an emphasis on faith as the human response to God's initiative ... Lutherans, in their concern to affirm the primacy of redeeming grace, have emphasized the powerlessness to initiate life in God. Baptists, on the other hand, in their concern to affirm the place of human responsibility in relation to God, have emphasized the element of decision with regard to faith.'[40]

Hence works of service and divine praise are inseparable from faith. 'Lutherans and Baptists are agreed that the proper response to God's gracious initiative is one of thanksgiving and service. Lutherans and Baptists agree that faith leads to good works, the indispensable demonstration of faith's reality: "faith apart from works is dead" (Jas 2:26), or it is no faith at all. The faith in Christ by which alone we are saved is the faith which is sure to produce good works. Faith that works by love calls each believer to a life of dedication to others out of a sense of indebtedness and thanksgiving for what it has received ...'[41]

5.   *Lutheran/Orthodox dialogue*

There two documents to date in which Orthodox Christians have been directly involved in the justification debate, both with Lutherans.

The first is a 1977 common statement between the Russian-Orthodox Church and the Evangelical-Lutheran Church of Finland called 'Salvation as Justification and Deification'.[42] The document seems to consider 'deification', *théosis*, a central theological theme in oriental theology, as more or less equivalent to 'sanctification'. It explains that the saving work of Christ, Incarnate Word who died and rose for us, is, at one and the same time, a work of justification and of deification. This saving work is communicated to us principally through Baptism and the Eucharist. After mentioning several points of agreement, the document points out that some tensions do remain, for example, 'the Orthodox side believes that [the work of deification involves] ... the *cooperation of man with the salutary grace of God or opposition to it*, and it is in this that his freedom consists.'[43]

39 Ibid.   40 Ibid., no. 2 (p. 104).   41 Ibid., no. 4 (p. 105).   42 'Communique on the 4th Theological Conversations between Representatives of the Russian Orthodox Church and the Evangelical Lutheran Church of Finland', in *Journal of the Moscow Patriarchate* 1977/9, pp. 6of. For an introduction to these conversations, cf. ibid., pp. 58–6o. Italian translation in EO 4:560–585. The meeting also dealt with the topic 'Salvation and the Kingdom of Earth: the Object of Faith and Ethical task'.   43 Ibid., p. 61.

Specific points of divergence include, the document says, the following: the relationship between faith, hope and love in salvation; the question of personal certainty of salvation; the relationship between divine grace and man's free will in salvation; the exact meaning of 'faith'; the relationship between law and gospel.[44]

The second document, dated 1989, theological in character, extensive and rich, is the result of conversations between the Evangelical-Lutheran Church and the Orthodox Church in the United States of America.[45] In attempting to understand the central terms which describe the reality of God's relationship with the believer, *justification* (Lutherans) and *deification* (Orthodox), the document develops and makes explicit a two-pole Christology, centered respectively on Christ 'for us' and Christ 'in us'.

Also to be noted are the dialogues that have taken place between theologians of the Rumanian Orthodox Church and of the German Evangelical Church in 1988 on justification and deification.[46]

6. *Evangelical/Old Catholic dialogue*

There is one document, published in 1984, dealing in the main with Eucharistic intercommunion.[47] The preface to the document mentions that at the Bonner Conference of Union (1874) the Old Catholic Church distanced itself from the Roman Catholic doctrine of merit, and spoke of faith 'that acts through love, never without love, as the centre and condition for the justification of man before God'.[48] Specifically as regards justification, the document says: 'We are considered just and made just entirely by grace through faith on the basis of the saving work of Our Lord Jesus Christ, and not on the basis of our own works and merits. The Church is, therefore, the communion of justified sinners, who are enabled, through the action of the Holy Spirit, to lead a life of service to all mankind and in praise of God, the Father, the Son and the Holy Spirit.'[49]

7. *Methodist/Roman Catholic dialogue*

There are two documents of significance dealing with justification. The first, called

---

44 Cf. ibid.   **45** J. Meyendorff and R. Tobias (eds.), Canonical Orthodox Bishops in the Americas—Evangelical Lutheran Church in America—Lutheran Church, Missouri Synod, 'Christ "in us" and Christ "for us" in Lutheran and Orthodox Theology', in *Salvation in Christ: a Lutheran-Orthodox dialogue*, Minneapolis, 1992.   **46** Cf. the collection of papers edited by K. Schwarz, *Rechtfertigung und Verherrlichung (Theosis) des Menschen durch Jesus Christus*, Hermannsburg 1995. **47** 'Vereinbarung über eine gegenseitige Einladung zur Teilnahme an der Feier der Eucharistie', in *Ökumenische Rundschau* 34 (1985) 365–367.   **48** Thesis 5 of the Bonner Conference, in U. Küry, *Die Altkatholische Kirche*, Stuttgart 1966, p. 463. cf. C. Oeyen, 'Auf dem Weg zu einer evangelisch/alt-katholischen Eucharistie-Vereinbarung', in *Ökumenische Rundschau* 34 (1985) 362–364.   **49** 'Vereinbarung über eine gegenseitige Einladung . . .', op. cit., no. 3, in ibid., p. 366. Emphasis added.

the Honolulu Report (1981) deals principally with the action of the Holy Spirit.[50] Special attention is paid to the experience of conversion, and to the radically 'inherent' or 'regenerative' side of justification.

'. . .Today from every side we hear the question once posed by Paul. "Wretched man that I am! Who will deliver me from this body of death?" (Rom 7:24). With or without their knowing it, the questioners are asking about justification: how may a sinner find a gracious God? how may a meaningless life be given a meaning? The Holy Spirit is present and active within us throughout the entire *experience of conversion*, which begins with an awareness of God's goodness and an experience of shame and guilt, proceeds to sorrow and repentance, and ends in gratitude for the possession of a new life given us through God's mercy in Jesus Christ . . . Justification is *not an isolated forensic episode*, but is part of a process which finds its consummation in *regeneration and sanctification, the participation of human life in the divine* . . . Here, of course, the key concept is "prevenience", a concept emphasized by both the Council of Trent and John Wesley. Always it is the Spirit's special office to maintain the divine initiative that precedes all human action and reaction. The Holy Spirit is God himself, present and active in human hearts and wills, "nearer to us than breathing, closer than hands or feet". This is why, when some wrongly denied the Church's latent sense of the Spirit's prevenience, the Church's positive response was rightly to reaffirm the truly splendid title: "Lord and Giver of Life".'[51]

'In justification God through the atoning work of Christ restores a sinner to a right relationship with himself. In such a restoration, both the initiative, the agency and the consummation is the ministry of the Holy Spirit as he brings Christ to us and leads us to him. When a sinner is led to Christ and receives him, he is re-born and given the power to turn away from a life curved back upon itself toward a "new life", opened out to love of God and neighbour . . . Thus the tragic malignancies of sin may be healed . . . And this is justification: *to be regarded and treated as righteous, for Christ's sake; and yet also to be put in the way of becoming righteous*. All this is done by the initiative of the Father's redeeming mercy, manifested in the Son's atoning grace, through the Holy Spirit's activity in our hearts . . . The Holy Spirit sanctifies the regenerate Christian. Sanctification is a process that leads to perfect love. Life in the Spirit is human life, lived out in faith, hope and love, to its utmost in consonance with God's gracious purposes in and for his children.'[52]

The second document, prepared in England, is entitled *Justification – A Consensus Statement*, and was published in 1988[53] as an interim statement on the question

---

50 Original: J. Hale (ed.), *Proceedings of the Fourteenth World Methodist Conference, Honolulu, Hawaii, 21–28 July 1981*, World Methodist Council, Lake Junaluska 1982, nos. 12–18 (pp. 86–87). Also in *Information Service* 15 (1981) 84–86. Italian translation of the entire document in EO 1:2123–2182. **51** J. Hale (ed.), op. cit., nos. 13–14. Emphasis added. The reference to Trent is to be found in DH 1525. **52** Ibid., nos. 15; 18. Emphasis added. **53** Cf. English Roman Catholic-Methodist Committee, 'Justification – A Consensus Statement', in *One in Christ* 28 (1992) 87–91, slightly modified in respect of the original version published in *One in Christ* 34 (1988) 270–273. Italian translation of the earlier version in EO 4:1616–1631.

of justification.[54] Its findings have a lot in common both with statements, already mentioned, in which Methodists were involved, and also with the 1987 ARCIC-II document we will examine presently. All in all, one can appreciate a considerable doctrinal affinity between Catholic and Methodist spirituality and theology insofar as they relate to justification. The document may be divided according to the *historical and doctrinal* issues it examines.

From the *historical* standpoint, the document holds that, though the doctrine on justification has been traditionally divisive between Catholics and Protestants, it is commonly held nowadays that division is due to a considerable degree to historical misunderstandings and to differences of emphasis. After a brief perusal of Tridentine and Reformed doctrines of justification, it insists that 'justification does not stand on its own. Justification and sanctification go together as two sides of the one coin: distinct but belonging together'.[55]

It then goes on to explain that whereas John Wesley, founder of the Methodists, was initially on the side of the Reformers and opposed to Rome, he took exception to Luther's remarks on good works and the law, and developed a doctrine of grace and justification based not only on Scripture but also on the Greek Fathers and Catholic writers such as Sts John of the Cross, Theresa of Avila and Francis de Sales. He insisted above all on 'the need for good works and sanctification, meaning by that the continuing gift of the Holy Spirit that leads slowly and painfully towards holiness'.[56] The result of such holiness is, for Wesley, 'to have a heart so all-flaming with the love of God as continually to offer up every thought, word and work, as a spiritual sacrifice, acceptable to God, through Christ'.[57] This kind of strong biblical piety is also to be found among Catholics, the document continues, citing some prayers of St Alphonsus de Liguori.

From the *doctrinal* angle, the document affirms that Methodists and Catholics alike hold that 'the grace of God comes first, the initiative in salvation rests with God . . . The person who is saved is saved by grace *with* free consent (in the case of an adult) but not saved by free consent.'[58]

But it adds that several problems and tensions do remain between Methodists and Catholics. One is the category of *merit*, which seems, the document says, to imply that the person can in some ways 'put pressure on God'. The biblical notion of 'reward' would, perhaps, be more accurate, it suggests.

Another is in the area of the *completion* of sanctification, necessary to obtain the reward of eternal life. The document states that 'Methodists and Catholics are united in confessing that perfect holiness is necessary before a person can see God face to face (cf. Heb 12:14). When a person has reached in this life a measure of holiness which falls short of perfection, then it is believed that this perfection is conferred in the transition from this life to eternal life.'[59]

---

54 In respect of the interim value of document, cf. 'Justification – A Consensus Statement', op. cit., p. 91.   **55** Ibid., p. 88.   **56** Ibid.   **57** Words of Bishop Ussher cited by Wesley, in ibid., p. 89.   **58** Ibid.   **59** Ibid., p. 90.

Of particular interest therefore is the respective understanding of the doctrine of *purgatory*, envisaged, according to the document, by Methodists as a more or less instantaneous action, by Catholics as a lengthy, drawn-out process. The point of contention in this area relates principally to the need for and nature of prayer offered by the Church for those being purified. For Catholics this is an important aspect of Christian piety, and is expressed particularly through the celebration of the Eucharist in suffrage for the dead, and by the application of indulgences for them. For Methodists, conversely, prayer for the dead is liturgically optional, and indulgences play no part in teaching and practice.

In any case, the document concludes, 'Catholics and Methodists agree that all who are in Christ, whether in this life or the next, constitute one family in Christ'.[60]

8. *Anglican/Roman Catholic dialogue*

In 1986 a significant, though non-authoritative, statement was prepared by ARCIC-II on the topic of salvation and justification in the Church.[61] The document, entitled 'Salvation and the Church', has drawn considerable attention.[62]

Problems pending It is made clear that, though fundamental agreement does exist between Anglicans and Roman Catholics on the doctrine of justification,[63] and di-

---

60 Ibid.   **61** ARCIC-II, *Salvation and the Church. An Agreed Statement by the Second Anglican-Roman Catholic International Commission*, London 1987; also published in *One in Christ*, 23 (1987) 157-172. Italian translation in EO 3:1–23. The initiative of ARCIC-II goes back to the encounter between Pope John Paul II and Archbishop Robert Runcie on the occasion of the former's visit to Canterbury in 1982. The non-authoritative character of *Salvation and the Church* is referred to not in the document itself but in a preface drawn up later by the co-chairmen, C. Murphy-O'Connor and M. Santer (cf. 'Salvation and the Church', op. cit., p. 157).   **62** Cf. the response of the Congregation for the Doctrine of the Faith, 'Observations and Commentary on ARCIC-II's "Salvation and the Church" (18.11.1988)', in *Origins* (1988) 429–434. Commentaries include: A.E. McGrath, *ARCIC-II and Justification: an evangelical assessment of 'Salvation and the Church'*, Oxford 1987; idem., 'Justification: The New Ecumenical Debate', in *Themelios* 13 (1988) 43–48; D. Valentini, 'A Contribution to the Reading of the ARCIC-II Statement on "Salvation and the Church" ', in *Information Service* 63 (1987) 41–53; R.G. England, 'Salvation and the Church: A Review Article', in *Churchman* 101 (1987) 49–57; P. Avis, 'Reflections on ARCIC-II', in *Theology* 90 (1987) 451–460; C.F. Allison, 'The Pastoral and Political Implications of Trent on Justification', in *One in Christ* 24 (1988) 110–127; D.A. Scott, ' "Salvation and the Church" and theological truth-claims', in *Journal of Ecumenical Studies* 25 (1988) 428–436, followed by a response by J.R. Wright, ' "Salvation and the Church". A Response to David Scott', in ibid., pp. 437–444; M.C. Boulding, 'The ARCIC Agreement on Salvation and the Church', in *Doctrine and Life* 39 (1989) 452–458; G.H. Tavard, 'Justification in Dialogue', in *One in Christ* 25 (1989) 299–310. Of special interest from a historical perspective, though written before the document was published, is H. Chadwick's study, 'Justification by Faith: a Perspective', in *One in Christ* 20 (1984) 191–225; and also A.E. McGrath, *Iustitia Dei* . . . , op. cit., vol. 2, pp. 98–134 on the doctrine of justification among Anglicans.   **63** 'Above all it was agreed that the act of God in bringing salvation to the human race and summoning individuals into a community to serve him is due solely to the mercy and grace of God, mediated and manifested through Jesus Christ in his ministry, atoning death

vergences are of less weight than those existing between Protestants and Roman Catholics,[64] difficulties that do remain all stem from the problem of 'explaining how divine grace is related to human response'.[65] Of these difficulties, four are dealt with in detail. Since division between Rome and the Anglicans did not come about on account of doctrinal divergences as such, certainly in respect of justification, such divergences as did arise were occasioned more by the fact of separation from Rome, than by the conscious development of a new doctrine.[66] The four differences are as follows.

The first lies in the proper understanding of *faith* and how exactly it relates to the person's confidence in his or her own being saved, Protestants falling into subjectivism in Catholics' eyes, Catholics tending towards legalism and scrupu-losity, as Protestants see things.

Secondly, on the question of the nature of *justification* of the sinner, whether this is solely imputed and thus extrinsic (Protestant tendency) or truly imparted and thus inherent (Catholic), the document notes: 'Anglican theologians of the sixteenth and seventeenth centuries saw imputed and imparted righteousness as distinct in the mind, but indissoluble in worship and life'.[67]

Thirdly, there arose the question of *good works and merit*. The dispute between Catholic and Reformation theologians is well known. Yet 'Anglican theologians of the Reformation, taking "by faith alone" to mean "only for the merit of Christ", also held good works to be not irrelevant to salvation, but imperfect and therefore inadequate. They saw good works as a necessary demonstration of faith, and faith itself as inseparable from hope and love.'[68]

Fourthly, though less explicitly, the *rôle of the Church*. Protestants generally thought Catholics took away from the exclusive mediatorship of Christ by overemphasizing the Church's rôle, where Catholics took it that Protestants were abandoning or devaluing the Church's ministry and sacraments, divinely appointed means of grace. Anglicans have traditionally attempted to establish a *via media* between the two positions.

---

and rising again. It was also no matter of dispute that God's grace evokes an authentic human response of faith which takes effect not only in the life of the individual but also in the corporate life of the Church' (*Salvation and the Church*, op. cit., no. 3).   64 Cf. ibid., no. 2.   65 Ibid., no. 3. 66 Take for example Thomas Cranmer's third homily in his *First Book of Homilies* (1547), theologically close to Calvin and probably based on Melanchthon's *Loci communes* (1535), of which article 11 of the *Thirty-nine Articles* (1562–63) reproduces the following phrase: 'We are accounted righteous before God, only for (*propter*) the merit of our Lord and Saviour Jesus Christ by Faith, and not for our own works or deservings. Wherefore, that we are justified by (*per*) Faith only, is a most welcome Doctrine, and very full of comfort . . . ' Given the efforts of Cranmer to explain justification in this way, Bucer and Fagius could say in 1549 that 'the doctrine of justification is purely and soundly taught' in England (cf. P.E. Hughes, *The Reformation in England, vol. 2: Religio depopulata*, London 1953, p. 97). According to McGrath this was certainly not the case in the whole of England at that time: cf. A.E. McGrath, *Iustitia Dei* . . . , op. cit., vol. 2, p. 102. On article 11 of the *Thirty-nine Articles*, cf. H. Chadwick, 'Justification by faith . . .', op. cit., pp. 210–213. 67 'Salvation and the Church', op. cit., no. 5.   68 Ibid., no. 6.

Content of 'Salvation and the Church'   After this introduction, the document goes on to develop the relationship between salvation and the four corresponding areas just mentioned: faith (nos. 9–11), justification (nos. 12–18), good works (nos. 19–24), Church (nos. 25–31). The following points are of special interest.

On faith and assurance of grace the document has the following to say. 'The Holy Spirit makes the fruits of Christ's sacrifice actual within the Church through Word and Sacrament: our sins are forgiven, we are enabled to respond to God's love, and we are conformed to the image of Christ. The human response to God's initiative is itself a gift of grace, and is at the same time a truly human, personal response . . . Our response to this gift must come from our whole being. Faith, therefore, not only includes an assent to the truth of the gospel but also involves commitment of our will to God in repentance and obedience to his call; otherwise faith is dead (Jas 2:17). Living faith is inseparable from love, issues in good works, and grows deeper in the course of a life of holiness . . . [Hence] Christian assurance is not presumptuous. It is always founded upon God's unfailing faithfulness and not upon the measure of our response... The word of Christ and his sacraments give us this assurance . . . Christians may never presume on their perseverance but should live their lives with sure confidence in God's grace.'[69]

The plurivalence of the term 'salvation' is pointed out in connection with other terms such as reconciliation, expiation/propitiation, redemption/liberation, adoption, sanctification and justification. Specifically the document states that 'justification and sanctification are two aspects of the same divine act . . . when God promises the removal of our condemnation and gives us a new standing before him, this justification is indissolubly linked with his sanctifying recreation of us in grace . . . God's grace effects what he declares: his creative word imparts what it imputes. By pronouncing us righteous, God also makes us righteous. He imparts a righteousness which is his and becomes ours.'[70]

And it continues: 'the remission of sins is accompanied by a present renewal, the rebirth to newness of life. Thus the juridical aspect of justification, while expressing an important facet of the truth, is not the exclusive notion in the light of which all other biblical ideas and images must be interpreted. For God sanctifies as well as acquits us.'[71]

The document makes it quite clear that good works are the natural result of grace, and receive a divine reward.[72] 'As justification and sanctification are aspects

69 Ibid., no. 11.   70 Ibid., no. 15. To this text, which rings unmistakably of Trent's *unica causa formalis*, is appended some words of the Anglican divine Richard Hooker (*Laws of Ecclesiastical Polity* 5: 61, 11) whose writings reflect to some degree a doctrine of *duplex iustitia* often considered quite representative of Anglicanism.   71 'Salvation and the Church', op. cit., no. 18.   72 'The works of the righteous performed in Christian freedom and in the love of god which the Holy Spirit gives us are the object of God's commendation and receive his reward' (ibid., no. 23). 'The language of merit and good works . . . when properly understood, in no way implies that human beings, once justified, are able to put God in their debt. Still less does it imply that justification itself is anything but a totally unmerited gift. Even the very first movements which lead to justification, such as repentance, the desire for forgiveness and even faith itself, are the work of God as

of the same divine act, so also living faith and love are inseparable in the believer. Faith is no merely private and interior disposition, but by its very nature is acted out: good works necessarily spring from a living faith. They are truly good because, as the fruit of the Spirit, they are done in God, in dependence on God's grace.'[73]

Glossing the notion that 'salvation involves participating in the humanity [of Christ]',[74] the document makes it clear that the individual Christian acts in the realm of grace with *true freedom*: 'In restoring us to his likeness, God confers freedom on fallen humanity. This is not the natural freedom to choose between alternatives, but the freedom to do his will . . . Inasmuch as we are recreated in his "own image and likeness", God involves us in what he freely does to realize our own salvation . . . Thus from the divine work follows a human work: it is we who live and act in a fully human way, yet never on our own or in a self-sufficient independence. This fully human life is possible if we live in the freedom and activity of Christ who, in the words of St Paul, "lives in me" (Gal 2:20).'[75]

As such a Christian can sin, and is called daily to repentance.[76] 'The Church is entrusted by the Lord with authority to pronounce forgiveness in his name to those who have fallen into sin and repent'. And the following point is made, with a view to giving due weight to penitential discipline. 'The Church may also help them to a deeper realization of the mercy of God in asking for practical amends for what has been done amiss. Such penitential disciplines, and other devotional practices, are not in any way intended to put God under obligation. Rather, they provide a form in which one may more fully embrace the free mercy of God.'[77]

Lastly as regards the rôle of the *Church* in justification, it is stated that the Church is a sign, steward and instrument. It is a sign of salvation and the gospel, insofar as it *'embodies and reveals the redemptive power contained in the gospel*. What Christ achieved through his cross and resurrection is communicated by the Holy Spirit in the life of the Church'.[78] It is besides a *steward* of the gospel, insofar as it is *enjoined by God himself to perpetuate and communicate the divine gift of salvation*. In this task, of course, 'the Church is servant and not master of what it has received . . . Its power to affect the hearer comes not from our unaided efforts but entirely from the Holy Spirit'.[79] And finally it is an instrument for the realization of God's eternal design. Though the Holy Spirit can act outside the visible confines of the Church, it is in her 'that the gospel becomes a manifest reality'.[80] Being an instrument, the document points out, means that the Church is 'called to be *a living expression of the gospel*, evangelized and evangelizing, reconciled and reconciling, gathered together and gathering others'.[81] In other words, it is an *instrument* of salvation more or less in that it is a sign of salvation.

The document states that insofar as the Church is *at once* sign, steward and instrument of God's design, it can be considered as a *sacrament* of God's saving

he touches our hearts by the illumination of the Holy Spirit' (ibid., no. 24).   [73] Ibid., no. 19.   [74] Ibid.   [75] Ibid.   [76] Cf. ibid., no. 21.   [77] Ibid., no. 22.   [78] Ibid., no. 26. Emphasis added.   [79] Ibid., no. 27. Emphasis added.   [80] Ibid., no. 28.   [81] Ibid. Emphasis added.

work, the credibility of which is limited by the sins of its members, the shortcomings of its human institutions, the scandal of division.[82] Hence the Church, living in the midst of the world, though 'always in need of renewal and purification, is already here and now a foretaste of God's Kingdom in a world still awaiting its consummation . . . Until the Kingdom is realized in its fullness, the Church is marked by human limitation and imperfection'.[83]

The document concludes by saying that 'we are agreed that this [justification] is not an area where any remaining differences of theological interpretation or ecclesiological emphasis, either within or between our Communions, can justify our continuing separation. We believe that our two Communions are agreed on the essential aspects of the doctrine of salvation and on the Church's rôle within it.'[84]

Evaluation of 'Salvation and the Church' Leaving aside the fact that the Vatican statement on this document failed to ratify its conclusions,[85] is not easy to assess what the *Salvation and the Church* has actually achieved. Of course the simple fact that the document was brought to a successful conclusion, is significant; besides, many valuable points were made, among them, in my view, the reflection on the interplay between ecclesiology and justification, and the Christologically based understanding of human freedom and faith response: man is *freed* not only *by Christ*, but is *made free* (and responsible) *in Christ*.[86] Yet the following observations, among others,[87] could be made.

1. Many complex theological questions have been presented in a dense though unquestionably brief document. However, language tends to be 'symbolic' and at times somewhat vague, perhaps intentionally so. Treatment of issues might be considered excessively 'therapeutic'.[88]

2. An unresolved tension seems to remain between 'justification' and 'salvation'. On the one hand, the impression is given that the question of justification as such should be given secondary value, and subordinated to other biblical concepts, particularly that of 'salvation'. On the other, all the topics studied in the document are totally linked up with the justification debate. Of course, historically speaking, the cause of separation between Catholics and Anglicans was not related to a clash on the topic of justification, and in that sense it has been asked why the topic of justification (or salvation) has been raised in Anglican-Roman Catholic dialogue in the first place.[89]

---

82 Cf. ibid., no. 29.   83 Ibid., no. 30.   84 Ibid., no. 32.   85 Cf. Congregation for the Doctrine of the Faith, 'Observations and Commentary on ARCIC-II's "Salvation and the Church"', op. cit., no. 1.   86 Cf. 'Salvation and the Church', op. cit., no. 19.   87 Other questions which need to be further explored include: the understanding of faith and its relation to baptism and Church; the question of the assurance or otherwise of grace; the link-up between natural human freedom, good works and redemption by Christ.   88 Cf. D.A. Scott, ' "Salvation and the Church" and Theological Truth Claims', op. cit., pp. 430–432.   89 Cf. G.H. Tavard, 'Justification in Dialogue', in *One in Christ* 25 (1989) 305.

Perhaps the wish not to put justification in the forefront explains why a significant option was taken in the document, that of subordinating the doctrine of justification (which relates to a past 'event' and a present 'situation') to that of salvation (which has strongly eschatological connotations).[90]

3. The Catholic point of reference for the document is undoubtedly Trent, yet it is not specified what kind of Anglicanism it takes as point of departure.[91] The question of the *unica causa formalis* of justification, perceived by many Anglican divines in the sixteenth century as the key point of divergence with Rome, is not treated.[92] From

---

90 Cf. A.E. McGrath, *ARCIC-II and Justification* . . . , op. cit., pp. 40–42.   91 H. Chadwick ('Justification by faith . . .', op. cit., p. 214) indicates that three broad patterns are to be found among sixteenth century Anglicans, specifically as regards interpretation of the *Thirty-nine Articles*: a humanistic-liberal school inspired by Erasmus, an evangelical school close to Calvin, and a philo-Catholic tendency which saw little difference between the *Articles* and Trent (for example that of C. Davenport). Commenting on the findings of ARCIC-I, the Congregation of the Doctrine of the Faith had observed in 1982: 'It would have been useful – in order to evaluate the exact meaning of certain points of agreement – had ARCIC indicated their position in reference to the documents which have contributed significantly to the formulation of the Anglican identity (The *Thirty-nine Articles* of Religion, *Book of Common Prayer*, *Ordinal*) in those cases where the assertions of the Final Report seem incompatible with these documents. The failure to take a stand on these texts can give rise to uncertainty about the exact meaning of the agreements reached' (Section A, 2, iii, in *Acta Apostolicae Sedis* 74 (1982) 1065). The commentary of the same congregation on *Salvation and the Church* makes reference to this observation: Congregation for the Doctrine of the Faith, 'Observations and Commentary on ARCIC-II's "Salvation and the Church". . .', in *Origins*, op. cit., pp. 434, note 5. Cf. also J.R. Wright, ' "Salvation and the Church": A Response to David Scott', op. cit., pp. 438f.; G.H. Tavard, 'Justification in Dialogue', op. cit., p. 308. One of the Anglican members of the ARCIC-II commission, J.R. Wright ('Martin Luther: An Anglican Ecumenical Appreciation', in *Anglican and Episcopalian History* 56 (1987) 320–323) has shown that the Anglican doctrine on justification in the sixteenth century differed considerably from Luther's. P. Avis ('Reflections on ARCIC-II', op. cit., p. 458) has it that Hooker's view 'is not the only doctrine of justification to be found within Anglicanism'.   92 The Evangelical Anglican Richard Hooker stated that the 'grand question, which hangeth yet in the controversy between us and the Church of Rome, is about the matter of justifying righteousness', ('A learned discourse of Justification', in W. Speed Hill, L. Yeandle and E. Grislis (eds.), *The Folger Library Edition of the Works of Richard Hooker*, vol. 5, Cambridge (Mass.)/London 1990, pp. 105–169, here no. 3, p. 109). He also judged 'the opinion of the Lutherans' to be 'damnable' (ibid., no. 17, p. 125). On Hooker's doctrine on justification, cf. L.W. Gibbs, 'Richard Hooker's *Via Media* Doctrine of Justification', in *Harvard Theological Review* 74 (1981) 211–220; H. Chadwick, 'Justification by faith . . .', op. cit., pp. 215ff.; P.E. Hughes, *Faith and Works: Cranmer and Hooker on justification*, Wilton 1982; C.F. Allison, 'The Pastoral and Political Implications of Trent on Justification', in *One in Christ* 24 (1988) 112– 127, especially pp. 119–123. Many other Anglican divines of the period were in agreement with Hooker. Three observations could be made. *Firstly*, one of the latter, John Davenant, Bishop of Salisbury, agreed with Robert Bellarmine in saying that the key issue dividing the two sides related to the formal cause of justification. Where Bellarmine, defending Trent's *unica causa formalis*, held that 'We learn [from Rom 5:17] that to be justified by Christ is not to be accounted or pronounced just, but truly to be made and constituted just by obtaining of inherent righteousness, not imperfect justice, but justice that is absolute and perfect' (*De Iustificatione II*, 3, in *Opera Omnia VI*, 212), Davenant said: 'We do not deny that inherent righteousness is infused into the justified by Christ . . . but we affirm that . . . in this life it is inchoate and imputed, and therefore not the cause

what we have seen, however, it would seem that the document comes quite close to
Trent on this very point[93] as on others, while seeming to distance itself from the
principal tenets of Evangelical Anglican thought.[94] The Vatican commentary on *Salvation and the Church* seems to confirm the point, stating clearly that divergences
remaining between Catholics and Anglicans 'principally concern certain aspects of
ecclesiology and of sacramental doctrine',[95] and not as such elements related to salvation and justification. Tavard would say that 'in Anglicanism, Luther's theology
of justification has never been much at home'.[96]

---

of our justification, but the appendage' (*Disputatio de Iustitia Habituali et Actuali* (1631), Eng., tr.,
London 1844, pp. 164f.). And Hooker had it that 'the righteousness, wherewith we shall be clothed
in the world to come, is both perfect and inherent. That whereby here we are justified is perfect,
but not inherent. That whereby we are sanctified, inherent, but not perfect' ('A learned discourse
of Justification', op. cit., pp. 127f.) and also: 'we participate Christ partly by imputation, as when
those things which he did and suffered for us are imputed unto us for righteousness; partly by
habitual and real infusion, as when grace is inwardly bestowed while we are on earth, and afterwards more fully both our souls and bodies made like unto his in glory' (ibid.). *Secondly* disagree-
ment in respect of the formal cause of justification may also be expressed in terms of whether or
not sin *remains* in the justified. Bellarmine, following Trent (DH 1515 and 1529) held that nothing
of sin remains, closing the door on the possibility of Luther's *simul iustus et peccator*. Davenant and
others held that something of sin does remain: 'Whether by infusion or inherent grace, whatever
hath the true nature and proper character of sin is forthwith eradicated and entirely taken away in
the justified. We deny it, the Papists affirm it . . . *For* according to our adversaries the formal cause
of justification expels by inhesion whatsoever is in itself hateful to God, or worthy of punishment'
(*Disputatio de Iustitia* . . . , op. cit., pp. 18; 227). *Thirdly*, the doctrine of Hooker, Davenant and
other Anglicans comes close in real terms to the theory of 'double justice' (cf. R. Hooker, 'A Learned
Discourse of Justification', op. cit., no. 21, p. 129), mooted at Regensburg, rejected by both Luther
and Trent, and popularized in England by Reginald Pole and others. According to Allison, 'the
force of the arguments of the minority at Trent [defending 'double-justice'] was not unlike the
Anglican criticism of inherent righteousness being the formal cause of justification' (J.F. Allison,
'The Pastoral and Political Implications of Trent . . .', op. cit., p. 121). On Anglicanism and justification in general, cf. H. Chadwick, 'Justification by faith: a perspective', op. cit., pp. 201-220;
A.E. McGrath, *Iustitia Dei* . . . , op. cit., vol. 2, pp. 98–111; idem., *ARCIC-II and Justification* . .
. , op. cit., pp. 15–29; J.F. Allison, 'The Pastoral and Political Implications of Trent . . .', op. cit.,
pp. 119ff.   93 Cf. 'Salvation and the Church', op. cit., no. 15.   94 Thus Evangelical Anglican
authors such as R.G. England (*Justification today: the Roman Catholic and Anglican Debate*, Oxford
1979) and A.E. McGrath (*ARCIC-II and Justification* . . . , op. cit.) considered the question of
justification to be central to the ecumenical encounters between Anglicans and Roman Catholics.
Certainly the latter author was dissatisfied with 'Salvation and the Church'. Cf. also the 1988 *Open
Letter to the Anglican Episcopate* (Nottingham 1988) signed by many Evangelical Anglicans, published shortly before the Lambeth Conference, and taking exception to many findings of both
ARCIC-I and II. The letter requested clarifications in the following areas: a definition of faith with
stronger emphasis on *fides est fiducia*; distinguishing between justification (instantaneous, relating
to our standing before God), and sanctification (gradual, relating to our own character); real disagreements between Reformers and Trent; elaboration of the doctrine of Atonement; spelling out
the implications for justification doctrine of Roman Catholic teaching on purgatory, penance, indulgences, the Mass, the rôle of Mary and the saints; the question of salvation outside the visible
bounds of the Church.   95 Congregation for the Doctrine of the Faith, 'Observations and Commentary on ARCIC-II's "Salvation and the Church" ', op. cit., no. 3.   96 G.H. Tavard, *Justification* . . . , op. cit., p. 68.

4. For the first time in a document on justification, an in-depth theological reflection on rôle of the *Church* is made. This widening of perspectives is to be warmly welcomed. As the 1993 Lutheran-Catholic document *Church and Justification* has come to show, the doctrines of justification and salvation must be ecclesiologically contextualized, and the three aspects of the Church's reality, action and mission described by the *Salvation and the Church* (as sign, steward, instrument) are completely to the point. However, little attempt is made to clarify the actual *link-up* between justification and the Church, and the impression remains therefore that the ecclesiological side of the doctrine of justification is left somewhat out on a limb.

It may be, however, that the lack of integration between 'Church' and 'justification' in the document responds rather to a definite ecclesiological option, according to which the Church is considered in a 'functional' way as being *posterior to* or *the result* of justification and salvation of sinners, and its principal task as that of offering corporatively a credible witness of the gospel to the world. In fact the Vatican observations on *Salvation and the Church* had the following to say concerning the chapter 'The Church and Salvation'. 'The rôle of the Church in salvation is *not only to bear witness* to it, but also and above all, to be the *effective instrument* – notably by means of the seven sacraments – of justification and salvation. This essential point needs to be further elaborated, especially in relation to *Lumen gentium*. [Besides] it is particularly important to draw more clearly the distinction between the holiness of the Church as universal sacrament of salvation on the one hand, and its members, who in some measure are still given to sin, on the other.'[97]

In its commentary on these observations, the Vatican document remarks that 'the commission presents a rather vague conception of the Church, which seems to lie at the base of all the difficulties that have been pointed out', specifically that it 'does not sufficiently keep in mind the sacramental dimension of salvation, alluding only briefly to the post-baptismal sacraments, which are the privileged means of the communication of grace [Eucharist, Penance] . . .'.[98]

Referring to the central rôle of ministry and the celebration of the Eucharist,[99]

---

97 Congregation for the Doctrine of the Faith, 'Observations and Commentary on ARCIC-II's "Salvation and the Church" ', op. cit., no. 2, d). The two points, both centered on the 'sacramental' quality of the Church as such, are closely linked. cf. P. O'Callaghan, 'The Mediation of Justification and the justification of Mediation. Report of the Lutheran/Catholic Dialogue: "Church and Justification: Understanding the Church in the Light of the Doctrine of Justification" (1993)', in *Annales Theologici* 10 (1996) 147–211, especially pp. 185–188; and 'The Holiness of the Church in "Lumen Gentium" ', in *Thomist* 52 (1988) 673–701. 98 Congregation for the Doctrine of the Faith, 'Observations and Commentary on ARCIC-II's "Salvation and the Church". . .', in *Origins*, op. cit., pp. 433; 432. Cf. for example, 'Salvation and the Church', no. 9ff. on faith and justification, in which no mention is made of the link-up between faith and baptism, 'sacrament of faith'. The same could be said regarding the assurance of justification, linked not only with faith, but also with the Church as a sacramental reality. 99 'This once-for-all atoning work of Christ, realized and experienced in the life of the Church and celebrated in the Eucharist, constitutes the free gift of God which is proclaimed in the Gospel. In the service of this mystery the Church is entrusted with a responsibility of stewardship. The Church is called to fulfill this stewardship by proclaim-

the commentary appended to the Vatican observations asks does *Salvation and the Church* (no. 27)

> really indicate recognition of the 'propitiatory value' of the Eucharistic sacrifice? And does the term 'realize' imply therefore an authentic actualization of this sacrifice through the mediation of an ordained minister, whose priesthood differs essentially from the common priesthood of the faithful . . . The importance of these questions will be readily grasped, because when this doctrine is not fully accepted, the rôle of the Church in the furtherance of salvation risks *being limited to witnessing to a truth that it is incapable of efficaciously making present*, a truth which then risks being reduced to a subjective 'experience' which does not bear within itself the guarantee of its redemptive power.[100]

The point being made is a critical one: if the Church is not capable (particularly through its ordained ministry) of making salvation effectively present, then what right does it have to consider itself and present itself as a witness to and steward of the divine truth and power it is supposed to communicate and perpetuate? In other words, it does not seem sufficient to say that the Church's 'instrumentality' in respect of salvation can be expressed merely as a call 'to be a living expression of the gospel, evangelized and evangelizing . . .'[101]

9. *Minor Lutheran-Reformed/Catholic documents on justification*

Before examining the three principal Lutheran/Reformed-Catholic documents on justification, it is worth while mentioning three other interesting local statements. Firstly, attention should be drawn to the statement on justification drawn up by an ecumenical discussion group of Catholics and Lutherans in Norway, published early in 1991, and based principally on the American document *Justification by faith* (USA) that we shall examine presently.[102]

Secondly, the 1991 statement *Towards a Common Understanding of the Church* prepared by the Reformed/Roman Catholic International Dialogue,[103] which is highly significant particularly in respect of its development of the relationship be-

ing the gospel and by its sacramental and pastoral life' ('Salvation and the Church', no. 27). 100 Congregation for the Doctrine of the Faith, 'Observations and Commentary on ARCIC-II's "Salvation and the Church". . .', in *Origins*, op. cit., p. 433. Emphasis added. 101 'Salvation and the Church', no. 28. 102 Cf. Catholic-Lutheran Discussion Group in Norway, 'Justification', in *Church Information Service*, Oslo 1991. Italian translation in EO 4:1809-1890. It is made up of four sections, one biblical, 'The Gospel on justification' (nos. 9–17), two anthropological, 'What does "becoming justified" involve?' (nos. 18–36), 'Faith, grace and justification' (nos. 37–54), and one ecclesiological: 'Grace, means of grace and the Church' (nos. 55–72). 103 Reformed/Roman Catholic International Dialogue, *Towards a Common Understanding of the Church*, Geneva 1991.

tween justification, Christology and ecclesiology. The following way of expression is of particular interest. 'Together we confess the Church, for there is no justification in isolation. All justification takes place in the community of believers, or is ordered toward the gathering of such a community. Fundamental for us all is the presence of Christ in the Church, considered simultaneously as both a reality of grace and a concrete community in time and space. Christ himself acts in the Church . . . Justification by grace through faith is given us in the Church. This is not to say that the Church exercises a mediation complementary to that of Christ, or that it is clothed with a power independent of the gift of grace. The Church is at once the place, the instrument, and the minister chosen by God to make Christ's word heard and to celebrate the sacraments in God's name throughout the centuries.'[104]

Lastly, the 1992 statement prepared by the Mixed Catholic-Protestant Committee in France on ethics,[105] is of interest. It is theologically focussed on the doctrine of justification by faith as the 'centre of Scripture'.

MAJOR LUTHERAN-REFORMED/CATHOLIC DOCUMENTS ON JUSTIFICATION

I have grouped major Lutheran and Reformed common statements with the Catholic Church together, not only because Lutheran and Reformed doctrines have much in common, but also because the three dialogues with Catholics (USA Lutheran, German Reformed, International Lutheran) have played a decisive rôle in the genesis of a gradually consolidated consensus on the doctrine of justification between Catholics and Lutherans. In the following pages, we shall look only at some fundamental elements of these documents, because they will be cited and used extensively in the final chapter of this work.

1.   *'Justification by faith' (USA, 1984)*

Justification by faith (1984, abbreviated USA) is the most extensive document to date dealing exclusively with the doctrine of justification. It is the result of a six-year study jointly made by scholars' committees appointed by the Roman Catholic Bishops' Committee for Ecumenical and Interreligious Affairs in the United States, and the Lutheran World Federation.

Justification by faith is the seventh in a series of thoroughly elaborated documents, started in 1965, on such topics as 'The Status of the Nicene Creed as Dogma of the Church', 'One Baptism for the remission of sins', 'The Eucharist as Sacrifice', 'Eucharist and Ministry', 'Papal primacy and the universal Church', 'The

---

104 Ibid., nos. 80; 86 (pp. 30–33). Emphasis added.   105 Cf. Comité Mixte Catholique-Protestant en France, *Choix éthiques et communion ecclésiale*, Paris 1992, I, 2. Italian translation of the entire document in EO 4:753–878; on justification, nos. 779–782.

teaching authority of the Church' and recently 'The one mediator, the saints, and Mary'. The document on justification has been considered by some as the high point of these conversations.[106] It is an extensive, carefully studied document, occupying over 80 pages in the English edition,[107] and has received a good reception from ecumenists worldwide.[108]

The most notable feature of *Justification by faith* is in the extensive attention it pays to the historical dimension of the doctrine of justification from the period of the Reformation up to the mid-1960's,[109] and this was done, the document says, with a view to understanding 'how disagreements over justification that were once irresolvable may now not be church-dividing.'[110] This form of historical reconstruction is of considerable interest theologically and ecumenically, as it shows how personal views of and approaches to the issues involved, as well as political and social factors of many kinds, often conditioned and coloured the real issues in a decisive way. The other two major sections of the paper, 'Reflection and Interpretation'[111] and 'Perspectives for Reconstruction'[112] (mainly on the biblical question) offer a more analytical approach.

Declared points of convergence   In its final stages, *Justification by faith* subscribes to a sort of interpretative 'fundamental affirmation', offers a dozen elements of 'material convergence', and then a final common declaration.

---

106 Cf. G.H. Tavard, 'The Contemporary Relevance of Justification by Faith', op. cit., p. 131.   **107** Cf. H.G. Anderson, et al. (eds.), 'Justification by faith', in *Lutherans and Catholics in Dialogue VII*, Augsburg Publishing House, Minneapolis 1985, pp. 8–74. Italian translation: Commissione ecumenica cattolico-luterana USA, 'Giustificazione per fede', in *Il Regno Documenti* 29 (1984) 162–190 and EO 2:2759–2925. The same volume edited by H.G. Anderson et al. gathers a significant collection of essays used in the preparatory phase of the document, to which may be added the scriptural study undertaken by J. Reumann, *'Righteousness' in the New Testament: 'Justification' in the United States Lutheran-Roman Catholic Dialogue; with responses by Joseph A. Fitzmyer; Jerome D. Quinn*, Philadelphia/New York/Ramsey 1982.   **108** Official responses include: National Conference of Catholic Bishops, 'An Evaluation of the Lutheran-Catholic Statement: "Justification by Faith" ', in *Ecumenical Trends* 19 (1990) 53–58; others (of the Evangelical Lutheran Church of America and of the Missouri Synod of the Lutheran Church, as well as the one just mentioned of the U.S. Bishops) may be found in: T. Rausch, 'Responses to the US Lutheran-Roman Catholic Statement on Justification', in *One in Christ* 29 (1993) 333–353. Other commentaries include: J.F. Hotchkin, 'Reflections on dialogue and justification', in *Ecumenical Trends* 13 (1984) 62–64; R.J. Goeser, 'Commentary on U.S. Roman Catholic-Lutheran Statement on Justification', in *Ecumenical Trends* 13 (1984) 81–85; G.H. Tavard, 'The Contemporary Relevance of Justification by Faith', in *One in Christ* 21 (1985) 131–138; A.E. McGrath, *ARCIC-II and Justification . . .* , op. cit., pp. 31–50; C.J. Peter, 'A Moment of Truth for Lutheran-Catholic Dialogue', in *Origins* 17 (1987/88) 537–541; G.H. Tavard, 'Justification in Dialogue', in *One in Christ* 25 (1989) 299–310; J. Reumann, ' "Justification by Faith" in the Lutheran-Roman Catholic Dialogue and Beyond: Reflections over a Decade', in *Lutheran Forum* 23 (1989) 21–24; C.E. Braaten, 'Lutherans and Catholics in Dialogue VII', in *Justification...* op. cit., pp. 118–123; J. Wicks, 'U.S. Bishops Welcome Document on Justification', in *Ecumenical Trends* 19 (1990) 49–52.   **109** Cf. USA 5–93.   **110** USA 5.   **111** Cf. USA 94–121.   **112** Cf. USA 122–160.

The 'fundamental affirmation' attempts to express a kind of spiritual common-ground between Lutherans and Catholics, and is stated in the following terms:

> Our entire hope of justification and salvation rests on Christ Jesus and on the gospel whereby the good news of God's merciful action in Christ is made known; we do not place our ultimate trust in anything other than God's promise and saving work in Christ.[113]

The first part of this statement amounts to a general declaration of the 'primacy of grace' in justification, the second points *to the way in which we appropriate* the grace of justification promised us, that is, the concretizing of our faith response: trusting *'ultimately'*, the document says, in nothing other than God's merciful promise. The term 'ultimate trust' is important, and recurs on several occasions, explicitly and implicitly, throughout the statement. The way in which such an ultimate trust is understood is central to the whole debate, for it provides the decisive test of the human and ecclesial quality of the doctrine of justification. Certainly the following affirmation should be noted: 'It must be emphasized that our *common affirmation* that it is *God in Christ alone whom believers ultimately trust does not necessitate any one particular way* of conceptualizing or picturing God's saving work.'[114]

Twelve points of 'material convergence' are listed. Since between Catholics and Lutherans there would seem to be general consensus on the question of the 'primacy of grace', that is on the theological preponderance of merciful divine initiative, of the twelve only those texts are mentioned which relate directly to *what goes to make up the human faith response*, in other words, the theological elements by which *humans express their 'ultimate trust' in God*, since it is on this point that views tend to diverge more decisively between Lutherans and Catholics.

> 3. As a consequence of original sin all human beings stand in need of justification even before they commit personal sins. Those in whom sin reigns *can do nothing to merit justification*, which is the free gift of God's grace. Even the *beginnings of justification*, for example, *repentance, prayer for grace, and desire for forgiveness*, must be God's work in us. 4. We remain God's creatures even when ruled by sin. *We retain the human freedom to make choices among created goods, but we lack the capacity to turn to God without divine help* . . . 6. Scripture, the proclamation of the word, and the sacraments are means whereby the gospel, as the power of God for salvation, *comes concretely to individuals to awaken and strengthen justifying faith*. 7. In justification we receive by faith the effects of Christ's action on our behalf. *Justifying faith is not merely historical knowledge or intellectual conviction, but a trustful, self-involving response to the gospel*. 8. *Justifying faith cannot exist without hope and love*; it necessarily

113 USA 157; also in USA 4.   114 USA 158.

issues in *good works*. Yet *the justified cannot rely on their own good works or boast of their own merits* as though they were not still in need of mercy. 9. Sin no longer reigns in the justified, yet they remain *subject to sinful inclinations and the assaults of sin* so that, when left to their own powers, they fall repeatedly. Of themselves they remain capable of losing justification, but, because of the great mercy of God in Christ, *they may firmly trust and hope that God will bring them to final salvation* . . .12. The priority of God's redeeming will over every human action in bringing about ultimate salvation is recognized in both our traditions by the classic doctrine of predestination.'[115]

The document is suggesting, if I am not mistaken, that the points of 'material convergence' on justification constitute statements which both Catholics and Lutherans could accept together, though each one might consider the content of such statements in a different way. Now the question should be asked at this stage: is agreement or convergence of such a kind reliable? Might there not be the danger of covering up of true divergences which remain all the while?

The final four-point common declaration is likewise one of spirit rather than of content; instead of dealing with the reality of justification and human response, it advocates the use of the doctrine of justification as a general interpretative principle for theology and the whole life of the Church.[116]

---

[115] USA 156. Emphasis added. The remaining points are as follows (all from USA 156): 1. Christ and his gospel are the source, center, and norm of Christian life, individual and corporate, in church and world. Christians have no other basis for eternal life and hope of final salvation than God's free gift in Jesus Christ, extended to them in the Holy Spirit. 2. The prerequisite of final salvation is righteousness. To be saved one must be *judged righteous* and *be righteous*. 5. Justification, as a transition from disfavor and unrighteousness to favor and righteousness in God's sight, is totally God's work. By justification we are both declared and made righteous. Justification, therefore, is not a legal fiction. God, in justifying, effects what he promises; *he forgives sin and makes us truly righteous.* 10. The eternal reward promised to the righteous is a gift, for it depends wholly on God's grace in Christ, the one mediator between God and fallen humanity. 11. The *good works of the justified, performed in grace, will be recompensed by God*, the righteous judge, who, true to his promises 'will render to everyone according to his works' (Rom 2:6) . . . [116] The text is as follows: 'We can make together, in fidelity to the gospel we share, the following declaration: 1. We believe that God's creative graciousness is offered to us and to everyone for healing and reconciliation so that through the Word made flesh, Jesus Christ, 'who was put to death for our transgressions and raised for our justification' (Rom 4:25), we are all called to pass from the alienation and oppression of sin to freedom and fellowship with God in the Holy Spirit. It is not through our own initiative that we respond to this call, but only through an undeserved gift which is granted and made known in faith, and which comes to fruition in our love of God and neighbor, as we are led by the Spirit in faith to bear witness to the divine gift in all aspects of our lives. This faith gives us hope for ourselves and all humanity and gives us confidence that salvation in Christ will always be proclaimed as the gospel, the good news for which the world is searching. 2. This gospel frees us in God's sight from slavery to sin and self (cf. Rom 6:6). We are willing to be judged by it in all our thoughts and actions, our philosophies and projects, our theologies and religious practices. Since there is no aspect of the Christian community or of its life in the world that is not challenged by this gospel, there is none that cannot be renewed or reformed in its light or by its power. 3. We have

The Theological Question   The second section of *Justification by faith* is entitled
'Reflection and Interpretation',[117] and it represents the principal analytical section
of the document. It begins by presenting what must surely be the central thesis of
the statement regarding Catholic and Lutheran understandings of the doctrine of
justification: 'it is evident that many of the difficulties have arisen from *the contrasting concerns and patterns of thought in the two traditions*'.[118] The purpose of this section therefore is to 'describe and interpret the historic concerns and thought patterns of Lutheran and Catholic understandings of justification before . . . [turning]
in the third part to a consideration of convergences in biblical exegesis and theological understanding.'[119]

The central thesis, contained in the following two paragraphs, is that the Catholic vision of grace and justification is vouched principally in *transformational language*, whereas the Lutheran view is for the most part in *declarative or juridical language*.[120]

> *Lutherans* generally emphasize *God's address to sinners* in the good news of
> Christ's life, death, and resurrection; theology and doctrine should serve
> proclamation so as to *exclude reliance on self for salvation*. They therefore fo-
> cus on safeguarding the absolute priority of God's redeeming word in Jesus
> Christ. The *unconditionality of God's love for fallen humankind* implies that
> the fulfillment of the promise of salvation depends on nothing else but the
> gift of faith by which believes trust in God. *Catholics*, while not rejecting the
> absolute priority of God's saving action, are generally speaking more con-
> cerned with *the renewal and sanctification of the created order*, an efficacy which
> Lutherans, for their part, do not deny.[121]

These different concerns entail notably different patterns of thought and discourse. 'The Catholic concerns are most easily expressed in the transformationist
language appropriate to describing a process in which human beings, created good
but now sinful, are brought to new life through God's infusion of saving grace . . .
Lutheran ways of speaking, on the other hand, are shaped by *the situation of sinners
standing before God (coram Deo) and hearing at one and the same time God's words of
judgement and forgiveness in law and gospel*. Attention is here focussed on this discon-

encountered this gospel in our Churches' sacraments and liturgies, in their preaching and teaching, in their doctrines and exhortations. Yet we also recognize that in both our churches the gospel
has not always been proclaimed, that it has been blunted by reinterpretation, that it has been
transformed by various means into self-satisfying systems of commands and prohibitions. 4. We
are grateful at this time to be able to confess together what our Catholic and Lutheran ancestors
tried to affirm as they responded in different ways to the biblical message of justification. A fundamental consensus on the gospel is necessary to give credibility to our previous agreed statements
on baptism, on the Eucharist, and on forms of church authority. We believe that we have reached
such a consensus' (USA 161–164).   117 Cf. USA 94–121.   118 Cf. USA 94.   119 USA 94.   120
Cf. USA 94–95.   121 USA 95. Emphasis added.

tinuous, paradoxical and simultaneous double relation of God to the justified, not on the continuous process of his transforming work.'[122]

The contrast between the two ways of expressing the Christian mystery is explicitated in six areas, each of which clearly presented and tightly reasoned. 1. The imputational or forensic character of justification; 2. The sinfulness of the justified; 3. The sufficiency of faith; 4. The doctrine of merit; 5. The doctrine of satisfaction; 6. The criteria by which Christian life and doctrine are to be judged.

1. As regards *forensic justification*, the difference between Lutheran and Catholic approaches lies, according to the document, in the fact that for the former God *declares* the sinner just, for the latter in that God *makes* the sinner just. Where Lutherans fear Catholic doctrine 'could tend to throw believers back on their resources',[123] Catholics wonder whether or not an 'emphasis on forensic justification . . . if not accompanied by other themes, could unintentionally encourage a certain disregard for the benefits actually imparted through God's loving deed in Christ'.[124]

For Catholics, justification is certainly unconditional on God's side, but it may be conditioned by man. 'Justification depends on faith, which in turn depends on the word of God, mediated through the Scriptures and the Church . . . In the execution of God's saving plan there may be conditions, which, without restricting God's power and freedom, condition the created effects of his powerful decrees. In efficaciously willing the effect, of course, God also wills the conditions and provides for their realization.'[125]

For Lutherans, the Catholic doctrine of the infusion of grace, by which sin is forgiven, 'makes it difficult to express adequately the unmerited character of God's forgiving mercy . . . Catholics . . . may think that the Lutheran position is too narrowly focussed on the "consolation of terrified consciences" and does not take sufficient account of the doxological dimension of the response of faith, i.e. the praise of God for his transformative indwelling.'[126]

2. Of course one of the principal reasons why Lutherans insist on forensic justification in the first place lies in the fact that *human sinfulness* remains even in the justified. 'While granting that justification unfailingly effects inner renewal (including the gifts of the Holy Spirit, sanctification, and good works), Lutherans see this renewal as a lifelong struggle against sin both as unrighteousness and self-righteousness . . . Sin . . . remains and is in need of continued forgiveness.'[127] The 'sinfulness' which remains, and requires 'a lifelong struggle against sinful tendencies, is termed concupiscence by Catholics. But *concupiscence*, according the Council of Trent, is not "truly and properly sin in those born again." '[128]

Sin in the true sense, that is guilt (*reatus culpae*), producing divine displeasure, is

122 USA 96. Emphasis added.   123 USA 100.   124 Ibid.   125 USA 100.   126 USA 101.   127 USA 102.   128 Ibid.

completely eliminated by the sanctifying action of the Holy Spirit, according to Catholic doctrine. In other words, man's justified state, in which sin has been banished and destroyed by God's transforming and sanctifying action, is *not incompatible* with the persistence of sinful inclinations.

Lutherans would tend to feel uncomfortable at this position, for man is *simul iustus et peccator*.[129] Indeed they fear Catholic doctrine 'may cause the Christian to be anxious or complacent, and in either case insufficiently reliant on God's promise of mercy'.[130] But likewise 'Catholics fear that the Lutheran position may lead to a certain neglect of good works or may not adequately motivate the believer to give praise and thanks to God for the healing and transforming effects of his redemptive action in us.'[131]

3. The next theme dealt with relates to the *kind of faith* that is *sufficient* for justification. Catholics understand that true faith must be 'accompanied (or perhaps better intrinsically qualified) by the gift of love (*caritas*)',[132] what was termed by the Scholastics *fides caritate formata*. Lutherans of course do not deny that true faith cannot but be living and operative. Again it is a question of priority: Catholics maintain that 'the indwelling the Holy Spirit brings about in believers not only assent and trust but also a loving commitment that issues in good works'.[133] Lutherans fear not so much the reality of the Holy Spirit's action inspiring the Christian to works of charity, but rather the possibility that on their own account Christians in fact would take complacency in carrying out such good works, attempting to prove to God that they are just, 'relying on their own activity rather than on the saving work of Christ'.[134] Understandably therefore they fear 'speaking of sinners actively cooperating in their own justification'.[135]

4. The question of *merit* moves in the same direction. Lutherans, while admitting in an eschatological sense that God 'rewards' the just, traditionally saw in the doctrine of merit a clear indication of Catholic 'Pelagianism' which 'could lead to a legalism that derogates from the unconditional character of God's justifying word'.[136] Catholics however hold that merit is itself the work of grace, 'presupposing a charity which proceeds from God'.[137] It is the contrast between 'the Catholic doctrine of merit *ex gratia*, and the Lutheran doctrine of promise'.[138] In fact 'Lutherans are primarily intent on stressing the saving character of the unconditional promises God addresses to human beings and on preventing Christians from being left to their own resources, whereas the Catholic preoccupation is to make sure that the full range of God's gifts, even the crowning gift of a merited destiny, is acknowledged.'[139]

---

129 Cf. ibid.   130 USA 102.   131 Ibid.   132 USA 105.   133 Ibid.   134 USA 106.   135 Ibid.
136 USA 110.   137 USA 111.   138 USA 112.   139 Ibid.

5. *Satisfaction*, from a theological stand-point, has quite a lot in common with merit, although in a strict sense it is a Christological issue. 'In the sixteenth century both Lutherans and Catholics were convinced that, as far as eternal punishments were concerned, Christ through his sufferings and death gave full satisfaction for all sin, original and personal.'[140]

In later times, Catholics experienced difficulties with the doctrine of satisfaction, especially as understood by Protestants in terms of 'penal substitution. The former wondered how exactly could Christ substitute in us and for us what in principle we could only do for ourselves, that is our arduous faith-assent to justifying grace, thus partaking in Christ's own satisfaction. The Protestant view of satisfaction, understood in the main in terms of penal substitution, got around the difficulty by holding that the human will is not essentially involved in the process of justification. Even if this is so, the Protestant explanation begs the question in respect of the meaningfulness of such a substitution: how is it possible that *only* Christ could satisfy?; how do we benefit really from such satisfaction?

Understandably, Lutherans are uneasy about the Catholic teaching that 'the sufferings of the saints, united in a mysterious way with those of Christ himself, could "fill up" what was lacking in Christ's sufferings (cf. Col 1:24)'.[141] *Justification by Faith* explains that the doctrine is acceptable 'not as regards intrinsic value but as regards the application to particular times, places, and persons'.[142] Thus 'the sufferings of penitent sinners and of the innocent can be prayerfully applied, in union with the immeasurable satisfaction given by Christ, to beseech God's mercy and pardon.'[143]

This issue is an important one insofar as it relates directly to many of the practical differences between Lutherans and Catholics, particularly as regards indulgences, Mass offerings, devotion to the saints and purgatory.[144]

6. The last theological issue *Justification by Faith* examines is that of *the criteriological or hermeneutical rôle of the doctrine of justification*, which is enormously significant in contemporary reflection on the question, especially among Lutherans, for whom justification is principally 'a critical principle by which to test what is authentically Christian. The principle of justification by faith, understood as the correlative of the sole mediatorship of Christ, was accepted as the article by which the Church must stand or fall. Lutherans believe that this principle has continuing validity, *since the tendency of Christians to rely on their own devices rather than on Christ is unabating*. While granting that the principle of justification by faith alone must not be employed to erode the fullness of the apostolic heritage and of the means whereby this heritage is to be mediated in any given time and place, they believe that this principle retains its critical importance.'[145]

---

140 USA 113.   141 USA 114.   142 Ibid.   143 USA 116.   144 Cf. ibid.   145 USA 117. Emphasis added.

Catholics at times have the impression that for Lutherans, who certainly do not deny the need for structural elements in the provision of salvation, 'to speak of "Christ alone" or "faith alone", could lead, contrary to [their] intentions . . . to the position that the grace of Christ is given *apart from the external word of Scripture*, Christian preaching, the sacraments, and the ordained ministry.'[146]

Lutherans, on the other hand, while aware 'of the dangers of neglecting the means of grace and fostering individualism in the Church'[147] are wary of the opposite extreme, that 'the rites and orders of the Church [be] . . . imposed as *conditions for salvation*, [being] . . . valid only as the free unfolding of the obedience of faith.'[148]

The same criterion should be applicable, according to Lutherans, to the exercise of the papacy and the magisterial office in the Church, as well as to official Catholic teachings on Mary and the cult of the saints. The section concludes as follows: 'Lutherans, *primarily intent upon emphasizing God's unconditional saving promises and upon purifying the Church* from superstition, corruption and self-glorification, continue to press for a more thoroughgoing application of justification by faith as a critical principle. Catholics, *concerned with protecting the fullness of God's gifts* as granted through Christ in the Holy Spirit, are on guard against criticism that might erode the Catholic heritage.'[149]

Concluding this section on the respective content and thought-forms of Catholic and Lutheran doctrines on justification, the document makes the following proviso: 'Some of the consequences of the different outlooks seem irreconcilable, especially in reference to particular applications of justification by faith as a *criterion* of all Church proclamation and practice.'[150] It is interesting to note, however, that the text speaks of '*a* criterion' and not '*the* criterion',[151] as some of the participants of the dialogue had wished.[152]

The Hermeneutical Question   Following on directly from the reflection just made on the hermeneutical/critical rôle of the doctrine of justification, the third and final section of the *Justification by Faith*, entitled 'Perspectives for Reconstruction', attempts to move towards a *common biblical perspective* on the doctrine of justification and its implications. 'Extensive attention has been given to biblical passages bearing on righteousness/justification by faith and its relation to the love and good works expected of a Christian', the document states.[153]

For this dense and scholarly part of the document to be fully appreciated, it should be read in conjunction with a more comprehensive survey done of biblical themes relating to justification undertaken by J. Reumann.[154] Many of these topics

146 USA 118.   147 USA 119.   148 USA 119, citing the Malta Agreement, no. 29.   149 USA 120.   150 USA 121. Emphasis added.   151 Cf. C.E. Braaten, *Justification* . . . , op. cit., p. 7.   152 For example, G.O. Forde, *Justification by Faith*, Philadelphia 1990; idem., 'Justification by faith alone', in *Dialog* 27 (1988) 260–267.   153 USA 123.   154 Cf. J. Reumann (ed.), *'Righteousness' in the New Testament: Justification in Lutheran-Catholic Dialogue*, Philadelphia/New York 1982, with responses by J.A. Fitzmyer and J.D. Quinn. cf. also the biblical contributions to the

will be considered again in the second part of this work, 'New Perspectives on Justification', especially in respect of the exact nature of 'justification by faith' and that of 'the justice of God'.[155]

Seven areas closely related to justification are discussed,[156] the third one being of special relevance.

1. *New Testament interpretation of the Old Testament*. Pauline doctrine of justification is based in fact on key passages[157] and personages (Abraham, for example) of the Old Testament.

2. *The origin of the New Testament term 'justification'*. Though there seems to be no evidence that Jesus himself used the term, and that it is to be found for the first time in an explicit fashion in Paul's writings, it is likely that justification language and theology existed *before* Paul penned a developed theology on the subject.

3. *The understanding of 'justification' in the context of early Christian preaching, especially to the Romans and Galatians*. Recent studies have shown that Paul's doctrine is richer and more flexible than Luther would have given him credit, in identifying justice with *iustitia aliena*. Besides, 'justification' is not the only term, though perhaps it is the principal one, used by Paul to describe God's saving power in Christ. Also, it is clear that justification doctrine is not to be understood *exclusively* in the light of debates with Judaizers in Galatia and Rome; in other words, the notion of 'faith alone' (cf. Gal 2:16) is not exactly the same thing as 'without the works of the law'. It is likewise pointed out that justification is not a mere past or future event, but a presently-acting eschatological reality which offers to the individual no water-tight guarantee of salvation.

4. *New Testament doctrine on justification in Pauline epistles of doubtful Pauline authorship*. These texts (for example, Ephesians, Colossians, pastoral letters, etc.) take less interest in justification as such, and more in its effects.

5. *New Testament justification doctrine in non-Pauline New Testament texts*. Synoptics, Johannine texts and Hebrews pay little attention, generally speaking, to the doctrine of justification.

6. *Justification theology in the epistle of James*. This epistle provides a key area for the Lutheran-Catholic debate: the strong link-up between faith and works responds not to an anti-Pauline strain in James, but to an antinomistic one; besides the letters of James and Paul have different understandings of the notion of 'works'.

7. *New Testament theology of 'merit'*, which is, in fact, closely related to that of 'reward', 'recompense'.

volume in which Justification by faith is published: H.G. Anderson et al., (eds.), *Justification by Faith. Lutherans and Catholics in Dialogue VII*, Minneapolis 1985: J.A. Fitzmyer, "Justification by Faith and "Righteousness" in the New Testament', in ibid., pp. 77–81; J.D. Quinn, 'The Scriptures on Merit', in ibid., pp. 82–93; J.A. Burgess, 'Rewards, but in a Very Different Sense', in ibid., pp. 94–110. 155 Cf. especially pp. 169–194 below. 156 Cf. USA 122–148. 157 Cf. e.g. Gen 15:6; Hab 2:4, on faith and 'justice'; Is 46:3, 51:5-8 etc. on God's merciful saving action; etc.

The following paragraph attempts to sum up the findings of the previous section, speaking of the doctrine of justification as 'the centre of Scripture'. Of course the degree to which this notion becomes acceptable will depend on the attitude one adopts toward the question of the 'canon within the canon', that is the relative value attributable to particular books of Scripture (Paul, and within the Pauline *corpus*, Romans and Galatians) and the way they are interpreted.[158]

> It is righteousness/justification which emerges in Paul and elsewhere as *an image and concept of prime importance*, at times, as in Romans, *the central or dominant image*, for expressing what God has done in Christ and thus for expressing the Gospel. Along with this emphasis there is also found in the New Testament writings a stress, though on the whole *not as great, on the consequent deeds of the righteous Christian* and on the recompense that awaits them ... Paul ... thinks of justification as *simply 'by grace' and 'through faith' without additions or qualifications* ... In brief, a faith centered and forensically conceived picture of justification is of major importance for Paul and, in a sense, for the Bible as a whole, although *it is by no means the only biblical or Pauline way* of representing God's saving work.[159]

The final section of *Justification by Faith* deals with growing convergence on the question of justification between Catholics and Lutherans, most of which have been mentioned above. The document concludes realistically in the following terms: 'what has emerged from the present study is a convergence (though not uniformity) on justification by faith considered in itself and of itself, and *a significant though lesser convergence on the applications of the doctrine as a criterion of authenticity* for the Church's proclamation and practice'.[160]

Clarification of this distinction (between 'material' convergence on specific, dogmatic, aspects of justification theology, and 'formal' convergence on the overall determining or authenticating rôle of this doctrine) is enormously significant, is one of the conspicuous merits of this statement, and will be at the heart of the second part of this work. The document we will now study, 'Justification of the sinner' (1985), part of the *Lehrverurteilungen—kirchentrennend* project in Germany, deals in the main with the former elements of justification theology, whereas the one afterwards, *Church and Justification*, deals in the main on the latter element: justification as a criteriological principle for testing and authenticating the life of the Church and the spirituality of Christians.

Evaluation of 'Justification by Faith'   It goes without saying that *Justification by Faith* is an excellent document, in many ways a model of ecumenical statements: biblically, historically and speculatively painstaking and thorough; balanced,

---

158 Cf. USA 147f.   159 USA 146. Emphasis added.   160 USA 152.

unprecipitated and serene; realistic in its conclusions. Though the presence of 'contrasting theological perspectives and structures of thought'[161] may be noted (Catholics preferring transformational language linked with Church and sacraments, Lutherans a proclamatory and therefore existential and dialectical way of expressing the relationship between God and man), important areas of convergence (not coincidence) emerge. In *that* sense, it should be said that *Justification by faith* may be better considered a working document rather than a consensus statement. It offers a serious attempt at sifting through an enormous quantity of theological and historical information, and to establish a meaningful dialogue between Lutherans and Catholics unthinkable in other times.

Reactions to the document, though slow in coming, have been positive for the most part.[162] The substantially favourable response of the US National Council of Catholic Bishops in 1990[163] pointed out three areas still in need of attention, areas which the document itself more or less recognizes: the use of justification as a hermeneutical or criteriological principle; the need for 'adequate agreement' on purgatory, the papacy, the rôle of the saints; and the need to reach a mutual recognition of *ministry* before Eucharistic intercommunion can be envisaged. In fact all three are closely linked one with the other. Lutheran difficulties with Catholic doctrine in the area of purgatory, papacy, the saints, ministry, and suchlike, stem in the main from the possibility that the latter might adversely condition the magnanimity of God's saving in power in Christ, and thus come under the critical scrutiny of the doctrine of justification as a criteriological principle, that is, as a powerful affirmation of the unconditionality of God's promise of merciful pardon independently of preceding 'works'.

The 1991 response of the Evangelical Lutheran Church in America[164] dealt likewise the latter point, and affirmed that 'we believe it is especially important for us as Lutherans to recognize that when the Catholic dialogue partners in the common statement explicitly endorse the comprehensive critical function of the gospel in the Church, they do so in the same terms in which the statement in its historical section sums up the insistence of the Reformers . . . that justification by faith is the "heart of the gospel" . . . We believe that . . . the dialogue has reached a criteriological and not only material agreement on justification.'[165]

But it adds: 'the common statement does not distinguish as clearly as it might between agreement *that* the gospel is the critical norm for all churchly belief and practice, and agreement on *what* should result from application of that norm in particular cases. Or one could say it does not distinguish adequately between the

---

161 USA 121.   162 Cf. A.E. McGrath, *ARCIC-II and Justification* . . . , op. cit., pp. 30–37.   163 National Conference of Catholic Bishops, 'An Evaluation of the Lutheran-Catholic Statement: "Justification by Faith" ', in *One in Christ* 29 (1993) 335–342.   164 Evangelical Lutheran Church in America, 'An Evaluation of the Lutheran-Catholic Statement "Justification by Faith" ', in *One in Christ* 29 (1993) 342–349.   165 Ibid., p. 348.

specification of the gospel as critical norm and the application of that norm . . .
[Thus] *Particular application of the gospel as critical norm represents the greatest area
of uncertainty in the justification statement and in the ongoing Lutheran-Roman
Catholic dialogue, both nationally and internationally.*'[166]

The point is an important one. One thing is to say that the doctrine of justification, emphasizing the unconditionality and magnanimity of God's saving promises
in Christ, should be applicable as a critical principle to the life of the Church and of
each Christian; quite another thing is when or how it should be applied in particular
cases.

The 1992 response of the Lutheran Church (Missouri Synod) to *Justification by
Faith* is considerably more circumspect,[167] cautioning 'against an exaggerated assessment of the achievements of the Lutheran-Roman Catholic Dialogue in its statement on justification by faith'.[168] This caution must be observed, it says, given 'the
fundamental doctrinal differences still exist between Roman Catholicism and Lutheranism'.[169] Apprehension is expressed that the document does not clarify sufficiently the following incontrovertible points of Lutheran doctrine:

— that works, though '*fruits* of faith', in no way 'intrinsically qualify justifying
faith';[170]

— that justification as a criteriological principle is not one among many for 'avoiding practical abuses and false theological teachings'. 'Rather, it is grounded and
rooted in the prophetic and apostolic Scriptures and is of the very essence of the
gospel itself, from which the Church lives and upon which it is built and by which
it is corrected when necessary';[171]

— that justification is a primary, not secondary, metaphor in the New Testament, 'referring to all the fullness and richness of the biblical language of God's
saving grace in Christ'.[172] 'We therefore reject as contrary to Scripture any understanding of the doctrine of justification which would include in God's forensic justification of the sinner "transformist view which emphasizes the change wrought in
sinners by infused grace".'[173] The doctrine of justification, strictly speaking, has to
do with what God has done in Christ *for* us, not what he does *in* us.'[174]

2.   *'Justification of the sinner' (Germany, 1986)*

The *'Lehrverurteilungen—kirchentrennend?' project   Justification of the sinner* (1986),
a chapter in the volume prepared by the work-group of evangelical and Catholic

---

166 Ibid. Emphasis added.   **167** Lutheran Church-Missouri Synod, 'A Response to the US Lutheran-Roman Catholic Dialogue Report VII, "Justification by Faith" ', extracts in *One in Christ*
29 (1993) 349–353.   **168** Ibid., p. 349.   **169** Ibid., p. 350.   **170** Ibid.   **171** Ibid., pp.
350f.   **172** Ibid., p. 351.   **173** USA 158.   **174** Lutheran Church-Missouri Synod, 'A Response
to the US Lutheran-Roman Catholic Dialogue Report VII, "Justification by Faith" ', op. cit., p.
351. This statement seems to be referring to the 1989 Lutheran-Orthodox statement, that Missouri Synod Lutherans were involved in, in which the two Christological approaches are confronted: Christ 'for us' (Lutheran); Christ 'in us' (Orthodox). cf. note 45 above.

theologians in Germany with a view to possibly revising the mutual condemnations of the time of the Reformation, is the principal document in the German ambit dealing *ex professo* with justification.[175] It is undoubtedly one of the key documents within the process of ever-growing consensus between Lutherans and Catholics on the topic of justification.[176] The document is best known as *Lehrverurteilungen – kirchentrennend?* ('The doctrinal condemnations, do they still divide?') and will be abbreviated as 'LV'.

The project of possibly revising the doctrinal condemnations of the sixteenth century (of Lutherans by Trent, of Catholic doctrine by the *Confessio Augustana*, the *Apologia*, etc.)[177] is part of an initiative encouraged by Pope John Paul II during his pastoral visit to Germany in 1980.[178] His interest in this project, its continuation and completion, is conspicuous. At a Catholic-Lutheran international symposium at Farfa in 1995 he said the following. 'A particularly important target of this dialogue has been obtained when the doctrine of justification has become a central question and we must look forward confidently to the document which Lutherans and Catholics are working on and which intends to express a common understanding of this central topic of our faith'.[179] On the occasion of an audience with a delegation of the Evangelical-Lutheran Church of America, the Pope observed regarding the doctrine of justification that 'we must pray together to obtain a common understanding of this central theme of our faith'.[180]

Finally, in the address he gave at Paderborn in 1996 to representatives of the Evangelical churches and the Evangelical-Catholic Ecumenical Work Group, making reference to the *Lehrverurteilungen—kirchentrennend?* project, he said:

> Thanks to this study, many controversies of the sixteenth century appear today in a new light. Hurdles have been crossed that preceding generations

175 Ökumenischer Arbeitskreis Evangelischer und Katholischer Theologen (K. Lehmann and W. Pannenberg, eds.), 'Rechtfertigung des Sünders', in *Rechtfertigung, Sakramente und Amt im Zeitalter der Reformation und heute (1985): 'Lehrverurteilungen – kirchentrennend?'*, Göttingen/Freiburg i. Br. 1986, pp. 35–75. English translation: K. Lehmann and W. Pannenberg, 'The Justification of the Sinner', in *The Condemnations of the Reformation Era. Do they still divide?*, Minneapolis 1990, pp. 29–69. **176** For a brief history of the document and the reactions to it until 1994, cf. H.-A. Raem, 'Katholische und lutherische Lehrverurteilungen – weiterhin kirchentrennend?', in *Una Sancta* 49 (1994) 302–307. **177** Cf. the studies of W. Pannenberg, K. Lehmann, G. Wenz, H.H. Eßer (Lutheran Confessional Statements), E. Iserloh (Luther and Trent), K. Kertelge, V. Pfnür (*Confessio Augustana, Apologia*, Smalcald Articles), F. Beißer (*Formula Concordiae*), J.F.G. Goeters & K. Lehmann (Heidelberg Catechism and Trent), O.-H. Pesch (Trent), in K. Lehmann (ed.), *Lehrverurteilungen – kirchentrennend? . . .*, op. cit. **178** Cf. John Paul II, *Address to Members of the Evangelical Church*, Magonza (17 November 1980), in *Insegnamenti di Giovanni Paolo II, III/2* (1980), Vatican City 1980, pp. 1253–1257. The address, based on the letter to the Romans, mentions Luther's injunction not only to hold on to Christ (*was Christi ist*) but also to what belongs to Christ (*was sein ist*). **179** John Paul II, in *Osservatore Romano*, 16 March, 1995. **180** Ibid., 11–12 December, 1995. cf. H.-A. Raem, 'I rapporti con i Luterani nell'anno 1995', in *Osservatore Romano* 22–23 January, 1996, p. 7; E.I. Cassidy, 'The Pontifical Council for Promoting Christian Unity in 1993', in *One in Christ* 30 (1994) 199–215.

considered insurmountable. This progress has been made possible because, methodologically, careful attention was paid to the distinction between the content of the faith and its verbal formulation.[181] This distinction is, in fact, one of the important elements of ecumenical accord . . . The unity to which we aspire requires a genuine agreement regarding the content of the faith. It does not affect the binding character of the doctrine of the Church . . . Faced with the seriousness and quality of the study 'The Condemnations of the Reformation Era – Do they still divide?', it was not only fair but also obligatory to examine conscientiously and carefully the scope of its findings.[182]

The document in fact deals with many areas besides that of justification, though the latter is doubtlessly of fundamental importance. John Paul II noted that

> The study 'The Condemnations of the Reformation Era. Do they still divide?' must be commended for having deeply studied a wide range of areas of agreement and convergence in essential aspects of the faith . . . A considerable degree of convergence (*weitreichende Annäherung*) has been established in the doctrine of justification. Examining the overall effect of the different common statements on the doctrine of justification, one gets the impression more and more that a basic agreement (*fundamental Übereinstimmung*) is being established in respect of the principal issues in our understanding of the message of justification. Even though all differences have not been eliminated, we can now ask ourselves in a more accurate way what weight do the remaining differences have.[183]

Content and method of 'Justification of the sinner'   The study 'Justification of the sinner', occupying forty-six pages of the *Lehrverurteilungen – kirchentrennend?* project, is situated after a long introduction dealing with interpretative and hermeneutical issues related to Scripture and Magisterium. The chapter on justification deals *in recto* with seven areas traditionally disputed between Lutherans and Catholics: the *depravity* or otherwise of human nature; the question of *concupiscence* and its possible sinfulness; human freedom in relation to grace; man's passivity or otherwise before God; justice imputed or imparted: the *forensic* and/or *inherent* quality of justification; justification through '*faith alone*', or through faith and charity; assurance or certitude of salvation; the value and theological nature of '*good works*', *merit*, etc.

An introductory section entitled 'The Antitheses, as they were hitherto understood' presents the seven areas one by one, indicating that, on the basis of authoritative statements on both sides, no possibility of reconciliation would seem to exist.[184]

---

181 Cf. John Paul II, *Enc. Ut Unum Sint* (1995) no. 81; Congregation for the Doctrine of the Faith, Decl. *Mysterium Ecclesiae* (1973), no. 5, par. 6.   182 John Paul II, Address 'Eine zukunftsträchtige Ökumene kann es nur geben, wenn wir uns selbstlos der Wahrheit stellen' (22 June 1996), no. 4, in *Osservatore Romano, Documenti* (26 June 1996), p. 4.   183 Ibid., nos. 4–5.   184 Cf. LV, pp. 30–36

The second section of the statement, its most extensive part, after laying down a series of principles for interpreting and evaluating the different issues, shows, generally in a quite convincing fashion, that, due to misunderstandings in the past and renewed theological research in recent times, a common understanding can be reached on all these questions[185] at least in the sense that 'Catholic doctrine does not overlook what Protestant faith finds important, and vice versa; and Catholic doctrine does not maintain what Protestant doctrine is afraid of, and vice versa.'[186] We shall come back to the seven specific areas, their development and content, in chapter six.

The four principles of interpretation mentioned by *Lehrverurteilungen – kirchentrennend?* are:[187]

1. 'The formulas of the doctrine of justification may sound abstract, but they have a specific background and a practical reference to Christian life in the Church'.[188] Specifically, 16th-century Protestants criticized some aspects of the then-common theology and praxis of penance and *sacramental confession*, defining their (new) theology of justification in respect of that praxis, and of the theology of sacramental conversion it implied. The Council of Trent, conversely, concentrated on *baptismal* justification and how this is lived out, and was concerned primarily with the integrity of Christian life and conduct.

2. 'It must not be our aim to prove that we are at one in structure of thinking and our trains of thought, let alone in our mode of expression'. Or put in negative terms: 'Are the "concerns" and interpretative stresses which are of primary importance in the doctrine of the one partner nevertheless so clearly maintained in the doctrine of the other that they can neither be overlooked nor misunderstood?'[189]

3. The third amounts to an application of the first two principles. 'No one can condemn and accuse of departing from Christian faith those who—experiencing the misery of their sins, their resistance to God, and their lack of love of God and their neighbour—in faith put their whole trust in the saving God, are sure of his mercy, and try in their lives to match up to this faith . . . Nor, on the other hand, can anyone condemn and accuse of departing from the Christian faith those who, deeply penetrated by the limitless power of God, stress above all, also in the event of justification, God's glory and the victory of his gracious acts on behalf of men and women, holding human failure and halfheartedness toward these gracious acts to be, in the strict sense, of secondary importance.'[190]

4. 'In our historical interpretation of . . . [the Tridentine decree on justification] . . . the principle applies: in case of doubt, the view closest to Augustine is to be

(following the English translation, cit.). 185 Cf. ibid., pp. 42–68. On the specific area of the assurance or otherwise of salvation (no. 6), a long *excursus* is included on 'Justification, Baptism and Penance': ibid., pp. 56–66. 186 Ibid., p. 53. 187 LV, pp. 39–42. 188 Ibid., p. 39. 189 Ibid., p. 40. 190 Ibid. Each side was afraid of the possible extremes the other side might go to. 'In the sixteenth century, Catholic theology was afraid that the result of the Reformers' doctrine of justification could be summed up as: no freedom, no new being, no ethical endeavour, no reward, no Church . . . Protestant theology was afraid that the result of the Catholic doctrine of justifica-

preferred'. The reason behind this principle, presumably, is that by interpreting Trent according to Augustine, as much common ground as possible between Catholics and Evangelicals can be maintained.[191]

The four interpretative principles can be summed up as follows: *differences between Evangelicals and Catholics must above all be related to their respective 'concerns', of which defined doctrines became conceptualized expressions; such differences of concern can be regarded as complementary*. Simply put, mutual condemnations do not correspond to differing 'truth-claims', but are principally the result of misunderstandings.

The principal, perhaps somewhat optimistic, conclusions of *Lehrverurteilungen— kirchentrennend?* are three.

The first two come back to the question of differing concerns versus 'truth claims'. Firstly, 'Where the interpretation of the justification of the sinner is concerned, the mutual sixteenth-century condemnations . . . *no longer apply to our partner in any sense that could divide the Churches*. This result has all the more weight, given that historical investigation into the dispute of the time shows that in many individual points the rejections did not, even at that time, meet the target of the opponents' real intention in what he said . . . We no longer fight against bogus adversaries, and we are careful to express ourselves in such a way that our partner does not misunderstand us . . . even if he is not himself able to adopt our way of thinking and speaking.'[192] And secondly, differences, if they do remain, do not in fact belong to the area of 'decisive differences of such a kind that the answer to them would decide about the true and false Church.'[193]

And the *third* has it that 'the doctrine of justification—and, above all, its biblical foundation—will always retain a special function in the Church. That function is continually to remind Christians that we sinners live solely from the forgiving love of God, which we merely allow to be bestowed on us, but which we in no way—in whatever modified a form—"earn" or are able to tie down to any conditions or preconditions. The doctrine of justification therefore becomes the touchstone for testing at all times *whether a particular interpretation of our relationship to God can claim the name of "Christian"*. At the same time, it becomes the touchstone for the Church, for testing at all times *whether its proclamation and its praxis correspond to what has been given to it by its Lord.*'[194]

Understandably the document has aroused considerable interest and a wide se-

---

tion could be summed up as: the triviality of sin, self-praise, a righteousness of works, purchasable salvation, a Church intervening between God and human beings' (ibid., pp. 40–41).   **191** According to the Göttingen document, this argument holds little water, because neither the Reformers nor Trent consistently held to Augustine's teaching (cf. D. Lange et al., 'An Opinion on "The Condemnations of the Reformation Era". Part One: Justification', in *Lutheran Quarterly* 5 (1991) 1–62, especially pp. 23f.).   **192** LV, p. 68. Emphasis added.   **193** Ibid.   **194** Ibid., p. 69. Besides, LV insists on several specific aspects to the theological approach to the problem, developed more extensively by the American document on justification (USA), especially the following four: the

lection of commentaries.[195] Five are of special interest: the critique of the members of Göttingen Evangelical Faculty of Theology, headed by J. Baur (1989–1991);[196] the comments of the Joint Committee of the United Evangelical Lutheran Church of Germany and the Lutheran World Federation's German National Committee

Christological foundation of justification; the need for a deeply *biblical* understanding of this doctrine; the fact that late scholastic doctrine of grace (against which Luther reacted and in respect of which Lutheranism is defined) differs significantly from high scholastic doctrine; and the contemporary emphasis on a *personalist* understanding of *faith* (cf. LV 36–39). **195** Including for example those of W. Härle, 'Lehrverurteilungen—kirchentrennend in der Rechtfertigungslehre?', in *Materialdienst des Konfessionskundlichen Instituts Bensheim* 38 (1987) 123–127; W. Kasper, 'Grundkonsens und Kirchengemeinschaft. Zum Stand des ökumenischen Gespräches zwischen katholischer und evangelisch-lutherischer Kirche', in *Theologische Quartalschrift* 167 (1987) 161–181; W. Löser, 'Lehrverurteilungen—Kirchentrennend', in *Catholica* 41 (1987) 177–196; K.H. Kandler, 'Rechtfertigung-Kirchentrennend', in *Kerygma und Dogma* 36 (1990) 325–347; W. Beinert, 'Den einen Glauben zur Ehre Gottes bekennen', in *Ökumenische Rundschau* 43 (1994) 37–46; idem., 'Do the condemnations of the Reformation era still confront the contemporary ecumenical partners?', in *Lutheran Quarterly* 8 (1994) 53–70; W. Pannenberg and T. Schneider (eds.), *Lehrverurteilungen – kirchentrennend?: Antworten auf kirchliche Stellungnahmen*, Göttingen 1994; H. Jorrisen, 'Kritische Erwägungen zur Stellungnahme der Deutschen Bischofskonferenz zur Studie "Lehrverurteilungen—kirchentrennend?" ', in *Catholica* 48 (1994) 267–278; H.-A. Raem, 'Katholische und lutherische Lehrverurteilungen – weiterhin kirchentrennend?', in *Una Sancta* 49 (1994) 302–307; H. Vorster, 'Ende gut, alles gut?: zur Rücknahme der reformatorischen Verurteilungen gegenüber der heutigen römisch-katholischen Lehre', in *Ökumenische Rundschau* 44 (1995) 92–98; D. Sattler, 'Neue Urteile zu den alten Lehrverurteilungen; die evangelischen Kirchen in Deutschland und die Studie des ökumenischen Arbeitskreises', in *Catholica* 49 (1995) 98–113; E. Lessing, ' "Lehrverurteilungen—kirchentrennend?": zur Bedeutung und zu den Grenzen eines ökumenischen Dokuments', in *Ökumenische Rundschau* 45 (1996) 24–38; J. Morales, 'Le vie del progresso ecumenico nella dottrina della giustificazione', in J.M. Galván (ed.), *La giustificazione in Cristo*, pp. 260–267. Cf. also the collection of commentaries on the document by K. Lehmann (ed.), *Lehrverurteilungen—kirchentrennend? Materialien zu den Lehrverurteilungen und zur Theologie der Rechtfertigung*, Freiburg i. Br. 1989. **196** The members of this Faculty offer a clear-cut and unequivocally critical study of *Lehrverurteilungen – kirchentrennend?*, point by point: D. Lange et al., *Überholte Verurteilungen?: Stellungnahme gegenüber 'Lehrverurteilungen— kirchentrennend?'; Die Gegensätze in der Lehre von Rechtfertigung, Abendmahl und Amt zwischen dem Konzil von Trient und der Reformation - damals und heute*, Göttingen 1991. English translation of the section on justification: D. Lange et al., 'An Opinion on "The Condemnations of the Reformation Era". Part One: Justification', in *Lutheran Quarterly* 5 (1991) 1–62. Cf. also the study, previous to the others, undertaken by J. Baur, member of the Göttingen Faculty: *Einig in Sachen Rechtfertigung?: zur Prüfung des Rechtfertigungskapitels der Studie des Ökumenischen Arbeitskreises evangelischer und katholischer Theologen: 'Lehrverurteilungen— kirchentrennend?'*, Tübingen 1989. In the same direction, cf. G. Martens, *Die Rechtfertigung des Sünders — Rettungshandeln Gottes oder historisches Interpretament? Grundentscheidungen lutherischer Theologie und Kirche bei der Behandlung des Themas 'Rechtfertigung' im Ökumenischen Kontext*, Göttingen 1992, pp. 273–321. To these criticisms, cf. the replies of U. Kühn and O.-H. Pesch, 'Rechtfertigung im Disput. Eine freundliche Antwort an Jörg Baur', in *Ökumenische Rundschau* 37 (1988) 22–46, and later, in extended form, Tübingen 1991; H. Schütte (ed.), *Einig in der Lehre von der Rechtfertigung!: mit einer Antwort an Jörg Baur*, Paderborn 1990; T. Mannermaa, 'Einig in Sachen Rechtfertigung?: eine lutherische Stellungnahme zu Jörg Baur', in *Theologische Rundschau* 55 (1990) 326–335; W. Pannenberg, 'Müssen sich die Kirchen immer noch gegenseitig verurteilen?', in *Kerygma und Dogma* 38 (1992) 311–330.

(VELKD & DNK/LWB) (1991);[197] an unpublished evaluation of the canons of Trent on justification by the Pontifical Council for Promoting Christian Unity (PCPCU) (1992);[198] the comments of the German Episcopal Conference (1994);[199] and the official reception statement of *Lehrverurteilungen – kirchentrennend?* by the General Synod of the United Evangelical Lutheran Church in Germany (1994).[200]

Lutheran reactions   Of particular interest from strictly theological standpoint is the reaction of the Göttingen Evangelical Faculty of Theology to *Lehrverurteilungen*, which does not limit its rejection of the document (in the area of justification) to a series of points of positive theology where misunderstandings and multiple interpretations could easily proliferate. It rejects the chapter on justification on a double front: in respect of the principles of interpretation and evaluation used, all four of them, and of the conclusions the document reaches. The Göttingen *Opinion* however considers the way of understanding justification doctrine expressed in the *Lehrverurteilungen* as trivial, relativistic and therefore unhelpful. Between Catholics and Evangelicals, it says 'two global soteriological concepts confront each other'.[201] 'When the study speaks of the differing but mutually compatible concerns or emphases of the various conceptions, it presupposes that the only thing that counts is that all these elements – grace, faith, Christ, will, works, and so forth – are represented everywhere, no matter in what shape or relationship.'[202]

The Göttingen document congratulates the authors of *Lehrverurteilungen – kirchentrennend?* for recognizing the doctrine of justification as the definitive nor-

197 Vereinigte Evangelisch-Lutherische Kirche Deutschlands (VELKD), *Lehrverurteilungen im Gespräch. Die ersten offiziellen Stellungnahmen aus den evangelischen Kirchen in Deutschland*, Göttingen 1993, pp. 57–160; on justification, pp. 77–102. The same volume contains comments on *Lehrverurteilungen—kirchentrennend?* by the Arnoldshainer Konferenz (AKf, 1991: pp. 17–56; on justification, pp. 27–33), and the Facharbeitskreise Faith-And-Order und Catholica-Fragen (1990, pp. 161–199; on justification, pp. 167–179). Cf. the comments of W. Pannenberg and T. Schneider (eds.), *Lehrverurteilungen—kirchentrennend?: Antworten auf kirchliche Stellungnahmen*, Göttingen 1994.   **198** Päpstlichen Rat zur Föderung der Einheit der Christen, 'Auswertung der Studie "Lehrverurteilungen—kirchentrennend?"' (Studiendokument nicht zur Veröffentlichung), Vatican City 1992. For a summary, cf. H.-A. Raem, 'Beachtlicher Beitrag zur Versöhnung der getrennten Christen, Gutachten des Einheitsrates zur deutschen Studie "Lehrverurteilungen— kirchentrennend?"', in *Kath. Nachrichtenagentur-Ökumenische Information*, no. 26 (23 June 1993) 13–16.   **199** Sekretariat der Deutschen Bischofskonferenz, 'Stellungnahme der Deutschen Bischofskonferenz zur Studie "Lehrverurteilungen – kirchentrennend?"' (4 February 1994; published 21 June 1994), in *Die deutschen Bischöfe*, no. 52, Bonn 1994. Cf. H. Jorrisen, 'Kritische Erwägungen zur Stellungnahme der Deutschen Bischofskonferenz zur Studie "Lehrverurteilungen – kirchentrennend?"', in *Catholica* 48 (1994) 267–278.   **200** 'Gemeinsame Stellungnahme zum Dokument "Lehrverurteilungen – kirchentrennend?"', common statement of the Protestant Churches of Germany (6 November 1994: AKf, VELKD, DNK), in *Ökumenische Rundschau* 44 (1995) 99–102; English translation in *Lutheran Quarterly* 9 (1995) 359–364. The Evangelical Lutheran Church of America, endorsing this document, recommended that it be used along with both the original document *Lehrverurteilungen – kirchentrennend?* and that of the Evangelical Faculty of Göttingen: cf. ibid., p. 359.   **201** D. Lange et al., 'An Opinion on "The Condemnations of the Reformation Era". Part One: Justification', op. cit., p. 21.   **202** Ibid., p. 22f.

mative principle of theology and Christian life, the centre of Christian faith.[203] However, it adds that if this principle were to be thoroughly applied to the specific aspects of the doctrine of justification treated at length in the main body of the document, one by one, it would have been impossible 'to reduce the differing justification doctrines to the sum of two complementary 'concerns'. In other words, conclusions one and two of *Lehrverurteilungen – kirchentrennend?* are incompatible with conclusion three. And the reason is this: the difference between Catholics and Evangelicals lies in 'an antithetical definition of the relationship between God and man'.[204] According to J. Baur of the Göttingen Faculty, humans cannot in any be considered before God as 'subjects'; no 'cooperation' of any kind can be envisaged.[205]

The point made by the members of the Göttingen Faculty, if valid, is highly significant: 'material' convergence on justification (as a doctrine) is only possible if 'formal' or 'fundamental' convergence (justification as a principle) is left aside. And vice versa: if the doctrine of justification is to be established as the full-blown guiding or hermeneutical principle for theology, for Christian and ecclesiastical life, then two objectively distinct 'doctrines' of justification result, one 'Catholic', the other 'Evangelical'. The contention is a serious one and we shall return to it in the second part of this work with the fundamental question: what would make it possible to obtain a convergence between Catholic and Evangelical theologies of justification on *simultaneously* 'material' and 'formal' terms?

The obvious question should now be asked: does the Göttingen *Opinion* represent the general position of Lutherans and Evangelicals on the question of justification? Although several Lutheran authors decisively reject their findings,[206] to a considerable degree, it would seem, the Göttingen *Opinion* is significant. In 1994 the General Synod of the United Evangelical Lutheran Church in Germany, representing virtually all Lutherans and Evangelicals in that country, presented a brief and authoritative statement, endorsed by the Evangelical Lutheran Church of America, containing a series of observations on *Lehrverurteilungen – kirchentrennend?* While accepting gladly the latter's admission of the rôle of the doctrine of justification as a global criteriological principal for the life of the Church and theology, it notes the following four basic differences between Catholic and Evangelical doctrine:

> (a) The understanding of grace as God's turning towards men (*extra nos*), or as a 'reality in the human soul' (*qualitas in nobis*); (b) the understanding of faith as trust in God's word of promise in the gospel, or as 'assent of the

---

203 Ibid., p. 55.   204 Ibid., p. 55f.   205 Cf. J. Baur, *Einig in Sachen Rechtfertigung?* . . . , op. cit., pp. 37ff.   206 According to U. Kühn and O.-H. Pesch, *Rechtfertigung im Disput* . . . , op. cit., pp. 21–32, Baur's thesis and that of the Göttingen *Opinion* does not coincide with the anthropology of the Reformation, but is rather a reading of 16th-century theology in the light of 19th-century philosophical problems. cf. also W. Pannenberg, 'Müssen sich die Kirchen immer noch gegenseitig verurteilen?', op. cit.

understanding to the revealed word of God', which must find form in hope and love; (c) the understanding of men's relationship to God under the consistent exclusion of the idea of merit or the interpolation of the concept 'to express the responsibility of men in spite of the gift-character of good works'; (d) the understanding of the relationship and differentiation of law and gospel.[207]

The fact is that all four correspond, quite closely, to salient elements of the Göttingen *Opinion*.[208]

Catholic reactions   A few points could be noted regarding official Catholic reactions. The observations made in the 1992 unpublished report on *Lehrverurteilungen— kirchentrennend?* of the Pontifical Council for Promoting Christian Unity, according to the summary prepared by Raem,[209] deal in the main with hermeneutical questions regarding how and to whom Trent's doctrinal definitions and *anathema's* apply. The basic principle established is the following: 'a difference in pure theological enunciation justifies no dogmatic condemnation'.[210] In respect of justification, the report analyzes the Tridentine canons, and one by one explains their origin, value, meaning and scope.[211] The document comes to the following carefully worded though significant conclusion: 'In spite of the absence of debate on the problem of law and gospel in these canons, we hold with *Lehrverurteilungen – kirchentrennend?* that can-

---

207 'Gemeinsame Stellungnahme zum Dokument 'Lehrverurteilungen—kirchentrennend?'' ', op. cit., in *Ökumenische Rundschau* 44 (1995) 100f.   **208** Göttingen takes the first two points (a) and (b) together: 'Reservations become stronger with regard to the "conception" of grace as a . . . *habitus*. Thereby the idea that righteousness "becomes your own" is evidently formulated at the expense of the idea that righteousness lies completely "outside ourselves, in Christ" (*extra nos, in Christo*) . . . At this point lies the main object of the Reformation's objection: the criticism of "trust in one's own natural power" . . . Against the document one must maintain that only in faith does righteousness lie at the same time "outside ourselves in Christ" and as such becomes our own . . . If one speaks . . . about the "essence of grace" without a single word about the significance of faith in this connection, one is bound to miss the true significance of grace and justification' (D. Lange, et al., 'An Opinion on "The Condemnations of the Reformation Era". Part One: Justification', op. cit., p. 28f.); for (c), on 'merit', the following is noted: 'The Reformation protest is directed against what the document points out as the legitimate "meaning" of the theological notion of "merit" and for the sake of which it is maintained after all, namely in terms of "human responsibility" ' (ibid., p. 32); for (d), on the relationship between faith and gospel, the Göttingen paper, at the very beginning of its critique of the LV's study of justification, asks 'what the all-determining centre of the details is. The enumeration [the seven areas] comprises all the essential points except for one blatant exception: the theme of 'law and gospel' which is deleted, and this despite the fact that the Tridentine decree on justification contains three canons on the subject [nos. 19–21]' (ibid., p. 24; on the question of law and gospel and its centrality, cf. especially ibid., pp. 16–17; pp. 43–44).   **209** Cf. H.-A. Raem, 'Beachtlicher Beitrag zur Versöhnung der getrennten Christen, Gutachten des Einheitsrates zur deutschen Studie "Lehrverurteilungen – kirchentrennend?" ', op. cit. pp. 13–16.   **210** 'Auswertung der Studie "Lehrverurteilungen – kirchentrennend?" ', op. cit., p. 7.   **211** Cf. ibid., pp. 23–34.

ons 1-33 of the decree on justification are not applicable to Lutheran teaching as this is expressed in its confessional statements.'[212]

The brief 1994 reply of the German Bishops' Conference[213] is quite positive in respect of the doctrine on justification. However it also makes note of a series of four 'open questions', not fully dealt with by *Lehrverurteilungen—kirchentrennend?*, the question of the preparation for and human cooperation in justification; the question of 'merit' and its relationship to 'reward' and 'making claim on God'; the rôle of the Church in justification, specifically in respect of its 'instrumental mediation of grace', though not indeed 'as a kind of reality "between" God and the sinner';[214] the need for the sacrament of Penance.[215] The section dedicated to justification concludes by saying that 'on the whole the study certifies . . . that in ecumenical dialogue a consensus on the doctrine of justification has been reached. However the open questions mentioned indicate the direction in which dialogue must be continued.'[216]

3. *'Church and justification' (1993)*

The document *Church and Justification* (1993, abbreviated CJ) was prepared jointly by the Lutheran World Federation and the Pontifical Council for Promoting Christian Unity.[217] It is not a document on justification as such (as the above-mentioned USA and German documents are), but it is undoubtedly *about* justification, insofar as it deals with the implications of this doctrine in respect of the Church, sacraments, ministry etc. In fact, *Church and Justification* is mainly about ecclesiology.

212 Ibid., p. 34.   213 Sekretariat der Deutschen Bischofkonferenz, 'Stellungnahme der Deutschen Bischofskonferenz zur Studie "Lehrverurteilungen – kirchentrennend?" ', op. cit.   214 Ibid., p. 11.   215 Cf. ibid., pp. 11 f. The acts of the penitent are mentioned: contrition, purpose of amendment, confession of sins, readiness to make reparation.   216 Ibid., p. 12.   217 Cf. Gemeinsame Römisch-katholische/ Evangelisch-lutherische Kommission, *Kirche und Rechtfertigung: das Verständnis der Kirche im Licht der Rechtfertigungslehre* (13 September 1993), Paderborn/ Frankfurt a. M. 1994. English translation: Lutheran-Roman Catholic Joint Commission, *Church and justification: understanding the Church in the light of the doctrine of justification*, Geneva, Lutheran World Federation/ Rome, Pontifical Council for Promoting Christian Unity, 1994, in *Information service* 86 (1994) 128–181. Italian translation in *Il Regno Documenti* 1994, 603–640 and also EO 3:1223-1538. For a presentation of the development of this document, cf. H.-A. Raem, 'The Third Phase of Lutheran-Catholic Dialogue (1986–1993)', in *Information Service* 86 (1994) 189-197, especially pp. 189–190. Other commentaries on *Church and Justification* include: S. Del Cura Elena, 'Radicación trinitaria de la "Koinônia" eclesial. Dios Trinitario e Iglesia en el documento del diálogo católico-luterano "Iglesia y Justificación" (1993)', in *Salmanticensis* 42 (1995) 211–234 (Italian translation in *Studi Ecumenici* 14 (1996) 183–207); H. von Wagner, 'Kirche und Rechtfertigung: zum Dokument aus der dritten Phase des katholisch-lutherischen Dialogs (1993)', in *Catholica* 48 (1994) 233–241; G. Bavaud, 'Le fruit d'un dialogue entre luthériens et catholiques: Le mystère de l'Église et celui de la justification', in *Nova et Vetera* 70 (1995) 50–65; H. Meyer, 'Ekklesiologie im Ökumenischen Gespräch und der katholisch/lutherische Dialog über "Kirche und Rechtfertigung" ', in *Kath. Nachrichtenagentur-Ökumenische Information no. 1* (5 Jan 1994) 5–16; idem., 'Der katholisch/lutherische Dialog über "Kirche und Rechtfertigung" ', in *Materialdienst der Ökumenischen Centrale* I/II, (1995) 68–82; T. Schneider, 'The Dialogue Report in the Present

Ecclesiology, an essential element of justification   A growing awareness has developed in recent decades that any Christian anthropology, or theology of grace and justification, that is divorced from ecclesiology, runs the risk of remaining individualistic.[218] And if individualistic, then exclusive of man's social dimension, and therefore, sooner or later, irrelevant to modern man. The social dimension of salvation and justification is essential, not accidental, to Christian anthropology. For humans not only produce society (in this sense society relates to them accidentally), but are produced by society (ontologically, personally, culturally). In the same way, the Church is the product of Christians (which is therefore a *congregatio fidelium*, a community of believers, the People of God) but also, inseparably, Christians *are produced* (that is constituted as such) by the Church (as a kind of *sacramentum salutis*, the Body of Christ).

Of course in real terms, Christians are 'made believers' by the action of Christ's Spirit, 'the Gospel',[219] in such a way that the fundamental 'social' quality of their *being Christian* is entirely based on their communion with *the* Communion of persons, the Father, the Son and the Holy Spirit. In that sense, humans are always 'alone', (better, *'dialogically' alone*), before their Creator, Redeemer and Sanctifier, in a foundational relationship that nothing or nobody can substitute or add to. And

---

Ecumenical Context: A Comment on "Church and Justification" ', in *Information Service* 86 (1994) 182–188; Lutheran-Roman Catholic Joint Commission, ' "Church and Justification". Understanding the Church in the light of the doctrine of justification. Report of the third phase of Lutheran-Roman Catholic international dialogue', in *Catholic International* 6 (1995) 329–347; D. Wendebourg, ' "Kirche und Rechtfertigung". Ein Erlebnisbericht zu einem neueren ökumenischen Dokument', in *Zeitschrift für Theologie und Kirche* 93 (1996) 84–100; H. Schütte, ' "Articulis stantis et cadentis ecclesiae": der Rechtfertigungsartikel in der Bedeutung für die Kirche', in *Bausteine für die Einheit der Christen* 36 (1996) 16–21; L. Ullrich, 'Genesis und Schwerpunkte des katholisch-lutherischen Dialogdokumentes "Kirche und Rechtfertigung" ', in *Catholica* 50 (1996) 1–22; S. Rostagno, 'Consenso tra cattolici e luterani', in *Protestantesimo* 51 (1996) 64-66; L. Sartori, 'Chiesa e giustificazione', in *Protestantesimo* 51 (1996) 131–152; G. Gaßmann, 'Lutheran-Catholic Agreement on Justification (I): a Historical Breakthrough', in *Ecumenical Trends* 25 (1996) 82–85; idem., 'Lutheran-Catholic Agreement on Justification (II): The Ecclesiological Dimension', in ibid., 97–103; idem., 'La dimensione ecclesiologica della giustificazione. Una prospettiva luterana', in J.M. Galván (ed.), *La giustificazione in Cristo*, Rome 1997, pp. 165–186; P. O'Callaghan, 'The Mediation of Justification and the justification of Mediation. Report of the Lutheran/Catholic Dialogue: "Church and Justification: Understanding the Church in the Light of the Doctrine of Justification" (1993)', in *Annales Theologici* 10 (1996) 147–211; A. Maffeis, 'Santità della chiesa e mediazione della salvezza', in *Studi Ecumenici* 14 (1996) 209–222; P. Rodríguez, 'La Iglesia, "creatura evangelii" ', in *Diálogo ecuménico* 31 (1996) 375–399; idem., 'La dimensione ecclesiologica della giustificazione. Una prospettiva cattolica', in J.M. Galván (ed.), *La giustificazione in Cristo*, Rome 1997, pp. 187–207. On chapter 5 of CJ, cf. M. Hauser, ' "L'autonomia del mondo": un concetto promettente nella teologia della giustificazione', in *Studi Ecumenici* 14 (1996) 223–231.   218 On the necessity of contextualizing the doctrine of justification ecclesiologically, cf. W. Pannenberg, *Systematische Theologie*, vol. 3, Göttingen 1993, p. 9; S. Pemsel-Maier, *Rechtfertigung durch Kirche? Das Verhältnis von Kirche und Rechtfertigung in Entwürfen der neueren katholischen und evangelischen Theologie*, Würzburg 1991.   219 Cf. P. Rodríguez, 'La dimensione ecclesiologica della giustificazione. Una prospettiva cattolica', op. cit.

in that sense, the doctrine of justification as a criteriological principle will always insist on the priority and unsubstitutable quality of God's saving action in Christ, and on the wholly personal, untouchable, faith response of the individual Christian.

However, the entire thrust of *Church and Justification* lies in its attempt to clarify the precise way in which the Church, as a visible institution founded by Christ (with its sacraments, ministry and preaching), is actually involved in the sanctifying and convoking action of Christ's Spirit. Christ's Spirit acts, certainly; the Church 'acts' as well: but how do the two 'actions' relate, coalesce, interact? Does the Church (in administering the sacraments, in preaching, etc.) do half the work, and Christ's Spirit the rest? Is the Church an essential (God-willed) *instrument* of God's action, or is it an accidental *sign, result or manifestation* of God's saving power? This is the key issue being dealt with in *Church and Justification*.[220]

Content of 'Church and Justification' Church and Justification is an enormous paper, occupying 151 pages in the original German text, with over 400 footnotes; it is also very wide-ranging, dense and tightly reasoned, rich and analytically unsparing, perhaps 'the most comprehensive and complex study ever published by an international bilateral dialogue'.[221] It is made up of five chapters.

The first,[222] entitled 'Justification and the Church', offers a brief introduction to the theme in hand, and provides a highly significant interpretative key for understanding the document, insofar as it places *both* 'Church' and 'justification' on the same plane: both are truths of faith, both are 'founded on the mystery of Christ and of the Trinity', both are 'unmerited gift of grace and challenge'.

The second chapter,[223] 'The Abiding Origin of the Church' deals with the *historical origins* of the Church, that is, its foundation by Christ, or divine origin, as a visible believing community.

The third chapter[224] is called 'The Church of the Triune God' and examines the *hidden and spiritual foundations*, as it were, of the Church, its underlying and determinative Trinitarian dimension. The key point made here is that *communion among Christians* (like their personal salvation) is not the result of their own efforts or merits, but is a partaking of the communion of the Father, the Son and the Holy Spirit, and thus as much the result of grace as justification itself.

> It is not primarily the communion of believers with each other which makes the Church *koinónia*: it is primarily and fundamentally the communion of believers with God, the triune God whose innermost being is *koinónia*. And yet the communion of believers with the triune God is inseparable from their communion with each other.[225]

220 The document is studied in detail in P. O'Callaghan, 'The Mediation of Justification and the justification of Mediation', op. cit. 221 H.-A. Raem, op. cit., p. 190. 222 CJ 1–9. 223 CJ 10–47. 224 CJ 48–106. 225 CJ 65.

The fourth chapter,[226] 'The Church as recipient and mediator of salvation', is the theological heart of the document, dealing with *what the Church is and does*, 'imparting life and salvation in faithfulness to its mission, which it has received from God',[227] what might be termed the 'sacramentality' of the Church. The chapter thoroughly explores the dialectic between the Church as a *congregatio fidelium* and as a *sacramentum salutis*.

The fifth and final chapter[228] 'The Mission and Consummation of the Church' looks at what God, in justifying the sinner through and in the Church, produces and brings about for the world: the eschatological kingdom of God.

In a very approximate way, it might be said that if chapters two and three relate to the efficient cause of justification, the fourth to its formal cause, the fifth chapter deals with the final cause: evangelization, kingdom of God, consummation.

In presenting the tensions existing between Lutheran and Catholic understandings of the Church, the document reiterates a single fundamental concern: 'Does the Lutheran doctrine diminish the reality of the Church?; does the Catholic understanding of the Church obscure the Gospel as it is explicitated by the doctrine of justification?'[229]

Lutherans insist, as they have always done, on the necessity of the preached word (the *verbum externum*) and the sacraments for salvation.[230] Yet they are concerned should the action of the Church (comprising the justified, who are just *but also* sinners) interfere at a significant level with God's merciful saving action (not with the divine action as such, of course, but with *human mediation, perception and reception* of it), and feel wary about the Church being considered as a kind of 'sacrament of salvation',[231] as Vatican Council II termed it.[232] Catholics, however, wonder

226 CJ 107–242.   227 CJ 107.   228 CJ 243–306.   229 CJ 173.   230 'The Gospel . . . is essentially an *"external word"*. That is to say it is always mediated through one or more individuals addressing one or more individuals . . . [The Gospel] . . . remains a message "from outside" and hearers remain dependent on its communication by one who proclaims it' (CJ 170).   231 On the notion of the sacramentality of the Church in Protestant thought, cf. for example G. Gaβmann, 'The Church as Sacrament, Sign and Instrument. The Reception of this ecclesiological understanding in ecumenical debate', in *Church, Kingdom, World*, Faith & Order Paper, no. 130, Geneva 1986, pp. 1–17; J.J. Degenhardt, J. Willebrands, H. Döring, H.J. Schulz and G. Gaβmann, P. Hünermann and H.J. Urban, *Die Sakramentalität der Kirche in der ökumenischen Diskussion*, Paderborn 1983; H. Luthe (ed.), *Christus-begegnung in der Sakramenten*, Kevelaer 1981. Many authors take clear exception to the idea of the Church as a 'sacrament'. For example G. Ebeling ('Worthafte und sakramentale Existenz. Ein Beitrag zum Unterscheid zwischer den Konfessionen', in *Wort Gottes und Tradition*, Göttingen 1964, pp. 197ff., and *Dogmatik des christlichen Glaubens*, vol. 3, Tübingen 1979, pp. 314ff.) sees this as the fundamental difference between Lutheranism and Catholicism. The same can be said for the unequivocal position of G. Maron, *Kirche und Rechtfertigung: eine kontroverstheologische Untersuchung, ausgehend von den Texten des Zweiten Vatikanischen Konzils*, Göttingen 1969, pp. 261–267. Cf. also M. Bernards, 'Zur Lehre von der Kirche als Sakrament. Beobachtungen aus der Theologie des 19. und 20. Jahrhunderts', in *Münchener Theologische Zeitung* 20 (1969) 29–54; E. Jüngel, 'Die Kirche als Sakrament?', *Zeitschrift für Theologie und Kirche* 80 (1983) 432–457; D. Wendebourg, ' "Kirche und Rechtfertigung". Ein Erlebnisbericht zu einem neueren Ökumenischen Dokument', op. cit., p. 93. G. Wenz fears that

does a conception of the Church seen not so much as the instrument of salvation,[233] but principally as its *sign*, not compromise its true nature. Would the Church in the Lutheran sense really be any more than a mere conglomeration of believers, the sum total of its members, the 'communional product' of those who are already justified, the visible and posterior union of those who have invisibly and previously believed and been justified?

Tensions between Catholics and Lutherans on this front are exemplified and clarified in respect of a series of controversial areas where the criteriological and reforming quality of the doctrine of justification is put to the test: the institutional continuity of the Church;[234] ordained ministry as an institution in the Church;[235] binding Church doctrine and the teaching function of the ministry, that is, magisterium;[236] Church jurisdiction and the legal ramifications of Christian ministry.[237] A considerable degree of convergence on the nature of the Church is established.

Church and justification, critical co-principles　The document repeatedly suggests that a *single criteriological principle* (that of justification by faith alone) should be applied or at least be applicable to every aspect of Christian life and practice, and especially to whatever is related to the institutional life of the Church. However, the notion of a *single* criteriological principle employed to interpret and correct every other aspect of Christian doctrine has been questioned on more than one occasion.[238] We shall return to this question later on.

sufficient distinction is not being drawn between the action of Christ and that of the Church (G. Wenz, *Einführung in die evangelische Sakramentenlehre*, Darmstadt 1988). Other authors such as K.A. Meißinger (*Der katholische Luther*, München 1952) see an openness of Luther to the concept of the Church as sacrament. It should be noted however that Luther speaks quite openly of the instrumentality of the Church, as J. Wicks shows (cf. 'Holy Spirit—Church—Sanctification: insights from Luther's Instructions on the Faith', in *Pro Ecclesia* 2 (1993) 150–172). **232** Cf. Vatican Council II, *Sacrosanctum Concilium* 5; 26 and *Lumen gentium* 1; 9; 48. The classical argument on the Church as 'protosacrament' is to be found in O. Semmelroth, *Die Kirche als Ur-Sakrament*, Frankfurt a. M. 1953; then in E. Schillebeeckx, *Christ the Sacrament of Encounter with God*, London 1963 and K. Rahner, *Kirche und Sakramente*, Freiburg i. Br. 1960. On the issue, cf. also C. Journet, 'Le mystère de la sacramentalité. Le Christ, l'Église, les sept sacrements', in *Nova et Vetera* 49 (1974) 161–214; G. Colombo, 'Dove va la teologia sacramentaria', in *La Scuola Cattolica* 102 (1974) 673–717; recently: S. Dianich, *Ecclesiologia. Questioni di metodo e una proposta*, Cinisello Balsamo 1993, pp. 75–85. **233** Lutherans accept the Church as an instrument in the following sense: '. . . if the Church *is the place where these means of grace become effectual* it follows that the Church itself is in a derivative sense an instrument of salvation . . . [insofar as] it is *the place where people participate in salvation* . . . In this sense it is true for Reformation theology too that there is no salvation outside the Church' (CJ 126). **234** Cf. CJ 174–181. **235** Cf. CJ 182–204. **236** Cf. CJ 205–222. **237** That is, canon law: cf. CJ 223–242. **238** Cf. for example C.J. Peter, 'Justification by faith and the need for another critical principle', in H. G. Anderson et al., *Justification by faith* (*Lutherans and Catholics in Dialogue*, VII), Minneapolis 1985, pp. 304–315. On the history of the theological thrust to establish the doctrine of justification as a criteriological principal, cf. H. Meyer, 'The doctrine of justification in Lutheran dialogue with other Churches', op. cit.

However, it should be noted that the document insists, directly and indirectly, that the rôle of the Church in 'providing' or 'mediating' God's saving power is *also* 'essential'. Since the very act of justification is a completely divine one, that is, saving grace originates from the non-human, from the Totally-other (it is, in Luther's terminology *extra nos, pro nobis*), the question of its mediation is not unimportant. The radical quality of the doctrine of justification by *faith alone* speaks of both the magnanimity of the divine saving will and the total incapacity of the human creature and sinner to attain salvation and pardon by its own resources. The true doctrine of justification therefore requires, necessarily yet paradoxically, the existence of some form of mediation between the two extremes, the divine and the human, a mediation which in some way must find common ground both with the divinity of the justifying God and with the soiled humanity of the unjustified sinner.

Insistence on the mediating quality of the Church, the very element that might, in Lutheran thinking, destroy or adversely condition the saving power of grace, may well be the factor which, at one and the same time (1) defends and maintains the infinite distance between the saving God and the creature whether saved or unsaved; (2) gives expression therefore to the fact that salvation is always 'received' by humans, that it always remains a *gift* (not only *in being received*, as semi-Pelagians hold, but in perpetually remaining so); and (3) ensures that 'faith alone' does not come mean 'faith without /independently of the Church', individualistic faith, but rather always remains 'ecclesial faith'. The Church in its mediating life and action in one sense is meant to *unite* God and man, and in practice may do so more or less effectively; but in another sense the Church *keeps them apart*, so to speak, in expressing the 'otherness' of God with respect to sinful humanity. Humans in and through the Church come to live God's own life, but can never dominate, or 'get a hold', as it were, of the divinity itself. And that is so because they not only live *in* the Church, 'producing' it as it were, but they also live *off* the Church, depending on it, receiving *from* it, or better, receiving (God's gifts) *through* it.

An elliptical hermeneutic   Hence it is fair to say that the document is structured, implicitly at least, on the basis of a kind of 'elliptical (or two-poled) hermeneutic', based that is on two criteriological principles: the 'justification principle' (expressing the gratuitous or unconditional quality of mankind's salvation by faith in the mercy of God in Christ: the individual side of justification), and the 'ecclesiological principle' (expressing the need of the historical Church for salvation, the need to belong to a tangible and visible saved and saving community in order to be justified: the social side of justification). The short introductory chapter to *Church and Justification* seems to move in this direction, placing justification and Church on the same plane, as two sides of the same coin.

At a principally *noetical level*, the doctrine of justification would act as a kind of criteriological principle for ecclesiology, in its theoretical and practical implications and manifestations, ensuring that the magnanimity of God's power and pardon is

not prejudiced, manipulated or blocked by human sinfulness. However, at a primordially experiential and practical level, the 'ecclesiological principle' in its turn should
act as a corrective for the Christian's lived experience of justification,[239] ensuring
that the kind of individualistic mysticism that could easily follow on from the notion
of immediate (non-mediated) justification would not degenerate into a kind of ex-
alted antinomistic pantheism.[240]

239 Speaking of the doctrine of justification as a criteriological principle, Rodríguez asks: 'can the
nature of the Church, its instrumentality and institutional dimension be really deduced from a
theological principle, or is it not rather inscribed on the plane of the historical and sovereign action
of God who reveals himself to man and communicates with him' (P. Rodríguez, 'La dimensione
ecclesiologica della giustificazione. Una prospettiva cattolica', op. cit., p. 206).   240 Of the latter
possibility, Luther's decisive distancing from the so-called *Schwärmer* in the late 1530's is highly
significant (cf. in chapter 2, pp. 34–36, the section entitled: 'The antinomian spiritualism of the
Schwärmer'). O.-H. Pesch observes: 'The criteriological function of the article on justification may
only be used in situations of crisis in the Church—otherwise it would become a law of faith which
would endanger the purity of faith as much as the demand for special works' ('Rechtfertigung und
Kirche. Die kriteriologische Bedeutung der Rechtfertigungslehre für die Ekklesiologie', in
Ökumenische Rundschau 37 (1988) 22–46, here, p. 40).

PART TWO

New perspectives on the doctrine of justification

CHAPTER FIVE

New perspectives on justification

'Justification' in exile? In the sixteenth century the doctrine of justification, with all its implications for personal, social and ecclesial life, was truly the *articulus stantis et cadentis ecclesiae*. The force with which it invaded every sphere of life was such that Christianity as a social reality has never been the same again. Luther, fired by an seemingly abstruse theological vision, had managed to touch a vital nerve in the fabric of medieval society. 'Justification of the sinner by faith alone' . . . justification of the *sinner*, by *faith*, by faith *alone*, that is, *independently of works* . . . each element of this programme hit home with enormous force, and compelled one and all to take position for or against.

However, things have changed considerably in the meantime. No longer does the doctrine of justification seem to be the flagship of reformed Christendom. Authors following on from Ritschl and other *Aufklärer*, belonging in the main to the liberal Protestant stream, felt no qualms in holding that the doctrine of justification was of predominantly historical interest, and thus of secondary importance in the theological sphere. A. Schweitzer in particular considered the doctrine of justification by faith alone a secondary crater off Paul's central crater of the doctrine of redemption, which is centered on the individual's mystical incorporation into the body of Christ.[1]

The reason for this change-about can be put down in part to the rise of modern secularism. Indeed for many authors, God's existence and action in the world came to be considered as holding little or no interest for contemporary emancipated humanity.[2] Interest was lost in God, and therefore in sin, hence in being justified, and so forth. Vittorio Subilia went so far as to say that in the minds of many people the problem of justification has been inverted: it is now a question of man's *justification of God*, not of God's justification of the sinner.[3]

But it must also be admitted that, even among believers, the notion of justification seems to have lost all relevance, insofar as it does not sufficiently express the social dimension of the human person and the ecclesial side of belief and Christian life. Gerhard Ebeling was honest enough to admit that the doctrine of justification

---

1 Cf. A. Schweitzer, *The Mysticism of Paul the Apostle*, London 1956 (orig. 1931), pp. 220–226. 2 On the impact of 'death of God' theologies which came to express this notion clearly, cf. J.L. Illanes, *Cristianismo, historia, mundo*, Pamplona 1972, passim. 3 Cf. V. Subilia, *La giustificazione per fede*, op. cit. (1976), pp. 343–351. Subilia, in saying this, is in fact glossing Luther's phrase *iustificatio Dei et credulitas in Deum idem est* (*Die Vorlesung über den Römerbrief*, WA 56: 226), 'the justification of God and belief in God are one and the same thing'.

is as meaningful to modern man as is the Egyptian sphinx.[4] Dietrich Bonhöffer said
that the controversies of the sixteenth century are simply 'unreal' for us; at best
evangelical Christians are 'historically' obliged to keep the doctrine of justification
on the back burner.[5] He asked: 'Has not the individualistic question of personal
salvation just disappeared off the map? Are we not all under the impression that
there are more important things to be concerned about?'[6]

For Paul Tillich the doctrine of justification by faith, which was discussed 'in
every house and workshop, in every market and inn in Germany, is now difficult to
understand even for our most intelligent scholars. This represents a breaking away
from tradition which has few parallels in history.'[7] Not many have expressed the
problem in so compact and incisive a way as Martin Buber when he said that he
refused to walk about with a redeemed soul in an unredeemed world.[8] To put it in
another way, attention is perceived to have shifted from the problem of man's personal eschatological salvation to that of the future of humanity as a whole. And
whereas the doctrine of justification faced up squarely to the former, it would seem
to have little to say to the latter. Hans-Martin Barth, reflecting on the apparent
divorce between traditional and contemporary reflection on the doctrine of justification on the one hand, and scientific anthropologies on the other,[9] sees the way
forward in directing attention, theologically, towards understanding human and
Christian 'identity' in the fullest sense.[10] W. Pannenberg takes a similar approach.[11]

However, as can be seen from the abundance of bibliography available on the
matter, theological reflection on the doctrine of justification seems to be alive and
well, commanding significant interest at least on the ecclesial and academic front.
Efforts at reinterpretation, some of them of a more philosophical bent (for example,
with Bultmann and Tillich), others more theologically inclined (for example those
of Holl and Ebeling), have abounded throughout the century, and the very copious-
ness of common ecumenical declarations shows that the doctrine has by no means
lost its interest and actuality. But might it not be that 'justification' has become a
kind of *theologumenon*, to be studied in 'closed-shop' by specialists of exegesis, history and theology?

What does 'justification' mean? The term *iustificare* is absent in classical Latin usage,[12] and is commonly found only in works of Christian theology,[13] in Latin trans-

---

4 Cf. G. Ebeling, *Dogmatik des christlichen Glaubens*, vol. 3, Tübingen 1979, pp. 195ff. 5 Cf. D.
Bonhöffer, *Widerstand und Ergebung. Briefe und Aufzeichnungen aus der Haft*, Munich 1970, p. 307;
313. 6 Ibid., p. 312. 7 Cf. P. Tillich, *The Protestant Era*, Chicago 1963, p. 224. 8 Cited by V.
Subilia, *La giustificazione per fede*, op. cit., p. 336. 9 Cf. H.-M. Barth, 'Giustificazione e identità',
in *Protestantesimo* 51 (1996) 116–130. As a point of departure, he takes the work of M. Beintker et
al. (eds.), *Rechtfertigung und Erfahrung. Für Gerhard Sauter zum 60. Geburtstag*, Gütersloh 1995.
10 Cf. H.-M. Barth, *Wie ein Segel sich entfalten. Selbstverwirklichung und christliche Existenz*,
München 1979. 11 Cf. especially W. Pannenberg, *Anthropology in Theological Perspective*, Philadelphia 1985. 12 Cf. P.G.W. Glare, *Oxford Latin Dictionary*, Oxford 1984, pp. 984–987. 13 Cf.
Various authors, *Thesaurus Linguae Latinae*, vol. 7/2, Leipzig 1979, pp. 712f.

lations of Scripture for example, in works of the Latin fathers, of the Scholastics and Reformers. According to St Augustine, the term means *iustum facere*, 'to make righteous'.[14] This understanding of the term came to be accepted generally within Christendom at least until the time of the Reformation, when, under the humanistic influence of Erasmus, Melanchthon and others, the Septuagint understanding of the classical Greek term δικαιοῦν, 'to *declare* just' was recuperated.[15] Whether or not the Augustinian Latin or the classical Greek understanding of the term (to 'make just', to 'declare just', respectively) corresponds more exactly to the Hebrew Biblical original *hasdîq* is a matter of scholarly dispute.[16] As we shall see presently, contemporary studies concerning the biblical roots of the terms 'justice' and 'justification' agree that the two aspects are compatible with one another, indeed, that they require and explain one another.[17]

In any case, it is quite clear that 'justification', to 'make'/'declare' just, is a clearly Christian concept, at the very heart of the biblical creationist, gift-centered vision of the world: *God's creative word declares and thus makes the sinner just.* And as a result (1) the Christian's 'remaining' just in God's sight never becomes something acquired or autonomously possessed, but perpetually remains a gift, declared and conferred; and (2) since *God* declares and makes the sinner just, by definition the sinner does not become just on his own account. All genuine Christian theology throughout the centuries, in widely differing ways, insists on this basic notion.

Yet the fact remains that the term 'justification' has lost, in the popular mind, virtually all the epoch-making religious connotations it once had. Spiritual ramifications that do remain in everyday language are historically tainted at best by a crudely predestinationist elitism. For most people 'to justify' means simply to demonstrate the truthfulness or validity of an affirmation, statement, or particular way of behaviour: to excuse, to exonerate, to defend, to vindicate, to maintain, to warrant . . . and all that within an exclusively human and 'secular' sphere. For a person to 'justify' something commonly means that they offer cogent reasons for holding on to a conscientiously taken position, and, if necessary, act thereon even in face of diverging positions and opposition of others. In other words, the one who 'justifies', that is the origin of 'justification', is no longer God, and the object is no longer the sinner. Rather, the person justifies *himself* or *herself* with a view to demonstrating that he or she has *not* contravened positive law or right reason, that is, has not become a 'sinner'. That is to say, his or her way of thinking or proposed way of acting

---

14 Cf. Augustine, *Ad Simplicianum* I, 2, 3; *Sermo* 131, 9; *Sermo* 292, 6; *Epist.* 160, 21, 52; *De Gratia et libero arbitrio* 6, 13. cf. G. Bavaud, 'La doctrine de la justification d'après Saint Augustin', in *Revue des Études augustiniennes* 5 (1959) 21–32; A.E. McGrath, *Iustitia Dei* . . . op. cit., vol. 1, pp. 30f., especially note 58.   15 In Greek the term has two meanings: the citizen's faithful observance of the law, and the rectitude of the judge in applying it (cf. for example Aristotle, *Eth. Nicom.* V: 1136 a30).   16 For an overview of the meaning and evolution of terms 'justice' and 'justification' in Hebrew, Greek and Latin texts, cf. A.E. McGrath, *Iustitia Dei* . . . op. cit., vol. 1, pp. 4–16.   17 Cf. pp. 185–194.

is considered not to be at variance with personal conscience, to the point that what others think or say or need make no substantial difference. This does not mean, of course, that God or the moral law are necessarily left out of the picture, but it does seem to involve and point to an individualistic ethical framework. An example of this may be seen in the way it is sometimes affirmed that 'circumstances' can justify a particular way of thinking or acting, in the face of a more commonly accepted or 'normal' way of acting; in other words, the concrete situation one is involved in may entitle one to act against the law or against common practice.

Perhaps the point is just there: humans 'justify' their positions or actions even in the face of differing attitudes and standards accepted by society at large, because in conscience, that is in the innermost shrine of their being, they perceive that in the heel of the hunt they will have account to *God alone* and not to the rest of society, and that *God* will 'justify' or defend them. So, it may be that the commonly-accepted present-day usage of the term 'justification' is, albeit in a somewhat secularized shape, in close *rapport* with a considerably developed ethical system, perhaps individualistic in nature. Luther's doctrine of the 'two kingdoms' can certainly be read in this direction: man's relationship to God and his relationship with society and created reality seem to move on simply distinct planes, each one having its own set of rules and values. Of course we have already seen that Luther strongly resisted all attempts at interpreting his strongly theocentric teaching in expressly individualistic, antinomian, or anti-ecclesial terms. Besides, his insistence on the 'forensic' character of justification in confessional circles certainly constituted a reminder of the presence and power of the transcendent divinity. But all in all it would seem that the terms 'justification' and 'to justify' in popular usage have come to respond to a secularized, somewhat individualistic view of ethics not unrelated to Luther's theology.

New developments   The question being asked in this chapter is the following: in spite of the diverse sensitivities and interests characterizing the present period of the life of the Church and the world, does Luther's doctrine of 'justification of the sinner by faith alone' retain its original revolutionary power? Does it still express the heart of the Gospel?

It should be noted that recent theological interpretations of the doctrine of justification need take into account not only exegetical advancement in the area of Pauline and Lutheran studies, but also, perhaps principally, theological development in the area of Christology. As we saw in chapter one (on Luther's understanding of justification), justification and Christology relate closely to one another. The recent challenging reformulations of the Pauline doctrine on justification we shall examine later on are rooted in traditions going back to Ritschl and the *Aufklärung*, that is in Protestant authors less and less cognizant of the strictly soteriological and Christological side of justification. Authors such as Albert Schweitzer,[18] P. Wernle[19]

---

18 Cf. especially A. Schweitzer, *Geschichte der paulinischen Forschung von der Reformation bis auf die*

and W. Wrede[20] were among the first to suggest that Paul's doctrine of 'justification by faith' was of primordially historical interest, being no more than a contingent reflection of his anti-Jewish polemic. The tendency marked the beginning of what Schoeps justly called the *Entlutherisierung Pauli*, the de-Lutherizing of Paul.[21]

The point they were making was certainly a valid one: the perennial value of Paul's doctrine could only be mapped and usefully employed if his theology and spirituality were historically contextualized. But their vision was undoubtedly conditioned by the fact that, in varying degrees, they maintained that there is a significant, perhaps decisive, discontinuity between the simple preaching and work of Jesus, the real object of Christian faith, and the sophisticated interpretation handed on to Christians by Paul, John and perhaps the other evangelists. For these authors, just as Paul's doctrine of justification was the direct result of his polemics with the Jews, so his Christology was little more than a kind of mythological projection of man's quest for salvation. In fact, due to liberal Protestantism, evangelical theologies of all kinds came under the sway of the distinction and tension perceived between the 'Jesus of history' (the authentic, simple, objective, real, human, though perhaps historically inaccessible Jesus 'in himself'), and the 'Christ of faith' (the personally or ecclesiastically projected and transmitted version of Jesus the Saviour, whether Pauline, Johannine, Nicean, Calcedonian, Lutheran, etc., the Christ 'for me').[22]

Developments in the doctrine of justification in the wake of Schweitzer's reinterpretation of Paul moved in two directions. *Firstly*, in the area of systematic theological reflection. Karl Barth, in spite of his undisguised opposition to liberal Protestantism, accepted that justification should not be taken as the central Christian doctrine, and attempted to shift the key-element of Christian theology and the Christ-event from salvation to revelation.[23] Other authors, such as Bultmann, Tillich and Ebeling accepted the classical Lutheran stance in respect of the centrality of the doctrine of justification, mainly as a fundamental interpretative, hermeneutical or criteriological principle, but reinterpreted its content and meaning in the context

---

Gegenwart, Tübingen 1911; and also his work *The Mysticism of Paul the Apostle*, op. cit. He noted that the doctrine of justification was merely a side-crater (*Nebenkrater*) of Paul's theology of redemption. 19 Cf. especially P. Wernle, *Der Christ und die Sünde bei Paulus*, Freiburg i. Br./ Leipzig 1897. 20 Cf. especially W. Wrede, *Paulus*, Tübingen 1907, p. 72: 'The Reformation has habituated us to considering the doctrine of justification as the central point of Paul. But it is not. In fact it is possible to present the whole of Pauline religion without hardly mentioning it, except in reference to the law . . . It appears only in the context of his conflict with Judaism. This is a measure of true import of this doctrine: justification is Paul's polemical teaching (*die Kampfeslehre*), understandable only on the basis of his confrontation with Judaism and Jewish Christianity, thought out only for this.' 21 H.J. Schoeps (*Paulus. Die Theologie des Paulus im Lichte der jüdischen Religionsgeschichte*, Tübingen 1959, p. 207) holds that Wrede was responsible for opening the process of 'de-Lutherizing' Paul. 22 On this tension and its applications, cf. my study 'Cristocentrismo y antropocentrismo en el horizonte del la teología', in J. Morales (ed.), *Cristo y el Dios de los cristianos. Actas del XVIII Simposio Internacional de Teología*, Pamplona 1997. 23 Cf. pp. 195– 197 below.

of modern circumstances vastly different from those obtaining in the time of Luther and the Reformation. We shall examine their positions in the coming pages.

The second area of interest is that of New Testament biblical exegesis. It should be noted that strictly exegetical critiques of Schweitzer's reinterpretation of Pauline doctrine were quite slow in coming from Lutheran and Evangelical biblical scholars. Those who insisted on the doctrine of justification by faith as the key expression of the Gospel and of faith in Jesus Christ include authors such as Hübner,[24] Reumann[25] and Westerholm.[26] However, it should be noted also that insistence on the centrality of justification has been contested significantly by other non-Catholic exegetes, such as Davies,[27] Strecker,[28] Sanders,[29] Dunn,[30] Räisänen[31] and J. Becker.[32]

In this chapter we shall examine some of the developments and implications of the doctrine of justification on the following four fronts:

1. Recent theological reinterpretations of the Lutheran doctrine of justification (Bultmann, Tillich, Ebeling);
2. Paul's and Luther's understanding of 'justification by faith alone';
3. The meaning of the 'righteousness of God' (*Iustitia Dei*);
4. The doctrine of justification and contemporary Lutheranism (Barth, the Lutheran World Federation's 1963 Helsinki conference, the influence of dialogue statements).

The chapter will be concluded with an evaluation of the rôle of justification as a hermeneutical or criteriological principle for theology and Christian life.

24 Cf. H. Hübner, *Das Gesetz bei Paulus*, Göttingen 1980 (English translation, *Law in Paul's thought: a Contribution to the Development of Pauline Theology*, Edinburgh 1986), and especially 'Pauli Theologiae Proprium', in *New Testament Studies* 26 (1980) 455–473.   25 Cf. J. Reumann, *'Righteousness' in the New Testament: 'Justification' in the United States Lutheran-Roman Catholic Dialogue; with responses by Joseph A. Fitzmyer; Jerome D. Quinn*, Philadelphia/New York/Ramsey 1982.   26 S. Westerholm, *Israel's Law and the Church's Faith. Paul and his Recent Interpreters*, Grand Rapids 1988.   27 Cf. W.D. Davies, *Paul and Rabbinic Judaism. Some Rabbinic Elements in Pauline Theology*, London 1965 (orig. 1948). For this author, justification is just one metaphor among others, used to describe liberation through Christ, and developed in a polemical context (cf. ibid., pp. 221f.).   28 Cf. G. Strecker, 'Befreiung und Rechtfertigung. Zur Stellung der Rechtfertigungslehre in der Theologie des Paulus', in J. Friedrich, W. Pöhlmann and H. Conzelmann, *Rechtfertigung (Festschrift für E. Käsemann zum 70. Geburtstag)*, Göttingen 1976, pp. 479–508.   29 Cf. especially E.P. Sanders, *Paul and Palestinian Judaism. A Comparison of Patterns of Religion*, London 1977; idem., *Paul, the Law, and the Jewish People*, Philadelphia 1983. We shall return to this author later.   30 Cf. Dunn's works cited throughout the next section.   31 Cf. H. Räisänen, *Paul and the Law*, Tübingen 1983.   32 Cf. J.C. Becker, *Paul the Apostle. The Triumph of God in Life and Thought*, Edinburgh 1989 (orig. 1980). Becker speaks of the doctrine of justification as a new kind of language, developed in Galatians, meant to actualize the theology of the Cross.

RECENT REINTERPRETATIONS OF THE LUTHERAN DOCTRINE OF
JUSTIFICATION

We shall examine three authors who have attempted to explain classical Lutheran doctrine on justification in modern terms, R. Bultmann, P. Tillich and G. Ebeling.

1.   *Justification by faith and human authenticity in R. Bultmann*

Rudolph Bultmann's theology is of special interest in the re-evaluation of the doctrine of justification, for the enormous influence his writings have had, if for nothing else. Bultmann attempted to reformulate Luther's doctrine of justification in modern parlance, in a mould, however, which Luther himself might well not recognize. His theological vision consists principally of an attempt *to give meaning to concrete human existence*, making use of the existentialist analysis of man and the world found in Martin Heidegger's *Sein und Zeit* and a somewhat subjectivist theology centered on the 'Christ of faith', negligent of the 'Jesus of history'.

For the early Heidegger,[33] man's 'way of being' (*Dasein*) is constituted essentially in such a way that he can transcend or go beyond himself and his immediate surroundings, experiencing and living in the midst of a tension between himself and the objective world. In this experience, man becomes conscious of and affirms his individuality (*Jemeinigkeit*). At the same time his encounter with the 'world' constantly offers him the possibility of opting between two form of existence, one authentic (*eigentlich*), the other inauthentic (*ineigentlich*). The latter is verified when man allows himself be overwhelmed by the surrounding 'world', thus 'falling' from authentic to inauthentic existence, eliminating all awareness of his essential distinction from the 'world', thus becoming uprooted (*entwurzelt*) from his proper way of being, and alienated from true human existence.[34]

Heidegger even went so far to point to Luther's doctrine of justification, in particular that of the assurance of salvation, as a case where existential analysis can be applied to the concrete reality of human life. Bultmann's theology of justification, in attempting to reformulate Luther's deeper theological intentions, seemed to prove Heidegger right.[35] The same could be said for Tillich. But is their interpretation of Luther correct?

According to Bultmann, man's *encounter with the preached word* (resulting from

33 Cf. A. de Waelhens, *La philosophie de Martin Heidegger*, Louvain 1943; A.E. McGrath, *Iustitia Dei* . . . op. cit., vol. 2, pp. 185f.   34 Cf. M. Heidegger, *Sein und Zeit*, Tübingen 1927, pp. 177ff.
35 On the validity or otherwise of a possible link-up between Luther and Heidegger, cf. H. Blumenberg, *Die Legimität der Neuzeit*, Frankfurt a. M. 1966; G. Ebeling, 'Gewißheit und Zweifel: Die Situation des Glaubens im Zeitalter nach Luther und Descartes', in *Zeitschrift für Theologie und Kirche* 64 (1967) 282–324; R. Lorenz, *Die unvollendete Befreiung vom Nominalismus: Martin Luther und die Grenzen hermeneutischer Theologie bei Gerhard Ebeling*, Gütersloh 1973, pp. 131–144.

the Christian *kerygma*) does not as such bring him face to face with objective revealed realities to be shared with other potential or actual believers, but rather offers him the possibility, in a free personal decision of faith, of opening his inauthentic existence to authentic existence based on the Christ-event (*Christusereignis*).
Reception of the preached word is what exposes and develops man's potentiality for
such existence (*Sein-Können*).

This process of man's attaining his true self through the faith-encounter with
the preached word, is, according to Bultmann, just another way of expressing the
Pauline and Lutheran message of justification by faith.[36] In other words, man ac-
quires his true selfhood only by believing. Performance of 'works of the law', conversely, cannot 'justify', or bring about 'authentic existence', because one must not
have anything *to boast of* before God.[37] The following words of Bultmann, a faultless
restatement of the classical Lutheran position in existentialist terms, are worth while
quoting at length:

> Because man's effort to achieve his salvation by keeping the Law only leads
> him into sin, indeed *his effort itself in the end is already sin*. It is the insight
> which Paul has achieved into the nature of sin that determines his teaching
> on the Law. This embraces two insights. One is the insight that *sin is man's
> self-powered striving* to undergird his own existence in forgetfulness of his
> creaturely existence, to procure his salvation by his own strength . . . that
> striving which finds its extreme expression in 'boasting' and 'trusting in the
> flesh' . . . The other is the insight that *man is always already a sinner*, that,
> fallen into the power of sin, he is always already involved in a falsely oriented
> understanding of his existence . . . [Hence] . . . he can find his salvation *only
> when he understands himself in his dependence* upon God the Creator.[38]

Self-justifying works are useless; man is a sinner and must recognize his complete
dependence on God. As faithful a rendering of Luther's doctrine of justification
could not be found. However, two closely-linked problematic aspects of Bultmann's
analysis should be noted.

Firstly, it should be pointed out that the starting point of Bultmann's understanding is not Christian revelation or the Christ-event as such, but the concrete
human situation, a humanly perceived and philosophically analyzed pre-compre-
hension (*Vorverständnis*) of man,[39] in the context of which Revelation is sounded *a*

---

36 Cf. R. Bultmann, *Glauben und Verstehen*, vol. 2, Tübingen 1964, p. 111.   37 Cf. R. Bultmann,
Theology of the New Testament, New York 1951, vol. 1, p. 283.   38 Ibid., p. 264.   39 Cf. R.
Bultmann, 'Das Problem der Hermeneutik' (1950), in *Glauben und Verstehen*, vol. 2, Tübingen
1961, pp. 211–223. On Bultmann's hermeneutics, cf. R. Marlé, *Bultmann et l'interprétation du
Nouveau Testament*, Paris 1966; L. Randellini, 'L'ermeneutica esistenziale in Bultmann', in Vari-
ous authors, *Esegesi ed ermeneutica. Atti della XXI Settimana Biblica dell'Associazione Biblica Italiana*,
Brescia 1972, pp. 35–70.

posteriori in search of a word of meaning.[40] Apart from the questionability of this approach from a purely methodological standpoint (starting with human plight and ending up with a theology of salvation),[41] some authors have criticized Bultmann for wanting to reduce the gospel to an analysis of the condition of natural man.[42] To this criticism Bultmann retorted that the gospel offers a specifically Christian answer to the common human problem of attaining authentic existence, quite distinct from secular understandings of the human condition.[43] However, E.P. Sanders, commenting on the text of Bultmann cited above, stated:

> It is not Paul's analysis of the nature of sin which determines his view, but his analysis of the way to salvation; not his anthropology, but his Christology and soteriology. Paul's own reason for maintaining [that man must not be justified by works of the Law] . . . is not that man must not think of procuring his own salvation, but that if the law could save, Christ died in vain (cf. Gal 2:21); and man does not find salvation by understanding 'himself in his dependence upon God the Creator', but by participating in the death of Christ, which assures his resurrection with Christ (cf. Rom 6:5).[44]

Secondly, Bultmann seems unable to avoid the doctrine of justification being formulated in narrowly individualistic terms. Part of this may well be due to his Heideggerian and existentialist leanings. Yet he also attempts to justify this view exegetically.[45] Disciples of his (for example, Ernst Käsemann), studying other aspects of Pauline theology such as the notion of participation in Christ's body,[46] and the cosmic aspects of his lordship,[47] in continuity with a line of interpretation initi-

40 Bultmann bases this approach on what he considers Paul's own missionary method: 'In Romans, where Paul is connectedly presenting the main issues of his message to a hitherto unknown congregation in order to legitimate himself as a genuine apostle, he . . . does not first present the salvation occurrence, the credibility of which would first have to be acknowledged. Instead he begins by exposing the plight of mankind, so that then the proclamation of God's salvation-deed becomes a decision-question' (R. Bultmann, *Theology of the New Testament* . . . , op. cit., p. 301). 41 Other biblical exegetes take an opposite view to Bultmann on the matter, holding that our need for a Saviour springs from the prior conviction that God has actually provided one (cf. E.P. Sanders, *Paul and Palestinian Judaism. A Comparison of Patterns of Religion*, London 1977, p. 443; cf. ibid., pp. 442–447; 474–511). 'Jesus Christ himself and the salvation based on and made available through his death on the cross, his resurrection, and his exaltation as Lord form the subject of Paul's proclamation' (G. Bornkamm, *Paul*, San Francisco 1971, p. 109). Cf. also F. Thielman, *From Plight to Solution. A Jewish Framework for Understanding Paul's View of the Law in Galatians and Romans*, Leiden 1989. 42 For example G. Kuhlman, 'Zum theologischen Problem der Existenz: Fragen an Rudolf Bultmann', in *Zeitschrift für Theologie und Kirche* 10 (1929) 28–57. 43 Cf. R. Bultmann, 'Die Geschichtlichkeit des Daseins und der Glaube: Antwort an Gerhardt Kuhlmann', in *Zeitschrift für Theologie und Kirche* 11 (1930) 339–364. 44 E.P. Sanders, *Paul* . . . , op. cit., p. 481f. 45 Cf. for example R. Bultmann, *Geschichte und Eschatologie*, Tübingen 1964, pp. 47ff., and his reply to Käsemann's critique: 'Δικαιοσύνη Θεου ', in *Journal of Biblical Literature* 83 (1964) 12–16. 46 Cf. for example, E. Käsemann, *Leib und Leib Christi*, Tübingen 1933. 47 Cf. for example, E. Käsemann, 'The Lord's Supper', in *Essays on New Testament Themes*, London 1964, pp. 117ff.

ated by A. Schweitzer,[48] insisted that 'the righteousness of God does not, in Paul's understanding, refer primarily to the individual and is not to be understood exclusively in the context of the doctrine on man'.[49] 'The Pauline doctrine of justification never took its bearings from the individual, although hardly anyone now realizes this',[50] Käsemann says, adding that the ecclesial, social and political implications of the individualistic understanding of justification are and have been enormously damaging to Christianity.[51]

This tendency may be confirmed, besides, by the fact that Bultmann consistently interpreted Pauline soteriology exclusively in the line of man's *new self-understanding in* the light of the gospel, carefully steering clear of anything related to his *real participation* in the body of the Risen Lord.[52] The notion of a 'new self-understanding' is clearly centered on the individual's experience and comprehension; that of 'real participation' on Christ's ecclesial or social body, and what God does, in Christ and the Church, for Christians and in Christians. He stated for example that there is 'no magical or mysterious transformation of man . . . [but rather] a new understanding of one's self takes the place of the old'.[53]

The revindication of the central and determinative rôle of participationist categories in Paul (centered mainly on a theology of εν Χριστοῦ),[54] in both a personal (or better, 'interpersonal') and ecclesiological sense,[55] even to the point of displacing the doctrine of justification by faith as a theological and interpretative centre, is well established nowadays.[56]

2. *Justification and doubt in P. Tillich*

Another author worth mentioning is Paul Tillich, again insofar as he attempted to reinterpret the perennial meaning of the doctrine on justification – what he called

48 Cf. A. Schweitzer, *The Mysticism of Paul the Apostle*, op. cit.; also A. Deißmann, *Paulus: eine kultur- und religionsgeschichte Skizze*, Tübingen 1925.   49 E. Käsemann, ' "The Righteousness of God" in Paul', in *New Testament Questions of Today*, London/Philadelphia 1969, p. 175.   50 E. Käsemann, 'Justification and Salvation History', in *Perspectives on Paul*, London/Philadelphia 1971, p. 73f.   51 Cf. ibid., p. 64.   52 Bultmann analyses the theology of εν Χριστοῦ within his ecclesiology (*Theology of the New Testament*, op. cit., vol. 1, pp. 311), affirms that the notion of being a 'member of Christ's body' is Gnostic in origin (cf. ibid., p. 310), and states the notion of partaking in the death of Christ is drawn from mystery religions (cf. ibid., pp. 311ff.), clearly envisaging an individualistic theology of redemption.   53 R. Bultmann, *Theology of the New Testament*, op. cit., vol. 1, pp. 268f. H. Conzelmann (*An Outline of the Theology of the New Testament*, London 1969, vol. 1, pp. 208-210 and passim) was of the same mind as Bultmann.   54 For a history of the discussion of the term until 1962, cf. M. Bouttier, *En Christ*, Paris 1962.   55 Cf. E. Käsemann, 'The Faith of Abraham', in *Perspectives on Paul* . . . , op. cit., p. 101; and W.D. Davies, *Paul and Rabinnic Judaism* . . . , op. cit., pp. 86–88.   56 Cf. for example E.P. Sanders, *Paul* . . . , op. cit., pp. 453–463 and the works of Dunn, Strecker, Davies and others mentioned above (notes 27–28). cf. A. Pitta, *Disposizione e messaggio della Lettera ai Galati: analisi retorico-letteraria*, Rome 1992. We shall return to this question later in this chapter (cf. pp. 206–208).

the 'Protestant principle' – in terms relevant and intelligible to modern man.[57] Like Bultmann, he begins with man's concrete sinful situation. To analyze it he characteristically employs his 'method of correlation' according to which Christian 'symbols' or doctrines are applied to concrete human situations with a view to understanding and resolving them.[58] In the nineteenth century, Tillich says, man's 'sin' was idealism, in the twentieth it is (or better it was, for he wrote on the subject in 1924) doubt (*Zweifel*) and despair. The 'symbol' or doctrine of 'justification by faith', as a definitive liberation from such a situation, lies therefore at the heart of the Christian message, insofar as it addresses a genuine human need: it means that man must learn *to accept that he is accepted* (or justified), *despite being unacceptable* (a sinner). His *acceptance of doubt* is identified with the 'faith' required in order to be 'justified'. The following text, from his work The *Protestant Era*, describes a kind of *Turmerlebnis* Tillich experienced in his early life, and offers a graphic and genuinely 'Lutheran' picture of the doctrine of justification:

> The step I myself made in those years [under Kähler and others] was the insight that the principle of justification through faith refers not only to the religious-ethical but also to the *religious-intellectual life*. Not only he who is in sin but also he who is in doubt is justified through faith. The situation of doubt, even doubt about God, need not separate us from God. There is faith in every serious doubt, namely the faith in the truth as such, even if the only truth we can express is our lack of truth. But if this is experienced in its depth and as an ultimate concern, the divine is present; and he who doubts in such an attitude is 'justified' in his thinking . . . You cannot reach God by the work of right thinking or by a sacrifice of the intellect or by a submission to strange authorities, such as the doctrines of the Church and the Bible . . . Neither works of piety nor works of morality nor works of the intellect establish unity with God. They follow from this unity, but they do not make it.

---

57 Cf. his early lecture entitled 'Justification and Doubt': P. Tillich, 'Rechtfertigung und Zweifel', from *Vorträge der theologischen Konferenz zu Gießen* (1924), in *Gesammelte Werke*, Stuttgart 1970, vol. 8, pp. 85–100; and also: 'The Protestant Message and the Man of Today', in *The Protestant Era*, London 1951, pp. 189–204; ' "You are accepted" ', in *The Shaking of the Foundations*, Harmondsworth 1969, pp. 153–163. On Tillich's doctrine of justification, cf. V. Subilia, *La giustificazione per fede* . . . , op. cit., pp. 183–188; C.J. Peter, 'Justification by Faith and the Need for Another Critical Principle', in H.G. Anderson et al. (eds.), *Justification by Faith* (Lutherans and Catholics in Dialogue VII), Minneapolis 1985, pp. 304–315; A.E. McGrath, *Iustitia Dei* . . . , op. cit., vol. 2, p. 187; C.E. Braaten, *Justification* . . . , op. cit., pp. 41–62.   58 'In using the method of correlation, systematic theology proceeds in the following way: it makes an analysis of the human situation out of which existential situations arise, and it demonstrates that the symbols used in the Christian message are the answer to these questions' (P. Tillich, *Systematic Theology*, vol. 1, Chicago 1951, p. 70). For a clear presentation and critique of P. Tillich's philosophical and theological construct, cf. J.L. Illanes, 'Teología Sistemática de Paul Tillich', in *Scripta Theologica* 6 (1974) 711–754.

They even prevent it if you try to reach it through them. But just as you are justified as a *sinner* (though unjust, you are just), so in the status of *doubt* you are in the status of truth . . . It is this radical and universal interpretation of justification through faith which has made me a conscious Protestant.[59]

In reflecting on justification in the context of man's interiority and personal experience, on the face of things Tillich offers, not unlike Bultmann, an somewhat individualistic rendering of Luther's doctrine of justification. However, this is not the whole truth. Tillich himself admitted that Protestantism in general, and its understanding of the doctrine of justification in particular, has historically tended towards an excessive interiorizing of the Christian message based on the personal relationship between God and the soul, and as such carries historical responsibility for the non-Christian character of modern social ethics.[60] However, Tillich's flight from excessive interiorizing and individualism, instead of being directed towards a renewed ecclesiology or appreciation of the Christian's belongingness to the body of Christ and the inter-personal character of salvation, tends more towards the terrain of social ethical responsibility, of a somewhat secularized commitment to the betterment of the world.

The subordinate and even problematic rôle of ecclesiology in Tillich may be seen in the fact that for him the doctrine of justification by faith alone is not merely one doctrine among many others; it is in a true sense a *principle*, the *Protestant* principle, which remains and should remain in perpetual dialectic tension with what he terms the 'Catholic substance', that is by opposing any identification of 'our ultimate concerns' with the Church's creations.[61] Among the latter, surprisingly, he includes the Scriptures, since their witness is 'also a conditioned expression of their own spirituality'.[62] The 'exclusive monotheism' of Israel, indicating as it does that Yahweh will not to tolerate rivals of any kind, is, like the 'Protestant principle', the prophetic principle which refuses to accept any kind of 'self-absolutizing and consequently demonically distorted church'.[63] The unconditional acceptance of the Church's authority which is demanded of Catholics offers, in Tillich's view, a clear case to which the 'Protestant principle' of the unconditionality of divine acceptance of the sinner must be applied.[64]

In fact, Tillich's understanding of the Church, and his insistence on its essential relativity and temporality is but a mirror of his Christology. Christ, for Tillich as for Bultmann, is of interest for what he means or signifies, not so much for what he is. Christ is 'the man who represents before those who live under the condition of existence what man is essentially'.[65] As a result, the living or visible body of Christ, the Church, is little more than the concrete and historically-conditioned product or

59 P. Tillich, *The Protestant Era* . . . , op. cit., pp. xiv-xv.   60 Cf. ibid., p. 204.   61 Cf. P. Tillich, *Systematic Theology*, vol. 1, op. cit., p. 42.   62 Ibid., pp. 42f.   63 Ibid., p. 252.   64 P. Tillich, *Systematic Theology*, vol. 3, Chicago 1963, pp. 238ff.   65 P. Tillich, *Systematic Theology*, vol. 2, Chicago 1957, p. 129.

aggregate of 'Christians', that is, of those who have found the true meaning and value of their lives through a faith-encounter with Christ. In other words, 'the Church' is the same thing as 'Christianity'. At heart, this understanding in turn reflects an essential incompatibility, in Tillich's mind, between the eternal fixity of the divine, and the historical concreteness of creatures (and the Church). 'It is through the negation, the sacrifice of the concrete-historical figure, both of Christ and of the Church, that Christianity can and must justify its pretension of being the definitive revelation'.[66]

3. *Justification as a theological hermeneutical principle in G. Ebeling*

Like Bultmann and Tillich before him, Gerhard Ebeling insists that the concept of justification must be shown to have an essential connection with human existence.[67] At justification a fundamental change takes place in man, a transfer from a state of non-existence (*Nichtsein*) to one of true existence (*Sein*). Though Ebeling does not consider himself either a philosopher or a biblical exegete, this transformation of man is to be understood in continuity with the existential analysis of Heidegger and Bultmann, that is, as a conversion from 'inauthentic' to 'authentic' existence,[68] based on the direct saving encounter with God's own word. He has consistently attempted to analyze and present the authentic, perennial thought of Luther. In fact Ebeling's work in the main deals with the question of theological hermeneutics or interpretation.

'Scripture interprets itself' Ebeling insists constantly that Luther's true understanding of the doctrine of justification goes far beyond a mere description of God's saving action in Christ and all this implies from an anthropological standpoint. 'Jus-

66 P. Tillich, *Systematic Theology*, vol. 1, op. cit., pp. 176f. Cf. J.L. Illanes, 'Teología Sistemática de Paul Tillich', op. cit., pp. 741ff. 67 G. Ebeling's principal works are *Evangelische Evangelienauslegung. Eine Untersuchung zu Luthers Hermeneutik*, Darmstadt 1962; *Das Wesen des christlichen Glaubens*, Tübingen 1959; *Wort und Glaube*, 2 vols, Tübingen 1960/69; *Theologie und Verkündigung*, Tübingen 1963; *Luther, Einführung in sein Denken*, Tübingen 1964; *Wort Gottes und Tradition: Studien zu einer Hermeneutik der Konfessionen*, Göttingen 1964; *Lutherstudien*, vol. 1, Tübingen 1971; *Einführung in die theologische Sprachlehre*, Tübingen 1971; *Dogmatik des christlichen Glaubens*, 3 vols, Tübingen 1979, especially vol. 3. Cf. in particular his article on Luther's hermeneutical revolution, 'Die Anfänge von Luthers Hermeneutik', in *Zeitschrift für Theologie und Kirche* 48 (1951) 172–230; summarized in English as: 'The New Hermeneutics and the young Luther', in *Theology Today* 21 (1964) 34–46. On his application of the doctrine of justification as a hermeneutical principle, cf. J.S. Preus, *From Shadow to Promise*, Cambridge (Mass.) 1969; P. Grech, 'La nuova ermeneutica: Fuchs e Ebeling', in Associazione Biblica Italiana, *Esegesi ed ermeneutica. Atti della XXI Settimana Biblica*, Brescia 1972, pp. 71–90; R. Marlé, *Parler de Dieu aujourd'hui. La théologie herméneutique de G. Ebeling*, Paris 1975, which we have drawn on considerably; M. Ruokanen, *Hermeneutics as an Ecumenical Method in the Theology of Gerhard Ebeling*, Helsinki 1982; W.G. Jeanrond, 'La nouvelle herméneutique', in *Introduction à l'herméneutique théologique*, Paris 1995, pp. 208–223. 68 Cf. P. Grech, op. cit., pp. 77–86.

tification', more than to dogmatic theology, belongs to fundamental theology; more than a *doctrine*, it is a *message*, more than a *content*, a *method*,[69] expressing the intrinsic link between saying and doing, between God's word and its saving effects. Justification for Luther thus became, according to Ebeling, a kind of *hermeneutical principle*[70] for properly interpreting the word of God, and for clarifying and criticizing the life and practice of the Church.

It should be stated from the beginning that for Ebeling the doctrine of justification is to be considered as a hermeneutical principle *at a strictly theological level*. In other words, justification as a hermeneutical principle has nothing whatever to do with some kind of abstract rule or philosophical system which measures *from outside* the reality of God's action in Christ, and interprets the true meaning of Scripture accordingly. He comments frequently on Luther's notion of 'Scriptura sacra sui ipsius interpres',[71] 'Holy Scripture interprets itself'; this phrase is exactly equivalent to and derived from the notion that Christ is present and acts *by himself*, and by himself *alone*. 'The history of Christ incarnate *is not repeated or duplicated by a cultual method* (a ministerial act, having its own power), nor is it actualized by a spiritualizing interpretation, but is only received in the very movement by which it makes itself present to the one who receives it in faith'.[72] And this is precisely what 'justification' by 'faith alone' means. 'The representation of the truth of God and of his grace, in Christ as well as in the Scriptures, is effected always in secret, not in seeing, but in hearing, in readiness to obey: in other words, by "faith alone" '.[73]

Ebeling's insistence on the 'justification by faith alone' as a strictly *theological* hermeneutic corresponds exactly to Luther's renowned 'sola' (*solus Christus, sola gratia, sola fides, sola scriptura*),[74] which means: nothing need be *added* to Christ, to grace, to faith, to Scripture, just as nothing need be *added* to God. Ebeling's hermeneutic intends to be strictly 'theological' in the sense that if it were anything other than theological, if it tried for example to get a vantage point on Christ outside Christ, or on Scripture outside Scripture, no longer would we have *solus Christus, sola scriptura*, etc. Luther would say that 'Scripture should not be interpreted except in the sense that man is nothing and Christ everything (*quod homo nihil sit, et solus Christus omnia*)'.[75] In Marlé's words, for Ebeling 'the fault of traditional hermeneutics as well as modern hermeneutics, whether humanistic or enlightened,

---

69 Ebeling intends to examine 'how content shapes method and how, at the same time, this method shows up this content' (*Evangelische Evangelienauslegung* . . . , op. cit., p. 359).   70 'Luther became a Reformer because of a new hermeneutics' (K. Bauer, cited by G. Ebeling, *Lutherstudien* . . . , op. cit., vol. 1, p. 5).   71 M. Luther, *Assertio omnium articulorum M. Lutheri per bullam Leonis X* (1520: WA 7: 97; 99). Cf. G. Ebeling, *Evangelische Evangelienauslegung* . . . , op. cit., pp. 297f. On this text, cf. W. Mostert, 'Scriptura sacra sui ipsius interpres. Bermerkungen zum Verständnis der Heiligen Schrift bei Luther', in *Lutherjahrbuch* 46 (1979) 60–96.   72 G. Ebeling, *Evangelische Evangelienauslegung* . . . , op. cit., p. 341f. Emphasis added.   73 R. Marlé, *Parler de Dieu aujourd'hui* . . . , op. cit., p. 52. Emphasis added.   74 Cf. especially G. Ebeling, ' "Sola scriptura" und das Problem der Tradition', in *Wort Gottes und Tradition* . . . , op. cit., pp. 91–143.   75 Cit., in G. Ebeling, *Evangelische Evangelienauslegung* . . . , op. cit., p. 454.

is not having seen, or not having dared to recognize the hidden character of revelation, of having wished to penetrate into the mystery by ways other than faith, of having wished to do other than to testify to this hidden character, that is, "to have wished that man would be something alongside Christ" '.[76]

Whether Christians have or have not seriously distorted the gospel of Jesus Christ by applying to it interpretative categories incompatible with its inner truth and power, as Ebeling holds, remains to be seen. But the point being made is undoubtedly a valid one. After all, the power of the Gospel, God's own definitive word in Christ, 'is living and active, sharper than any two-edged sword, piercing to the division of soul and spirit, of joints and marrow, and discerning the thoughts and intentions of the heart' (Heb 4:12). Thus, just as creation adds nothing to God, man and the Church add nothing to Christ, human response nothing to grace and faith.

Justification by faith as the hermeneutical principle Ebeling's reflection on the doctrine of justification as a hermeneutical principle is to be found in a section of his *Lutherstudien* dedicated to the Reformer's understanding of the nature of theology.[77] In the latter's 1532 *Enarratio* on Psalm *Miserere* we can read the following dense text: 'The knowledge of God and man is divine wisdom, it is theological in the proper sense. It is the knowledge of God and of man that relates both to the justifying God and to man the sinner, in such a way that the subject of theology is both man guilty and lost, and God who justifies or saves'.[78]

The object of theology for Luther is 'God and man', God and man *in their mutual relationship*. Of course, this is quite acceptable, although traditionally, one might have said that the object of theology is God, and *besides*, God in his relationship with man. The subject of theology for Luther is *also* God and man. This of course is a perfectly acceptable way of speaking: the theologian is one who partakes through faith in God's own knowledge.[79] Here, Luther undoubtedly takes a strictly 'economic' view of God and his saving action, reflecting only on what God does and says about himself and his saving action *insofar as this affects us*, thus virtually identifying theology with soteriology. And the reason he does so is as clear as it is significant: man *is* a sinner; God *is* a 'justifier' or saviour of man the sinner. In other words theology in its object and subject is totally determined and defined by the reality of

---

76 R. Marlé, *Parler de Dieu aujourd'hui* . . . , op. cit., p. 57. 77 For Ebeling's explicit reflection on 'justification' as a hermeneutical principle for theology and the life of the Church in Ebeling, cf. especially his *Lutherstudien*, vol. 1, Tübingen 1971, pp. 260–272, and also *Das Wesen des christlichen Glaubens* . . . , op. cit., pp. 162f. 78 'Cognitio dei et hominis est sapientia divina et proprie theologica. Et ita cognitio dei et hominis, ut referatur tandem ad deum iustificantem et hominem peccatorem, ut proprie sit subiectum Theologiae homo reus et perditus et deus iustificans et salvator. Quicquid extra hoc subiectum in theologia quaeritur aut disputatur, est error et venenum' (M. Luther, *Enarratio in Ps. 51* (WA 40/2: 328), cit. by G. Ebeling, *Lutherstudien* . . . , op. cit., vol. 1, p. 221). 79 'Sacra doctrina est scientia quia procedit ex principiis notis lumine superioris scientiae, quae scilicet est scientia Dei et beatorum' (Thomas Aquinas, *Summa Theologiae* I, q. 1, a.2, c.); 'sacra doctrina [est] velut quaedam impressio divinae scientiae, quae est una et simplex omnium' (ibid., a. 3, ad 2).

both man's sinfulness and God's active and merciful 'will-to-save', that is, by a proper understanding of the real relationship between God and man. Man's knowledge of God is completely determined by what he is (a sinner); and yet his knowledge of what he is (a sinner) is made known to him by what God does for him (saving, justifying). In the same *Ennaratio* on the Psalm *Miserere* Luther had insisted: 'we are not dealing here with the philosophical knowledge of man, which defines man as a rational animal and so forth. Such things are for science to discuss, not for theology. So a jurist speaks of man as an owner and master of property, and a physician speaks of man as healthy or sick. But a theologian discusses man as a sinner. In theology, this is the essence of man. The theologian is concerned that man become aware of this nature of his, corrupted by sins'.[80]

Sola experientia fit Theologum, Luther said.[81] And in Ebeling's terms, man's knowledge of himself, *cognitio hominis*, is necessarily a *cognitio peccati*, a knowledge of sin and under sin, whereas his knowledge of God, *cognitio Dei*, is a *cognitio gratiae*,[82] a knowledge of grace and under grace. The two forms of knowledge, human (*cognitio peccati*) and divine (*cognitio gratiae*), correspond to Luther's distinction between law and gospel.[83] 'What he [Luther] calls *cognitio hominis* is a particular modality of *cognitio Dei et hominis*, that is, a *cognitio* under the law; and what he terms *cognitio Dei* is likewise a specific modality of the *cognitio Dei et hominis*, this time under the gospel'.[84]

Hence for Ebeling

> what Luther takes as the *subjectum theologiae*, the *cognitio Dei et hominis*, understood as a concentration on *deus iustificans* and *homo peccator*, takes on, in his way of understanding things, the value of a criterion for authenticating every theological statement. It is on this very point that theology is distinguished from all other sciences, insofar as they visualize man under a particular aspect of his existence. Theology, conversely, deals with the very existence of man, with his fundamental situation as *homo peccator*, not therefore with what might be considered a partial factor within the limits of this life, but with the previous sign which affects it all . . . Whatever is not determined by this fundamental principle is vain wandering, even if it is presented as theology.[85]

The fact that one speaks 'of God' religiously, according to Ebeling, provides no guarantee that one is speaking in a truly theological fashion. If man does not speak of God while admitting that he is a sinner, his *cognitio Dei* may well not be a *cognitio*

---

80 M. Luther, *Enarratio in Ps. 51* (WA 40/2: 327).   81 M. Luther (WA *Tischreden* 1: 16).   82 Cf. G. Ebeling, *Lutherstudien* . . . op. cit., vol. 1, p. 260. Ebeling notes how L. Feuerbach makes specific mention of Luther (and not so much of Calvin and Zwingli) in his doctrine of 'God' as an *imago hominis*, projection of man's situation and necessities (cf. Luther, *Einführung* . . . , op. cit., p. 290).   83 Cf. *Lutherstudien* . . . , op. cit., vol. 1, pp. 261f.   84 Ibid., p. 270.   85 Ibid., p. 265.

proprie theologica.[86] 'The absolutely critical theological criterion for Luther is the knowledge of the situation of man before God.'[87]

Understandably, therefore, for Ebeling, 'Luther does not take the theme of *justificatio* as an optional theological topic alongside others; it is, rather, as it were, *the* "place" for speaking theologically in general, that is, the place where man is situated when talking about God, before God (*coram Deo*). And conforming to reality surely means to allow the *situation* of the word become the criterion of verification for the word, especially since it is God's own word . . . This is not whatever situation, but *the* situation of man . . . The relationship between *homo reus et perditus* and *deus iustificans vel salvator* belongs to fundamental theology.'[88]

In sum, 'justification' as the fundamental hermeneutical principle of Christian life offers a principle of discernment which 'operates the deepest possible interpenetration between the general experience man makes of himself and Christian knowledge of God.'[89] Within this context, man is no longer, as Luther would have said, a *peccator insensatus*, but rather a *peccator sentiens*.[90]

Let us see how Ebeling applies the doctrine of justification to different situations in the life of the Church and of Christianity in general.

Applying 'justification' as a hermeneutical principle: law and gospel The fundamental hermeneutical principle of 'justification' finds many expressions and applications in Christian theology and life.

At heart, it is expressed as a criterion for discerning, in the ambit of theology, personal and ecclesial Christian life, between 'letter' and 'spirit',[91] and, what comes to the same thing,[92] between 'law' (*cognitio hominis* as a *cognitio peccati*) and 'gospel' (*cognitio Dei* as a *cognitio gratiae*). Neither distinction should to be taken in a formal or metaphysical sense, but in an existential and methodological one, reflecting two radically different ways of living *coram Deo*.[93]

The proper function of the doctrine of justification is one of giving true meaning to all other doctrines. But it can only be understood as Luther saw it if it is identified with what is implied in the fundamental biblical distinction between 'law' and 'gospel' as the basic guiding principle of theological thought, and therefore as

86 Cf. ibid., pp. 265f.   87 Ibid., p. 266.   88 Ibid. On the centrality of the term 'coram' (especially *coram Deo, coram mundo*) in Luther, cf. ibid., pp. 218–230, and also R. Marlé, *Parler de Dieu aujourd'hui* . . . , op. cit., pp. 60-66.   89 G. Ebeling, *Lutherstudien* . . . , op. cit., vol. I, p. 296.   90 Cf. ibid.   91 Luther reflects on a very wide variety of terms running parallel to 'letter' and 'spirit'. He posits an irreducible opposition of the 'spiritualia' to the 'carnalia', the 'visibilia', to the 'invisibilia', the 'intelligibilia' to the 'sensibilia', the 'abscondita' to the 'manifesta', the 'interiora' to the 'exteriora', the 'divina' to the 'humana', the 'coelestia' to the 'terrena', the 'aeterna' to the 'temporalia', the 'futura' to the 'praesentia', etc. (cf. G. Ebeling, *Lutherstudien* . . . , op. cit., vol. I, p. 18; 20; 27; 37 f.; R. Marlé, *Parler de Dieu aujourd'hui* . . . , op. cit., p. 37). Cf. also Ebeling's 'New Hermeneutics and the Early Luther', op. cit., pp. 41–43.   92 The distinction between letter and spirit in a strict sense is identical to the distinction between law and gospel (cf. G. Ebeling, *Luther. Einführung* . . . , op. cit., p. 127).   93 Cf. R. Marlé, *Parler de Dieu aujourd'hui* . . . , op. cit., p. 37f.

the decisive standard of theological judgement.[94] In fact, the primary basis for understanding all points related to justification, whether systematic or practical, whether anthropological or ecclesiological, is a proper understanding of the relationship between 'law' and 'gospel', because this distinction, considered by Luther 'the greatest intuition of Christianity',[95] best expresses the abyss that exists between the merciful Creator and the sinful creature, the true relationship between God and man in the context of salvation,[96] and is thus the very core of theological epistemology.

In brief terms, it could be said that *under the law* (that is, outside or 'before' salvation or justification, man 'on his own'), humans are obliged to complete obedience, they experience nothing but failure, and do not achieve the expected, self-made, perfection they strive after. Under the law, man's perversion 'transforms all his deeds into means of self-assertion', of self-justification, 'being his own creator', 'resistance to one's own creatureliness', 'self-establishment and self-assertion as the driving force of action', 'fulfilling the will of God by one's own means'.[97]

Conversely, *under the gospel* (being saved and justified), 'man is *promised* that Christ has died for him and taken on his guilt'. In God's sight, 'Christ's righteousness becomes his own'; 'the believer is transplanted from himself into Christ . . . so that Christ himself becomes the new being of the sinner'. He is 'justified in his relationship to God and is a sinner according to his own quality (*simul iustus et peccator*)'. Faith, which effects this transplantation into Christ, 'fills man with an unconditioned trust in the grace of God', and places him on the way to sanctification, without, however requiring any 'anxious observation of his own progress or failure because his good standing before God is grounded in the righteousness of Christ'.[98]

Applying 'justification' as a hermeneutical principle: Christ and the Church; Scripture
The principal area for practical application of the doctrine of justification as a hermeneutical principle is the life of the Church, specifically in respect of its institutional relationship with Christ, and its rôle in the interpretation of Scripture.

Ebeling's criticism of what he sees to be an excess of institutionalism in the Catholic Church is particularly noticeable in his earlier works. He said that 'the history of Christ incarnate is not repeated by a cultual method (a ministerial act, having its own power), nor actualized by a spiritualizing interpretation, but *only received in the very movement by which it makes itself present to the one who receives it in faith*'.[99] This notion of the singularity, inimitability and once-and-for-all character

94 G. Ebeling, *Einführung* . . . , op. cit., p. 126.   95 M. Luther, *Serm. in Gal. 3*,1 (WA 36, 9, 28–29). Cf. *Formula Concordiae: Solida Declaratio 5*: 27, in T.G. Tappert et al. (eds.), *The Book of Concord*, op. cit., p. 563.   96 Cf. also G.O. Forde, 'Forensic Justification and Law in Lutheran Theology', in H.G. Anderson et al. (eds.), *Justification by faith (Lutherans and Catholics in Dialogue*, VII) . . . , op. cit., pp. 278–303. Cf. also Forde's earlier work *The Law-Gospel Debate: an interpretation of its historical development*, Minneapolis 1969.   97 Cf. D. Lange et al., 'An Opinion on "The Condemnations of the Reformation Era". Part One: Justification', op. cit., p. 16.   98 Ibid., pp. 17f.   99 G. Ebeling, *Evangelische Evangelienauslegung* . . . , op. cit., p. 341f. Emphasis added. The sacra-

of Christ's saving action is often termed by Ebeling the 'sacramentality of the history of Christ'. And he notes: 'if the unique sacramental meaning of the cross of Christ, in its "once and for all" character is denied, then Christ is no longer present.'[100]

For Catholics, as for Augustine, the fundamental way in which the mystery of God in Christ is present is in the *Church itself*, Ebeling says, and the result is that 'Christ is not present in spirit, with the testimony he gives, but only by the presence of the institutional, sacramental Church which is the Church of Rome'.[101] The Catholic Church has acted in this way, he claims, by *adding* to the work of Christ the Mass, the merits of the saints, the intercession of the Blessed Virgin. According to Marlé, paraphrasing Ebeling, 'in Christ's place, disguising him as it were, have been put human works, such as the reproduction of the sacrifice of the cross, the imitation of his abasement with monastic humility, contact with relics, holy places, and the like.'[102]

What happens in relation to the Church also happens in the interpretation of Scripture. Ebeling says that for Luther 'the bearer of the Holy Spirit is not the Church in its hierarchical structure, the Church as a magnificent historical entity, but Scripture as a testimony of the cross of Christ',[103] pure Scripture, without protection, without defence, under the *forma crucis*. For Luther, he says, Scripture stands in need of interpretation not because it is obscure, but rather that it begins to becomes obscure because it is interpreted and domesticated by the Church.[104]

Perhaps few contemporary authors have given to the fundamental tenets of Luther's doctrine, *solus Christus, sola fides, sola Scriptura*, the sense of freshness and authenticity that Ebeling has given them. In doing so he has paid signal service to the modern debate, showing that for Luther 'justification' is more a message than a systematic doctrine, more an authenticating criterion than an explanation of content. As with Bultmann and Tillich, however, it will still have to be seen how fully his vision respects the integrity of Christian doctrine, especially in respect of Christology and ecclesiology.[105]

---

mental significance of the Church is where Ebeling sees the most decisive difference between Lutherans and Catholics. cf. his 'Worthafte und sakramentale Existenz. Ein Beitrag zum Unterscheid zwischer den Konfessionen', in *Wort Gottes und Tradition* . . . , op. cit., pp. 197ff., and *Dogmatik des christlichen Glaubens* . . . , op. cit., vol. 3, pp. 314ff. Cf. P. O'Callaghan, 'The Mediation of Justification and the justification of Mediation. Report of the Lutheran/Catholic Dialogue: "Church and Justification: Understanding the Church in the Light of the Doctrine of Justification" (1993)', op. cit., especially pp. 180–184.   **100** G. Ebeling, *Evangelische Evangelienauslegung* . . . , op. cit., p. 291. According to Ebeling, 'the sacramental perspective is the only way of avoiding [Christianity being considered] on the one hand a past history, simply exemplary in character (speculatively or morally) and, on the other, a history of the works of holiness, where sacraments soon become instruments' (R. Marlé, *Parler de Dieu aujourd'hui* . . . , op. cit., p. 55).   **101** G. Ebeling, *Evangelische Evangelienauslegung* . . . , op. cit., p. 290.   **102** R. Marlé, *Parler de Dieu aujourd'hui* . . . , op. cit., p. 40.   **103** G. Ebeling, *Evangelische Evangelienauslegung* . . . , op. cit., p. 295. Luther says: 'Verbum Dei supra Ecclesiam est incomparabiliter, in quo nihil statuere, ordinare, facere, sed tantum statui, ordinari, fieri habet, tanquam creatura' (cit. in ibid.).   **104** Cf. ibid., p. 296. Cf. also ibid., p. 325 on Luther's defence of Scripture's natural clarity against Erasmus.   **105** We will return to Ebeling's doctrine later on in this chapter (cf. pp. 203–205).

4. *Man's 'search for a gracious God'*

Bultmann's, Tillich's and Ebeling's restatements of Lutheran doctrine of 'justification of the sinner by faith alone' undoubtedly go the existential heart of Luther's
own vision. All three speak in unequivocal terms of the doctrine of justification as a
kind of interpretative principle: Bultmann for demythologizing Scripture;[106] Tillich
as the 'Protestant principle' for finding the true Christ and defining authentic Christianity;[107] Ebeling, as a definitive *theological* hermeneutic for interpreting Scripture
and for examining and judging the life of the Church. All three wish to initiate their
reflection with the driving conviction of *solus Christus, sola fides, sola Scriptura*. However, in spite of their best intentions, it would seem that two traits run through their
widely diversified reflections: firstly, the presence of a *Vorverständnis* or pre-com-
prehension determined as much by modern philosophical systems, in which
Heidegger and Gadamer figure significantly, as by Christian Revelation;[108] and secondly an undoing of the essential linkup between God's action in Christ and the
action of the Church institutional, to a extent, in all probability, not envisaged by
Luther himself.

The reflection undertaken in modern times to the doctrine of justification offers
the opportunity of asking two questions, one fundamental, the other specific. The
fundamental question is this: where does man's search for Christian salvation or authenticity (being 'justified by faith alone', 'finding a gracious God') actually lead
him? Three replies could be made. His search may turn him in on himself, on his
interiority and spiritual experience; it may direct him towards the world and its
needs and challenges; it may lead him towards the Church as the historical space in
which the divine and risen Christ lives and acts. And *the specific question* is as follows: are these three quests compatible with one another or not? In other words, is
it possible for a Christian to live at one and the same time a life of integrated personal, social and ecclesial fulness? Or are these ways, in spite of a certain common
spirit, fundamentally exclusive of one another?

We have just seen that several Protestant authors throughout this century, while
attempting to reinterpret the doctrine of justification 'by faith alone' in such a way
as to make it more meaningful to the times we live in, did not quite manage to get it
out of the individualistic frame of mind centered on personal works that Lutheranism locked it up in. The following sections, respectively on Paul's own understand-

---

106 'Demythologizing is the radical application of the doctrine of justification by faith to the
sphere of knowledge and thought' (R. Bultmann, *Jesus Christ and Mythology*, London 1960, p. 84).
107 'By the power of what reality does the Protestant principle (namely, justification by faith alone)
exercise its criticism? There must be such a reality, since the Protestant principle is not mere
negation . . . The answer is: in the power of the New Being that is manifest in Jesus as the Christ.
Here the Protestant principle comes to an end. Here is the bedrock on which it stands and which
is not subject to its criticism. Here is the sacramental foundation of Protestantism, of the Protestant principle, and of the Protestant reality.' (P. Tillich, *The Protestant Era. . .* , op. cit., p. xxiii).
108 Cf. P. Grech, 'La nuova ermeneutica: Fuchs e Ebeling', op. cit., pp. 71–90.

ing of 'justification by faith alone, that is, without works' and on the full meaning of
the Pauline key notion 'the righteousness of God' will show how, in recent times,
the social and ecclesiological side of justification has been coming to the fore anew,
and how a properly understood ecclesiological contextualizing of the doctrine of
justification offers promising prospects for considering centuries-old differences
between Catholics and Lutherans in a new light.

PAUL AND LUTHER ON 'JUSTIFICATION BY FAITH ALONE'

Luther consistently envisaged his new perception of the Gospel, centered on the
doctrine of justification by faith, in terms of a repristination or rediscovery of St.
Paul's fundamental and determinative intuition. The context of his revolution constituted, as he saw it, an almost exact repetition of the situation Paul found himself
in when faced with the Judaizing movement within nascent Christianity. He applied the Pauline tension between 'faith' and 'works' (as expressed especially in
Galatians and Romans)[109] to the tension he perceived to exist between his personal
situation as a conscience-smitten monk seeking a merciful God, and the medieval
Church enslaved, as he saw it, to a religion of works far removed from the original
Gospel message of evangelical simplicity and freedom. The comparison Luther made
between the two historical situations, in spite of obvious religious and cultural differences that not even he denied, is highly significant. If Luther's contention was
true, his would be an epoch-making rediscovery of authentic Christianity, and by
insisting on 'justification by faith alone' he would be paying signal service to the
Church's evangelizing mission. His doctrine, as a re-expression of Paul's teaching,
would necessarily constitute a living statement of the permanent and perennial core
of Christian life and doctrine. And on the same account, the medieval Church Luther
encountered could well be accused of having severely prejudiced, at least in practice, the core belief of Christians, that God in his mercy had sent his only Son to
save his people from their sins.

However, in attempting to re-present authentic Christian teaching in terms of
the doctrine of justification by faith, Luther made two assumptions, both of which
were considerably mistaken.[110]

109 On the tension between the negative vision of the law in Galatians, and the positive one in
Romans, cf. J.W. Drane, *Paul, Libertine or Legalist? A Study in the Theology of the Major Pauline
Epistles*, London 1975, pp. 5 f.; 132–136; J. Gnilka, 'La dottrina paolina della giustificazione:
legge, giustificazione, fede', in *Annales Theologici* 10 (1996) 93–108, especially p. 94. 110 On
Paul's understanding of justification and the law, bibliography is very ample. I have drawn espe-
cially the ground-breaking work of E.P. Sanders, *Paul and Palestinian Judaism*, London 1977,
already cited, his *Paul, the Law, and the Jewish People*, Philadelphia 1983, and also J.D.G. Dunn,
Jesus, Paul and the Law: studies in Mark and Galatians, London 1990, especially his essays entitled
'The New Perspective on Paul', in ibid., pp. 183–206 and 'Works of the Law and the Curse of the
Law', in ibid., pp. 215–236; cf. also Dunn's popularized work with A.M. Suggate, *The Justice of
God. A Fresh Look at the Old Doctrine of Justification*, Carlisle 1993, pp. 7–48.

Paul's conversion and Luther's   Firstly, Luther took it for granted that Paul underwent more or less the *same conversion experience* that he (Luther) had undergone
before discovering the true meaning of *iustitia Dei*, the 'righteousness of God'. Before encountering Christ on the road to Damascus, Paul had, in Luther's mind,
suffered long with a distressed conscience. 'Wretched man that I am! Who will
deliver me from this body of death?' (Rom 7:24). The anguished confession contained in Romans 7 has been commonly applied by Lutherans to Paul's situation
before his conversion.[111] However, contemporary biblical exegesis is quite contented
to apply this passage from Romans to the situation of the converted Christian,[112]
and does not even exclude the possibility that for Paul it is not entirely autobiographical.[113]

And the fact is that elsewhere Paul does explicitly describe his personal situation
and mind-frame before conversion took place. In the letter to the Philippians he
boasts that he was 'blameless as regards righteousness within the law' (Phil 3:6); to
the Galatians he exclaimed he 'advanced in Judaism beyond many of my own contemporaries, so exceedingly zealous was I' (Gal 1:14). There is no reason to think
that Paul was riddled with anxiety and scruples before encountering the Risen Lord
Jesus on the road to Damascus. It is therefore fair to say that 'the Protestant reading
of Paul was a reading back of Luther's own experience into Paul. It was a retrojection
back into Paul's first-century self-testimony of what Krister Stendahl has called
"the introspective conscience of the West." '[114] In spite of Stendahl's thesis being
vigorously rejected by authors such as E. Käsemann and considered as a serious
threat to Protestantism,[115] it has come to be widely accepted nowadays. 'We can
safely subscribe to the now common opinion that Paul's critique of the law was not
born out of any personal moral difficulties. Paul was no Luther before Luther.'[116]

111 On this position the important study of K. Stendahl ('The Apostle Paul and the Introspective
Conscience of the West', in *Harvard Theological Review* 56 (1963) 199–215) should be taken into
account. This essay is reprinted in K. Stendahl, *Paul among Jews and Gentiles and other essays*,
Philadelphia 1987, pp. 78–96.   112 For a complete overview of the different positions, cf. J.D.G.
Dunn, *Romans* (Word Biblical Commentary 38), Dallas 1988, pp. 374–413, especially pp. 404ff.   113
For a comprehensive overview of the bibliography on the matter, cf. E.P. Sanders, *Paul . . .*, op.
cit., pp. 443; 479 (in notes). 'The fact that Paul can express the pathos of life under the law as seen
through Christian eyes does not mean that he had himself experienced frustration with the law
before his own conversion' (ibid., p. 443, note 4).   114 J.D.G. Dunn and A.M. Suggate, *The
Justice of God . . .*, op. cit., p. 14.   115 Cf. E. Käsemann, *Perspectives on Paul*, Philadelphia 1971,
pp. 60–78 (original 1969). Stendahl's later, more extensive, treatment of the question is to be found
in his *Paul among Jews and Gentiles . . .*, op. cit., pp. 1–77, and his reply to Käsemann in ibid., pp.
129–133. Käsemann in fact holds to an unswervingly Lutheran view of justification by faith alone:
'the true adversary of Paul is the pious Jew... as the realization of the religious man' ('Paul and
Israel', in *New Testament Questions of Today*, London 1969, pp. 183–187, here p. 184).   116 H.
Räisänen, *Paul and the Law*, Tübingen 1983, p. 231. 'Luther's doctrine of justification is not the
Pauline one' (W. Heitmüller, *Luthers Stellung in der Religionsgeschichte des Christentums*, Marburg
1917, p. 19). 'It is obvious that the difficulty of Luther is not that of Paul' (O. Kuss, *Der Römerbrief*,
Regensburg 1957, p. 134). 'In no case can we any longer take as obvious that Luther can be made
equal with Paul, nor rest on such a presupposition, nor much less can we explain Paul with Luther

Judaism in the time of nascent Christianity   In the second place, Luther took it for granted that the situation of the medieval Church was very similar to that of Judaism in the time of Paul, in that one and the other were steeped in a legalistic religious mentality based on an exacting performance of works and obtaining of merits.[117] Whether Luther's appraisal of medieval Christianity was accurate on a global scale need not be looked into at the present moment, although his judgement on the matter was, doubtless, to some degree simplistic. But certainly the Reformer was convinced, at least on the basis Paul's own testimony, that Judaism of the first decades of the Christian era was the epitome of narrow legalistic religious institutionalism.[118] Of course Jesus' far from commendatory depiction of the hypocritical legalism of many priests and leaders of the people, as present in the Gospels, only serves to confirm Luther's impression.

Yet recent studies on the fundamental spiritual traits of Judaism at the time of nascent Christianity – E.P. Sanders' ground-breaking *Paul and Palestinian Judaism* comes especially to mind – have shown quite clearly that Judaism in its different manifestations was not in the main a religion of 'works' in the Lutheran sense, but rather one of mercy and faith in God as Saviour.[119] Old Testament spirituality, expressed in wisdom literature, particularly the psalms, and also in intertestamentary spirituality, clearly perceived and expressed in Rabbinic-Tannaitic literature,[120] Qumran documents drawn from the Dead Sea Scrolls and the *Apocrypha* and *Pseudephigrapha* during the period 200 BC to AD 200,[121] may be characterized in terms

and Luther with Paul' (H. Pohlmann, *Hat Luther Paulus endeckt? Eine Frage zur theologischen Besinnung*, Berlin 1959, pp. 147f.).   117 This negative evaluation of first-century Judaism, substantially rejected by Sanders (*Paul* . . . , op. cit., pp. 1–12; 33–59) and others, can be traced back to highly influential works of authors such as F.W. Weber (*System der altsynagogalen palästinischen Theologie aus Targum, Midrasch und Talmud*, 1880; revised as *Jüdische Theologie auf Grund des Talmud und verwandter Schriften*, Leipzig 1897) and those who followed on from him, for example J. Wellhausen, E. Schürer, R.H. Charles and W. Bousset (*Die Religion des Judentums im späthellenistischen Zeitalter*, Tübingen 1966, orig. 1925). Through Bousset, R. Bultmann and his school undoubtedly take up many of Weber's findings (cf. for example R. Bultmann, *Primitive Christianity in a Contemporary Setting*, London 1956). For an influential defence of the antithesis between Judaism and Paul's doctrine in the English-speaking world, cf. H. St John Thackery, *The Relation of St Paul to Contemporary Jewish Thought*, London 1900.   118 On Luther's anti-Semitism, cf. H.A. Oberman, *Wurzeln des Antisemitismus. Christenangst und Judenplage im Zeitalter von Humanismus und Reformation*, Berlin 1981, pp. 123–183. See specifically the following works of Luther: *Von den Juden und ihren Lügen* (1543: WA 53: 417–522); *Von den lezten Worten Davids* (1543: WA 54: 28–100).   119 In support of this position, cf. also G.F. Moore's then neglected 1921 essay entitled 'Christian Writers on Judaism', in *Harvard Theological Review* 14 (1921) 197– 254, and its voluminous follow-up *Judaism in the First Centuries of the Christian Era: The Age of Tannaim*, 2 vols, Cambridge (Mass.) 1950.   120 The Tannaites were teachers, Pharisaic in inspiration, active from the foundation of the Grand Council of Jania (ca. AD 75) until the third century AD.   121 The possible exception being IV Ezra (cf. E.P. Sanders, *Paul* . . . , op. cit., pp. 409–418). 'On the whole . . . the author of IV Ezra without doubt gives us a correct presentation of the repercussion of the belief in the future judgement on the religious expressions of individual Jewish piety. All the many expressions of belief in God's grace and mercy appear to be denied' (J. Köberle, *Sünde und Gnade im religiösen Leben des Volkes Israel bis auf Christentum. Ein Geschichte*

of what Sanders called 'covenantal nomism', which he describes in the following terms:

> The 'pattern' or 'structure' of covenantal nomism is this: (1) God has chosen Israel and (2) given the law. The law implies both (3) God's promise to maintain the election and (4) the requirement to obey. (5) God rewards obedience and punishes transgression. (6) The law provides for means of atonement, and atonement results in (7) maintenance or re-establishment of the covenantal relationship. (8) All those who are maintained in the covenant by obedience, atonement and God's mercy belong to the group which will be saved. An important interpretation of the first and last points is that election and ultimately salvation are considered to be by God's mercy rather than human achievement . . . By consistently maintaining the basic framework of *covenantal nomism*, the gift and demand of God were kept in a healthy relationship with each other, the minutiae of the law were observed on the basis of the large principles of religion and because of the commitment to God, and humility before the God who chose and would ultimately redeem Israel was encouraged.[122]

That is to say, God's merciful call to Israel, the subsequent covenant and final salvation are *all by grace*; obedience to works of the law simply 'maintains one's position in the covenant, but does not earn God's grace as such'.[123] In other words, grace comes before law. Nomism, or observance of the law, is covenantal; it is an expression of the believer's wish to be faithful to the covenant. It cannot be held, therefore, on the basis of available documentation of the intertestamentary period 'that Judaism necessarily tends towards petty legalism, self-serving and self-deceiving casuistry, and a mixture of arrogance and lack of confidence in God . . . according to which one had to earn the mercy of God by minute observance of irrelevant ordinances.'[124]

God did not expect or require, under pain of punishment, a sinless perfection from his people. The whole sacrificial system, deeply rooted in the social and liturgical life of Israel, should be seen as a God-given means of conveying forgiveness to sinners. In that sense little or no fundamental contrast may be perceived between Paul's doctrine of justification and the Old Testament message of God's graceful and merciful generosity. God's fidelity is directed principally towards the 'commitments' he acquired, as it were, in establishing a covenant with Israel, rather than towards punishing infractions of the law for its own sake.[125]

des vorchristlichen Heilsbewußtseins, München 1905, p. 657). Sanders pays little attention to Sadducean and Pharisaic literature, in all probability because little of it is available (cf. *Paul . . .*, op. cit., pp. 426–428).   122 Ibid., pp. 422; 427.   123 Ibid., p. 420.   124 Ibid., pp. 427; 419.   125 A.E. McGrath (*The Intellectual Origins of the European Reformation*, Oxford 1987, pp. 77–85) holds that Luther does not hold to a 'covenental' view of reality, seeing in it an obscuring of grace. The covenantal view in fact was characteristic of the *via moderna*.

However, an important question remains. If Judaism and Christianity shared a more or less common theology of justification, of sin, grace and faith, where did the differences lie?[126] Why did Jesus berate the scribes and Pharisees for their legalism and hypocrisy? And more specifically, why did Paul convert? Why was his conversion such a radical one? What did he convert from? What did he convert to?

Covenant and Jews, Gentiles and sinners   The Jews did not doubt God's merciful generosity towards them, nor the grace of the covenant, nor their obligation in gratitude to fulfill the law, as a necessary sign of their recognition of God's goodness. The theology of election, followed on by observation of the law, the *Torah*, is at the very heart of Jewish spirituality and life.[127] Hence the sacred significance of circumcision, of avoiding 'unclean' foods, of protecting the holiness of the Temple, etc.

An important corollary, however, tended invariably to result from this outlook and spirituality: Israel came to consider itself a people set apart, God's own people, his favourites. This was true in an important sense. By inference, however, the other peoples of the ancient world tended to be considered not only as different, or distinct, but by the very fact that they were *not* under God's special protection and care, they were *Gentiles*, that is 'sinners', non-fulfillers of the *Torah*. The existence of the covenant not only bound Israel to observance of the Law as a kind of defensive barricade surrounding it and protecting it from defilement;[128] in practice it also induced them to take it for granted that the Gentiles were in some way *outside* the reach of God's favour and consideration.[129]

It is understandable that the question would spontaneously arise in the hearts of the Israelites: 'why did God chose my people to enter into a covenant with them, and not others, more powerful, more numerous, perhaps even more faithful?' Why were we invited and others excluded? What was the purpose of the covenant? Per-

---

126 Critiques of Sander's theory generally take him to task on this point; cf. for example M.D. Hooker, 'Paul and "Covenental Nomism" ', in M.D. Hooker and S.G. Wilson (eds.), *Paul and Paulinism. Essays in honour of C.K. Barrett*, SPCK Press, London 1982, pp. 47–56.   127 Cf. the interesting reflections of L. Klenicki, 'Exile and Return: Moments in the Jewish Pilgrimage to God (Responding to the Shoah)', in *Annales Theologici* 10 (1996) 485–503.   128 In the words of W.A. Meeks, 'Israel cannot be harmed by its opponents so long as it is a "people dwelling alone" (Num 23:9), "because in virtue of the distinction of their peculiar customs they do not mix with others to depart from the way of their fathers" (Philo, *Life of Moses* 1:278)' (W.A. Meeks, *The First Urban Christians*, Yale 1983, p. 97). For a incisive anthropological reflection on 'the social function of the Law', cf. J.D.G. Dunn, 'Works of the Law and the Curse of the Law', in *Jesus, Paul and the Law*, op. cit., pp. 216–219. Cf. also J. Neusner, *Judaism. The Evidence of the Mishnah*, Chicago 1981, pp. 72–75.   129 The following New Testament texts show this up the tendency to confuse 'Gentile' and 'sinner'. Paul told the first Christians to 'remember that at one time you, Gentiles by birth . . . , were at that time . . . aliens from the commonwealth of Israel, and strangers to the covenants of promise, having no hope and without God in the world' (Ef 2:11–12). Jesus himself taught: 'If you do good to those who do good to you, what credit is that to you? For even sinners do the same' (Lk 6:33; Matthew 5:47, written probably for Jewish converts, has: 'Do not even the Gentiles do the same?').

haps some light can be shed on the matter by reflecting on the real motives of Paul's conversion.

Paul, Apostle to the Gentiles, and the 'works of the law'   Paul was quite clear on the matter: he was converted *from being a persecutor of Christians*, the followers of Jesus, and not as such from being an 'observer of the law'. 'Then they cast him [Stephen] out of the city and stoned him; and the witnesses laid down their garments at the feet of a young man named Saul . . . [who was] consenting to his death. And on that day a great persecution arose against the Church in Jerusalem' (Acts 7:58–8:1).[130]

Memories of his earlier life in Judaism brought to Paul's mind *in the first place* his violent persecution of those who came to be his brothers and sisters in the faith (cf. Gal 1:13; 1 Cor 15:8–9; Acts 9:4; 22:7; 26:14). Some things had not changed. He persecuted out of 'zeal' ($\zeta\tilde{\eta}\lambda o\varsigma$: Phil 3:6; cf. Acts 22:3); now he preached the good news with unabated vigour (cf. 2 Cor 8:7; Phil 1:14). But the object of his zeal had certainly changed. Perceiving that Israel's covenant status and distinctiveness was under serious threat (see the discourse of Stephen in Acts 7), Saul, the ardent Pharisee, saw he was under strict obligation to defend the covenant and the law, and thus safeguard the privileges, prerogatives and distinctive quality of Israel.[131] He saw that though Christians considered themselves to be the continuity of Israel, they admitted Gentiles into their assemblies without requiring them to become Jews, nor to observe the prescriptions of the law.

In fact, Paul does not speak of his 'conversion' as a turning away from personal sin, an obtaining of personal mercy and forgiveness. His new life did not look inwards, but outwards. His was not so much, at least apparently, a personal changeabout, but rather *a change in mission*.[132] The effect of Christ's appearance on

---

130 On the nature and significance of Paul's conversion, cf. the works of J.D.G. Dunn, and in particular his 'The Justice of God. A Renewed Perspective on Justification by Faith', in *Journal of Theological Studies* 43 (1992) 1–22; idem., 'Paul's Conversion—A Light to Twentieth Century Disputes', in O. Hofius (ed.), *Evangelium—Schriftauslegung—Kirche*, Göttingen 1996.   131 On the delicate socio-political situation confronting Judaism in the years of early Christianity which induced the Jews, understandably, to believe that their distinctive religious and national prerogatives were under serious threat, cf. J.D.G. Dunn, 'The Incident at Antioch (Gal. 2.11-18)', in *Jesus, Paul and the Law*, op. cit., pp. 129–174, especially pp. 133–136.   132 That Paul's conversion was essentially a kind of 'commissioning', an apostolic vocation rather than a moral conversion, has been clearly established by E. Pfaff: 'Paul never spoke of his conversion but almost always of his vocation, connecting that event with his mission as an Apostle' (*Die Bekehrung des hl. Paulus in der Exegese des 20. Jahrhundert*, Rome 1942, p. 169). Cf. also J. Knox, *Chapters in a Life of Paul*, London 1954; J. Munck, *Paul and the Salvation of Mankind*, London 1959, pp. 11–35; U. Wilkens, 'Die Bekehrung des Paulus als religionsgeschichtliches Problem', in *Rechtfertigung als Freiheit: Paulusstudien*, Neukirchen 1974, pp. 11–32; M. Hengel, *Between Jesus and Paul*, London 1983, p. 53; K. Stendahl, *Paul Among Jews and Gentiles . . .*, op. cit., pp. 7–12; J. Blank, *Paulus: Von Jesus zum Christentum*, München 1982; S. Kim, *The Origins of Paul's Gospel*, Tübingen 1983, p. 56; J.D.G. Dunn, ' "A Light to the Gentiles", or "The End of the Law"? The Significance of the Damascus Road Christophany for Paul', in *Jesus, Paul and the Law*, op. cit., pp. 89–104; G. Pini, 'Vocazione di Paolo o conversione', in L. Padovese (ed.), *Atti del I Simposio di Tarso su San Paolo*

the road to Damascus was one of constituting him as an apostle or missionary to all peoples (cf. Gal 1:15–16; 1 Cor 9:1–2 and 15:8–10). The sin he turned from, which made of him 'the least of the apostles', *was to have persecuted the Church of God* (cf. 1 Cor 15:9), to have attempted frustrating God's *universal* saving will.

Conversion gave Paul a completely new way of looking at the Old Testament. God had not chosen Israel for its virtues, moral superiority to other peoples, or suchlike reasons. The benefit of the Gentiles was ever in his view.[133] The original promise to Abraham was ultimately directed towards the Gentiles: 'In you all the families of the earth shall be blessed' (Gen 12:3). Deutero-Isaiah had already expressed the notion in proclaiming who Israel was and what Israel was for: it would be 'a light to the nations, *that* my [God's] salvation may reach to the end of the earth' (Is 49:6; cf. Is 6; Jer 1:4–5).

In other words, Paul's insistence on justification 'by faith alone', that is without 'works of the law' was an expression of the fact that God was ready to accept Gentiles as his children, with the same privileges as Jews, without requiring them first to 'become' Jews, that is, to adopt a new culture, to observe an exact fulfillment of the *Torah*, to subscribe to ritual laws of purification, circumcision, etc. In the words of James Dunn: 'The Christian doctrine of justification by faith begins as Paul's protest not as an individual sinner against a Jewish legalism, but as Paul's protest on behalf of Gentiles against Jewish exclusivism.'[134]

When Paul criticizes the Jews for 'boasting', he is not referring in the first place to human complacency in 'works' performed. Rather he rejected Jewish insistence on an undeserved special status before God in respect of other peoples (cf. Rom 2:17; 23). The boasting of the Jews, in 'establishing their own righteousness' (Rom 10:3), might seem to imply that God is Lord of Jews only (cf. Rom 3:27–30).[135] Both Bultmann and Käsemann, following the classical Lutheran stance, understood this 'boasting' in an individualistic and personally self-confiding sense, as an expression of an attitude of self-relying achievement before God.[136] But this does not respond exactly to the mind of Paul nor to the circumstances nascent Christianity was facing up to.

Apostolo, Rome 1993, pp. 47–63; and many other authors. 'Again and again we find that there is hardly a thought of Paul's which is not tied up with his mission . . . The "I" of his writings is not "the Christian" but "the Apostle to the Gentiles" ' (K. Stendahl, op. cit., p. 12). 133 Cf. Rom 1:1–2; 3:29–31; 9; Eph 4:6; 1 Tim 2:4. 134 J.D.G. Dunn and A.M. Suggate, *The Justice of God* . . . , op. cit., p. 25. Authors besides E.P. Sanders who take up this position include N.A. Dahl, 'The Doctrine of Justification: its Social Function and Implications', in *Studies in Paul*, Minneapolis 1977, pp. 95–120; W.D. Davies, 'Paul and the People of the New Testament', in *New Testament Studies* 24 (1977–78) 4–39; L. Gaston, 'Paul and the Torah', in A.T. Davies (ed.), *Antisemitism and the Foundations of Christianity*, New York 1979, pp. 48–71. 135 Cf. J.D.G. Dunn, 'Works of the Law and the Curse of the Law (Gal 3:10–14)', in *Jesus, Paul and the Law*, op. cit., pp. 215–236 (here 221f.). 136 Cf. R. Bultmann, 'Καυχάομαι', in G. Kittel and G. Friedrich (eds.), *Theological Dictionary of the New Testament*, vol. 3, Grand Rapids 1965, pp. 648–654; *Theology of the New Testament*, op. cit., vol. 1, pp. 242f.; E. Käsemann, *Commentary on Romans*, London 1980, p. 102. Bultmann's position is also held by H. Hübner, *Das Gesetz bei Paulus*, Göttingen 1980, p. 102.

When Paul hits out against 'justification by works' there is no evidence that he is attempting to run down good deeds, sincere and persevering striving in fulfilling the law, understood as 'covenantal nomism' (Sanders), 'service of the law' (Lohmeyer),[137] or 'nomistic service' (Tyson).[138] The 'works of the law' Paul rejects refer in the main to ceremonial laws of different kinds, especially to circumcision and food laws, and not to moral prescription or observance as such.[139] 'The phrase ['works of the law'] refers not to an individual striving for moral improvement, but to a religious mode of existence . . . which demonstrates the individual's "belongingness" to the people of the law'.[140] The notion of living 'in the flesh' (Rom 2:28) denotes not merely an exterior, sinful and material lifestyle and attitude over against one which is interior, holy and spiritual, 'in the spirit', but rather the people of Israel taken in terms of their physical identity and racial kinship.[141] Hence not being 'in the flesh' is equivalent to 'not of works' (Rom 9:8; 11) in the sense that 'works of the law' demonstrate national identity, and constitute not individual right-eousness, but 'collective righteousness, to the exclusion of the Gentiles'.[142]

It should be noted that the precise technical term 'works of the law' may also be found in the Dead Sea Scrolls, which portray the life-style and religious practice of the Qumran communities.[143] As we saw above, these communities can be said to

---

137 Cf. E. Lohmeyer, *Probleme paulinischer Theologie*, Stuttgart 1955, p. 67. 138 Cf. J.B. Tyson, '"Works of the Law" in Galatians', in *Journal of Biblical Literature* 92 (1973) 423–431. 139 Cf. J.D.G. Dunn, 'Works of the Law and the Curse of the Law (Gal 3:10–14)', op. cit., p. 220, which reflects especially on Galatians 2:16 (cf. also ibid., pp. 225–230). The same can be said of Romans (cf. ibid., pp. 221f.). Cf. also K. Kertelge, 'Zur Deutung des Rechtfertigungsbegriffs im Galaterbrief', in *Biblische Zeitschrift* 12 (1968) 215; H. Räisänen, *Paul and the Law* . . . , op. cit., p. 259. Cf. also Dunn's essay 'A New Perspective on Paul', op. cit., pp. 183–206 and especially the symposium entitled *Paul and the Mosaic Law* (J.D.G. Dunn, ed.), Tübingen 1996, particularly the papers of H. Lichtenberger and M. Hengel. 140 J.D.G. Dunn, 'Works of the Law and the Curse of the Law (Gal 3:10-14)', op. cit., p. 220. The section entitled 'works of the law' (ibid., pp. 219–225) is of particular interest. 141 Cf. ibid., pp. 222f.; and also J.D.G. Dunn, 'Jesus—Flesh and Spirit: an Exposition of Romans 1.3–4', in *Journal of Theological Studies* 24 (1973) 44–49. 142 G. Howard, 'Christ the End of the Law: the Meaning of Romans 10:4', in *Journal of Biblical Literature* 88 (1969) 331–337 (here p. 336). 143 Cf. for example, 1 QS 5:21.23; 6:18; 11:2ff.; 4 QFlor 1:1–7; 4 Q, and the analysis of E. Lohmeyer, *Probleme paulinischer Theologie*, op. cit., pp. 33–74. This position is held by S. Schultz, 'Zur Rechtfertigung aus Gnade in Qumran und bei Paulus', in *Zeitschrift für Theologie und Kirche* 56 (1959) 155-185; J.D.G. Dunn, *Romans*, Dallas 1988, p. 154; J. Jeremias, *The Central Message of the New Testament*, London 1965, pp. 49ff.; B. Estrada-Barbier, 'La fede e le opere a confronto con il giudaismo', in J.M. Galván (ed.), *La giustificazione in Cristo*, Rome 1997, pp. 63–72. Several texts from the recently published 4QMMT Qumran manuscript (E. Quimron and J. Strugnell, *Qumran Cave 4 – V*, Oxford 1994, especially C27–30; F. García Martínez, *The Dead Sea Scrolls Translated: The Qumran Texts in English*, Leiden 1994, pp. 113–117) indicate quite clearly that common usage of the Pauline syntagma ἔργα νόμου ('opere della legge') refers not so much to fulfillment of ethical actions as such, but rather to particular prescriptions of the law which require obedience and serve as 'identity markers'. Of course, a perfect distinction between ceremonial and moral laws cannot be made: cf. E.P. Sanders, *Judaism. Practice and Belief*, London 1992. On the significance of the Qumran texts in this regard, cf. J.D.G. Dunn, '4QMMT and Galatians', in *New Testament Studies* 43 (1997) 147–153; and R. Penna, 'Le "opere

have practiced 'covenantal nomism'. Certainly they did they not consider they could *earn* God's favour or mercy by their works.[144] Rather, for them 'doing the law is *the condition for remaining elect . . .* of remaining in the covenant'.[145] However, the concrete existence of the members of the Qumran communities was characterized by an attempt to separate themselves consciously from other peoples, even of their own race, with a view to avoid being tainted by the world of sin and the defilement that surrounded them.[146] Thus, by persevering in their practice of the 'works of the law' they were distinguished to some extent from other Jews as a specially chosen part of Israel,[147] and certainly from the Gentiles, their 'enemies' and God's,[148] who are destined to destruction at the end of time.[149] Remaining within the covenant by persevering in good deeds was their way of maintaining and affirming their privileged status, of defining themselves as members of the covenant people.[150] To some degree it could be said that their fulfillment of the 'works of the law' pointed to an intention to monopolize God's favour and grace, and by implication, condition his merciful will to save *all* humanity.

And this is what Paul's conversion or newly-found mission consisted of: to announce to the world that the time had come for God's promises of universal salvation to be fulfilled. Dunn summarizes his apostolic mission and understanding of 'works of the law' in the following terms:

> The law serves both to identify Israel as the people of the covenant and to mark them off as distinct from (other) nations . . . 'Works of the law' refer not exclusively but particularly to those requirements which bring to sharp focus the distinctiveness of Israel's identity. It is because they have such a crucial rôle in defining 'Jewishness', membership of the covenant people, that circumcision and food laws feature so prominently in discussion of works of the law and righteousness. What lies behind so much of the debate is the identity crisis which Paul's work among the Gentiles precipitated among his fellow Jewish Christians.[151]

Jesus' condemnation of hypocrisy and legalism   A brief mention should be made of the fact that Jesus' forceful recrimination of the Jews, in particular of the 'scribes and Pharisees', seems to respond to his perception of a hypocritical, exterior legal-

della legge" in S. Paolo e 4QMMT", in *Ricerche Storico-Bibliche* 9 (1997).   **144** Cf. especially E.P. Sanders, *Paul . . .* , op. cit., pp. 305–312.   **145** Ibid., pp. 312; 320.   **146** Cf. ibid., pp. 312–316.   **147** Cf. ibid., p. 247.   **148** Cf. ibid., pp. 248ff. On the notion of the hatred of wicked outsiders as an *imitatio Dei*, cf. A. Jaubert, *La notion d'alliance dans le judaïsme*, Paris 1963, pp. 186–189.   **149** Cf. E.P. Sanders, *Paul . . .* , op. cit., p. 257.   **150** The documents of the Qumran community MMT 'preserves a vocabulary and manner of theologizing which left its mark on a wider spectrum of Jewish thought and practice, and it was just this sort of theologizing and practice which confronted Paul in Antioch and which he wrote Galatians to counter' (J.D.G. Dunn, '4QMMT and Galatians', op. cit., p. 153).   **151** J.D.G. Dunn, 'Works of the Law and the Curse of the Law (Gal 3:10–14)', op. cit., p. 223.

ism, a disregard for weightier matters of the law, an attitude in fact which would eventually be instrumental in his execution.[152] Paul's outright rejection of 'works of the law' for the sake of true 'faith in Christ Jesus' would seem to confirm this message, condemning all human self-righteousness in God's sight.

However, a closer look at the Gospel texts shows that Jesus' resolute condemnation of the hypocritical exteriorism of the scribes and Pharisees did not respond only to the possibility that they might be searching after *divine* approval of their good works, but rather to the fact that they sought approval *'from men'* (cf. Mt 6:2.5). His insistence on the preponderance of interior rectitude (cf. Mt 5–7) by no means implied that his disciples should not fulfil the law (cf. Mt 5:17ff.), but rather that their actions and thoughts be turned in all sincerity and simplicity towards their 'Father who is heaven' (Mt 5:16). Such sincere interiority was by no means lacking in Old Testament spirituality (cfr. for example Deut 6:5), nor, as we have seen, is it missing in the spirituality found in intertestamentary literature. Jesus' indignation towards 'the scribes and Pharisees' was motivated, so it would seem, by the way in which they relied on a scrupulous exterior fulfillment of the law, even to the point of neglecting the 'weightier matters', while excluding from God's favour those who did not fulfill the law with such exactitude. It was the legalistic 'exteriority' of their behaviour that belied the fact that they were excessively interested in impressing on others that *they* were God's favourites, the true Israel, and the rest were not. They attempted to 'stay in' by acting the part of the true Israelite. Jesus gives the reason for his remonstrances: 'Woe to you, scribes and Pharisees, hypocrites! *because* you shut the kingdom of heaven against men; for you neither enter yourselves, nor allow those who would enter to go in' (Mt 23:13). John the Baptist said to the Jews: *'Do not presume to say to yourselves, "We have Abraham as our father"* . . . Even now the axe is laid to the root of the trees; every tree therefore that does not bear good fruit is cut down and thrown into the fire' (Mt 3:9–10).

Though contemporary studies have certainly made a most welcome contribution towards taking the sharp edges off the negative understanding many Christians

152 Recent investigations, particularly in the area of comparative studies of Judaism and Christianity, commonly tend to redress the predominantly negative image the gospels seem to offer of 'the Jews' and especially of the Pharisee party, whose life and spirituality, we are told, have been consistently misrepresented in Christian theology (sic W.D. Davies, *The Setting of the Sermon on the Mount*, Cambridge 1964, pp. 256–315; J. König, *Jews and Christians in Dialogue*, Philadelphia 1979, chapters 4 & 6; F. Mussner, *Traktat über die Juden*, München 1979). Some authors, often Jews attempting to 'reclaim' Jesus, would go so far as to say that the Pharisees had no part in the death of Jesus (cf. for example H. Maccoby, *The Mythmaker: Paul and the Invention of Christianity*, London 1986, pp. 45–49; E. Rivkin, *What Crucified Jesus?*, Nashville 1984), and others that Jesus himself was a Pharisee (cf. J.T. Pawlikowski, *Christ in the Light of Christian-Jewish Dialogue*, New York 1982; H. Falk, *Jesus the Pharisee*, New York 1985; E.P. Sanders, *Jesus and Judaism*, Philadelphia 1985). Despite the real coincidence between Jesus' teaching and that of the Pharisees on many fronts, Christians generally do not see the latter position as tenable (cf. S. Westerholm, *Jesus and Scribal Authority*, Lund 1978, especially p. 128; J.D.G. Dunn, 'Pharisees, Sinners and Jesus', in *Jesus, Paul and the Law*, op. cit., pp. 61–86).

have had of the mind-frame and spirituality of the Jews, and especially of the Pharisees,[153] the *same message* comes across both in the teaching of Jesus and that of Paul:[154] the saving power of God is not limited to a restricted group of individuals who establish a boundary between themselves and the rest by insisting on the strict observance of a series of burdensome statutes and ceremonial regulations. Israel was elected as God's people so that his grace and salvation would reach to the ends of earth (cf. Acts 1:8). As we shall see now, there is a clear continuity between the message of Jesus and that of Paul, inseparable from that existing between the Jesus of history and the Christ of faith.

Paul, apostle of Jesus Christ   Paul's calling or 'commissioning' brought him to realize that he could no longer consider himself 'in' by ensuring that others stayed 'out'.[155] He could not truly remain a Christian were he not to strive to bring others, all others, 'in' with him: 'Woe to me if I do not preach the gospel!' (1 Cor 9:16).

At times it is suggested that Paul's vocation did not consist in the main of a commission to evangelize the whole world. Such a conviction would have arisen afterwards.[156] The nucleus of his vocation which resulted from the Damascus Christophany should be considered, rather, as the special union with, and knowl-

---

153 For a good overview, cf. J.D.G. Dunn, 'Pharisees, Sinners, and Jesus', op. cit., who comes to the following conclusions. For the Pharisees, 'the purity of the meal table was an important concern among many of the Pharisees of Jesus time' (ibid., p. 65); 'in the middle decades of the first century, Pharisees were characterized by zeal for the law and concern to practice that pattern of life which maintained the righteousness of the covenant and Israel's status as people of God' (ibid., p. 69). 'That there were at the time of Jesus a number of Pharisees, and probably a significant body of Pharisees, who felt passionately concerned to preserve, maintain, and defend Israel's status as the people of the covenant and the righteousness of the law . . . must be regarded as virtually certain' (ibid., p. 71); 'The more that members of the Jewish community departed from the standards which the Pharisees as a rule saw to be necessary to maintain covenant righteousness, the more likely these Pharisees would be to dub them "sinners" ' (ibid., p. 77). 'It is very likely that the portrayal of Pharisees, sinners, and Jesus in passages like Mark 2 and 7 accords very closely with the historical realities of Jesus' ministry and may not be discounted as a retrojection of later controversies into the period of Jesus' ministry' (ibid., p. 80). And finally, 'far from being left with an uncomfortable wedge between Jesus and Gentile Christianity, the overall perspective we have gained . . . enables us to recognize an important line of continuity between Jesus and his successors [Paul for example]. For behind the particular objections and charges levelled against Jesus was the central fact that Jesus was ignoring and abolishing boundaries which more sectarian attitudes had erected within Israel . . . [This] helps us see how a Christianity which broke through the boundaries of Israel's own distinctiveness sprang from a Jesus who posed such a challenge to the boundary between Pharisee and sinner' (ibid.). 'In other words, the recognition of the Jewishness of Jesus need not separate Jesus from the Christianity he founded, just as the recognition of the Christian significance of Jesus need not separate him from the faith of his own people' (ibid., pp. 80f.).   **154** Cf. J. Jeremias, *The Central Message of the New Testament* . . . , op. cit., pp. 51ff.   **155** The terminology is of E.P. Sanders, *Paul, the Law, and the Jewish People*, Philadelphia 1983.   **156** Thus for example J. Dupont, 'The Conversion of Paul, and its Influence on his Understanding of Salvation by Faith', in W.W. Gasque and R.P. Martin (eds.), *Apostolic History and the Gospel* (Festschrift F.F. Bruce), Grand Rapids 1970, pp. 176–194 (here p. 193); M.S. Enslin, *Reapproaching Paul*, Philadelphia 1972, pp. 64f.

edge of the crucified and risen Lord, who is the expected Messiah.[157] The 'content' of his new faith and calling lay in the fact that the Messiah should be identified with the crucified one.[158]

Of course the claim is substantially true. The occasion and *res* of Paul's conversion was undoubtedly his singular encounter and subsequent union with the crucified one who had risen from the dead by God's power, and on account of whom he knew 'nothing among you except Jesus Christ and him crucified' (1 Cor 2:2). Paul's whole life became a 'being with Christ', and as a result, an acting in conformity with this 'new being',[159] and a vision of all things 'in Christ'. But it should also be said that Paul's 'commissioning' to evangelize *was* a consequence, and a very direct one, of his personally turning towards Jesus Christ and incorporation into his 'body'. The true, personal object of his calling was indeed the Risen Lord Jesus Christ, whom he encountered on the road to Damascus, and whom he had previously persecuted in his members (cf. Acts 9:4–5). Yet turning away from persecuting the Christians and turning towards evangelizing the Gentiles did not result, for Paul, simply from a new *understanding* of the full meaning of the Scriptures and of the law, the culmination perhaps of an extended reflection on the reality of God's universal saving will, at best occasioned or consolidated by his encounter with Christ. Rather his vocation of universal evangelization was the *direct and necessary consequence* of his encounter with the Risen Lord. 'He who had set me apart before I was born, and had called me through his grace, was pleased to reveal his Son to me, *in order that* (ἵνα) I might preach him among the Gentiles' (Gal 1:15–16). These two elements that defined Paul's new life – being with Christ, preaching the good news everywhere – belong inseparably to one another, explain one another.[160] However, this intimate link-up between the content ('being with Christ') and consequences (universal evangelization) of Paul's conversion may be understood in two ways.

Some authors[161] suggest that, since Christians before Paul had already posed the alternative 'salvation through faith in Christ' / 'salvation through works of the law',

---

157 Cf. for example, H.G. Wood, 'The Conversion of Paul: Its Nature, Antecedents and Consequences', in *New Testament Studies* 1 (1954–55) 276–282; P.H. Menoud, 'Revelation and Tradition: The Influence of Paul's Conversion on his Theology', in *Interpretation* 7 (1953) 131–141.   158 It has sometimes been noted that Sander's theory of associating Jewish and Pauline 'covenental nomism' does not take the centrality of Christ sufficiently into account: cf. R.H. Gundry, 'Grace, Works, and Staying Saved in Paul', in *Biblica* 66 (1985) 1–38.   159 Cf. the interesting study of Phil 2:5 in A. Moreno García, 'Vivid entre vosotros lo que sois en Cristo: la tarea brota del don', in *La sabiduría del Espíritu: sentir en Cristo*, Rome 1995, pp. 265–278.   160 The fruitful tension between them may be perceived in Paul's words to the Philippians: 'To live is Christ, and to die is gain. If it is to be life in the flesh that means fruitful labour for me. Yet which I shall choose I cannot tell. I am hard pressed between the two. My desire is to depart and be with Christ, for that is far better. But to remain in the flesh is more necessary on your account' (Phil 1:21–24).   161 For example U. Wilkens, 'Die Bekehrung des Paulus als religionsgeschichtliches Problem', op. cit., pp. 11–32; P. Stuhlmacher, ' "Das Ende des Gesetzes": Über Ursprung und Ansatz der paulinischen Theologie', in *Zeitschrift für Theologie und Kirche* 67 (1970) 14–39; H. Weder, *Das Kreuz Jesu bei Paulus*, Göttingen 1981, pp. 187–193.

his encounter with Christ and subsequent faith in him meant simply that observance of the law was no longer a viable way to salvation, and had to be resisted with the same energy (ζῆλος) with which Christians had previously to be persecuted. In this sense, the coming of Christ would mark 'the end of the law [τέλος γὰρ νόμου] that everyone who has faith would be justified' (Rom 10:4). Paul's encounter with Christ on the road to Damascus would come to mean 'the bankruptcy of the law and the all-sufficiency of Christ'.[162] Likewise it is argued that, according to Paul, since Christ had been crucified, that is 'cursed by the law' (Gal 3:13), but had been vindicated by God, the law had lost all power of being God's instrument of salvation.[163] Clearly this is a restatement of the classical Lutheran position: justification by faith simply excludes seeking salvation by fulfilling works of the law.

Other authors argue that this position, though plausible, does not hold up when it is observed that in all probability most Christians in Paul's time 'did not see any antithesis between faith in Christ and a life regulated by the *Torah*'.[164] Besides, for Paul the Jew, before his conversion, the crucifixion of Jesus confirmed purely and simply that God had rejected and disavowed him, excluding him from the covenant (cf. Deut 27:58–68) in keeping Deuteronomy's injunction, 'Cursed is everyone who hangs on a tree' (Deut 21:23). On account of the crucifixion he took it that Christianity itself had been repudiated by God, and its members henceforth excluded from the divine promises. However, Paul's encounter with the Risen Lord, 'the Damascus road Christophany, must obviously have turned such a line of reasoning completely on its head, for it indicated clearly that God had accepted and vindicated this one precisely as the crucified'.[165] 'The curse which was removed by Christ's death . . . was the curse which had previously prevented [the covenant] blessing from reaching the Gentiles, the curse of a wrong understanding of the law . . . It was *that* curse which Jesus had brought deliverance from by his death'.[166] That the Gentiles came to be accepted by God is not, as it were, an historical accident, occasioned by excessive Jewish attachment to the letter of the law and subsequent falling from divine favour. Rather, it fitted into God's eternal design which came to fulfillment

---

162 J.D.G. Dunn, ' "A Light to the Gentiles", or "The End of the Law"? The Significance of the Damascus Road Christophany for Paul', op. cit., p. 92. On Rom 10:4, cf. especially M.A. Tabet, 'Rm 10,4 nel dialogo ebraico-cristiano', in J.M. Galván (ed.), *La giustificazione in Cristo*, Rome 1997, pp. 83–100. The discussion on Romans 10:4 has centered, understandably, on the two possible meanings of the term τέλος, 'termination' or 'fulfillment' (cf. also R. Bardenas, *Christ the End of the Law. Romans 10:4 in Pauline Perspective*, Sheffield 1985, pp. 7–37; J.D.G. Dunn, *Romans*, op. cit., pp. 589–591). 163 Cf. M.A. Tabet, 'Rm 10,4 nel dialogo ebraico-cristiano', op. cit., pp. 85–89; also, in greater detail, cf. Dunn's essay 'Works of the Law and the Curse of the Law', in ibid., pp. 215–236; E.P. Sanders, *Paul, the Law, and the Jewish People*, Philadelphia 1983, pp. 25f.; H. Räisänen, *Paul and the Law* . . . , op. cit., pp. 249ff.; S. Kim, *The Origin of Paul's Gospel*, op. cit., pp. 268–311. 164 For example, J.D.G. Dunn, ' "A Light to the Gentiles", or "The End of the Law"? The Significance of the Damascus Road Christophany for Paul', op. cit., p. 99. 165 Ibid., p. 100. cf. J.A. Fitzmyer, 'Crucifixion in Ancient Palestine, Qumran Literature and the New Testament', in *Catholic Biblical Quarterly* 40 (1978) 493–513. 166 J.D.G. Dunn, 'Works of the Law and the Curse of the Law', op. cit., p. 229.

in Christ, whose fidelity to 'the law', that is to doing the will of his Father, brought about his execution on the perceived charge of blasphemy. Belief in the crucified one as the Christ, or God's Anointed One, therefore, did not require the repudiation of the law as such, but meant rather that man could not be saved by a mere external observance, conditioned furthermore by a will to demarcate God's favour and restrict his saving will.[167]

Living 'in Christ' and living 'off Christ', Paul saw clearly that the purpose of God's special election of Israel (cf. Is 6; 49:1–6; Jer 1:4–5) was the salvation of all peoples, and, inseparably, that this universal salvific will culminated in the coming of the long-awaited Messiah, 'according to the *revelation of the mystery* which was kept secret for long ages but is *now disclosed* and through the prophetic writings *is made known to all nations*' (Rom 16:25f.). The coming of the Messiah coincides directly with the fulfillment of God's will and promise, the salvation of all peoples: thus Christ is the 'end', or 'fulfillment' and culmination (τέλος: Rom 10:4) of the law.[168] And so, Paul's two primary convictions (that Jesus Christ is the crucified-risen Lord in whom God has provided for the salvation of all mankind; that he [Paul] was called to be apostle to the Gentiles) go hand in hand, explain one another, require one another.[169]

The faith of Paul is no longer directed, as a zealous Pharisee, to the words of prophets already defunct, towards the impersonal *Torah*, which must be studied, understood, correctly interpreted and defended at all costs, but rather towards the Christ, Risen Lord and universal Saviour, Image and Wisdom of God made visible, who lives in the Church.[170] It is of its very essence a *fides Christi*, a faith directed towards and determined by Christ, faith *in* him. And it was none other than this newly-found, personally lived faith that spurred Paul on to evangelize all peoples without exception (cf. 2 Cor 5:14). Made a son of God in Christ,[171] incorporated into him and becoming a member of his body, Paul perceived directly and almost

---

167 The following text of Dunn's is worth citing: 'Christ in his death had put himself under the curse and outside the covenant blessing . . . , that is, put himself in the place of the Gentile! Yet God vindicated him! There, God is for the Gentiles; and consequently the law could no longer serve as a boundary dividing Jew from Gentile. In short, Christ in his death had effectively abolished this disqualification, by himself being disqualified. It is the out-working of this train of thought which we see unfolding in the incidents described in Galatians 2, and climaxing in 2.21: "If righteousness comes through the law, then Christ died in vain". Christ's death was effective, in Paul's view, precisely because it broke through the restrictiveness of the typical Jewish understanding of God's righteousness, and demonstrated that the grace of God was not to be experienced apart from the law' (ibid., p. 230).   **168** As is the common Patristic, Scholastic and Reformed reading of Rom 10:4 up to, though excluding, liberal Protestant authors such as A. Harnack. The notion of τέλος as the temporal end (cessation, abrogation of the law) is found for example in Conzelmann, Käsemann etc. (cf. M.A. Tabet, 'Rm 10,4 nel dialogo ebraico-cristiano', op. cit., pp. 85–89).   **169** Cf. J. Munck, *Paul and the Salvation of Mankind*, op. cit., pp. 41; 66ff.; E.P. Sanders, *Paul . . .*, op. cit., pp. 439–442. Paul's determining, driving faith in Christ is linked besides, at least to some degree, to his conviction of the nearness of the end of the age.   **170** Cf. especially S. Kim, *The Origins of Paul's Gospel*, op. cit., passim.

intuitively that 'in Christ Jesus you are all sons of God, through faith . . . [Therefore 'in Christ'] there is neither Jew nor Greek, there is neither slave or free, there is neither male nor female; for you are all one in Christ Jesus' (Gal 3:26; 28). And Paul saw that 'the Gospel which [Christians] took as their common starting-point [would be] . . . distorted in its fundamentals if . . . the outworkings of the gospel and Christology were not followed through',[171] that is if Judaizing Christians were to have their way in reinstating strict observation of the law in order to ensure salvation.

One final observation to tie up the question. 'Fulfillment of the law' in Christ did not mean for Christians its abrogation. But neither did it mean a mere quantitative improvement on the Jewish way of fulfilling the law.[173] If such were the case, the action of Christ's Spirit would be at the service of the law which would retain its primacy. Fulfillment of the law for the Christian originates from their belonging to Christ, in such a way that the law is carried out primarily by God through Christ's Spirit *in* the Christian, not so much *by* the Christian.[174]

Paul and Luther on 'justification by faith alone': a summary[175] From what we have seen it would seem that 'justification by faith without works of the law' meant some-

---

171 A. Pitta (*Disposizione e messaggio della Lettera ai Galati . . .* , op. cit.) maintains that the theological centre of Galatians is that of our divine sonship in Christ. Cf. also B. Byrne, *Sons of God, seed of Abraham: a Study of the Idea of the Sonship of God of all Christians in Paul against the Jewish Background*, Rome 1979.   172 J.D.G. Dunn, 'The Theology of Galatians', in *Jesus, Paul and the Law*, op. cit., pp. 242–264 (here p. 248).   173 This is the position held by C.E.B. Cranfield, 'St. Paul and the Law', in *Scottish Journal of Theology* 17 (1964) 43–68; idem., 'Has the Old Testament Law a Place in Christian Life? A Response to Professor Westerholm', in *Irish Biblical Studies* 15 (1993) 50–64; T.R. Schreiner, *The Law and its Fulfillment. A Pauline Theology of the Law*, Old Rapids 1993, especially pp. 149–178.   174 Cf. L.E. Keck, 'The Law and "the Law of Sin and Death" (Rom. 8:1–4). Reflections on the Spirit and Ethics in Paul', in J.L. Crenshaw and S. Sandmel (eds.), *The Divine Helmsman. Studies on God's Control of Human Events*, New York 1980, pp. 41–57.   175 Review articles on the debate we have considered abound. They include R.H. Gundry, 'Grace, Works, and Staying Saved in Paul', in *Biblica* 66 (1985) 1–38; B. Riecke, 'Paulus über das Gesetz', in *Theologische Zeitschrift* 41 (1985) 237–257; J.M.G. Barclay, 'Paul and the Law: Observations on Some Recent Debates', in *Themelios* 12/1 (1986) 5–15; idem., *Obeying the Truth: A Study of Paul's Ethics in Galatians*, Edinburgh 1988; J. Lambrecht, 'Gesetzesverständnis bei Paulus', in K. Kertelge (ed.), *Das Gesetz im Neuen Testament*, Freiburg i. Br. 1986, pp. 86–127; D.J. Moo, 'Paul and the Law in the Last Ten Years', in *Scottish Journal of Theology* 40 (1987) 287–307; F.F. Bruce, 'Paul and the Law in Recent Research', in B. Lindars (ed.), *Law and Religion. Essays on the Place of the Law in Israel and Early Christianity*, Cambridge 1988, pp. 115–125; G. Klein, 'Ein Sturmzentrum der Paulusforschung', in *Verkündigung und Forschung* 33 (1988) 40–56; S. Westerholm, *Israel's Law and the Church's Faith. Paul and his Recent Interpreters*, Grand Rapids (Michigan) 1988; T.R. Schreiner, 'The Abolition and Fulfillment of the Law in Paul', in *Journal for the Study of the New Testament* 35 (1989) 47–74; B.L. Martin, *Christ and the Law in Paul*, Leiden 1989; R. Penna, 'Il problema della legge nelle lettere di San Paolo', in *L'Apostolo Paolo. Studi di esegesi e teologia*, Cinisello Balsamo 1991, pp. 496–518; M.A. Seifrid, *Justification by Faith: the origin and development of a central pauline theme*, Leiden 1992; F. Thielman, *Paul and the Law: A Contextual Approach*, Downers Grove (Ill.) 1994.

thing quite different to Paul than it did to Luther. For the Apostle to the Gentiles it meant that we are justified or saved by *faith in Jesus Christ*, God's Son and our Saviour, and incorporation into his 'body', the Church, and not as such by passively *remaining within a privileged community* through the observation of certain exterior precepts, which in some way could localize God's favour and grace towards humanity. Hence justification is not merely a personal question for a Christian, with implications of a predominantly individualistic and interior kind, but an essentially ecclesiological one.[176] Certain 'works', or more exactly, certain forms of behaviour incompatible with faith in Jesus Christ, have to be avoided. But the works to be avoided are not, as such, those in which the individual strives to express gratitude to God and obedience to his will, but rather 'works' which, in their intentionality and performance, in one way or another reinforce one's belonging to the community of the saved *to the exclusion of others* from such a community, works that is of a ceremonial, social, perhaps 'ecclesiastical' kind.

As was noted above, many contemporary authors maintain a more classical (Lutheran) approach to this vast and complex exegetical question, holding that the Pauline 'works of the law' insofar as they are opposed to 'faith in Christ' refer to the law in general,[177] and not only to ceremonial laws and suchlike as boundary conditions reinforcing covenant identity.

Perhaps in real terms, the positions are not as far removed from one another as it might seem at first sight.[178] Lutheran doctrine rightly hits out at those who complacently seek to be pleasing to God on the basis of their own self-given justice. Now, does it really matter whether this attitude comes across as an individualistic striving to cross the divine favour barrier by the abundance or self-centered rectitude of good works, or as a societal endeavour to show God that in *his* sight one is worthier than the rest of humanity to receive and retain his gifts? Putting the same thing in positive terms: the sense of personal unworthiness and mistrust in one's own person and works resulting from the faith-perceived awareness of the abundant and merciful goodness of God, necessarily expresses itself in the joy of communicating that goodness to the *whole* of sinful mankind. Conversely, should God's gifts be monopolized or consciously withheld from others, this can only mean that one considers *oneself* naturally worthy *coram Deo* of receiving and retaining such gifts in the

---

176 On the question of the ecclesiological aspects of justification among biblical exegetes cf. especially W. Klaiber, *Rechtfertigung und Gemeinde. Ein Untersuchung zum paulinischen Kirchenverständnis*, Göttingen 1982; A. von Dobbeler, *Glaube als Teilhabe. Historische und semantische Grundlagen der paulinischen Theologie und Ekklesiologie des Glaubens*, Tübingen 1987, pp. 97ff.; J. Roloff, *Die Kirche im Neuen Testament*, Göttingen 1993.   177 Cf. especially H. Hübner, *Das Gesetz bei Paulus*, Göttingen 1980; S. Westerholm, *Israel's Law and the Church's Faith . . .* , op. cit.; J. Reumann, *Righteousness in the New Testament . . .* , op. cit.   178 S. Westerholm in particular has maintained that behind the 'social function of the law' (Dunn) is to be found the more fundamental issue of the relationship between personal salvation and human activity (cf. S. Westerholm, *Israel's Law and the Church's Faith . . .* , op. cit.; 'Paul and the Law in Romans 9–11', in *Paul and the Mosaic Law*, J.D.G. Dunn (ed.), op. cit., pp. 215–237).

first place, when others are not considered to be worthy of such a standing. As Dunn comments:

> It is important to appreciate that both emphases are rooted in a fundamental assertion of the sufficiency of faith; both protest against any attempt to add or require something more than faith on the human side when computing what makes a person acceptable to God. The difference which become apparent in earlier chapters [of Galatians] is that the added factor against which Paul himself was protesting was not individual human effort, but the assumption that ethnic origin and identity is a factor in determining the grace of God and its expression. Ethnic origin and identity is a different way of assessing human worth, but one more fundamental than the question of ability to perform good works. What Paul protested against was even more insidious—the assumption that the way people are constituted by birth rules them in or rules them out from receiving God's grace. Paul's protest was not against a high regard for righteousness, against dedicated devotion to God's law. It was rather against the corollary to such devotion: that failure to share in that devotion meant exclusion from the life of the world to come, and that the majority of peoples of the world were in principle so excluded.[179]

It is not mistaken for a Christian to strive to fulfill God's commandments with all the God-given energies he or she has received. Besides it is impossible for a Christian not to belong to the saved community, the Church, Christ's own 'body'. However, to be faithful to the inner truth of this 'incorporation', it is necessary for each and every Christian to strive to communicate the Gospel of Christ to the whole of humanity.

THE MEANING OF THE RIGHTEOUSNESS OF GOD ('IUSTITIA DEI')

As we saw in the first chapter, Luther's new understanding of the biblical (specifically Pauline) term *iustitia Dei*, the righteousness of God, is theologically situated at the very inception of his reflection on the nature of justification. He insisted that the Christian should not consider and confide in the *attribute* of divine justice (*iustitia Dei* in subjective genitive), against which he might *calibrate* his own justice and act accordingly, but rather the gracious *action* of God justifying the sinner (*iustitia Dei* in objective genitive). He sees in this reading a rediscovery of the true Paul, especially when the latter exclaims:

> For I am not ashamed of the gospel: it is the power of God (δύναμις γὰρ Θεου) for salvation to every one who has faith, to the Jew first and also to the

179 J.D.G. Dunn, 'The Influence of Galatians in Christian Thought', in *The Theology of Paul's Letter to the Galatians*, Cambridge 1993, pp. 133–145 (here 143f.).

Greek. For in it the righteousness of God (Δικαιοσύνη Θεου) is revealed through faith for faith; as it is written, 'The righteous shall live by faith' (Rom 1:16–17).[180]

However, in recent decades the term *iustitia Dei* has come under considerable scrutiny at the level of biblical exegesis.[181] The discussion has been centered on two points. Firstly, the significance of the term in the overall context of Pauline theology. This we have examined, in part, in the last section. Secondly, recent discussion has attempted to explain what exactly the genitive construction Δικαιοσύνη Θεου refers to: is an objective genitive being used, denoting righteousness as a gift of God to man and counting before God, or is it a subjective genitive, referring to an attribute (justice) of divine being and action, according to which he gives to each one according to his deeds?[182]

Different understandings of 'the righteousness of God'   For Luther, certainly, the objective genitive understanding of the 'righteousness of God' prevails, emphasizing as it does the unconditional gift-character of salvation.[183] God attributes justice to the sinner, whose actions whether sinful or upright no longer deserve (or 'merit') retribution. Righteousness (*iustitia aliena*) thus remains extrinsic to the one who is justified, yet the latter is no longer without hope, but is accepted by God and liberated in order to live a new life. As we saw earlier, Luther wished to avoid anything which could smack of a narrowly *retributive* notion of divine justice, seeing in this the possibility and danger of attributing to man a justice of his own before God.[184]

---

180 On this text, cf. K. Kertelge, *'Rechtfertigung' bei Paulus*, Münster 1967, pp. 93ff.   181 On the discussion, cf. the works of K. Kertelge, *'Rechtfertigung' bei Paulus*, Münster 1967; M.T. Brauch, 'Perspectives on "God's righteousness" in recent German discussion', in an appendix to E.P. Sanders, *Paul and Palestinian Judaism* . . . , op. cit., pp. 523–542, both of which I have followed closely. Of particular importance is the conference of E. Käsemann, 'Gottesgerechtigkeit bei Paulus', in *Zeitschrift für Theologie und Kirche* 58 (1961) 367–378, the reply of R. Bultmann, 'Δικαιοσύνη Θεου', in *Journal of Biblical Literature* 83 (1964) 12–16, as well as the studies of Käsemann's disciples C. Müller, *Gottes Gerechtigkeit und Gottes Volk: Eine Untersuchung zu Römer* 9–11, Göttingen 1964, and P. Stuhlmacher, *Gerechtigkeit Gottes bei Paulus*, Göttingen 1966. Cf. A. di Marco, Δικαιοσύνη, Δικαίωμα, Δικαίωσις, in *Laurentianum* 24 (1983) 46–75; D.A. Campbell, *The Rhetoric of Righteousness in Romans* 3.21–26, Sheffield 1992, pp. 138–156.   182 On the different implications of one or the other rendering, cf. J.A. Ziesler, *The Meaning of Righteousness in Paul. A Linguistic and Theological Enquiry*, New York-London 1972.   183 Cf. for example M. Luther, *De Servo Arbitrio* (WA 18: 768 f.): 'Faith of Christ (*fides Christi*) in Latin means the faith Christ has, but in Hebrew our faith in Christ. Just as the justice of God (*justitia Dei*) means in Latin the justice which God has, whereas in Hebrew it means the justice that comes from God and which man has before God'. More or less the same thing can be said of Augustine's interpretation (cf. for example *De gratia et libero arbitrio* 12: 24).   184 On the notion of the retributive justice of God in the Scholastic period, cf. H. Denifle, *Die abendländischen Schriftausleger bis Luther über 'Iustitia Dei' [Röm I.17] und 'Iustificatio'*, op. cit.; H. Bornkamm, 'Justitia dei in der Scholastik und bei Luther', in *Archiv für Reformationsgeschichte* 39 (1942) 1–46.

The weakness of Luther's position lies in its inability to adequately found an ethical system meaningful in the religious sphere on the basis of his doctrine of *iustitia Dei*. Understandably, his vision of things was lost by the prevailing moralism of liberal 19th-century exegetes and theologians,[185] who tended to consider the term in an ethical-abstractive mode (Δικαιοσύνη Θεου in subjective genitive) which Luther had perceived to have infected the Church and Christian spirituality of his own time.

Of course the objective genitive understanding of Δικαιοσύνη Θεου favoured by Luther is quite common in Paul's writings. In the letter to the Philippians, for example, he speaks of the Christ he wants to gain, while 'not having a righteousness of my own, based on the law, but that which is through faith in Christ, the *righteousness from God* that depends on faith' (Phil 3:9: literally, 'that is supported by faith'). The righteousness of God is thus clearly opposed to any possible righteousness on Paul's own part. Similarly in the letter to the Romans, we read: 'Being ignorant of the righteousness that comes from God, and seeking their own, they did not submit to God's righteousness' (Rom 10:3).[186] So it would seem that Paul speaks of righteousness predominantly on *God's* part, not man's. Righteousness, therefore, can only be an entirely 'free gift' (Rom 5:17) of God, independent of human works.

However, the term Δικαιοσύνη Θεου taken in the subjective genitive sense is also to be found in the epistles of St Paul. It denotes the justice of God insofar as this is *bestowed on us*, imputed to us, thus justifying us, as the personified power of God constituting and defining the redeemed community. Again in the letter to the Romans, Paul states that in the Gospel 'the righteousness of God is revealed through faith' (Rom 1:17). The purpose of redemption as worked by Christ, he says, 'is *to show God's righteousness*, because in his divine forbearance he had passed over former sins' (Rom 3:25).[187] Later he speaks of sinners who, 'being ignorant of the *righteousness that comes from God*, and seeking to establish their own . . . did not submit to God's righteousness' (Rom 10:3).

The reappearance of the subjective genitive reading of Δικαιοσύνη Θεου in Protestant circles towards the end of the last century is due in part to development in philological studies,[188] in part to the notion, developed by H. Cremer on the basis of his study of the Old Testament notion of divine justice (sᵉdáqâ), that justice in God is primarily relational (or 'economic') and not essential (or attributive), and is closely linked with God's faithfulness to the covenant he established with man, and man's behaviour within such a covenant. Δικαιοσύνη Θεου, in other words, expresses nei-

185 Cf. especially A. Ritschl, *Die christliche Lehre von der Rechtfertigung und Versöhnung*, op. cit., vol. 2 (1874), pp. 318 f. and H. Cremer, *Die paulinische Rechtfertigungslehre in Zusammenhange ihrer geschichtlichen Voraussetzungen*, Gütersloh 1900. Also cf. P. Kölbing, 'Studien zur paulinischen Theologie', in *Theologische Studien und Kritiken* 68 (1895) 7–51; T. Häring, ΔΙΚΑΙΟΣΥΝΗ ΘΕΟΥ *bei Paulus*, Tübingen 1896; E. Kühl, *Der Brief des Paulus an die Römer*, Leipzig 1913, pp. 38–46. 186 On Rom 10:3, cf. K. Kertelge, *Rechtfertigung . . .*, op. cit., pp. 103ff. 187 On Rom 3:21–26, cf. ibid., pp. 8off. 188 Cf. especially T. Häring, ΔΙΚΑΙΟΣΥΝΗ ΘΕΟΥ *bei Paulus*, op. cit., p. 13.

ther God's action nor his essential attributes, but rather is a reflection of the conduct of one who acts in the context of a pact or covenant.[189]

Understandably, many authors, Catholics among them, opted for a midway position between the two readings, understanding the term 'the righteousness of God' as a *genitivus auctoris*; Δικαιοσύνη Θεου would thus mean the righteousness coming from God, attributed to man and founding his relationship with God.[190] However, the influential studies of R. Bultmann, following likewise in the general line of *genitivus auctoris*, come to understand divine justification principally as a divine 'action or event',[191] or more specifically, 'as an *eschatological* action and *eschatological* event',[192] and thus a pure gift of God. Righteousness, therefore, for Bultmann 'is a forensic term. It does not mean the ethical quality of a person . . . but a relationship. That is, δικαιοσύνη is not something a person has on his own; rather it is something he has in the verdict of the forum . . . "Righteousness" then is the "favourable standing" that a person has in the eyes of others'.[193] The sinlessness of one who has been justified is not, for Bultmann, equivalent to ethical perfection, but lies in the fact that God no longer 'counts' man's sin against him.[194] Bultmann's interpretation, as we have already noted, is centered on the individual, who is not ontologically transformed by God's power, but simply lives within a transformed historical situation offering him the opportunity of making an authentic decision of obedient faith.[195] For Bultmann, in other words, the righteousness of God, remaining both eschatological and forensic, is taken in a classically Lutheran sense.

Recent reinterpretations of 'the righteousness of God'   Of particular interest in a renewed understanding of the formula has been E. Käsemann's 1961 brief study 'The justice of God according to Paul'.[196] This essay undoubtedly has marked a turning point in the debate on justification, even though Catholic exegetes before him, such as Lyonnet, had already arrived at many of his conclusions.[197]

---

189 Cf. H. Cremer, *Die paulinische Rechtfertigungslehre* . . . , op. cit., pp. 33ff.   190 Cf. for example R. Cornely, *Epistula ad Romanos*, Paris 1896, pp. 68–70; F. Prat, *La théologie de Saint Paul*, vol. 2, Paris 1930, pp. 291–300; R. Lemonnyer, 'Justification', in *Dictionnaire de Théologie Catholique* 8/2, 2058–75; M.-J. Lagrange, *Epître aux Romains*, Paris 1950; L. Cerfaux, 'Justice, Justification', in *Dictionnaire de la Bible, Supplément* 4 (1949) 1471–1496; A. Nygren, *Der Römerbrief*, Göttingen 1954; O. Michel, *Der Brief an die Römer*, Göttingen 1963. According to the latter, the justice of God is 'both the judicial verdict of God and his eschatological gift of salvation' (ibid., p. 45).   191 Cf. R. Bultmann, *Theology of the New Testament*, op. cit., vol. 1, pp. 282–287 (here 286). Cf. also his 'Δικαιοσύνη Θεου', op. cit. Cf. M. Brauch, ' "God's Righteousness" in Recent German Discussion', op. cit., pp. 526ff. Bultmann's line is followed by E. Jüngel, *Paulus und Jesus*, Tübingen 1962, p. 45.   192 Cf. R. Bultmann, *Theology of the New Testament*, op. cit., vol. 1, p. 286.   193 R. Bultmann, *Theology of the New Testament*, op. cit., vol. 1, p. 272.   194 Ibid., p. 276f.   195 Cf. ibid., 274f.; paragraph 38.   196 Cf. E. Käsemann, 'Gottesgerechtigkeit bei Paulus', op. cit. English translation, used here: ' "The Righteousness of God" in Paul', in his *New Testament Questions of Today*, London/Philadelphia 1969, pp. 168–182.   197 Cf. S. Lyonnet, 'De "iustitia Dei" in Epistola ad Romanos', in *Verbum Domini* 25 (1947) 23–34; 118–121; 129–144; 193–203; 257–263. He understands the righteousness of God *essentialiter activitas salvifica Dei* (ibid., p. 139). 'Iustitia Dei ad quam provocat Apostolus ea est quam invocabat Psalmista vel Daniel, Isaiasque annuntiaverat

Käsemann's study attempted to overcome the stalemate established by the apparently incompatible interpretations that follow on from the opposed genitives. Against Bultmann,[198] he pointed out that the notion of 'the righteousness of God' is not Paul's in an original and exclusive sense, but is to be found in the Old Testament, intertestamentary literature and in other writings of the New Testament, where it has quite a concrete and independent meaning which Paul assumes and reworks.[199] Judaism, Käsemann says, speaks of God's righteousness neither in terms of a personal ethical quality, nor as a pure gift, but *as a relationship of fidelity within a covenant community*. 'Originally signifying trustworthiness in regard to the community, it [the term 'righteousness'] came to mean the rehabilitated standing of a member of the community who had been acquitted of an offence against it'.[200] The 'righteousness *of God*' thus expresses the divine action whereby the sinner is rehabilitated and reconciled. The term 'runs parallel to the other similar expressions, the "energy', the "love", the "peace", the "wrath" of God and that these, equally, can be used in personified form and can connote divine power'.[201] Käsemann's central thesis is the following:

> God's power becomes God's gift when it takes possession of us and so speak, enters into us, so that it can be said in Gal 2:20, 'It is no longer I who live, but Christ who lives in me.' This gives us a proper understanding of the double bearing of the genitive construction: the gift which is being bestowed here is

tempore messianico revelatam iri, nempe activitas Dei qua Deus iustus quidem est, non vero in quantum reprobos damnat . . . , sed qua populum suum restaurat et a peccati servitute eum liberat seu iterum secum coniungat, aliis verbis qua iustificat' (ibid., p. 135). cf. also S. Schmidt, 'S. Pauli "iustitia Dei" notione iustitiae, quae in V.T. et apud S. Paulum habetur, dilucidata', in *Verbum Domini* 37 (1959) 96–105, who completely avoids identifying divine righteousness with God's saving activity. 'Iustitia Dei (in V.T.) non est dicenda nec exclusive nec essentialiter salvifica . . . non est identificanda cum eius bonitate et misericordia . . . sed consistit in conformitate actionis Dei cum Esse divino ipso' (ibid., p. 101). **198** On the discussion, cf. H. Hübner, 'Existentiale Interpretation der paulinischen "Gerechtigkeit Gottes". Zur Kontroverse R. Bultmann-E. Käsemann', in *New Testament Studies* 21 (1974/75) 462–488. **199** Käsemann mentions Deut 33:21; Dan 6:10; Jas 1:20; 1 QS 11:12; Mt 6:33. To support his assertions, he relies on the findings of A. Oepke, 'Δικαιοσύνη Θεου bei Paulus in neuer Beleuchtung', in *Theologische Literaturzeitung* 78 (1953) 257–263. On this point as in others, Paul is not in conflict with the Jewish-Christian tradition, but approves and accepts it because he sees in it 'a legitimate announcement of Christ' (K. Wegenast, *Das Verständis der Tradition bei Paulus und in den Deuteropaulinen*, Neukirchen 1962, p. 79). Against the position of Käsemann (that 'righteousness of God' is a previously existing technical term), cf. E.P. Sanders, *Paul and Palestinian Judaism*, op. cit., p. 494, and H. Thyen, *Studien zur Sündenvergebung im Neuen Testament und ihren alttestamentlichen und jüdischen Voraussetzungen*, Göttingen 1970, pp. 56ff. For an analysis of this material, especially of the Qumran documents, cf. K. Kertelge, *Rechtfertigung* . . . , op. cit., pp. 27ff., and for non-Pauline New Testament texts, cf. ibid., pp. 63–67. **200** E. Käsemann, ' "The Righteousness of God" in Paul', op. cit., p. 172. **201** Ibid., p. 173. 'Thus Rom 1:17 and 3:31 speak of this righteousness revealed in an earthly epiphany, Rom 10:6 portrays it as itself speaking and acting; while it appears in 1 Cor 1:30 as the direct manifestation of the Christ, and in 2 Cor 5:21 as that of the community' (ibid.).

never at any time separable from its Giver. It partakes of the character of power [*Machtcharakter der Gabe*], insofar as God himself enters the arena and remains in the arena with it.[202]

In other words, the righteousness of God should not be understood merely as an exterior *gift of God*, but also as the power of God which makes man just. Käsemann develops this idea in the context of other elements of Pauline theology which clearly express how the power of God always accompanies and follows his gift.[203] To describe this unitary character of righteousness, he uses terms such as the *Machtcharakter der Gabe* (the power character of gift), God's *heilsetzende Macht* (saving power).

Käsemann makes it quite clear that God's righteousness cannot be considered simply as an abstract property of the divine nature, because if it were, it would be impossible to relate it to its equivalents (divine faithfulness, for example, which is always linked to the life of the covenant community)[204] and corollaries (for example the making-over to a human being of a property of the divine nature).[205] 'The key to this whole Pauline viewpoint is that power is always seeking to realize itself in action and must indeed do so. It does this with greatest effect when it no longer remains external to us but enters into us and, as the apostle says, makes us its members'.[206] Thus man's transformation (*Existenzwandel*) though real, nonetheless always remains a gift. Hence 'every gift of God which has ceased to be seen as the presence of the Giver and has therefore lost its character as a personal address, is grace misused and working to our destruction. Justification and sanctification must therefore coincide, provided that by justification we mean that Christ takes power over our life.'[207] He concludes by saying that 'Δικαιοσύνη Θεου is for Paul God's sovereignty over the world revealing itself eschatologically in Jesus . . . the rightful power with which God makes his cause to triumph in the world which has fallen away from him and which yet, as creation, is his inviolable possession.'[208] Justification is thus equivalent to 'new creation'.

This interpretation of Δικαιοσύνη Θεου made by Käsemann, of course, goes to

---

202 Ibid.   203 He mentions the following examples. 'Just as, according to 2 Cor 12:9 and 13:3f., the power of God is at the same time active as a gift within us, so the Spirit who effects the resurrection of the dead is at the same time the πνεῦμα ἐν ἡμῖν, so, too, Christ, whom Paul already hails as Lord of the world, not only gives himself for us but also dwells and lives in us. While χάρις means primarily the power of grace, nothing could be more concrete than its individuation in the χάρισμα bestowed on each of us. The love of God in Rom 8:39 is the power from which nothing can separate us; in Rom 5:5 it is the gift poured out into our hearts' (ibid., p. 174).   204 Cf. ibid. and also E. Käsemann, 'Zum Verständnis von Römer 3.23–26', in *Exegetische Versuche und Besinnungen*, Göttingen 1960, pp. 96–100.   205 Cf. E. Käsemann, ' "The Righteousness of God" in Paul', op. cit., p. 174.   206 Ibid., p. 175.   207 Ibid.   208 Ibid., p. 180. R. Bultmann, in his reply to Käsemann's paper ('Δικαιοσύνη Θεου', in *Journal of Biblical Literature* 83 (1964) 12–16), reaffirms his own position regarding the 'gift-quality' of Δικαιοσύνη Θεου and does not admit that Paul radicalized and universalized the concept, understanding it as God's power and saving activity bringing about a new creation.

the very heart of the justification debate, for it has contributed towards overcoming, in principle, the perceived incompatibility between 'forensic' and 'effective' justification. For the most part the general thrust of his position has been accepted by biblical exegetes, such as his own disciples C. Müller[209] and P. Stuhlmacher,[210] and also by K. Kertelge,[211] J. Reumann,[212] J.D.G. Dunn[213] and J.A. Fitzmyer.[214] Other authors, such as H. Conzelmann[215] and G. Klein,[216] retracing the steps of Bultmann, take an opposite view. However, it is interesting to note that Käsemann's approach

---

209 C. Müller, (*Gottes Gerechtigkeit* . . . , op. cit.) explains that Paul's doctrine 'is permeated by an eschatological creation-tradition, in terms of the right of the Creator over against his Creation, and that this creation-tradition characterizes the essential nature of the Pauline doctrine of justification throughout' (M. Brauch, ' "God's Righteousness" . . .', op. cit., p. 529). ' "God's Righteousness" is therefore the victory of God in which his universal claim vis-à-vis the world prevails' (C. Müller, *Gottes Gerechtigkeit* . . . , op. cit., p. 26). 'The "realization of God's right" (*Rechtsverwirklichung*) among the "new" people of God is not experienced in terms of an abstract norm or imputed idea, but in terms of a relationship in which God is really Lord and in which his Lordship is realized in the concrete life . . . As Creator, God is not vindicated, i.e., his right is not established, until man submits to the "forensic" judgement' (M. Brauch, ' "God's Righteousness" . . .', op. cit., pp. 530f.; cf. C. Müller, op. cit., pp. 74f.). **210** P. Stuhlmacher (*Gottesgerechtigkeit bei Paulus* . . ., op. cit.) develops Käsemann's thesis carefully. The 'righteousness of God' is God's own creating-power ('the power of the creating Word of God', ibid., p. 175) which in the gospel moves through the world, creates faith and thus inaugurates God's new world (cf. ibid., pp. 83 f.; cf. M. Brauch, ' "God's Righteousness" . . .', op. cit., pp. 531–533). At the same time God's re-creating power provokes a real response on man's part, in such a way that justification for Paul means 'the obligating, renewing calling of the individual, by the power of God, into the realm of encounter with God which has been opened by Christ. This renewing calling culminates in service' (*Gottesgerechtigkeit bei Paulus* . . . , op. cit. p. 258). **211** Cf. K. Kertelge ('*Rechtfertigung' bei Paulus*... op. cit.) According to Kertelge, ' "forensic" judgement is at the same time "effective" judgement, because the judgement of God has creative power (cf. ibid., p. 123). God's action is not exhausted in simply an external decree (a purely forensic declaration) but signifies the effective creation of a new reality through God. This new creation does not involve the establishment of a static ontology within man, but a 'relational reality' (*Beziehungsrealität*), 'which consists of nothing except a new relationship between God and man created by God, the content of which is, from the side of God, Lordship, and from the side of man, obedience' (ibid., p. 127). **212** Cf. J. Reumann, *'Righteousness' in the New Testament*, Philadelphia/New York 1982. 'Righteousness/ justice/ justification terminology in the Hebrew Scriptures is "action-oriented", not just "status" or "being" language' (ibid., p. 15f.). **213** Cf. J.D.G. Dunn, *Romans*, op. cit., pp. 40–42; 287f.; 338f. **214** Cf. J.A. Fitzmyer, *Romans. A New Translation with Introduction and Commentary* (Anchor Bible, no. 33), New York 1992, pp. 257–263 (here p. 262). **215** H. Conzelmann ('Die Rechtfertigungslehre des Paulus: Theologie oder Anthropologie?', in *Evangelische Theologie* 28 (1968) 389–404) reaffirms the existentialist-anthropological approach of Bultmann, insisting that 'Pauline theology must be interpreted anthropologically, since Christology and soteriology come together in the salvation-event which is proclaimed to man in the kerygma' (ibid., pp. 391f.). According to Conzelmann, when Paul uses the term 'righteousness of God', 'he speaks of man's own righteousness, given to him by God *sola gratia*' (M. Brauch, ' "God's Righteousness" . . .', op. cit., p. 538). Conzelmann clearly rejects Käsemann's *Machtcharakter der Gabe*, since 'the content of the kerygma . . . is exclusively gospel, bearer of righteousness, Paul knows of no power-aspect of God which can be isolated' (op. cit., p. 399). **216** Cf. G. Klein, 'Gottes Gerechtigkeit als Thema der neuesten Paulus-Forschung', in Various authors, *Rekonstruction und Interpretation*, München 1969, pp. 225–236.

has been almost literally endorsed by the USA dialogue statement *Justification by Faith*:

> Recent biblical scholarship sees the righteousness of which Paul speaks both as a gift from God and, in some passages, as an attribute or quality of God, a power exercised on behalf of sinful humanity to save and justify (*heilsetzende Macht*). This widespread consensus in the modern understanding of Δικαιοσύνη Θεου, according to which it is an attribute of God, but also his power present in his gift, should help us further to go beyond the divisive issues of the sixteenth century.[217]

Divine righteousness and the doctrine of justification   From his fundamental premise, Käsemann draws several corollaries. The following three could be mentioned.

Firstly, no discontinuity or tension need be posited between the sacramental and ethical aspects of Christian life. 'In these circumstances there is no longer any real tension between sacraments and ethics . . . If a transformation of our existence is really effected in baptism and if God's Word does posit a new creation, this cannot help but mean a change of lordship. The new Lord cuts us off from what we were before and never allows us to remain what we are at any given time . . . We no longer exist simply for ourselves and cannot therefore simply dig in behind what we have received. Only so long as we keep on the pilgrim way and allow ourselves to be recalled daily to the allegiance of Christ, can we abide in the gift which we have received and can it abide, living and powerful, in us.'[218] In other words, Paul's understanding of justification 'by faith, without works' does not involve as such a breaking with the traditional Jewish view on the matter.

Secondly, Käsemann makes it clear, against Bultmann, that Paul's doctrine of justification, in spite of the appearances, is at odds with *individualism* of any kind, since it binds the saved human being both to God and to the community. In other words, divine righteousness establishes a relationship, a dialogue. 'It is true that Paul does, for the purpose of the mordant polemic against the Jewish motif of the "covenant people" portray the believer, and him alone, as the recipient of salvation. But the emergent character of the individual human being is to be seen here in immediate relation to the divine will for salvation, now directed towards the whole world and no longer limited by the confines of the law.'[219]

This goes to confirm what we have seen in the previous section:[220] Paul speaks of justification 'by faith alone' in apparently individualistic terms not with a view to undermining the Christian's 'belongingness' to the 'body' of Christ, which is of course determinative for a believer, nor to undo divine righteousness understood as a 'relationship', but to avoid Israel's election and privilege being considered in an elitist or restricted way.[221]

217 USA 131.   218 E. Käsemann, ' "The Righteousness of God" in Paul', op. cit., pp. 175f.   219 Ibid., p. 181.   220 Cf. 169–185.   221 To be noted is the contrast between Käsemann's attempt to over-

Finally, Käsemann sees the possibility of overcoming the tension, at the centre of the justification debate, between God's 'declaring righteous' and his 'making righteous' the sinner. He explains, albeit in somewhat actualistic terms, that 'according to 1 Cor 12:2f., God's power, in contrast to the power of the false gods, is not silent but bound up with the Word. It speaks to us in love and judgement so that we experience the pressure of its will, and by means of the Gospel, sets us in the posture (which it alone determines) "before the face of Christ" . . . This righteousness is the possibility of access to God, in which we have peace . . . and are reconciled with God . . . But a Lord that is no assured possession and is not subordinated to our arbitrary disposal . . . The status of a Christian under such lordship is no fantasy or ideological programme . . . Thus the divine presence posits reality. But whether or not this remains a living reality and whether or not the Christian status in the eyes of God . . . is preserved by obedience—these things are bound up with the actualization of the promise.'[222]

'Forensic' and 'effective' justification Thus no contrast or contradiction need be posited between 'forensic' and 'effective' justification, between *declaring* just and *making* just.[223] In the words of Kertelge, 'the value man must have before God as a condition for salvation, is not constituted for Paul by the moral rank of man, but is created by a divine decree, that is by God himself . . . Divine judgement contains creating power. The justification of the sinner does not only have a forensic value, but, as forensic, also an "effective" power'.[224] In brief terms, 'God's righteousness is his acting out of the obligation [the covenant] which he took upon himself in creating the world and in choosing Israel to be his people'.[225]

come an individualistic understanding of Christianity espoused by Bultmann, and that expressed some years later in which he strongly criticizes K. Stendahl's reminder that Luther's interpretation of Paul was also fundamentally individualistic. See note 115 above.   **222** E. Käsemann, ' "The Righteousness of God" in Paul', op. cit., pp. 176f.   **223** The same point is made by P. Bovati, *Re-establishing justice: legal terms, concepts and procedures in the Hebrew Bible*, Sheffield 1994 (original Italian, 1986). Bovati, after a thorough research into the legal terminology employed in the Old Testament, distinguishes between two kinds of judgement: *rib* and *mishpát*. The first, usually translated as 'quarrel' or 'controversy', refers to the re-establishment of a broken relationship between two sides through the conceding of pardon and an act of mercy, which mitigates anger of the offended party. Often a mediator or intercessor is present on the side of the one guilty. The second procedure, *mishpát*, usually translated as 'judgement', is a specification of the first, in which a completely impartial third party dictates sentence between the litigants. In the Old Testament, God at times is presented as the judge between conflicting parties; more commonly he is the accuser, insofar as he is personally involved. St Paul, logically, works within these coordinates, yet for him the process of justification always refers to *rib*, never to *mishpát*. In other words, justification is never a simple remission or absolution of the fault, but always the re-establishment of interpersonal relationship between two estranged parties. The notion of pure 'forensic justification' is unknown. Justification on the contrary involves regeneration, renewal of a broken relationship. On this cf. also C. Breytenbach, *Versöhnung. Eine Studie zur paulinischen Soteriologie*, Neukirchen 1989; C.K. Barrett, *Paul. An Introduction to his Thought*, London 1994.   **224** K. Kertelge, *'Rechtfertigung' bei Paulus* . . . , op. cit., p. 123.   **225** J.D.G. Dunn and A.M. Suggate, *The Justice of God* . . . , op. cit., p. 37.

Kertelge points out that this 'new creation' does not involve for Paul the establishment of a static ontology within man, but rather a 'relational reality' (*Beziehungsrealität*), 'which consists of nothing other than a new relationship between God and
man created by God, the content of which is, from God's side, Lordship, and from
man's, obedience'.[226] Though we will still have to see what exactly such a 'relational
reality' consists of, the same author holds that 'it is the forensic-eschatological structure of Paul's concept of justification which guards against a Gnostic simplification
of "justification" in the sense of a purely present possession of salvation. Such a
simplification is clearly seen in an interpretation of the Pauline concept of justification which considers it as a transformation of man's nature out of which the new
ethical life results almost automatically'.[227]

THE DOCTRINE OF JUSTIFICATION AND CONTEMPORARY LUTHERANISM

In spite of the state of academic and ecclesial irrelevance it seemed to have fallen
into, the doctrine of justification 'by faith alone' has in recent times come to the fore
in theological discussion, particularly among Lutherans. Three reasons for this
phenomenon may be suggested.

In the first place, as we have seen in the last chapter, the exigencies and urgency
of the ecumenical movement have pressed all sides to confront the inner core and
historical roots of their respective understandings of Christ, of the Church and of
Christianity in the world, in fruitful, though demanding and wide-ranging studies,
particularly in the critical area of justification.

Secondly, ground-breaking work of theologians and exegetes, principally Lutheran and Evangelical, has come to offer a better appreciation and understanding
of the meaning and application of the doctrine of justification. Renewed studies of
Luther's own writings have shown that his Christ-centered understanding of justification is quite at odds with the 'forensic' or extrinsic categories that have often
been pressed on it (see chapters one and two),[228] and is nearer than is often realized
to the *unica causa formalis* which is at the heart of Trent's decree on justification
(chapter three).[229] Besides, we have considered the fact that the divine act of justification is not only forensic or declarative, but effective as well, conferring on the
believer, in a 'new creation', the reality promised by God's word.[230] And lastly, we
have seen that insistence on the article of justification 'by faith alone', that is 'without works of the law', does not only mean that the Christians should avoid taking

226 K. Kertelge, *'Rechtfertigung' bei Paulus* . . . , op. cit., p. 127.   227 K. Kertelge, *'Rechtfertigung'
bei Paulus* . . . , op. cit., p. 159. R. Reitzenstein (*Die hellenistischen Mysterienreligionen nach ihren
Grundgedanken und Wirkungen*, Leipzig 1927, pp. 258–261) finds in hermetic literature traces of a
view of justice which equates the gift of God with a natural quality or power of the soul over which
man retains disposal.   228 Cf. pp. 19–69 above.   229 Cf. especially pp. 80–83 above.   230 Cf.
pp. 185–194.

personal satisfaction or complacency in their good works, considering perhaps that they can win God's favour and positively contribute towards their salvation. Good works should also avoid becoming expressions of ecclesial complacency, considering it sufficient to belong to a saved community, the Church: openness to God's grace and total confidence in his merciful love must be expressed in terms of a universal missionary spirit and commitment so that the saving power of God may reach the very ends of the earth.[231]

In the third place, Lutherans have had to face up to and reassess their understanding of the doctrine of justification on two specific occasions: in response to the challenge to traditional Lutheran doctrine on justification made by theologians such as Karl Barth, which has served 'to sharpen the question of Lutheran identity',[232] and on the occasion of the Lutheran World Federation general meeting in Helsinki in 1963.

1.   *A contribution to the justification debate: Karl Barth on the meaning of justification* [233]

The entire theological construct of the evangelical theologian Karl Barth doubtlessly constituted for all twentieth century evangelical Christians, and to some degree for Catholics as well, an explosive *cri-de-coeur* in the face of liberal Protestantism's relapse into a theology of practical works-righteousness. However, his profound criticisms of Lutheranism, especially in respect of the central rôle of the doctrine of justification, have not been kindly received by Lutherans. While admiring Luther's effort to place Christ at the centre of Christian life and reflection, Barth criticized his distinction between law and gospel, seeing in it an acknowledgment of a dark, unknown, enigmatic side in God, expressing itself in terms of mysterious forces at work in history and nature, in an unhealthy mysticism leading to political conservatism and unwillingness to espouse change in society, and in the potentially secularizing virtualities of Luther's doctrine of the 'two kingdoms'.[234] Specifically, Barth does not recognize that the doctrine of justification constitutes the article 'by which the Church stands or falls'.

Interestingly enough, however, Barth understands the doctrine of justification as such in a decidedly forensic fashion, not out of keeping with a classical Lutheran stance.[235] The difference between Barth and Lutheranism lies in the fact that whereas the former's is a theology of *revelation*, Lutheranism is a theology of *salvation*. Hence, faith for Barth is correlative exclusively to revelation/ignorance, whereas for

---

231 Cf. pp. 169–185 above.   **232** Cf. C.E. Braaten, *Justification* . . ., op. cit., p. 64.   **233** Cf. C.E. Braaten, *Justification* . . . , op. cit., pp. 63–79 and A.E. McGrath, *Iustitia Dei* . . . , op. cit., vol. 2, pp. 170-184, which has been followed closely. Also cf. J. Alfaro, 'Justificación barthiana y justificación católica', in *Gregorianum* 39 (1958) 757–769; G. Colzani, 'La dottrina della giustificazione alla prova della storia. La proposta barthiana ed il dibattito ecumenico', in *Annales Theologici* 10 (1996) 119-146.   **234** Cf. C.E. Braaten, *Justification* . . . , op. cit., pp. 64f.   **235** Cf. especially K. Barth, *Church Dogmatics 4/1: The Doctrine of Reconciliation*, Edinburgh 1956, pp. 514–642.

Lutherans, it pairs off with salvation/sin. And hence 'faith alone' for Barth would mean that we have no way of knowing God and his design to save mankind other than by positive revelation culminating in Christ. For Lutherans of course it means that nothing other than God's action in Christ can save us, by awakening our unconditional faith in him. In the words of Wingren, criticizing Barth, 'it is exactly this framework which is questionable. "Revelation" stands in the place where "justification", or "forgiveness of sin", i.e., the gospel in the essential meaning of that word, ought to stand. If "justification" stands at the centre, it is assumed that man already knows something; yes, that God has already "revealed" himself through his work in creation (cf. Rom 1:20), although he has not disclosed his plan of salvation in this creation'.[236]

God, according to Lutherans, reveals himself in two ways, through creation and the law for condemnation, and through Christ and the gospel for salvation.[237] But in both cases there is a real knowledge of God. For Lutherans 'the human being stands under the divine wrath and judgement, *not without knowledge but without excuse, and thus guilty*. The gospel enters a situation where God and human beings have already been involved with each other, delivering a new righteousness apart from the law . . . [Thus] in the light of justification, bondage rather than ignorance defines the great chasm between God and humanity'.[238]

On one occasion Tillich made the following observation: 'One can distinguish two ways of approaching God: the way of overcoming estrangement and the way of meeting a stranger'.[239] Clearly Lutheranism envisages the former, just as Barth does the latter. According to Barth, man knows simply nothing of God or of his personal situation *coram Deo* without positive revelation.[240] The prime activity of God is not to save man (for Barth, all humans, included in God's eternal 'yes' to Christ, will eventually be saved),[241] but to 'bridge the epistemological gap between God and the godless world'.[242] Christianity in other words should be understood primarily in cognitive terms. Understandably therefore, since the doctrine of justification is not a reply to human ignorance but to human guilt, Barth considered Lutheran insistence on it excessive.[243] His position in respect of the critical function of justification is to be found in his critique of E. Wolf's programmatic and influential study 'The

236 G. Wingren, *Theology in Conflict: Nygren, Barth, Bultmann*, Edinburgh/London 1958, pp. 28f.   237 Cf. G. Wingren, *Schöpfung und Gesetz*, Göttingen 1960.   238 C.E. Braaten, *Justification . . .*, op. cit., pp. 74; 77. Emphasis added.   239 P. Tillich, 'Two Types of the Philosophy of Religion', in *Theology of Culture*, New York 1964, p. 10.   240 Understandably, Barth resisted all efforts to revive natural theology and ethics, particularly E. Brunner's notion of *Schöpfungsoffenbarung*, which he termed a 'return to the fleshpots of Egypt'. Cf. E. Brunner, *Natur und Gnade*, Tübingen 1934, passim; *Der Mensch im Widerspruch*, Zurich 1937, pp. 165ff.; and the reply of K. Barth, *Nein! Antwort an E. Brunner*, 1934, especially pp. 16f.; 24 ff.   241 Cf. K. Barth, *Church Dogmatics 2/2: The Doctrine of God*, Edinburgh 1957, pp. 175–194.   242 C.E. Braaten, *Justification . . .*, op. cit., p. 72. On the potential 'agnosticism' of Barth's reflection, and its capacity to spawn secularized or 'death-of-God' theologies, cf. J.L. Illanes, *Cristianismo, historia, mundo*, Pamplona 1972, p. 14.   243 Cf. K. Barth, *Church Dogmatics 4/1 . . .*, op. cit., pp. 518ff.

Doctrine of Justification as the Centre and Limit of reformed Theology'.[244] Wolf, following Luther, argues that God's salvific activity (*subjectum theologiae*) takes its meaning from the centrality of justification, beyond which everything is erroneous and poisonous (*error et venenum*).[245]

Though the doctrine of justification served its purpose in certain moments of the history of the Church, Barth admits, dogmatics should not universalize 'the needs and necessities of the moment . . . In the Church of Jesus Christ this doctrine has not always been *the* Word of the Gospel, and it would be an act of narrowing and unjust exclusiveness to proclaim and treat it as such.'[246] He concludes: 'We need a greater freedom than that which is allowed us if we move only within the framework of the Reformation doctrine of justification . . . The *articulus stantis et cadentis ecclesiae* is not the doctrine of justification as such, but its basis and culmination: the confession of Jesus Christ, in whom are hid all the treasures of wisdom and knowledge.'[247] Lutherans of course do not dispute this much: Christ is the basis and centre of theology. The point is that they express their faith in Christ as the basis and culmination of justification in terms of the *solus Christus*, which is the exact equivalent, in Christological terms, of the doctrine of justification of the sinner *sola fide*, by faith alone.

All in all, the fact remains that the Barth's theology is not as such a theology of salvation and justification, but a theology of revelation,[248] and therefore more in keeping with the content (whatever of the spirit) of the *Aufklärung* than with the theology of Luther. In McGrath's words: 'For Barth and the *Aufklärer*, Christ is supremely the revealer of the knowledge of man's true situation, by which man is liberated from false understandings of his situation . . . Barth's new emphasis on the theocentricity of theology . . . is not associated with a revival in interest in the *articulus justificationis*'.[249]

2. Helsinki 1963: towards a Lutheran understanding of justification

A key moment in the development of modern Lutheran doctrine on justification was the Helsinki meeting of the Lutheran World Federation in 1963.[250] The final

---

244 Cf. E. Wolf, 'Die Rechtfertigungslehre als Mitte und Grenze reformatischer Theologie', in *Pereginatio*, vol. 2, München 1965, pp. 11–21. On Barth's critique of Wolf, cf. A.E. McGrath, 'Karl Barth and the Articulus Iustificationis: the Significance of his Critique of Ernst Wolf within the Context of his Theological Method', in *Theologische Zeitschrift* 39 (1983) 349–361.   **245** E. Wolf, 'Die Rechtfertigungslehre . . .' op. cit., p. 14 (cf. M. Luther, WA 40/2: 328). Barth's criticism is to be found in his *Church Dogmatics* 4/1 . . . , op. cit., pp. 521f.   **246** Ibid., p. 523.   **247** Ibid., p. 527.   **248** And that in spite of Hans Küng's optimistic rapprochement between Barth's and Catholic teaching on justification in the 1950's (cf. H. Küng, *Justification: the Doctrine of Karl Barth and a Catholic Reflection*, New York 1964).   **249** A.E. McGrath, *Iustitia Dei* . . . , op. cit., vol. 2, p. 183 f. cf. idem., 'Karl Barth als Aufklärer? Der Zusammenhang seiner Lehre vom Werke Christi mit der Erwählungslehre', in *Kerygma und Dogma* 30 (1984) 273–283.   **250** Cf. C.E. Braaten, *Justification* . . . , op. cit., pp. 12–15.

document produced, *Justification today*,[251] is generally considered unsatisfactory in that it did not provide a single 'reformed' doctrine on justification. But the discussions were relevant and far-reaching in that they concentrated on the problem of justification in the present-day context, that is, in a period when sin, guilt and redemption no longer seemed to be at the centre of human consciousness, Christian life and theological reflection. Alienations other than those of personal sin and guilt needed to be addressed by the *articulus stantis et cadentis ecclesiae*, for example poverty and oppression (political theologies), intellectual doubt (Tillich), etc. The *terminus a quo* of salvation and of God's action in the world needed to be amplified and diversified in order to overcome the individualism rampant in some forms of evangelical Christianity, and give the doctrine of justification the centrality it once enjoyed.

Taking advantage of advances made in Luther research, biblical studies, analytical and existentialist philosophies, psychology, the Federation's principal intention was to express in clear terms the rôle of the doctrine of justification as a fundamental Christian principle for assessing and criticizing in a Christian manner the value of modern attempts at self-justification through scientific humanism, utopian socialism and totalitarian ideologies. In an address to the assembly G. Gloege stated:

> With the doctrine of justification we not only have one doctrine alongside other ones, but rather the very criterion which determines our every thought, every word and action before God.[252]

As things turned out, the assembly was unable to come up with a consistent, unitary statement on justification. The variety of positions taken can be attributed to a clear conflict in the interpretation of the doctrine of justification present at the meeting. Many Lutherans held on to a more traditional view of the doctrine, centered on a strictly forensic understanding of imputed righteousness, and on the wrath of God towards individual human sin.[253] However, a different vision of things, inspired by the writings of authors such as Karl Holl[254] and Gerhard Ebeling,[255] had for several decades been having an ever-growing influence on Lutheran thought. It should be noted that both sides intended quite positively to establish and consolidate *Lutheran identity*, and to do so by returning to the *authentic* Luther. They way in which this should be done, however, was a matter of dispute. Two areas should be especially noted.

251 Lutheran World Federation, 'Justification today', in *Lutheran World* 12 (1965), 1, suppl., 1–11.   252 G. Gloege, in E. Wilkens (ed.), *Helsinki 1963; Beiträge zum theologischen Gespräch des Lutherischen Weltbundes. Im Auftrage des Deutschen Nationalkomitees des Lutherischen Weltbundes*, Berlin 1964, p. 327.   253 Their principal point of reference was probably the 1862 work of T. Harnack, *Luthers Theologie mit besonderer Beziehung auf seine Versöhnungs- und Erlösungslehre*, 2 vols, 1862–1885, reissued in 1927.   254 Cf. K. Holl, *Gesammelte Aufsätze zur Kirchengeschichte*, 3 vols, especially vol. 1, Tübingen 1927.   255 Cf. pp. 161–168 above.

Firstly, Karl Holl, considered by many as the founder of modern *Lutherforschung*, distinguished in a Kantian way between justification in an 'analytical' sense, and justification in a 'synthetical' sense.[256] *Synthetic justification* may be defined as a declarative divine judgement whereby the sinner is justified solely on the basis of Christ's work; here, justification is taken in a purely 'forensic' way, as a legal fiction. According to Holl, this view was not shared by Luther; it was Melanchthon who understood and expressed it as such, and later on popularized it, making it the prevalent hallmark of classical Lutheranism. Luther's understanding of justification, conversely, was *analytic*, according to Holl, in the sense that God *really makes the sinner righteous*, in such a way that justification is a *reale Gerechtmachung* of the sinner. Luther in his earliest writings did not hold to a doctrine of double justice, nor does he juxtapose *Rechtfertigung* and *Gerechtmachung* (justification and 'making just'), but retains an integrative combination of the two. Were God not to really make the sinner righteous, he would be a untrue to himself, in treating the sinner as righteous when in fact he is not so. In a sense, this places regeneration logically *prior* to justification: God declares us righteous because he has made us righteous; in a sense justification *follows* regeneration, not the other way around. Both in our examination of Luther's own doctrine in the context of later developments in Lutheranism, and our analysis of the biblical doctrine of *iustitia Dei* in terms of *Machtcharakter der Gabe* would seem to substantially corroborate the validity of Holl's analysis.

Secondly, perhaps the most novel and enduring aspect of the reformulation of justification doctrine by these authors, especially Ebeling, is their insistence on the strictly hermeneutical and interpretative rôle of the *articulus stantis et cadentis ecclesiae*.[257] Let us examine it now.

3. *The centrality of justification as a critical or hermeneutical principle*

Karl Barth was quite right of course in saying that the doctrine of justification had had a lot of ups and downs throughout the history of the Church. Historically speaking even Lutheranism 'has refused to centre its theology upon the one article of justification'.[258] This article, he says, had not always, everywhere and for everyone (*semper, ubique et ab omnibus*) been the centre and norm of Christian faith and doctrine.[259] In fact, the very opposite is the case. And taking the side of the main sweep of Church tradition he says that 'we need a rather greater freedom than that which is allowed us if we move only within the framework of the Reformation doctrine of justification'.[260]

256 Cf. K. Holl, 'Die Rechtfertigungslehre in Luthers Vorlesung über den Römerbrief mit besonderer Rücksicht auf die Frage der Heilsgewißheit', in *Gesammelte Aufsätze . . .*, op. cit., vol. 1, pp. 111–154; and idem., 'Luthers Bedeutung für den Fortschritt der Auslegungskunst', in ibid., pp. 544–582. 257 The USA document explains that though this aspect of the doctrine of justification was 'of little direct importance at Helsinki . . . [it] has since become increasingly influential' (USA 88). 258 K. Barth, *Church Dogmatics 4/1 . . .*, op. cit., p. 527. 259 Cf. ibid., p. 524. 260 Ibid., p. 527.

To some degree, the chorus of voices that nowadays reclaim the centrality of the *articulus stantis et cadentis* would seem to explain Barth's protest. M. Kähler claimed that he constructed his entire dogmatics on this principle.[261] His disciple P. Tillich's affirmation of the structural centrality of the 'Protestant principle' moves in the same direction, as we saw earlier.[262] R. Bultmann declared that his demythologization programme is theologically underpinned by the doctrine of justification by faith alone.[263] W. Pannenberg on one occasion claimed that one of his major works, *Anthropology in Theological Perspective*, is implicitly guided by the article of justification by faith alone.[264] Other authors think alike.[265]

Of course it is important to clarify what exactly Lutherans mean when they say that the doctrine of justification is central to the whole of Christian life and theology. Specifically they maintain that we may not be *conscious* of the doctrine of justification acting as a kind of hermeneutical or critical principle over Christian life and theology. We may not apply it intentionally, but, whatever denomination it receives, it is present and active nonetheless in all genuine Christian life and theological reflection, in that the action of Christ's Spirit, whether we realize it or not, is always effective in the life of the Church. This way of understanding has generally come to be appreciated by Catholic theologians.[266]

The following words of R. Jenson explain that the doctrine of justification is central to Christian reflection though not always, perhaps, at an explicit level. 'This dogma [justification by faith alone] is not a particular proposed content of the Church's proclamation along with other contents. It is rather a metalinguistic stipulation of what kind of talking – whatever about contents – can properly be procla-

---

261 M. Kähler (*Zur Lehre von der Versöhnung*, Leipzig 1898) constructed his soteriology against Ritschl's, systematically situating the doctrine of justification at the centre.   262 Cf. pp. 158–161 above.   263 'Demythologizing is the radical application of the doctrine of justification by faith to the sphere of knowledge and thought' (R. Bultmann, *Jesus Christ and Mythology* . . . , op. cit., p. 84).   264 Cf. C.E. Braaten, *Justification* . . . , op. cit., p. 72. cf. W. Pannenberg, *Anthropology in Theological Perspective*, Philadelphia 1985.   265 G.O. Forde is a champion of hermeneutical use of the article as a *Richtschnur* (plumbline) by which theology and Church teaching is to be assessed and criticized. He has termed this article 'a matter of life an death' (cf. his *Justification by Faith*, Philadelphia 1990) and has occasionally expressed frustration upon seeing it spoken of as only one criterion among others. 'Justification by faith alone is thus seen as the "article by which the church stands or falls" because it directs and drives towards speaking that word which calls forth faith and to which faith alone is the possible answer. It insists that where the church no longer speaks this word it has lost its reason for being' (G.O. Forde, 'Justification by faith alone', in *Dialog* 27 (1988) 260–267). Likewise, R.W. Bertram stakes everything on justification as a hermeneutical principle (cf. R.W. Bertram, 'Faith alone justifies. Luther on "Iustitia fidei" ', in H.G. Anderson et al. (eds.), *Justification by faith* (*Lutherans and Catholics in Dialogue*, VII) . . . , op. cit., pp. 172–184).   266 W. Kasper ('Grundkonsens und Kirchengemeinschaft', in *Theologische Quartalschrift* 167 (1987) 161–181): 'The doctrine of justification is no longer Church-dividing. The central question is how the justification event acts as a hermeneutical principle and critical standard of the entire Christian faith'. Cf. also G. Tavard, 'The Contemporary Relevance of Justification by Faith', in *One in Christ* 21 (1985) 131–138; 'Justification in Dialogue', in *One in Christ* 25 (1989) 299–310.

mation and word of the Church. It does not say: "Talk about justification and faith". It is perfectly possible to talk about these subjects, even mimicking the Reformers, and proclaim the purest works-righteousness. Rather, it says, "Whatever you talk about, do so in such a way that the justification your words open to your hearers is the justification that faith apprehends rather than the justification that works apprehend". It is this metalinguistic character of the proposed "justification by faith" dogma that makes it a doctrine by which the Church stands or falls.'[267]

H.E.W. Turner points out that justification by faith is the hidden heart of all Christian life and spirituality, whose consequences 'positively . . . include a relationship to God which includes commitment and surrender as an indispensable ingredient, the understanding of the Christian life (which includes Christian conduct) as a response to God's saving initiative in Christ, with the marks of gratitude, dependence, and responsive love. Negatively it stands as a beacon light against any attempt by the Church to absolutize itself, to turn itself from a penultimate into an ultimate, to forget that it is still *in via* and not yet *in gloria*, the pilgrim people of God.'[268]

And even more explicitly, G. Ebeling has it that 'the idea that justifying faith be identified with faith in the doctrine of justification must be rejected with utmost decisiveness. To say it even more pointedly: nobody has any need of having the slightest premonition of the so-called doctrine of justification in order to partake of justifying faith. Or the other way around, an exact theological knowledge of the doctrine of justification on no account assures partaking of the faith that justifies'.[269]

EVALUATION OF THE RÔLE OF JUSTIFICATION AS A HERMENEUTICAL PRINCIPLE

Three observations should be made in respect of the foregoing reflections. In the first place, the fact is, as Barth noted, that genuine Christianity has been lived by countless Christians throughout extended periods in which 'justification' was by no means recognized as the predominant article of faith, whether on a hermeneutical level or on the level of content. In that sense, justification as a fundamental hermeneutical or critical principle may only be regarded *as one among several equivalent principles* which are in a position to gauge and detect genuine Christianity, whatever they may be.

Secondly, as Kertelge points out, the doctrine of justification and divine righteousness, as a clear expression of the δύναμις of the Gospel (cf. Rom 1:16), is central and determinative to Paul's thought and to Christianity itself *as a message or kerygma*,

267 E.W. Gritsch and R.W. Jenson, *Lutheranism: The Theological Movement and its Confessional Writings*, Philadelphia 1976, pp. 42–43. 268 H.E.W. Turner, 'Justification by Faith in Modern Theology', in M.E. Glasswell and E.W. Fasholé-Luke, *New Testament Christianity for Africa and the World*, London 1974, pp. 100; 111. 269 G. Ebeling, *Das Wesen des christlichen Glaubens* . . . , op. cit., pp. 119–120.

and not so much from the standpoint of its content. The point he makes is that the kerygma, or preaching of the Church, is always 'the truth insofar as it is communicated to man perceiving what is true (*wahr-nehmend*)'.[270]

Thirdly, any fundamental interpretative principle for gauging, and convalidating practical manifestations of personal and ecclesial Christian life, must needs be properly situated in respect of the foundation of such a principle (Christ)[271] and of its living context (the Church's *universal mission*).[272] According to Kertelge, the message or doctrine of 'justification' fulfills this very function: 'it develops as a movement of thought following on from the demands of the situation of the moment which the preaching of the gospel brings with it. Yet it is not only the result of the missionary situation, but in its movement follows on from the primary commencement founded on the "revelation of Jesus Christ" (cf. Gal 1:12).'[273]

In spite of the fact that A. Schweitzer, W. Wrede and others accorded centrality to the Pauline doctrine of our mystical incorporation into Christ through Baptism,[274] and not to the doctrine of justification, which was considered simply as an element of Paul's anti-Jewish polemic,[275] Kertelge has it that the doctrine of justification can be considered as a key expression of the very heart of Pauline theology,[276] because (1) the fact that this teaching is 'polemic' does not mean it is transitory;[277] (2), given that 'the essential content of the gospel is that salvation is unconditionally a gift of grace',[278] which 'justification' expresses; and (3) that 'Paul is not interested so much in the truth of the gospel as such, or in overcoming the law, but in the effectiveness of the saving message of the gospel'[279] in which 'Jesus is preached as the Christ, that is, as the salvation of mankind'.[280] And in doing so Kertelge makes it clear that the central rôle of the *message* of justification is not the same thing as its would-be absoluteness. In brief terms, Paul's doctrine of 'justification of the sinner by faith alone' offers a succinct summary of his understanding of Christ, man and salvation at the

---

270 K. Kertelge, *'Rechtfertigung' bei Paulus* . . . , op. cit., p. 286.   271 O. Kuss has it that 'the unity of Pauline theology does not reside principally in the perfect concatenation of different elements . . . but rather, above all, in the perception of the reality that is in Jesus Christ; this is the object which the theology of the Apostle strives, in close communion with tradition, to understand ever anew, using terminology and ideas which are in constant flux' (O. Kuss, *Der Römerbrief* . . . , op. cit., p. 131).   272 Cf. A. Oepke, *Die Missionspredigt des Apostels Paulus. Eine biblisch-theologische und religionsgeschichtliche Untersuchung*, Leipzig 1920, pp. 40–76.   273 K. Kertelge, *'Rechtfertigung' bei Paulus* . . . , op. cit., p. 289.   274 Sic. especially A. Schweitzer, *Geschichte der paulinischen Forschung* . . . , op. cit., pp. 130–134, followed by F. Buri (*Die Bedeutung der ntl. Eschatologie für die neuere protestantische Theologie*, Zürich 1935, pp. 155f.) and H.J. Schoeps, *Paulus. Die Theologie des Paulus im Lichte der jüdischen Religionsgeschichte*, Tübingen 1959, pp. 206; 216.   295 Sic. especially W. Wrede, *Paulus* . . . , op. cit., p. 72.   276 He does so drawing on the works of H.D. Wendland, A. Schlatter, G. Schrenk, M. Dibelius, W.G. Kümmel, E. Käsemann, and also Catholics such as O. Kuss (*Der Römerbrief* . . . , op. cit., pp. 129-131), R. Schnackenburg, 'Die paulinische Theologie', in *Lexikon für Theologie und Kirche*, 2nd ed., 8: 220–228) and L. Cerfaux (*Le Chrétien dans la théologie de saint Paul*, Paris 1954, pp. 343–428).   277 K. Kertelge, *'Rechtfertigung' bei Paulus* . . . , op. cit., p. 295.   278 Ibid.   279 Ibid., p. 296.   280 Ibid., 294.

very heart of the Christian dynamic. A similar understanding is to be found in the writings of J. Reumann.[281]

Anthropology, soteriology and sin   Kertelge also points out that the 'message' of justification, no matter how central it may be, inevitably carries 'theological presuppositions' of its own. In particular, it takes for granted that man's true and common 'theological' situation is that of *being a sinner*, in other words, 'under the law', powerless to free himself, enslaved to sin. 'Paul's doctrine on justification is located theologically by the human situation before Christ and without Christ, therefore by his anthropology.'[282] Besides, '*the very Christ-event is already presented in an interpreted form* . . . Paul interprets the Christ-event in function of man, and founds in this way a new theological self-understanding of man.'[283]

The core of the entire debate lies on this very point: man for Luther *is* a sinner; God, in Christ, *is* his Saviour. In other words justification remains as the interpretative centre of Scripture and the hermeneutical principle for criticizing every aspect of the Church's life and Christian spirituality only *as long as* man is considered *exclusively* as a sinner and God *exclusively* as his Saviour. The question must be asked, in the light of Scripture: is that *all* that can be said about man in his relationship to God? Is that all that can be said of God and his saving action over man? Or, to put it slightly differently, is *man being a sinner* and *God being a Saviour* all that we are in a position to say, as Christians, of ourselves and God?

This would seem to be the thrust of Luther's own teaching. In his commentary on Romans (1515) he had it to say that the ultimate purpose of the whole of Scripture is to bring a person to 'becoming a sinner' in their own estimation. Such a 'conversion' is 'the purpose of *every* word of Scripture and *every* divine operation'.[284] And in 1538, as we saw earlier, he said that 'the jurist speaks of man as an owner and master of property, and a physician speaks of man as healthy or sick. But the theologian discusses *man as a sinner*. In theology, this is the essence of man. The theologian is concerned that man become aware of this nature of his, corrupted by sins'.[285]

Difficulties with G. Ebeling's hermeneutics   This brings us back to Ebeling's careful analysis of the doctrine of justification as the fundamental Lutheran hermeneutic of Christian life and practice. He expressed the core of Luther's intuition as follows:

> Luther does not take the theme of *justificatio* as a optional theological topic alongside others; it is, rather, as it were, the 'place' for speaking theologically

281 Cf. especially J. Reumann, *'Righteousness' in the New Testament*, Philadelphia/New York 1982. 282 K. Kertelge, *'Rechtfertigung' bei Paulus* . . . , op. cit., p. 300.   283 Ibid., p. 302. Emphasis added.   284 M. Luther, *Die Vorlesung über den Römerbrief* (WA 56: 233). Emphasis added.   285 M. Luther, *Enarratio Psalmi LI* (WA 40/2: 327). On this text, cf. J. Wicks, 'Living and Praying as "Simul Iustus et Peccator",' in *Gregorianum* 70 (1989) 521–548 (especially p. 526ff.).

in general, that is, the place where man is situated when talking about God, before God (*coram Deo*). And conforming to reality surely means to allow the situation of the word become the criterion of verification for the word, especially since it is God's own word . . . This is not whatever situation, but the situation of man . . . The relationship between *homo reus et perditus* and *deus iustificans vel salvator* belongs to fundamental theology.[286]

However, it has been argued that Ebeling's establishment of justification as the hermeneutical or critical principle of Christian life and spirituality is faulty insofar as it intends to be self-standing, exclusively theological and non-metaphysical: man face to face with the Word of God *experiences himself* as a sinner, and *God* as his saviour, and little more need be said. 'The greatest problem of Ebeling's hermeneutical method is that of pre-understanding . . . Unlike Bultmann, Ebeling pays no attention to the criticism of pre-understanding (*Vorverständnis*). For him the problem of the hermeneutical method is solved through the self-efficiency of the word. Ebeling says " . . . the content and object of hermeneutics is the word event as such." '[287] In this his dependence on Heidegger is apparent.[288] Ebeling's concept of the word functions in the service of his existentialized theology of creation.[289] It could be said that the whole of his thinking is characterized by the effort to provide an *existentially understood conception of the theology of creation*. 'God as Creator of man is the main definition of revelation.'[290]

In sum, for Ebeling, the 'message' of justification, insistence upon this article as the fundamental Christian criteriological or hermeneutical principle, would act as a day-to-day existential reminder of who God is and who man is *coram Deo*, in other words, the reality that man is a sinner and God his merciful Saviour. But the point is that the Christian is not only a sinner, and God not only his Saviour, that the Christian is not only a 'sinner loved by Jesus Christ', a sinner who remains as such, but besides, a 'sinner who loves Jesus Christ',[291] that is, a sinner loved by God and made a lover of God. If this is the case, if God is not only Saviour but also Father,

286 G. Ebeling, *Lutherstudien* . . . , op. cit., vol. 1, p. 266.   287 M. Ruokanen, *Hermeneutics as an Ecumenical Method in the Theology of Gerhard Ebeling*, Helsinki 1982, p. 137, which cites Ebeling's *Wort und Glaube I* . . . , op. cit., p. 334f. 'Because the subject matter under interpretation is verified on the basis of its existential function', writes Ruokanen, 'the truth of the matter cannot be concluded by means of a formula. Verification takes place in "the blink of an eye" as man experiences the encounter with the secret of reality. A biblical text cannot have a permanent, generally valid significance; the essence of the Christian faith is perceived by an existential *affectus* in a concealed, sacramental event in which the word underlying all reality addresses man . . .' (M. Ruokanen, op. cit., p. 137).   288 M. Heidegger (*Sein und Zeit I*, Tübingen 1927, p. 153) defines the hermeneutical circle as 'die VorStruktur des Daseins selbst'. In his later works (for example *Unterwegs zur Sprache*, Frankfurt a. M. 1985, p. 254) Heidegger understood that man's *Vorverständnis* consists of the linguistic conditions of understanding.   289 Cf. M. Ruokanen, *Hermeneutics as an Ecumenical Method* . . . , op. cit., p. 205f.   290 G. Ebeling, *Wort und Glaube I* . . . , op. cit., p. 368.   291 This expression was often used by Blessed Josemaría Escrivá.

and man not only sinner but child, would the 'message' of justification of he sinner by faith alone, though unique in Christian life and thought, not have to be adapted to some degree?

Two elements of adaptation or amplification could be suggested, the first related to creation as God's own work, and the second to the divine filiation of Christians.

Glorifying God in his works   In a preparatory study for the 1984 USA statement *Justification by Faith*, C.J. Peter spoke of the need for 'another critical principle' to be applied to the theology and life of the Church alongside that of justification, in order to account theologically for what Tillich called 'the Catholic substance', and not only 'the Protestant principle'.[292] He said that

> The criterion of justification by faith alone is an imperative to keep the churches free from idolatry. But that is not the only temptation the churches face. They need another critical principle to warn them that they may run the risk of blasphemy . . . To fail to recognize the divine where it is in fact being mediated or embodied because the mediating agency or embodying symbols are touched by sin may well involve both insolence and arrogance with regard to the divine.[293]

Speaking of the 'ultimate trust' all Christians must place in God, he asks the question: 'is a desire to trust and hope *ultimately* in God *alone* leading people to refuse to trust or even disdain ecclesial institutions where God has promised through Jesus Christ to be present and operative with his Spirit and grace?'[294] The point is made on several occasions throughout the dialogue statement *Justification by faith*, especially when it makes reference to the central place in Christian spirituality of praising God 'for his transformative indwelling.'[295]

The document *Church and Justification* moves in the same direction. It 'is structured, implicitly at least, on the basis of a kind of "elliptical (two-poled) hermeneutic", based that is on two criteriological principles: the "justification principle" (expressing the gratuitous salvation of mankind by faith in the mercy of God in Christ, the individual aspect of justification), and the 'ecclesiological principle' (expressing the need of the Church for salvation, the need to belong to a saved community in order to be saved, the social aspect of justification) . . . One might suggest that the criteriological role of the 'justification principle' is applicable above all as a theoretical point of reference for the *practical living-out* of the ecclesiality of being Christian; while the 'ecclesiological principle' is applicable as a practical – visible, tangible – criterion of verification of the theoretical principle of justification. In a sense one could say that the *doctrine of justification taken in a double perspective is the single*

292 Cf. C.J. Peter, 'Justification by faith and the need of another critical principle', in H.G. Anderson et al. (ed.), *Justification by faith (Lutherans and Catholics in Dialogue, VII)*, op. cit., pp. 304–315. 293 Ibid., p. 309.   294 Ibid., p. 310.   295 Cf. USA 101; 103.

criterion for validating the entire reality of Christian life: looking at the matter from a Protestant perspective, the principle could be applied to ensure that *the existence of ecclesial structures* would not condition the magnanimity of the divine promise of salvation and justification, that human sinfulness and meanness would not block out, or totally distort, divine holiness and bounty; looking at it from a Catholic standpoint, that the *systematic calling into question of ecclesial structures* would not have exactly the same effect, in straining the link between saving power of God and created reality'.²⁹⁶

Divine pardon and divine filiation Luther pointed out, quite rightly, that many of the saints considered themselves at one and the same time sinners *and* justified by God. 'While the saints keep their sin ever in mind and implore righteousness from God according to his mercy, thereby they are considered righteous by God'.²⁹⁷ The question however comes to this: do the saints consider themselves *sinners loved by God in Christ*, or rather sinners who are *really made children of God*, and are thus *no longer sinners*, strictly speaking, but rather redeemed brothers and sisters of Jesus Christ and thus prodigal children of God?

A. Pitta, in a recent study of the letter to the Galatians,²⁹⁸ has argued cogently that the fundamental theological thrust of this critical Pauline epistle does not lie so much in *justification and the law*, but rather in *divine filiation*, the new dignity in which justified Christians are constituted by their 'new creation' as sons and daughters of God. On the basis of a rhetorical-literary analysis of the epistle, he concludes that the principal thesis of the gospel is progressively explained by Paul in terms of Abrahamitic filiation and life according to the Spirit, with their relative implications. Thus, the centrality of the Pauline gospel dethrones the question of the relationship between faith and the law which, while not to be ignored, is seen to be functional in respect of divine filiation, realized in Christ, by the gift of the Spirit.²⁹⁹

Of course the theological context in which Christians do consider themselves sinners is one of divine pardon, justification, which in turn can only be understood and fully appreciated in the context of God being Father and Christians in Christ becoming his adopted children.³⁰⁰ God, in other words, reveals his paternity in par-

296 P. O'Callaghan, 'The Mediation of Justification and the Justification of Mediation', op. cit., pp. 151; 210f. **297** M. Luther, *Die Vorlesung über den Römerbrief* (WA 56: 269). This theme is developed by J. Wicks (op. cit.), who brings to bear testimonies of several saints. **298** Cf. A. Pitta, *Disposizione e messaggio della Lettera ai Galati: analisi retorico-letteraria*, Rome 1992. **299** Cf. ibid., pp. 212–214. **300** Blessed Josemaría Escrivá, as a result of his profound experience of the fatherly, pardoning power of God, stated pithily that 'sólo los padres saben perdonar': only parents know how to forgive. He expresses the relationship between divine pardon and the divine filiation of Christians in very graphic terms. 'Our Lord . . . is not a tyrannical master or a rigid and implacable judge: he is our Father. He speaks to us about our lack of generosity, our sins, our mistakes; but he does so in order to free us from them, to promise us his friendship and his love. Awareness that God is our Father brings joy to our conversion: it tells us that we are returning to our Father's house . . . This divine filiation is the basis of the spirit of Opus Dei. All men are children of God

doning his children. But the opposite is not consistently true. For God to be Father and for Christians to be his children, it is not *necessary* for God to be their Saviour and his children be sinners; this would only be the case if should human beings be considered sinners *constitutionally*, such as might involve an unwarranted confusion between creation and fall/sinfulness.[301]

Certainly Christ, in living out his eternal and constitutional Filiation, especially on the Cross, should not be linked with or dialectically identified with sinfulness, as Luther[302] (to a certain degree) and more so Calvin[303] and Barth[304] tend to hold.[305] Christ is eternally the Father's beloved Son, in whom he is well pleased (cf. Mt 3:17) and Christians, 'in Christ', become not only nor principally 'reconciled sinners', but rather 'children in the Son'.[306] The *analogatum princeps* of Christian life and

... A child of God treats the Lord as his Father. He is not obsequious and servile, he is not merely formal and well-mannered: he is completely sincere and trusting. Men do not scandalize God. He can put up with all our infidelities. Our Father in heaven pardons any offence when his child returns to him, when he repents and asks for pardon . . . Human life is in some way a constant returning to our Father's house. We return through contrition, through the conversion of heart which means a desire to change, a firm decision to improve our life and which, therefore, is expressed in sacrifice and self-giving. We return to our Father's house by means of that sacrament of pardon in which, by confessing our sins, we put on Jesus Christ again and become his brothers, members of God's family.' (Josemaría Escrivá, *Christ is Passing By* . . . , op. cit., no. 64; cf. also idem., *Furrow*, Dublin 1988, no. 65; *The Forge*, Dublin 1988, no. 332). On the non-mutual though clarifying relationship between divine filiation and divine pardon, cf. P. O'Callaghan, ' "That everything may be for his glory': the Paternity of God, Christ's own perspective', in Various authors, *Preparing for the year 2000*, New Hope / Rome 1996, pp. 207–218.   301 A marked tendency towards confusing man's creaturely condition with his fallen or sinful state may be detected among some Evangelical authors, for example, P. Althaus, *Die christliche Wahrheit*, Gütersloh 1952, pp. 383 ff.; K. Barth, *Church Dogmatics* 4/1 . . . , op. cit., pp. 478–513; E. Brunner, *Der Mensch im Widerspruch*, Zurich 1941, pp. 105–143; idem., *Die christliche Lehre von Schöpfung und Erlösung*, Zurich 1950, pp. 101–131; P. Tillich, *Systematic Theology*, vol.2, op. cit., pp. 29–44.   302 Cf. especially Luther's 1531–35 commentary on Galatians, in particular on Gal 3:13 (WA 40/1: 437f.).   303 J. Calvin: 'The Creed sets forth what Christ suffered in the sight of men, and appositely speaks of the invisible and incomprehensible judgement which he underwent in the sight of God in order that we might know not only that Christ's body was given as the price of our redemption, but that he paid a greater and more excellent price in suffering in his soul the terrible torments of a condemned and forsaken man . . . Yet we do not suggest that God was ever inimical or angry toward him . . . This is what we are saying: he bore the weight of divine severity, since he was stricken and afflicted (Is 53, 5) by God's hand and experienced all the signs of a wrathful and avenging God. Therefore by his wrestling hand to hand with the devil's power, with the dread of death, with the pains of hell, he was victorious and triumphed over them, that in death we may not now fear those things which our Prince has swallowed up (cf. 1 Pet 3:22 Vulg.).' (*Institutiones Christianae* II, 16: 10-11; English translation, *Institutes of the Christian religion*, 2 vols, Grand Rapids 1979 f., vol. 1, pp. 516f.). For further texts, cf. J. Rivière, *Le dogme de la Rédemption. Étude théologique*, Paris 1914, pp. 389–393.   304 K. Barth: 'He (Christ) stands before the Father at Golgotha burdened with the actual sin and guilt of man and of each individual man, and is treated in accordance with the desserts of man as the transgressor of the divine command' (*Church Dogmatics* 2/2 . . . , op. cit. p. 58).   305 Cf. A. Aranda, 'Dio ha assunto in Cristo il peccato dell'uomo', in J.M. Galván (ed.), *La giustificazione in Cristo*, Rome 1997, pp. 211–225.   306 Cf. F. Ocáriz Braña, *Hijos de Dios en Cristo: introducción a una teología de la participación sobrenatural*, Pamplona 1972. On the relationship

spirituality is not the reconciled sinner but the son or daughter of God. Perhaps Catholic teaching on the total sinlessness of the Virgin Mary is a critical case in point: Christian faith is not correlative to sin alone.

Conclusion   It should now be quite clear that doctrine of justification by faith alone, if it is to be successfully applied to Christian life and spirituality as a determinative, critical and hermeneutical principle, needs to go beyond the purely existential reading of the human situation which considers man primordially as a sinner, and God only as his Saviour. It needs to take into account the fact that man, alongside the experience of sinfulness and pardon, really encounters the goodness of God both through the reality of creation and through his personal filiation in Christ's Spirit.

between Cross and justification, cf. A. Ducay, 'Croce e giustificazione nella Chiesa. Una lettura ecumenica alla luce della soteriologia giovannea', in J.M. Galván (ed.), *La giustificazione in Cristo*, pp. 248–259.

CHAPTER SIX

The doctrine of justification

This (final) chapter will attempt to present the doctrine on justification not as such as a 'message', or critical principle, but as a systematic or dogmatic doctrine, as a key element of Christian anthropology. Its purpose is reflect on the elements involved in eventually establishing what might be termed 'material consensus' between Lutherans and Catholics on justification. It will be based principally on the various bilateral statements on justification we have already presented. Of special importance of course are the German document *Lehrverurteilungen – kirchentrennend?* (abbreviated as LV), and the American statement *Justification by Faith* (abbreviated as USA).

Firstly we shall examine the reality of the *human subject* being justified *coram Deo*, that is, man face to face with justifying grace, under two headings: (1) the human being's 'passivity' towards and 'cooperation' with grace, and (2) human sinfulness and concupiscence. Then we will look at the two-fold *reality of justification*: God forgiving sin and making the sinner just (3). Finally, we shall consider *what grace effects* in those justified: good works (4) and assurance of saving grace (5).

Besides attempting to reflect on the dogmatic content of the doctrine of justification, and the possible tensions between the Lutheran and Catholic understandings, I intend to bring up two other issues as each heading is considered, both of which have been taken up in chapter five. Firstly, a brief doctrinal history of the evident tensions and even contradictions existing between Catholics and Lutherans on the disputed questions, and the way in which exegetical and historical research, especially in recent decades, has contributed towards taking the sharp edges off these oppositions. Secondly, insofar as this is possible, an application to each of the above-mentioned points of the doctrine of justification taken as a hermeneutical and criteriological principle, with a view to ensuring that eventual agreement, though inevitably imperfect, may become 'formal' and not only 'material'.[1]

---

1 Elsewhere I have argued that serious doctrinal convergence between Lutherans and Catholics on the question of justification will never be possible unless the doctrinal (material) and fundamental/criteriological (formal) aspects of the question are considered together, and temper one another *mutually* (cf. P. O'Callaghan, 'L'uomo giustificato, nuova creatura in Cristo. Una riflessione intorno all'attuale dibattito ecumenico', in J.M. Galván (ed.), *La giustificazione in Cristo . . .* , op. cit., pp. 129–164). Cf. also the 'Concluding Reflection', pp. 239–249 below.

THE HUMAN SUBJECT 'CORAM DEO':
HUMAN POWERLESSNESS AND 'COOPERATION'

1.   *Tensions pending between Catholics and Lutherans*

Catholics have traditionally considered excessive the insistence Lutherans seem to place on the radical perversion of human nature due to sin, suspecting that this might well involve a substantially negative attitude towards the work of creation, or a certain divine arbitrariness in respect of humans, enslaved by sin and incapable of doing anything good, or even anything worth while. Lutherans, on the other hand, fear that Catholics, in speaking with excessive optimism of the goodness of created nature and the value of 'good works', might well be placing excessive trust in such works, to the detriment of faith and confidence in God, which constitute the very heart of the Christian message. Divine grace would thus be envisaged as a kind of supplement to human nature, and man would be, in the fullest sense of the term, a free cooperator or 'partner' of God. The reformers taught that by sin 'human beings have lost their liberty and power to do what is morally good, and to fulfill God's commandments out of love love and not merely outwardly, for their own credit or out of fear of punishment.'[2]

The Lutheran *Formula of Concord* (1577) repeats the idea on several occasions. 'We believe, teach, and confess that original sin is not a slight corruption of human nature, but that it is so deep a corruption that nothing sound or uncorrupted has survived in man's body or soul, in his inward or outward powers . . . We believe that in spiritual and divine things the intellect, heart and will of unregenerated man cannot by any native or natural powers in any way understand, believe, accept, imagine, will, begin, accomplish, do, effect, or cooperate . . . Hence according to its perverse disposition and nature the natural free will is mighty and active only in the direction of that which is displeasing and contrary to God.'[3]

2.   *Resolving the tensions: human freedom* coram creaturis *and* coram Deo

To some degree the problem and related tension have not been well stated. The nature and exercise of the human will in relation to other creatures is objectively different from the nature and exercise of the human will before God. *Coram creaturis*, that is, face-to-face with other creatures, man can act freely and intelligently, in the sense that he can choose one thing or another, bring a project to completion along with other people, use and modify what he encounters, acquire rights and duties. Before God, *coram Deo*, however, things are objectively different: in the order of nature and of grace, of creation and of redemption, man is totally dependent on his Creator, Redeemer and Sanctifier, insofar as he has received all things – even the

2 LV 30f.   3 *Formula Concordiae*, Epitome 1: 8, in T.G. Tappert et al., (ed.), *The Book of Concord* . . . , op. cit., p. 467.

very faculty of created freedom – from God. In real terms, therefore, man cannot be said to directly *co-operate* with God, if this were taken to mean that he *adds*, as it were, something to what God has already given him. *Objectively speaking*, humans exercise their spiritual faculties of intelligence and will in gratefully receiving God's gifts or in ungratefully rejecting them. Perhaps the essence of the sin of idolatry lies in the human attempt to dominate and manipulate God and his action over creatures, just as man tends to do over other creatures. And the fear Lutherans had of Catholic doctrine and practice was on this very point.

When Luther said that the human will is essentially enslaved, in his own words that *servum arbitrium* is the *cardo rerum*,[4] it would seem that he wished above all to affirm divine transcendence and complete human dependence on God. Insofar as this is the case, Catholics and Lutherans have a great deal in common. But Trent's decree on justification does speak of 'cooperation',[5] and Catholic theology has never let go of this idea. But how is this compatible with affirming the transcendence of God and the complete receptivity of man?

3. *Tensions remaining: how passive is human receptivity to grace?*

Understandably, the nature of the Christian's passivity or receptivity before God (in positive terms, his or her having received all things natural and supernatural from God) critically determines the nature of the cooperation involved in human response to grace. Man is passive to grace, yet active in Christian life, completely receptive to God, yet fully cooperative with him. It is commonly held by both Catholics and Protestants that human response to grace is *itself* an 'effect' of grace. But this notion is understood somewhat differently by the different sides, as the following three observations show.

Firstly, the whole question of the relevance of the doctrine of justification and of Christian life lies on the very point being dealt with: how *meaningful and human* is our acceptance (or rejection) of God's gifts and grace? Man's action certainly 'adds' nothing to the gift of God, in the sense that humans are in no position to *donate* anything of their own *to God* to pay back in part for or to supplement the gift they have received. Nonetheless humans in receiving God's grace do 'add' (to themselves, not to God) the reality that divine grace has been, in them, 'made really existent'. And of course, they could have refused to do this, falling into sin. In other

---

4 Cf. M. Luther, *De Servo Arbitrio* (WA 18: 786). On this fundamental work of Luther's, cf. the analysis of L.F. Mateo-Seco, *M. Lutero. Sobre la libertad esclava*, Madrid 1978. Pesch affirms that on this point 'Luther holds on to Catholic tradition over against a humanistic understanding of freedom [that of Erasmus]' (O.-H. Pesch, 'Gottes Gnadenhandeln als Rechtfertigung des Menschen', in Various authors, *Mysterium Salutis IV/2: Das Heilsgeschehen in der Gemeinde: Gottes Gnadenhandeln*, Einsiedeln 1973, pp. 831–920, here p. 854). In the same line, cf. H.J. McSorley, *Luther: Right or Wrong?: an ecumenical-theological study of Luther's major work The Bondage of the Will*, Minneapolis 1969; H. Vorster, *Das Freiheitsverständnis bei Thomas von Aquin und Martin Luther*, Göttingen 1965.   5 Cf. DH 1525; 1554 etc.

words, divine grace and the human act of response or acceptance are not gifts of God (or 'effects of grace') in exactly the same sense. For if they were, justification and Christian life would be simply reduced to a divine theatre of little tangible relevance to the human situation. Man would be as involved in being justified as a piece of tinderwood would be in a bonfire.

Lehrverurteilungen – kirchentrennend? clarifies the point quite well. Catholic teaching, in toning down the Reformed teaching on the depravity of human nature, 'does not fall short of the insights of the Reformation: grace is not something *added* to human endeavours, as it were. It *enables* the human being to take the first step toward salvation, and hence all succeeding stages as well.'[6] And Protestants are well aware that their view 'can even today give rise to the misunderstandings that God justifies a person quite arbitrarily, without that person's being affected or involved. According to Protestant conviction, justification is necessarily bound up with the preaching of God's law, which indicts the sinner and awakens his desire for the free pardon of the gospel.'[7]

Secondly, the reason why humans must allow themselves receive the grace of justification as a pure gift is, according to *Lehrverurteilungen – kirchentrennend?*, due to the fact that they are 'completely imprisoned *by the power of evil*'.[8] But does this mean that human incapacity to do anything of value *coram Deo* must be attributed to the *sinfulness* of humans? Would it not more correct to say that such incapacity is more fundamentally due to our created condition, that is to our having a finite, totally received, existence? Are perhaps the notions of sinfulness and creatureliness being confused here? *Lehrverurteilungen – kirchentrennend?* alludes to such a possibility in saying that 'according to the Catholic view, this also shows the inner theological connection between "creation" and "redemption": the justifying act of God is directed toward the man or woman in need of redemption, who is not totally "replaced" by God's grace, but who is awakened to a new life.'[9]

'Creation' and 'redemption', deeply linked of course . . . but distinct as well. According to Catholic doctrine, justification neither eliminates nor enters into conflict with the *creaturely condition* of man, but it does enter into mortal combat with his *sinful condition*; conversely, for Protestants, to an significant degree it eliminates neither, for man remains *simul iustus et peccator*. Could it be perhaps that creatureliness and sinfulness are being put on the same plane?

The *last* of the three observations follows on directly. At an ontological and thematic level, it is possible to distinguish between the action of the Creator/Redeemer

---

6 LV 42.   7 LV 43. The following point is made in the commentary on *Lehrverurteilungen—kirchentrennend?* by the VELKD: 'The strict emphasis on the passivity of human beings concerning their justification never meant, on the Lutheran side, to contest the full personal participation in believing; rather it meant to exclude any cooperation in the event of justification itself' (Vereinigte Evangelisch-Lutherische Kirche Deutschlands, *Lehrverurteilungen im Gespräch* . . . , op. cit., p. 84: 3-8).   8 Ibid. 'Outside the saving activity of God, liberty is merely what Peter Brunner calls "liberty inside a prison" ' (ibid., 43).   9 LV 43.

and that of the creature/sinner. Yet at a concrete and existential level it may not be strictly necessary or even possible to hold that the Christian's 'ultimate trust'[10] in God alone requires renouncing all trust in creatures, all complacency in one's own actions and faculties, as Lutherans often insist.[11] In other words, it is not really possible *at a practical and existential level* to say where confidence in God ends, and trust in creatures begins. This is especially the case when we consider that creatures were made by God for our enjoyment and in order to facilitate our doing his will. Or yet again: the concrete choices made by humans, choices by which they truly exercise their freedom and dominion and build up the earthly city, are such choices unrelated to God, and ultimately to the life of grace? It would seem therefore that a distinction between God's action and man's, and a radical subordination of the latter to the former, however valuable and necessary it may be at the level of thematic and metaphysical reflection, is not readily applicable to the concrete existential human situation.

The Göttingen Faculty critique of *Lehrverurteilungen – kirchentrennend?* examines the nature of man's 'pre-justified' or 'depraved' state in a way which considers unjustified human reality *coram Deo* at best as neutral, in such a way that it is impossible to affirm simultaneously 'cooperation' in one's own justification and 'passivity' in respect of God's grace. 'Since the very definition of man is that he is a being before God, the perversion of the relationship to God means his own "radical" depravity . . . If the depravity or the sin of man is defined thus one can maintain neither that there is "still good" remaining in the sinner which could stand up before God; nor anything good – or bad – can be found in the sinner, which would make sin something external and not personal . . . If *the good supposedly remaining in the sinner* is defined as the freedom which makes him able to prepare for justification, then justification is not understood as the radically new beginning by which divine grace brings man into the right relationship to God . . . The reference to grace preceding justification permits the conclusion that there is something in the sinner that precedes justification and that is exempt from radical corruption, and thus does not need transformation through the grace of justification: *the will of man, the possibility of reacting freely to God's action.*'[12]

Catholic doctrine would generally hold that, previous to receiving the grace of justification, there is something 'in' humans, even as sinners, which is capable of accepting or receiving supernatural gifts, a *potentia obedentialis* for grace,[13] closely

---

10 Cf. USA 4; 157.   11 *Lehrverurteilungen—kirchentrennend?* says: 'Both [Lutherans and Catholics] are concerned to make it clear that . . . human beings cannot . . . cast a sideways glance at their own endeavours, not even "partly", and not even after their regeneration through the Holy Spirit . . .' (LV 46).   12 D. Lange et al., 'An Opinion on "The Condemnations of the Reformation Era". Part One: Justification', op. cit., p. 25. Emphasis added.   13 For Augustine, human nature 'is a great nature, for it is capable of and can partake in the highest nature' (*De Trinitate* XIV, 6). Ripalda stated in fact that Augustine is *primus inventor potentiae obedientialis* . . . cf. also Thomas Aquinas, *De virtutibus in commune*, a. 10, ad 2; ad 13.

related to *human free will*, by which man can in fact truly accept (or reject) God's grace, while adding nothing to its content as such. In that sense man could be said to really 'cooperate' in his justification, in that divine grace seeks and finds an authentically human 'register' in the unjustified sinner, the work of creation ('image of God', Gen 1:27) though not of justifying grace. The Göttingen *Opinion*'s understanding of the definition of man envisages no such presence. 'One must insist that the radicality of sin, understood against the background of the relationship to God, completely excludes any possibility of a free reaction to his act and any possibility of preparing himself.'[14]

THE HUMAN SUBJECT 'CORAM DEO': CONCUPISCENCE AND SIN

1. *Different understandings of human sinfulness*

The dispute over the exact nature and theological relevance of disordered human concupiscence was central to the Reformation debate.[15] Catholic doctrine, clearly defined during Trent's fifth session, held that concupiscence, though deriving from sin and inclining towards sin, is not sin as such, but perverse inclination, non-essential to human nature.[15] Such 'sinfulness' does not arouse divine wrath or deserve divine punishment except in the case that it is actualized in personal sin, that is when humans give free consent to temptation. Theologically speaking, therefore, concupiscence is simply not sin, though it is associated with sin and derives from it, and thus may be bound up with complex and often powerful unconscious sinful inclinations of all kinds. In fact Catholic moral theology, spirituality and penitential practice has traditionally distinguished carefully between temptation (sinful concupiscence) and consent (personal sin), and seen its prime rôle in resolving the former by means of resolving the latter.[17]

Lutherans, however, usually insist that concupiscence is sinful in the true and proper sense of the word, in such a way that the Christian is in reality *simul iustus et peccator*, inseparably both just and sinner. Such concupiscence is not merely an (unfortunate) natural quality within man, making perseverance in friendship with God particularly arduous. Rather it is a true opposition to God, not to be understood moralistically or empirically, but theologically. Man experiences this inner opposition to God as a *striving to be like God*,[18] as an almost incurable 'propensity to

---

14 D. Lange et al., 'An Opinion on "The Condemnations of the Reformation Era". Part One: Justification', op. cit., pp. 25f.   15 G. Bavaud, 'La justification par la foi. Quelle est la racine de la divergence entre catholiques et protestants?', in *Nova et Vetera* 68 (1993) 250–262, here p. 261, considers the question of sin, theologically considered, as the key issue of divergence between Catholic and Lutheran doctrine.   16 Cf. DH 1515.   17 As regards the different ways Catholics and Lutherans have come to grips with the notions of sin as such and 'unconscious sin', cf. the suggestive study of C.F. Allison, 'The Pastoral and Political Implications of Trent on Justification', in *One in Christ* 24 (1988) 112–127.   18 Cf. *Apologia* 2: 7; 14; 24.

trust one's own righteousness',[19] producing a *cor incurvatum in seipsum*.[20] For Luther, in Ebeling's words, 'all sin is lack of faith, despising the first commandment, being turned in on oneself, not wanting God to be God, hence, not wanting to recognize oneself a sinner'.[21] Concupiscence for Lutherans, therefore, is to be identified with humans' attachment to 'works' which is both insuperable and pernicious, in detriment to their trust and confidence in God.

2. *A converging understanding of sin and sinfulness*

Over the years, the waters have settled somewhat on this particular front.[22] Catholics, following the guidelines of Trent, have come to appreciate more fully the spiritual (and not only carnal) aspects of the perverted inclination that derives from original sin.[23] It has likewise become apparent that Lutheran insistence on the full sinfulness of concupiscence was significantly conditioned by its opposition to and rejection of a typically Nominalistic understanding of the doctrine of original sin.[24] Lutherans were aware of the following three understandings of original sin put forward by Gabriel Biel:[25]

—the optimistic view of Anselm followed by Scotus, Ockham and the Nominalists, according to which original sin consists principally of the *absence* of original righteousness; concupiscence is considered to be of secondary importance;[26]

— that of Aquinas, Alexander of Hales and Bonaventure, according to whom concupiscence is the 'quasi-material cause' of original sin, and the privation of justice is the 'quasi-formal cause';[27]

— that of Peter Lombard and many Augustinians, for whom original sin, 'a morbid quality of the soul', is identified with 'the vice of concupiscence';[28] it came to include all kinds of inordinate desire, of *amor sui*.[29]

---

19 USA 25.　**20** Cf. LV 44.　**21** G. Ebeling, *Martin Lutero. L'itinerario e il messaggio* . . . , op. cit., pp. 69f.　**22** Cf. especially C. Baumgartner, 'Concupiscence', in *Dictionnaire de Spiritualité* 2 (1953) 1343-1373; and also B. Stöckle, *Die Lehre von der erbsündlichen Konkupiszenz in ihrer Bedeutung für das christliche Leibethos*, Ettal 1954; P. Wilpert, 'Begierde', in *Reallexikon für Antike und Christentum* 2, pp. 63–78; K. Frölich, 'Justification Language in the Middle Ages', in H.G. Anderson et al. (eds.), *Justification by Faith* . . . , op. cit., pp. 143–161, especially pp. 144–146.　**23** Cf. C. Baumgartner, 'Concupiscence', op. cit., coll. 1363ff.　**24** On the doctrine of original sin in the Middle Ages, cf. H. Rondet, *Le péché originel dans la tradition patristique et théologique*, Paris 1967; J. Gross, *Entwicklungsgeschichte des Erbsündendogmas seit der Reformation*, Munich 1972; L. Scheffczyk, 'Urstand, Fall und Erbsünde von der Schrift bis Augustin', and H. Köster, 'Urstand, Fall und Erbsünde von der Schrift in der Scholastik', volumes 2/3 a & b (1981 & 1979), respectively, of M. Schmaus et al. (eds.), *Handbuch der Dogmengeschichte*, Freiburg i. Br./Basel/Vienna 1951ff.　**25** The three are mentioned in LV 44.　**26** Cf. especially R. Martin, 'La question du péché originel dans saint Anselme', in *Revue de Sciences Philosophiques et Théologiques* 5 (1911) 735–749; P. Vignaux, *De saint Anselme à Luther*, Paris 1976. cf. also O. Lottin, *Psychologie et morale aux XIIème et XIIIème siécles*, vol. 4/3: 1, Louvain 1954, pp. 9–306 (on Anselm and Aquinas).　**27** Cf. ibid.; W.A. van Roo, *Grace and Original Justice according to St Thomas Aquinas*, Rome 1955. On St Thomas, cf. especially *De Malo*, q. 4, a. 2; *Summa Theologiae I-II*, q. 82, a. 3.　**28** Cf. P. Lombard, *II Sent.*, D. 30, q. 2, a. 1, 1a.　**29** Of the three, this position was closest to Luther's own.

Lutherans[30] resolutely rejected the first position (probably Biel's own),[31] rightly holding it impossible for humans to completely fulfill the material demands of the commandments with their natural strengths alone, since nature has been deeply damaged by sin. By extension, they would probably also reject the second position, but would be much more at home with the third. In fact, for the first time in the history of theology, Lutheranism came to identify original sin and concupiscence.[32]

3. *The theological statute of 'concupiscence'*

The divergence between Catholics and Lutherans is on this very point. Both hold that sinful inclination, often violent and apparently insuperable, remains throughout the lifetime of humans, even after the reception of Baptism. But whereas Lutherans term this reality 'sin', Catholics, insisting on the distinction between temptation and sin, between inclination and consent, do not. Of course this is quite in keeping with the Catholic understanding on the reality of human freedom *coram Deo*. So, one may ask, in what way can Catholics and Lutherans eventually come to hold the same doctrine?

Lehrverurteilungen – kirchentrennend? expresses the common teaching in the following terms. 'The doctrines laid down by Trent and by the Reformers are at one in maintaining that original sin, and also the concupiscence that remains, are in contradiction with God, a disqualification in his eyes which precedes all ethical or unethical action . . . that it is the object of a lifelong struggle . . . [but that it] no longer cuts that person off from God.'[33]

This way of speaking is not common in Catholic theology, though the content is probably quite acceptable. But is this explanation true to the Lutheran position? The memorandum prepared by the Faculty of Göttingen would probably say it is not. 'Is the concupiscence remaining in the baptized still to be regarded as sin? Therein lies the question of content, whether the baptized person is still a sinner.

In fact his doctrine followed that of Giles of Rome and Gregory of Rimini: cf. A. Zumkeller, 'Erbsünde, Gnade und Rechtfertigung im Verständnis der Erfurter Augustinertheologen des Spätmittelalters', in *Zeitschrift für Kirchengeschichte* 92 (1981) 39–59.   30 On the doctrine of original sin in Lutheran Confessional documents, cf. W. Breuning and B. Hägglund, 'Sin and Original Sin', in G.W. Forrell and J.F. McCue, *Confessing One Faith. A Joint Commentary on the Augsburg Confession by Lutheran and Catholic Theologians*, Minnesota 1982, pp. 94–116.   31 That Luther (and Melanchthon) were specifically rejecting Biel's position has been shown by P. Vignaux, 'Luther lecteur de Gabriel Biel', in *Église et théologie* 22 (1959) 33–52; H.A. Oberman, *The Harvest of Medieval Theology* . . . , op. cit.; and V. Pfnür, *Einig in der Rechtfertigungslehre?* . . . , op. cit., pp. 68–77.   32 Cf. K. Frölich, 'Justification Language in the Middle Ages', op. cit., p. 146. This is understandable, firstly because of the traditional distinction between *fomes* and *reatus*; secondly because of Abelard's insistence that only the application of the individual will can make for true sin (cf. A. Teetaert, 'Le péché originel d'après Abélard', in *Estudis Franciscans* 40 (1928) 23–54), and thirdly because Anselm's theory had got across the point that concupiscence was not a positive *habitus*, but simply remained in the baptized due to a lack of supernatural help, a position more or less taken up by Aquinas.   33 LV 46. cf. also USA 102.

Lehrverurteilungen — kirchentrennend? tacitly denies it . . . by contrasting the being of the one baptized and the being of those still in original sin . . . *Against precisely this notion* the Reformation's position is that *sin remains active also in the baptized*, and that the justified person is at the same time a real sinner. There can no arguing, therefore, that his sin no longer separates him from God, since it is "'no longer sin in the real sense", and that it is, as it were, "only damnable hypothetically". In itself, concupiscence is indeed sin and therefore damnable.'[34]

So which of the two is the true Lutheran position on the matter? A brief reflection on two aspects of Luther's own teaching (his portrayal of the Christian as *simul iustus et peccator*, and the distinction between *peccatum regnans* and *peccatum regnatum*) may help to clarify the impasse.

For Lutherans the doctrine of *simul iustus et peccator* means the following: when we look at Christ, we discover God's own righteousness, but when we consider ourselves, we encounter only sin. Man is thus just and a sinner really and simultaneously. However, the question is: is this compenetration of justice and sin in the Christian to be taken in an existential and spiritual sense, in which case it would be quite acceptable for Catholics,[35] or must it be understood literally, ontologically? Of course Catholics traditionally fear that Lutherans, insisting on 'forensic' or imputational justification, and excluding justification in terms of regeneration and interior renewal, held to the second option. However, though many of Luther's own texts do not easily allay such fears,[36] others, for example Melanchthon, seem to do so.[37]

---

34 D. Lange et al., 'An Opinion on "The Condemnations of the Reformation Era". Part One: Justification', op. cit., p. 26. Emphasis added.   35 On a predominantly existentialist and spiritual understanding of this phrase, to be found to some degree in the writings of many saints, cf. the following works: R. Kösters, 'Luthers These "Gerecht und Sünder zugleich" ', in *Catholica* 33 (1964) 48–77; K. Rahner, ' "Just and Sinner" ', in *Theological Investigations*, London 1974, pp. 218–230; A. Brandenburg, *Martin Luther gegenwärtig. Katholische Lutherstudien*, Paderborn 1967, p. 109; J. Wicks, 'Living and Praying as "Simul Iustus et Peccator" ', in *Gregorianum* 70 (1989) 521–548; H. Meyer, 'The doctrine of justification in Lutheran dialogue with other Churches', in *One in Christ* 17 (1981) 106–114, with further bibliography.   36 'Verum vos scitis nos esse quidem iustos, puros, sanctos, esse etiam peccatores, iuiustos et damnatos, sed diverso respectu: sumus etiam iusti, quod ad reputationem seu misericordiam Dei in Christo promissam, hoc est propter Christum, in quem credimus . . . Sed secundum formam aut substantiam, seu secundum nos, sumus peccatores iuiusti et damnati, quia certe nihil est in tota natura hominis, quod opponi possit iudicio Dei' (*Die dritte Disputation gegen die Antinomer*, 1538: WA 39/1: 492f.).   37 At Worms in 1541, Melanchthon and Eck subscribed to the following formula which is close to the doctrine of Thomas Aquinas and canon 5 of Trent's session on original sin (DH 1515): 'Forma Concordiae in doctrina de peccato originali, proposta a Catholicis in conventu Wormat . . . "Fatemur unanimi consensu, omnes ab Adam propagatos secundum legem communem nasci cum peccato originali, et ita in ira Dei. Est autem peccatum originale carentia iustitia originalis, debitae inesse, cum concupiscentia. Consentimus etiam, in baptismo remitti reatum peccati originalis cum omnibus peccatis per meritum passionis Christi. Manere autem, non solum apostolicis scripturis sed ipsa etiam experientia docti sentimus concupiscentiam, virium naturae infirmitatem, morbum. De quo quidem morbo in renatis inter nos convenit, quod manet materiale peccati originis, formali

This is where Luther's distinction between *peccatum regnans* (sin acting and reign-
ing in the sinner) and *peccatum regnatum* (sin controlled, beaten and made ineffec-
tual in the Christian by the power of Christ) should be evoked.[38] The question is
this: should 'controlled (or beaten) sin' in the justified (that is, concupiscence) be
actually *called* 'sin' if in real terms it no longer objectively prejudices man's sanctification and eternal salvation? Or more specifically: what does Christ's justifying
action over the sinful believer actually consist of? Does it correspond merely to an
actualistic or dynamic view of grace, the rôle of which would be to keep sin constantly at bay, like a stopper in a dam? Or should it be said that man's sinful condition is truly (if gradually) eliminated?

Taken in respect of the Christian *experience* of justification, the question could
be asked in another way: is the Christian, intent on trusting God to the exclusion of
all else, obliged *as a believer* to mistrust systematically all his or her inclinations,
sentiments and spontaneous leanings and propensities, seeing in them the inevitable sign and symptom of sinful concupiscence? Or put the other way around: if one
is to admit that man is not completely perverted at an ontological or ethical level,
should it not be possible for the empirical and sensitive to become the *locus* and way
of the believer's experience of Christ's Spirit?

It should now be clear that the articulation between the forgiveness of sins (justification) and regeneration through grace (sanctification) is really what is in the
offing.

THE REALITY OF JUSTIFICATION: FORGIVENESS OF SIN AND SANCTIFICATION

1. *Tensions pending between Lutherans and Catholics*

Should human nature be permanently corrupted or perverted by sin, what would it
mean to say that humans can become, through Baptism, 'truly' children of God (cf.
1 Jn 3:1), brothers and co-heirs with Christ, temples of the Spirit? If justification is
'forensic', how can it be inhering and effective, involving a real incorporation into
the body of Christ? Catholics traditionally feared Protestant insistence on 'forensic'
or 'imputative' justification, seeing in it a tacit denial of God's power to sanctify and
recreate the sinner, and insisted that forgiveness of sins is simply inseparable from
the divinizing regeneration of the sinner by grace, which transforms the soul, makes

---

sublato per baptismum. Materiale autem vocamus peccatum, et ipsam humanae naturae
deprivationem, quod ad rem ipsam attinet, est quiddam repugnans legi Dei, quemadmodum Paulus
quoque peccatum adpellat. Ad eandem rationem in scholis compendio doceri solet, manere in
baptizato originalis peccati materiale, formale vero, quod reatus est, auferri" ' (*Corpus Reformatorum*
4: 32; 86; cf. J. Eck, *Apologia pro principibus catholicis* (1543), p. 154).   38 The distinction is developed in Luther's dispute against B. Latomus in 1521, the so-called *Rationis Latomianae confutatio*
(WA 8: 96–105). cf. W. Breuning and B. Hägglund, 'Sin and Original Sin', op. cit., pp. 99f.

it holy, and initiates the process of sanctification. Whatever of the logical priority between 'forgiveness of sins' and 'regeneration through grace' ('synthetic' or 'analytic' justification) the two cannot be dissociated in reality. Trent said as much by insisting on the *unica causa formalis* of justification.

Protestants on the whole, however, considered Catholic doctrine mistaken in the following sense. It seemed that for Catholics the believer, from the moment of justification, was in possession of a sort of divine quality, a 'created grace', over which he or she would be able to exercise some kind of autonomous dominion, whether of merit or of demerit.[39] Carrier of a sort of divine 'organism', Christians could consider themselves exonerated from the obligation of offering *perpetual praise to God* for his gifts, particularly for the pardon of sins and the constant action of the Holy Spirit. The 'state of grace' would become, in real terms, a 'work', a pretext for practical ethical autonomy. Melanchthon, in fact, constantly reprimanded Catholics for their tendency to understand grace as an installed *habitus* in the soul which would promote trust in the Christian's own strength and make it possible for them to love God with their own natural powers.[40] Although nowadays many Lutherans do not consider that the doctrine of grace as a *habitus* necessarily involves the Christian in spiritual possessiveness or complacent self-seeking,[41] the fact is that over the centuries Lutherans have feared that the Catholic understanding of justifying grace would in a first moment inspire Christians with an attitude of pride and self-sufficiency before God, and in a second moment, almost as a consequence, would give rise to a fearful and terrorized conscience in those who realize they are not *doing enough* to please God.[42]

In other words, whereas Protestants in speaking of justification place the emphasis on the forgiveness of sins, Catholics are more conscious of authentic sanctification, that is, of the fact that divine forgiveness brings about the regeneration or divinization of the sinner. Let us examine the question more closely, in particular looking at the relationship (1) between justification and sanctification, and (2) between 'uncreated' and 'created' grace.

2. *Re-evaluation: the continuity between justification and sanctification*

In the first place, as we have seen, modern biblical scholarship generally accepts that justification involves two complementary and mutually conditioning elements:

---

39 Cf. the presentation of different positions in H. Meyer, 'The doctrine of Justification in the Lutheran Dialogue with Other Churches', op. cit., p. 94f.   40 Cf. P. Melanchthon, *Apologia* 2:9–11; 17f.; 4:287-197;316-318. Cf. LV 48f.   41 Cf. especially V. Pfnür, *Einig in der Rechtfertigungslehre?* . . . , op. cit., pp. 76–77. Pfnür points out that the weakness of the *habitus* theory of grace during the late Middle Ages lay in its tenuous relationship with moral life. The *habitus* of grace would do no more than facilitate upright action the human will is already capable of.   42 On the importance of the 'therapy of terrorized consciences' as a point of departure for Lutheranism, cf. USA 22; 24; 39; 62.

the forgiveness of sins (*Sündenvergebung*), and making the sinner truly righteous (*Gerechtmachung*).

The traditional point of contention is expressed between Lutheran and Catholic understandings of the doctrine of justification is on this very point: where the former considered justification in an imputational and forensic way (God *decrees* the remission of sin), the latter identified it as the real renewal of the sinner (God forgives sin in regenerating the sinner). In different ways, strangely enough, *both sides* wished to make the same point. Both wanted to insist on the sovereign and transcendent action of God in justification. Lutherans did so by holding that *only God* can forgive sin and thus cannot be conditioned by human merits or pre-conditions, whereas Catholics understand that precisely because justification is a *divine* pardon, and not a merely human one, it must be effective and re-creative.

Research into Luther's own doctrine and into the origins of Reformation thought has shown that Protestants by no means rejected the doctrine of 'sanctification' or renewal by grace, but just insisted that it is distinct from justification, posterior to and initiated by it.[43] Calvin, in particular, maintains a clear distinction between the two, but insists principally on sanctification, not justification, arguing, at least in polemical writings, that justification relates to sanctification as heat does to the thing that is heated.[44] The tension between the two is linked likewise to Luther's distinction between 'grace' (the divine action of justification) and 'gift' (the result of that action).[45] As we saw earlier, it was particularly in the context of his polemic with the *Schwärmer*, his antinomistic, excessively enthusiastic, followers, that Luther came to insist resolutely on the necessity of both good works and sanctification, as the authentic and necessary fruit of justification. In sum, no fundamental opposition need be posited between 'forensic' and 'effective' justification in Luther's teachings.

Justification by Faith summarizes recent exegetical findings in the following terms.

> Luther at times attributed to his predecessors an identification of the biblical 'justice of God' (*iustitia Dei*) with God's punitive, vindictive justice. He himself preferred to speak of the 'righteousness of God' as an alien righteousness (*iustitia aliena*) that God gives on account of faith in Christ. It alone is 'die Gerechtigkeit die vor Gott gilt', is of value before God. Historians of doctrine today usually admit that Luther's medieval predecessors did not as a rule identify *iustitia Dei* with a punitive justice. In any case recent biblical scholarship sees the righteousness of which Paul speaks both as a gift of God

---

43 Cf. above pp. 31–34.   44 Cf. J. Calvin, 'Les Actes du Concile de Trente avec le reméde contre la poison', in *Recueil des opuscules*, Geneva 1566, p. 943.   45 Cf. M. Luther, *Rationis Latomianae confutatio* (WA 8: 107); A. Bellini, 'La giustificazione per la sola fede', op. cit., pp. 55f.; LV 48; 60f.; J. Wicks, 'Living and Praying as "Simul Iustus et Peccator" ', in *Gregorianum* 70 (1989) 521–548 (especially pp. 534–537).

and, in some passages, as an attribute or quality of God, a power exercises on behalf of sinful humanity to save and justify: *heilsetzende Machte* [Rom 3:5; Käsemann]. This widespread consensus in the modern understanding of Δικαιοσύνη Θεου, according to which it is an attribute of God, but also his power present in his gift, should help us further to go beyond the divisive issues of the sixteenth century.[46]

Perhaps one of the key biblical expressions which links the two elements is to be found Romans 5:5: 'the love of God is poured into our hearts by the Holy Spirit who is given to us' (Rom 5:5). *Lehrverurteilungen—kirchentrennend?* has the following to say.

New Testament exegesis teaches us today that the Protestant way of talking about the righteousness which exists and is efficacious 'outside us' (*extra nos*) has a proper biblical foundation . . . (cf. 1 Cor 1:30; Rom 6: 6 f.; 7:4). Yet the idea of grace 'poured into' the soul and 'adhering' to it (*adhaerens*) clearly also has a sound biblical basis. For the love of God which remains 'outside us' is nonetheless 'poured into our hearts' (Rom 5:5), being identical with the gift of the Holy Spirit . . . and as such, it unites us with Christ, fills us with confidence and joy, and makes us capable of a new life, which we nevertheless never owe to ourselves in any way, since it is fellowship with Christ and the gift of the Holy Spirit . . . In this way New Testament exegesis has initiated a step forward to which we cannot ascribe too great an importance . . .[47]

3. *Re-evaluation: created and uncreated grace; Romans 5:5*

In recent times Catholic theology has recuperated to an important degree the fundamental preponderance, the personal and interpersonal meaning of 'uncreated grace', that is of divine re-creating action on the Christian,[48] and in doing so has managed to overcome a certain popular tendency of talking about grace in terms of a kind of thing or inert substance (*Verdinglichung des Gnades*).[49] But is also true that the complementary trend of downplaying the significance and rôle of created grace

46 USA 131. The phrase 'die Gerechtigkeit die vor Gott gilt' is to be found in M. Luther, WA *Deutsch Bibel* 7: 30f.   47 LV 48.   48 On the recuperation of the notion of uncreated grace and its proper relationship with created grace, cf. M.J. Scheeben, *I misteri del cristianesimo*, Brescia 1960 (orig. 1865), pp. 151–184; 605–644. On this work, cf. K. Eschweiler, *Die zwei Wege der neueren Theologie. Georg Hermes—M.J. Scheeben*, Augsburg 1926; G. Tanzella-Nitti, *Mistero trinitario ed economia della grazia. Il personalismo soprannaturale di M.J. Scheeben*, Roma 1997; G. Colombo, 'Sull'antropologia teologica', in *Teologia* 20 (1995) 223–260 (here 232). Other authors of importance in this regard were Lessius, Petavius, J.A. Möhler, J.H. Newman.   49 On the way in which 'created' or 'sanctifying' grace became depersonalized and considered more and more as an inert object during the later Middle Ages, due to discussions on the nature of merit and mediation, cf. C. Möller, 'La grâce et la justification', in *Lumen Vitae* 19 (1964) 532–544, especially pp. 539f.

has meant, at times, that free human response to grace (faith) has tended to become somewhat confused with the 'gift of grace' as such, that is, with the very action of the Holy Spirit.[50]

It should be noted that investigation into the history of dogma has brought out many useful and interesting elements for our reflection on the relationship between created and uncreated grace. It has been shown that, whatever practical consequences and spurious theological and spiritual interpretations Christians may have drawn from the Catholic doctrine of *gratia creata* around the time of the Reformation, this doctrine originated in the Middle Ages in a clearly *anti-Pelagian* context.[51] Of special importance was Peter Lombard's identification, taking up the anti-Pelagian thrust of Augustine's teaching, of infused charity with the very action of the Holy Spirit: 'the Holy Spirit is itself the love or charity by which we love God and neighbour'.[52] Though the position of Lombard was shared by some medieval authors of a mystical bent (Pascasius Radbertus, Hugh of St Victor, William of St Thierrey, and particularly Richard Fishacre[53]), and is not far from the actualistic-dynamic view of grace common among Lutherans, it was never accepted by the principal Scholastics: Albert the Great, Aquinas, Bonaventure.[54]

50 K. Rahner also insisted on the preponderance of the uncreated and personal side of grace: cf. his study 'Some Implications of the Scholastic Concept of Uncreated Grace', in *Theological Investigations*, vol. 1, London 1974, pp. 319–346; 'Questions of a Controversial Theology on Justification', in *Theological Investigations*, vol. 4, London 1974, pp. 189–218. Employing the immediacy of beatific vision as an analogy for understanding the life of grace, he holds that created grace is in reality a secondary, even superfluous, element in justification. The corollary of this stance is a certain actualist understanding of grace according to which 'not only the grace of divinization, but even the acceptance of this gift must, according to all theological sources, be characterized as grace. Hence the acceptance of the divine gift of justification is itself part of the gift' (K. Rahner, 'The Word and the Eucharist', in *Theological Investigations*, vol. 4, op. cit., 253–281, here p. 257). cf. USA 79–80 and also A. Dulles, 'Justification in contemporary Catholic theology', in H.G. Anderson, et al. (eds.), *Justification by faith . . .* , op. cit., pp. 256–277.   51 On the issue, cf. especially P. Vignaux, *Justification et prédestination au XIV siècle: Duns Scot, Pierre d'Auriole, Guillaume d'Occam, Grégoire de Rimini*, Paris 1934; J. Auer, *Die Entwicklung der Gnadenlehre in der Hochscholastik, mit besonderer Berücksichtigung des Kardinals Matteo d'Acquasparta*, Freiburg i. Br. 1942, vol. 1, pp. 86–166; G. Philips, *L'union personnelle avec le Dieu vivant*, Leuven 1989, pp. 91; 99; 124; 157; 177; 186; 202. On the relationship between created and uncreated grace, J.M. Alonso, 'Relación de causalidad entre la gracia creada e increada en santo Tomás de Aquino', in *Revista Española de Teología* 6 (1946) 3–59; J.L. Ruiz de la Peña, *El don de Dios. Antropología teológica especial*, Santander 1991, pp. 347–351; C. Möller, 'La grâce et la justification', op. cit., pp. 537–541.   52 'Ipse idem spiritus sanctus est amor sive caritas, qua nos diligimus Deum et proximum' (P. Lombard, *I Sent.*, D. 17, a. 1 & 6). On Lombard's theology of grace, cf. J. Schupp, *Die Gnadenlehre des Petrus Lombardus*, Freiburg i. Br. 1932; G. Philips, op. cit., pp. 67–76.   53 Fishacre understood the union between the Holy Spirit and the soul in parallel to the union between the two natures of Christ: just as in Christ the divine and the human unite in a single person in a necessary and permanent fashion, so also the Spirit and the human will form a real, though free and soluble, union. cf. F. Pelster, 'Das Leben und die Schriften des Oxforder Dominikanerlehrers Richard Fishacre (d. 1248)', in *Zeitschrift für Katholische Theologie* 54 (1930) 518-553; A.M. Landgraf, 'Caritas und Heiliger Geist', in *Dogmengeschichte der Frühscholastik, I: Gnadenlehre 1*, Regensburg 1952, pp. 220–237; G. Philips, op. cit., pp. 71–73.   54 Cf. G. Philips, op. cit., pp. 101–173.

The fact is of course that Augustine had by no means identified infused charity with the action of the Holy Spirit,[55] in spite of Lombard's efforts to prove the contrary. Yet, with a view to countering the tendency to identify infused charity purely and simply with the action of the Holy Spirit, a distinction developed over the Scholastic period between *gratia increata* (the action of God's Spirit on the soul) and *gratia creata* (the effect of such action, produced continually by God in the soul), and was consolidated principally in commentaries on Lombard's *Sentences*.[56] It expressed an attempt to avoid confusing the distinction natural/supernatural (both 'created' effects) with that of creature/Creator, that is to insist on divine transcendence over man in both the natural and the supernatural sphere.[57]

During the Middle Ages, for example in the doctrine of Thomas Aquinas, it became quite clear that insistence on the doctrine of 'created grace' is in fact an *exact corollary* of affirming the transcendence and unconditioned quality of God's gracious self-giving. Aquinas holds that the grace of God (*favor Dei*) necessarily 'places something in the soul' (*ponit aliquid in anima*).[58] By the very nature of things, God's love or favour cannot encounter in man anything 'previous' that would induce him to consider man benevolently. The way God loves man is not, as occurs among humans, by *encountering* in him some preexistent goodness inducing such love. Rather the only way God can love is *to give man* such goodness *ex novo*, whether by creating, redeeming or sanctifying, in that sense *making* him good and, as a result, lovable. In other words, if God did not effect a real change in man by forgiving him (turning him from being unforgivable to being forgivable), such forgiveness would be either meaningless in reality, or hedged in intention. In that sense *pure* 'forensic' or imputed justification, may not be altogether inconsistent with an anthropomorphic vision of God's action, detectable to some degree in Calvin's writings.[59] The humanistic origins of the Reformation notion of forensic justification, particularly in Melanchthon, should be kept in mind,[60] as should its Nominalistic roots.[61]

Also to be noted is the fact that Lombard's identification of infused charity with

---

55 Cf. ibid., op. cit., pp. 39–42.   56 The first to develop the distinction systematically was Alexander of Hales (d. 1245) in his *Summa Fratris Alexandri*: cf. G. Philips, op. cit., pp. 77–100; J. Auer, 'Textkritische Studien zur Gnadenlehre des Alexander von Hales', in *Scholastik* 15 (1940) 63–75. 57 Cf. K. Frölich, 'Justification Language in the Middle Ages', op. cit., especially pp. 146ff.   58 Cf. Thomas Aquinas, *Summa Theologiae I-II*, q. 110, a.1. He gives expression to this fundamental assertion by explaining that grace is a *qualitas animae* (ibid., a. 2). cf. also his *III Contra Gentiles* 150 (ed. Marietti, no. 3233). This aspect of the argument is appreciated by Lutheran theologians: cf. for example H. Meyer, *The doctrine of Justification in the Lutheran Dialogue with Other Churches*, op. cit., pp. 95ff.   59 Cf. J. Calvin, *Institutiones Christianae III*, 2: 2.   60 Cf. pp. 46–49 above.   61 R. Jolivet, in an important essay (*La notion de substance. Essai historique et critique sur le développement des doctrines d'Aristote à nos jours*, Paris 1929) pointed out that main-line Scholasticism was well able to cope with the categories of *qualitas* and *habitus* being applied to grace. By contrast, nominalistic thought envisaged such elements more or less as substantial adjuncts either completely substituting the sinful person, or subsisting alongside him. It is understandable that the latter conception would be rejected by Luther.

the action of the Holy Spirit takes as a starting point his interpretation of Romans 5:5 ('the love of God poured into our hearts by the Holy Spirit who is given to us'),[62] a text which was central also for Augustine.[63] Although John Chrysostom[64] and Ambrosiaster[65] held that the expression 'the love of God' (ἀγάπη τοῦ θεοῦ) meant 'the love of God by which God loves us', Augustine and others taught that it referred to the love by which *we love God*. Modern commentators,[66] commonly following Nygren's critique of Augustine's theory of love,[67] generally take the former interpretation, closer to Lombard's, taking note of Romans 5:8, a few verses later, which says: 'God shows us his love for us in that *while we were yet sinners* Christ died for us'.

It should be noted, however, that St Augustine's doctrine on the love of God is considerably more subtle than Nygren's study of him would seem to allow.[68] Augustine holds, as do many contemporary biblical scholars,[69] that the 'love of God poured out' on us provides to some degree a direct experiential encounter with God's grace.[70] But perhaps his most pertinent gloss on Rom 5:5 is to be found in his commentary *De spiritu et littera*, which reads as follows:

> The love of God is poured into our hearts not insofar as he loves us, but insofar as he makes us lovers of his (*qua nos facit dilectores suos*), just as the justice of God is the gift which makes us just (*qua nos facit iustos*).[71]

62 Cf. P. Lombard, *Collectanea* (*Glossa Ordinaria*): PL 191: 1298–1534 (here 1381 C).   63 Augustine cites this key text over 200 times, often commenting on it extensively. cf. A.-M. La Bonnardiére, 'Le verset paulinien Rom., v. 5 dans l'Œuvre de saint Augustin', in Various authors, *Augustinus Magister*, Paris 1954, vol. 2, pp. 657–665.   64 John Chrysostom, *Comm. in Rom., Sermo 9*.   65 Ambrosiaster, *Comm. in Epistolas Paulinas* (CSEL 81/1: 154; 288; 81/2: 28; 54).   66 Cf. for example U. Wilkens, *Evangelisch-katholischer Kommentar zum Neuen Testament*, 3 vols, Zürich 1978, vol. 1, pp. 300–305; J.A. Fitzmyer, *Romans* . . . , op. cit., pp. 397f.; J.D.G. Dunn, *Romans* . . . , op. cit., vol. 1, pp. 252–254; etc.   67 Cf. A. Nygren, *Eros und Agape: Gestaltwandlungen der christlichen Liebe*, Gütersloh 1930, 2 vols, passim. There are several other works of that period which strongly criticize what was considered as Christian (Patristic) espousal of the pagan category of *eros*, inappropriately integrating it with that of *agape*, divine love; cf. especially H. Scholz, *Eros und Caritas. Die platonische Liebe und die Liebe im Sinne des Christentums*, Halle 1929; E. Brunner, *Der Mensch im Widerspruch*, Zürich 1937; K. Barth, *Church Dogmatics 4/2*, Edinburgh 1956, pp. 726–783.   68 Cf. A.-M. La Bonnardiére, op. cit., pp. 658–662, for the wide variety of interpretations of Rom 5:5 given by Augustine. Cf. also G. Hultgren, *Le Commandement d'amour chez Augustin. Intérpretation philosophique et théologique d'après les écrits de la période 386–400*, Paris 1939. Nygren's study has been criticized on several occasions. cf. especially J. Burnaby, *'Amor Dei'. A Study of the Religion of St Augustine*, London 1938; R. Holte, *Béatitude et Sagesse. Saint Augustin et le probléme de la fin de l'homme dans la philosophie ancienne*, Paris 1962, pp. 208–213; 261–263; M.C. D'Arcy, *The Mind and Heart of Love: Lion and Unicorn, a Study in Eros and Agape*, London 1954; J. Pieper, *Über die Liebe*, Munich 1972; and especially V. Capánaga, 'Interpretación agustiniana del amor. Eros y Agape', in *Augustinus* 18 (1973) 213–278.   69 Cf. J.D.G. Dunn, *Romans* . . . , op. cit., p. 253; H. Schlier, *Der Römerbrief*, Freiburg i. Br. 1977, *in hoc loco*.   70 Cf. Augustine, *Tr. in Io*. 6:10, which, citing Rom 5:5, indicates the experience of fraternal charity as a clear sign of the presence of the Holy Spirit in the heart; *Sermo* 5: 4–6, on the consolation the pouring out of the Holy Spirit produces; *In I Io*. 8: 12, which says that love is a sign of the inhabitation of the Holy Spirit.   71 Augustine, *De spiritu et littera* 32: 56 (CSEL 60: 215).

On the same text from the letter to the Romans he comments in *De Trinitate* that the Holy Spirit 'makes of each one a lover of God and of neighbour'.[72] And elsewhere, he confirms the notion, saying: *amare Deum, Dei donum est*.[73] The love of God, poured out by the Holy Spirit, has an absolute priority over human response, but at the same time such a pouring out of divine love effects a recreative, divinizing response on the believer, making of him a lover of God and, inseparably, of neighbour.[74]

Indeed, Luther had said that, when loved by God, the Christian becomes 'divine, heavenly',[75] and by remaining in this love, 'is a god'.[76] But in this process, as Nygren points out, 'the subject, properly speaking, of Christian love is not man, but God himself . . . man is but a channel, a conduit which transports divine love'.[77] This is the impression Luther generally gives in his own writings; though God's love is indeed creative, man remains passive and sinful: *amor Dei non invenit sed creat suum diligibile. Amor hominis fit a suo diligibili*:[78] 'divine love does not find but creates the lovable object; human love derives from the lovable object'. And elsewhere, 'we are gods through the love which makes us charitable towards our neighbour; in fact, divine nature is no more than pure benevolence . . . goodness and benevolence which constantly pour out good things profusely on every creature'.[79] However, although in his commentary on Rom 5:5 Luther indeed contrasts *charitas Dei* to the vile love of the creature (concupiscence, the *cor incurvatum in seipsum*), he states clearly that we do truly love God due to the pouring out of the *charitas Dei* on us. His words are: 'this love is called the "love of God" because thanks to it we love God alone, in which there is nothing visible, nothing to be experienced, nothing in which one can place one's trust'.[80] And he insists that 'it is not enough to possess the gift if the giver is not also present . . . In fact only to [the gift of] love does the Apostle attribute the presence and at the same time the gift of the Spirit given to us with love.'[81]

Augustine was probably the first among the Fathers to explain theologically not only that God in the Spirit loves without measure, unconditionally, but that the Spirit himself is Love,[82] prior to, as it were, and independently of donating himself to creatures. And therefore when God gives, he gives or donates what he is, *Love itself*, reproducing *ad extra* his own life and reality. This is why Augustine insists that the love of God poured out on believers makes them not only 'receivers of gift', but also 'lovers of the God who loved them', and, as a direct result, lovers of their fellow human beings.[83] And at the same time the grace which sanctifies never be-

72 Idem., *De Trinitate XV*, 17: 31–32.   73 Idem., *Sermo 297*: 1.   74 Cf. especially V. Capánaga, op. cit., passim.   75 M. Luther, *Sermon 2* (1532: WA 36: 439).   76 Ibid., 437.   77 A. Nygren, *Eros und Agape* . . . , op. cit., vol. 2, p. 557.   78 M. Luther, *Heidelberg Disputation*, thesis 28 (WA 1: 365).   79 M. Luther, *Sermon no. 1*, 1532 (WA 36: 423).   80 Idem., *Die Vorlesung über den Römerbrief* (WA 56: 307). cf. ibid., 306–309.   81 Ibid., 308.   82 Cf. Augustine, *De Trinitate XV*, 17: 31.   83 Cf. the brief though convincing study on deification in Augustine by V. Capánaga, 'La deificación en la soteriología agustiniana', in Various authors, *Augustinus Magister*, Paris 1954, vol. 2, pp. 745–754.

comes a possession of human beings to which they might appeal before God, but is and remains *entirely dependent on the salvation-constituting activity of the gracious God*.[84]

The foregoing discussion is significant on many fronts, not least in that it provides a solid theological basis for a doctrine of 'created grace' fully cognizant of the priority of 'uncreated grace'.[85] But it is especially important on the following point: a phrase very similar to Augustine's one just mentioned (from *De Spiritu et littera*) is employed by Trent to explain the critical *unica causa formalis* of justification: 'iustitia Dei, non qua ipse iustus est, sed *qua nos iustos facit*'.[86] In other words, just as the *amor Dei* is not to be identified exclusively with the dynamic relationship established by divine donation to man, but refers primordially to the triune God whose eternal essence is identified with Love itself, and is capable of creating divine lovers out of humans, so also, for Augustine, *iustitia Dei* describes not merely a divinely established right relationship between God and man, but truly effects righteousness in man: God is righteous and truly makes man righteous.[87]

Of course, the contemporary trend to downplay the significance and rôle of created grace has also meant, in practice, that free human response (faith) to grace has tended to become confused with the 'gift of grace', itself, that is, with the very action of the Holy Spirit on the Christian. This tendency, quite common in Lutheran theology, leads us to the next point, on the rôle of faith and grace in justification.

4. *Tensions remaining: grace vs. faith*

In Lutheran confessional statements and theology, it is not uncommon to encounter a certain confusion or, better, equivalence between faith and grace: to say that 'man is justified by (or through) grace' is much the same as to say that 'man is justified by faith'.[88] This point is understandable in a Lutheran context insofar as it reflects that fact that faith is not a 'work' and has little *thematic* content; rather it constitutes the very core of the union established between God and man by grace, of what God's justifying action achieves in man. For Luther, as we saw above, 'faith is a work of God, not of man . . . Other faculties act with us and through us. Only this one acts in us but without us (*in nobis et sine nobis*)'.[89] 'Faith is *being taken by God*, allowing him to act'.[90]

---

84 Cf. LV 47–53, quoting Bonaventure's notion of God's grace by which we possess God because he in the first place possesses us: *habere est haberi* (cf. *Breviloquium V*, cap. 1: *Opera omnia*, ed. Quaracchi, 5, 253 a).   85 On whether or not Augustine developed a doctrine of 'created grace', cf. G. Philips, 'Saint Augustin a-t-il connu une "grâce créée"?', in *Ephemerides Theologiae Lovanensis* 47 (1971) 97–116; P.G. Riga, 'Created Grace in St Augustine', in *Augustinian Studies* 3 (1972) 113–130.   86 Augustine, *De Trinitate XIV*, 12: 15, in DH 1529.   87 Cf. G. Bavaud, 'La doctrine de la justification d'aprés Saint Augustin', in *Revue des études augustiniennes* 5 (1959) 21-32; A.E. McGrath, *Iustitia Dei* . . . , op. cit., vol. 1, pp. 23-36.   88 Cf. for example *Confessio Augustana IV*.
89 M. Luther, *De captivitate Babylonica* (WA 6: 530).   90 A. Bellini, 'La giustificazione per la sola fede', op. cit., p. 45.

According to Lutherans, faith, as the supreme expression of what justifying grace achieves *in man*, includes communion with Christ, as well as charity and hope. For Catholics, the response of faith, though impossible without God's grace (and in that sense it is fully God's gift) deeply involves human free will and creaturely response, both of the individual and of the Church. *Lehrverurteilungen – kirchentrennend?* admits quite candidly that 'if we translate from one language to another, then Protestant talk about justification through faith corresponds to Catholic talk about justification through grace; and on the other hand, Protestant doctrine understands substantially under the one word "faith" what Catholic doctrine (following 1 Cor 13:13) sums up in the triad "faith, hope and love".'[91] As can be seen, the issue is closely related to that of the weight given to creaturely freedom in responding to grace.

5.   *Tensions remaining: ontological vs. actualistic understanding of grace*

The difference between Lutheran and Catholic understanding of justification clearly responds to different emphases and concerns which *Justification by faith* has described respectively as 'proclamatory' and 'transformational',[92] and *Lehrverurteilungen – kirchentrennend?* as 'forensic' and 'effective'.[93] However, even after the difference in perspective is taken into account, certain variances do remain between the two approaches. Whereas Lutherans see man's confidence as directed *exclusively* towards God's promise and *saving action*, Catholics 'include' (or at least do not exclude) as a partial object of this confidence the created 'state of sanctifying grace', precisely insofar as such trust is founded entirely on the salvation-constituting activity of God who is faithful to his promises and therefore worthy of being trusted by man. The question remains: why would or should Lutherans be unhappy with human trust being directed to some degree towards such a 'state of grace'?

The reason I believe is to be found once more in the predominantly actualistic/dynamic view of grace common in Lutheranism, which Catholic theology does not altogether share. Lutherans consider the 'sanctification' that follows on from 'justification' principally as a renewal of life (*Eneurung des Lebens*),[94] whereas Catholics regard it primarily as a stable ontological recreation of the Christian which serves, one might say, as a springboard for a new life. And of course one thing is to direct one's trust towards divine life created by grace in the believer (what Catholics do when they joyfully consider their 'own' holiness and divine filiation and praise God for it), quite another to direct it towards those good actions which in principle should derive from the action of Christ's Spirit in us. The following words of Bellini offer an interesting explanation of what is in the offing.

> When the Reformation affirms that sanctification follows justification necessarily . . . *it does not mean a sanctification of man in his being*, an ontological

---

91 LV 52; cf. ibid. 50.   92 Cf. USA 8; 20; 90f.   93 Cf. LV 48.   94 Cf. ibid.

sanctification, as Catholic theology would say, but a moral sanctification . . .
In fact sanctification [for Protestants] is simply that new life which the Christian, justified in the goodness of judgement and the mercy of God, begins to
carry out under the action of the Holy Spirit present in him.[95]

In other words, where Catholic theology speaks of a stable ontological sanctification
of man, a created grace, which expresses itself *a posteriori* in the obligation and
reality of a life lived according to the Gospel, Protestants prefer in general a dynamic vision of sanctification as a result of the direct action of Christ's Spirit on us,
in us and through us: grace is simply the action of Christ's Spirit in the Christian.
But is this really the same thing as 'sanctifying grace' (*gratia gratum faciens*), or
'created grace'? Or does it make that much difference whether we take one or the
other position, as long as the transcendence of divine action is affirmed?

To some degree, I think, it does. Lutheran theology tends, from what we have
seen, to hold that 'grace' is purely and simply the immediate and personal action of
Christ's Spirit on man, who 'creates' faith in him,[96] and transforms moral action
directly, in such a way that 'good works' are, in an almost exclusive sense, the 'fruit'
of grace, divine works in man. The human subject, passive in itself, active only
insofar as God acts in it, is left somewhat in the shade. Of course such a unilaterally
actualistic and dynamic understanding of grace, although commonly reflected in agreed
statements on justification,[97] is not a universally held position among Lutherans.
However, as we shall see in the next section, some of the consequences of this understanding of grace, at the very heart of the tensions remaining between Lutherans
and Catholics must be taken into account.

LAW, WORKS AND GOSPEL IN CHRISTIAN LIFE

1.   *The correct relationship between God and man: law and gospel*

The Göttingen *Opinion*'s principal criticism of *Lehrverurteilungen – kirchentrennend?*
is that the latter does not thoroughly apply the doctrine of justification as a
hermeneutical or criteriological principle for Christian and ecclesiastical life to the
different dogmatic aspects of justification doctrine it examines. The Göttingen paper argues that 'if [this] had been taken seriously, one would not have been able to
reduce the differing justification doctrines to the sum of two complementary "concerns". For the difference between the two is an antithetical definition of the relationship between God and man.'[98]

95 A. Bellini, op. cit., p. 69.   96 LV 47: 'There can be "cooperation" *only* in the sense that in faith
the heart is involved, when the Word touches it and creates faith'.   97 USA 101: 'For them
[Lutherans] God's justifying act of forgiveness is itself the cause or constant power of renewal
throughout the life of the believer'.   98 D. Lange et al., 'An Opinion on "The Condemnations of
the Reformation Era". Part One: Justification', op. cit., p. 55f.

The same study states that *Lehrverurteilungen – kirchentrennend?* examines several aspects of the doctrine of justification 'except for one blatant exception: the theme of "law and gospel" which is deleted . . . At this point . . . the inevitable question would have had to be posed about the different centres of the doctrines of justification and their relationship with one another . . . The [fundamental] concern of the doctrine of justification, namely the correct determination of the relationship between God and man, does not come into view as the guiding principle of that doctrine . . . This is a deficit which corresponds to the neglect of the theme of "law and gospel" in the document.'[99]

And earlier on, the Göttingen *Opinion* insists that 'the doctrine of justification is not just one dogmatic article among others, but the theological formulation of the event which marks the *centre of Christian faith* . . . That is so because justification is *the truth about the relationship between God and man*; that is, in the event of justification, God is truly God, and man truly man – standing before God. *From this perspective, all the other primary statements of the Reformation doctrine of justification are to be understood* . . . [This] means that justification is God in action whereby for Christ's sake he forgives the sinner, and grants him the righteousness of Christ so that man, lost in his sin, through this gracious condescension, is newly established and determined. That God enters this relationship of grace with man is the content of the *gospel*. Its true meaning becomes understandable only from the correct distinction from and relationship to the *law*.'[100]

In other words, according to this study, the basis for understanding all points related to justification, whether systematic or practical, whether anthropological or ecclesiological, is a proper understanding of the relationship between 'law' and 'gospel', because this distinction, considered by Luther 'the greatest intuition of Christianity',[101] best expresses the abyss that exists between the merciful Creator and the sinful creature, the true relationship between God and man in the context of salvation.

In brief terms, it could be said that *under the law* (that is, outside or 'before' salvation or justification, man 'on his own'), humans are obliged to complete obedience, they experience nothing but failure, the cannot achieve their expected, self-made, perfection. Under the law, man's perversion 'transforms all his deeds into means of self-assertion', self-justification, 'being his own creator', 'resistance to one's own creatureliness', 'self-establishment and self-assertion as the driving force of action', 'fulfilling the will of God by one's own means'.[102]

Conversely, *under the gospel* (being saved and justified), 'man is promised that Christ has died for him and taken on his guilt'. 'Christ's righteousness becomes his

99 Ibid., p. 24.   100 Ibid., p. 16.   101 M. Luther, *Serm. in Gal.* 3,1 (WA 36, 9, 28–29). cf. *Formula Concordiae: Solida Declaratio* 5: 27, in T.G. Tappert et al. (eds.), *The Book of Concord*, op. cit., p. 563.   102 Cf. D. Lange et al., 'An Opinion on "The Condemnations of the Reformation Era". Part One: Justification', op. cit., p. 16.

own'; 'the believer is transplanted from himself into Christ . . . so that Christ himself becomes the new being of the sinner'. He is 'justified in his relationship to God and sinner according to his own quality (*simul iustus et peccator*)'. Faith, which effects this transplantation into Christ 'fills man with an unconditioned trust in the grace of God', and places him on the way to sanctification, without, however any 'anxious observation of his own progress or failure because his good standing before God is grounded in the righteousness of Christ'.[103]

2. Different understandings of 'law' and 'gospel'

Of course, the understanding of the categories of 'law and gospel', in content and application, is not unvaried among Lutherans. The key issue lies in the different ways in which Lutheran controversy has understood the so-called 'uses' of the law: for Luther and for many of his interpreters (probably also for the authors of the Göttingen *Opinion*), the law has two 'uses'; for Melanchthon, Calvin[104] and mainline sixteenth century Lutheranism, taken up by the *Formula of Concord* (1577), it has three. *Justification by faith* describes the different 'uses' of the law as follows.

> The theological distinction between law and gospel raised questions about the relation of law to the chronology of the life of the justified. Does the distinction between divine demand [law] and divine promise [gospel] lead to an end of the law at some point in time? Luther, holding to his view of the justified person as simultaneously righteous and sinful (*simul iustus et peccator*), stressed only *two uses of the law*: one is for the restraint of sin through political authority (*usus legis politicus*); the other is for the disclosure of sin through accusation and exhortation (*usus legis theologicus* or *paedagogicus*, also called *elenchticus*). Under the pressure of the antinomian controversies, the *Formula of Concord*, apparently fearing a separation between law and gospel, which would lead to individualistic 'enthusiasm' (*Schwärmerei*), held that believers 'require the teaching of the law'; under the heading of 'the third function of the law', it insisted on the preaching of the law to believers 'so that they will not be thrown back on their own holiness and piety and under the pretext of the Holy Spirit's guidance set up a self-elected service of God without his Word and commands'.[105]

In other words, one position holds that the law is but profane and accusatory, linked exclusively with man's insuperably corrupted condition, opposed to the gospel of mercy and pardon; the other *adds* that the law is, besides, a vehicle of God's word, and therefore inseparable from his love and mercy. The question of the legitimacy

---

103 Ibid., pp. 17f.   104 Quite explicitly so: cf. his *Institutiones Christianae II*, 7.   105 USA 61.

of such an addition has been the object of considerable controversy among Lutherans.[106]

The problem is quite a practical one: must the preaching of the Gospel *include* the preaching of the law? In other words, is the 'law' completely on the side of sin and accusation, or is it an integral part of the Gospel, offering man the possibility of doing God's will and thus acquiring liberation and salvation? Catholic doctrine on the matter would seem to be the following. On the one hand, as an expression of the material fulfillment of the commandments, the law does not suffice for justification, and under Christ it no longer mercilessly accuses and enslaves the believer, who joyfully turns towards the pardon promised by God in Christ.[107] On the other hand, as a concrete expression of the word and will of God, any refusal to fulfill the law (preferring 'one's own' will) is sinful, is a lack of faith. Law therefore belongs, in a differentiated way, both to the realm of sin and to that of the Gospel. But is this in accord with the Lutheran position?

The following reflection on the rôle of 'good works' in Christian life should clarify the issues somewhat.

3. *The rôle of 'works' in Christian life: tensions between Catholic and Lutheran positions*

Though the rôle of 'works' has traditionally constituted one of the most contentious issues in Catholic-Reformed controversy (the question of 'merit' comes especially to mind), it would seem nowadays that major differences, based to a considerable degree on misunderstandings, no longer remain on this particular front.

Reformers consistently held that 'it is of the essence of God's justifying act to exclude all merit'.[108] Luther said that the 'righteousness fanatics', as he called them, 'are not willing to receive grace and eternal life for nothing from him [God]; they desire to earn both through their works'.[109] Yet the Council of Trent does not hesitate to say that the justified can truly merit an 'increase of grace, eternal life and the attainment of that eternal life, and increase of glory', in virtue of 'the grace of God and the merit of Jesus Christ, whose living member he is'.[110] In brief terms, where Lutherans fear God's gifts not being accepted *as gifts*, and the resultant 'self-glorification of human beings in their works',[111] Catholics, understanding 'merit' Christologically and in terms of the biblical doctrine of 'reward', consider Lutheran misgivings unfounded in respect of God's charge to bring forth good fruit, and his promise to reward it.

---

106 Cf. for example W. Joest, *Gesetz und Freiheit: Das Problem des tertius usus legis bei Luther und die neutestamentliche Paränese . . .* , op. cit.   107 'Since the justified remain exposed to the onslaught (*Zugriff*) of sin throughout their lives, they also remain exposed to the law's accusation and, believing the gospel, they turn in faith unreservedly to God's merciful grace in Christ, which alone declares and makes them just.' (LV 35).   108 Ibid.   109 M. Luther, *In ep. S. Pauli ad Galatas* (1531–35: WA 40/1: 224).   110 Conc. Trid., *sess. VI de Iustificatione*, canon 32 (DH 1582).   111 LV 66.

According to *Lehrverurteilungen – kirchentrennend?* Catholic doctrine of merit does not necessarily involve vain complacency in one's own works, but is rather 'a way of expressing the responsibility of human beings and the eschatological structure of grace'.[112] And just as Trent makes it clear that man cannot, as such, place any claims on God, Lutherans 'uphold the responsibility of human beings just as firmly as they do the eschatological structure of justification'.[113]

However, the Göttingen *Opinion* calls into question the notion of 'human responsibility' which the doctrine of 'merit' expresses, seeing in it a contradiction of 'the gift-character of grace . . . unavoidably [abandoning] the Christian to uncertainty about his salvation . . . The talk of "merit", or of "responsibility" in a way corresponding to it, presupposes that the Christian's relationship to God is one of law'.[114] It adds that 'the biblical talk of "reward", which is something quite different, does not correspond with merit... and cannot be reconciled with it.'[115] Commenting on *Lehrverurteilungen—kirchentrennend?*'s insistence that the Reformers also uphold human responsibility, the Göttingen *Opinion* adds that 'it is not as a responsibility *for obtaining salvation*, but *for the preservation of salvation* already received. The Christian, who on earth has grace only when struggling against his own sin until, after death, God renders that grace ultimately victorious . . . , runs the risk of becoming lazy in this struggle and thus losing the received salvation'.[116] 'Responsibility' for Lutherans, it says, therefore points to *perseverance in grace received*, and not so much to *earning an increase in grace*.

Tensions, clearly, do remain between Lutherans and Catholics. Luther taught consistently that 'good works' are the *fruit and natural/necessary outcome* of grace and faith,[117] that they 'reveal salvation',[118] that 'works save us externally, that is, they testify to our being just . . . , external salvation [showing] up the good tree, as its fruit'.[119] Earlier on we made reference to Lutheranism in respect of human free will in salvation, and of the Lutheran tendency to affirm a unilaterally actualistic and dynamic understanding of grace,[120] that is, avoiding the category of 'created grace' while insisting on that of 'uncreated grace'. The same issue comes up here. If human free will, itself a created gift of God, does not 'contribute' to justification even the acceptance of grace, if God's grace is simply identified with the action of Christ's Spirit on the believer, then, logically, 'good works' would simply be the *direct result* of divine justifying grace. Such good works are not denied, of course, but since 'grace' seems to be taken here as little more than the immediate personal action of

---

112 LV 67.   113 Ibid.   114 D. Lange et al., 'An Opinion on "The Condemnations of the Reformation Era". Part One: Justification', op. cit., p. 33.   115 Ibid., p. 61, note 60.   116 Ibid., p. 33. Emphasis added.   117 Cf. M. Luther, *Disputatio de fide infusa et acquista* (1520: WA 6: 94). On the continuity between faith and works in Luther, cf. P. Manns, 'Absolute and Incarnate Faith: Luther on Justification in the Galatians' Commentary of 1531–1535', op. cit.; G. Ebeling, *Luther. Einführung in sein Denken* . . . , op. cit., pp. 177–197.   118 M. Luther, *Die Promotionsdisputation von Palladius und Tileman* (1537: WA 39/1: 254).   119 Idem., *In ep. S. Pauli ad Galatas Comm.* (WA 40/1: 96).   120 Cf. pp. 221–226.

the Spirit on the human person, making him or her a believer, it would seem that human ethical action is simply *transformed directly by God* in such a way that 'good works' are, in an exclusive sense, the 'fruit' of grace, 'divine works in man', who behaves as a passive spectator, and not the 'good works *of* man' in which he is fully involved. In such a situation, it is easy for our personal collaboration to be considered unneeded and meaningless. Catholics generally pay more attention to the phenomenology of ethical behaviour, considering the need the Christian has of *applying* himself or herself to the fulfillment of the commandments of God in order to be true to the justified state, and effectively carry out 'good works'.

At heart, I believe, the difference lies in the manner in which the so-called *tertius usus legis* is integrated with the other two 'uses' of the law. In other words, if, apart from acting as a correlative to sin and non-salvation, 'the law' is also seen to express the need to positively fulfill the will of God as expressed in the commandments, then it would not sufficient to say simply that 'good works' are solely the result of God's grace acting in us.

ASSURANCE OF SAVING GRACE

The theological value of human experience and involvement in justification is particularly significant in dealing with the controversial issue of *assurance* or *certitude* of salvation.[121] Before the Reformation took place, in fact, the question of the assurance or otherwise of personal saving grace had not generally be developed in a theological fashion. Aquinas and others had spoken of the signs and indications the Christian can experience of the action and of the 'state' of grace (joy for the things of God, despising the things of the world, not being conscious of mortal sin, etc.)[122] But with Lutheranism, the topic came strongly to the fore, perhaps in spite of itself, and as a result took on a certain consistency in Catholic theology,[123] especially on account of the treatment it received during the discussions between Thomists and Scotists at the Council of Trent.

---

121 Cf. LV 34–35; 53–56; USA 24; 33; 158–159. At times the two words 'assurance' and 'certitude' are considered equivalent when in reality they are not. The first expresses, generally speaking, a certitude obtained due to the promise of help *from another*; the second refers more to pure subjective certainty. cf. Vereinigte Evangelisch-Lutherische Kirche Deutschlands, *Lehrverurteilungen im Gespräch* . . . , op. cit., p. 92; and also O.-H. Pesch, 'Gottes Gnadenhandeln als Rechtfertigung des Menschen', op. cit., pp. 871–877. 122 Cf. Thomas Aquinas, *Summa Theologiae I-II*, q. 112, a. 5, c.; *De Veritate*, q. 10, a. 10; *In II Cor.* 12: 1 f., lect. 1 (ed. Marietti, nn. 440 457). On this topic, cf. E. Neveut, 'Peut-on avoir la certitude d'être en état de grâce?', in *Divus Thomas (Piacenza)* 37 (1934) 321–349; O.-H. Pesch, *Theologie der Rechtfertigung bei Martin Luther und Thomas von Aquin*, Mainz 1967, pp. 748–757; S. Pfürtner, *Angoisse et certitude de notre salut: Luther et Saint Thomas au-delà des oppositions traditionelles*, Paris 1967. 123 The critical rôle of human experience has been of particular importance in recent times in Catholic theology. cf. especially J. Mouroux, *L'expérience chrétienne: Introduction à une théologie*, Paris 1952.

1. *Tensions pending*

Luther asked: 'Why did Christ say: "Whose sins you shall remit, they are remitted" if not because they are not remitted unless a man believe they are remitted when the priest remits them? . . . Nor does the remission of sin and the bestowal of grace suffice, but a man must also believe that it is remitted . . .'[124] Elsewhere he says that if one 'doubts and is uncertain, then he will indeed not thereby be justified, but rejects grace'.[125] And in the *Apologia* to the *Confessio Augustana*, we read that 'faith alone, looking to the promise and believing with full assurance that God forgives because Christ did not die in vain, conquers the terrors of sin and death. If somebody doubts that his sins are forgiven, he insults Christ because he thinks that his sin is greater and stronger than the death and promise of Christ.'[126] Luther, in other words, linked *assurance of forgiveness of sins directly with Christian faith*. He as much as said: if we do not *believe* we *are* forgiven, then we are not in fact forgiven. In the words of Pesch, Lutherans hold that 'while I accept him, while I attach myself to Christ in faith, while I relate to myself and my sin what God has done for me in Christ, I become certain of my salvation. Faith and certainty of salvation are one and the same thing.'[127]

Understandably, the Council of Trent retorted by condemning those who say that 'man is absolved from his sins and justified because he believes with certainty that he is absolved and justified; or that no one is truly justified except he who believes he is justified, and that absolution and justification are effected by faith alone'.[128]

2. *Re-evaluation of positions*

In the context of such declarations and counter-declarations, it has not been uncommon to attribute to Luther's affirmations a crass religious subjectivism, and see in him a significant forerunner of modern idealistic and existentialist philosophies.[129] Nevertheless, over the time of the Reformation it can be seen that, whatever of later developments, the two sides were not very far apart on this particular question. Cardinal Cajetan at the Diet of Augsburg in 1518 made it clear that faith must be completely certain of divine forgiveness, not dissociating, however, such faith from

124 M. Luther, *Resolutiones Disputationum et indulgentiarum virtute*, concl. 7 (1518: WA. 1: 543).   125 M. Luther, *Acta Augustana* (1518: WA 2: 13).   126 *Apologia*, 4: 148f., in T.G. Tappert et al., (ed.), *The Book of Concord . . .* , op. cit., p. 127.   127 O.-H. Pesch, 'Gottes Gnadenhandeln als Rechtfertigung des Menschen', op. cit., p. 873.   128 Conc. Trid., *sess. VI de Iustificatione*, canon 14 (DH 1564). cf. canon 13.   129 Cf. for example J. Maritain, 'Luther, or The Advent of the Self', in *Three reformers: Luther, Descartes, Rousseau*, London 1966, pp. 3–50; P. Häcker, *Das Ich im Glauben bei Martin Luther*, Graz/Wien 1966. On the relationship and contrast between Luther and Descartes, especially in respect of epistemological 'certitude', cf. G. Ebeling, 'Gewißheit und Zweifel. Die Situation des Glaubens im Zeitalter nach Luther und Descartes', in *Zeitschrift für Theologie und Kirche* 64 (1967) 282–324.

reception of the sacraments.[130] In other words, doubt regarding one's own salvation, if existent, derives not from God's will, nor from the sacrament's inefficacy, but, as *Lehrverurteilungen – kirchentrennend?* says, from inadequacy on the recipient's side, on whose part 'a doubt is justified, because the recipient can never be sure whether he has laid himself sufficiently open to the efficacy of the sacrament'.[131] However, it would seem that Lutherans wanted to go further than this, urging Christians not to merely *endure* personal uncertainty with Christian patience, but to see such uncertainty as a relapse into sin, and to trust completely in the true effectiveness of the absolution they receive from outside (*extra nos*). In other words, 'the person tempted should not look at himself, his sin and his doubt. He should look to Christ and his fellowship with him, founded on baptism and continually promised anew in repentance'.[132]

Cajetan considered this position somewhat mistaken in that it seemed to imply that assurance of salvation would be founded on one's subjective state or feelings. Lutherans on their side took it that 'the rejection of their view meant that their opponents had a positive interest *in keeping believers in a state of uncertainty*, and that for these ends they would not even shrink from implying a doubt in the reliability of Christ's promises,'[133] a claim, of course, that is impossible to verify historically. Besides, Luther virtually identified Catholic doctrine on the matter with the 'contritionist' teaching of G. Biel, who saw 'perfect' contrition as a condition for sacramental absolution, a condition or 'work' bound to leave the Christian uncertain as to efficacy of the administration of the sacrament.

According to *Lehrverurteilungen – kirchentrennend?*, however, it should be added that, in this quest for a gracious God, Luther 'wished in fact to give *increased importance* to the power of the keys and to absolution, with an emphatic stress on faith in the Word of promise'.[134] He sincerely wished and intended to place no trust whatsoever in 'good works', nor in any kind of personal experience of divine favour towards himself. In fact, quite in keeping with the canons of the Council of Trent, he wished to avert 'security and self-conceit about one's own condition and a complacent certainty of being in grace, self-deception about one's own weakness, insufficient fear of losing grace, comforting 'feelings' as criterion, moral laxness under appeal to the assurance of salvation, and – even more – security of predestination'.[135] It is quite fair to say that the kind certainty of grace sought by Luther was not the one rejected by Trent.[136]

130 Cf. J. Wicks (ed.), *Cajetan responds: a reader in reformation controversy*, Washington 1978; C. Morerod, *Cajetan et Luther en 1518: édition, traduction et commentaire des opuscules d'Augsbourg de Cajetan*, Fribourg (Suisse) 1994. On the controversy, cf. G. Hennig, *Cajetan und Luther: ein historischer Beitrag zur Begegnung von Thomismus und Reformation*, Stuttgart 1966. 131 LV 53. 132 LV 54. 133 LV 54f. Emphasis added. 134 LV 55. Emphasis added. On the debate regarding 'contritionism' and 'attritionism' between Lutherans and Catholics, cf. G. Bavaud, 'La justification par la foi. Quelle est la racine de la divergence entre catholiques et protestants?', op. cit. 135 LV 56. 136 Cf. J. Alfaro, 'Certitude de l'espérance et certitude de la grâce', in *Nouvelle Revue Théologique* 94 (1972) 3–42, here p. 29.

3. *Tensions remaining; the Christian's 'experience of the Spirit'*

The Christian's assurance of the presence of saving grace is expressed in terms of 'looking towards God'; faith, from which assurance of salvation derives, is grounded on the reality of God's promise in Christ, not on our own strengths, resources, experiences or achievements. Catholics and Lutherans would be happy enough to admit that; objectively speaking, Christians can and should place their confidence, or 'ultimate trust' in God alone, insofar as only he can offer an assurance which is experienced as certitude.[137] The Göttingen *Opinion* says more or less the same thing: 'God is conceived as the power that brings about certitude . . . [he is] experienced as the one present to man . . . [and] in a lively fashion determines man in the centre of his person . . . By faith alone God makes his presence felt by word and sacrament in the Holy Spirit . . . The ground of assurance is God himself who brings men to faith by making himself present in the Word through the Holy Spirit. This divine presence, in the confidence of faith, produces through itself the certainty the believer experiences.'[138]

Notice however how assurance of salvation is brought about according to the Göttingen *Opinion*. God, it says, 'makes his presence felt . . . in the Word through the Holy Spirit . . . producing through itself the certainty of the believer',[139] which involves, on our part, 'looking away from our own experience'. This is where the difficulty lies. The fact is that certain forms of *created mediation* may be encountered and experienced by the believer as inextricably *linked with* the saving and assuring power of God: the preaching and sacraments of the Church, interior or exterior personal experience of God's gifts, etc. Lutherans tend to fear that such created mediations may become, perhaps partially, perhaps unwittingly, object of the confidence the Christian wishes to direct entirely towards God. The Göttingen paper insists that *faith* brings certainty insofar as it 'transposes us into Christ';[140] it is nothing else but 'the receiving organ, created in the act of receiving'.[141] Conversely, Catholics hold that without such mediations, the word of God and his saving power would be like a sealed fountain, and of little *human relevance* to believers. Hence a certain tension remains on this point between the Catholics and Lutherans.

The problem remaining could be presented in the following terms. God in communicating the gift of faith to the sinner, thus making him a believer, communicates his grace and thus brings about a certain assurance of being under the power of saving grace. But since this 'experience' is not *produced* by man, but exclusively by God, it is by its very nature an 'experience of the Spirit'. And at the same time, such

137 On God as the fountain-head of justification in an anthropological context, cf. J.M. Galván, 'La giustizia di Dio, sorgente della giustificazione', in J.M. Galván (ed.), *La giustificazione in Cristo*, pp. 117–128.   138 D. Lange et al., 'An Opinion on "The Condemnations of the Reformation Era". Part One: Justification', op. cit., p. 31.   139 Ibid.   140 Ibid., p. 32.   141 Ibid., p. 61, note 55. On the notion of faith as 'pure organ of reception', etc., cf. E. Wolf, op. cit., pp. 11–21; P. Althaus, *Die Theologie Martin Luthers* . . . , op. cit., pp. 202; 374 etc.

an experience is received by *man*, and is meant to assure *him*. Thus the 'experience of the Spirit' must be, in a very real sense, a *human* experience, in the sense that man must be in a position to experience it, and to experience it *meaningfully*, assuringly, humanly. Now Luther, certainly in his earlier writings, tended to reject whatever possibility of a *human experience* of faith.[142] In later works, dealing with the positive content of faith, he accepts the notion of experience, but only insofar as it is understood as an *experience of the Spirit*, disconnected therefore from the senses. 'The meaning of the Holy Spirit', von Löwenich says, 'consists in this: what is considered as his work is taken away from any purely empirical causality . . . Yet, not allowing itself be reduced to the ambit of the empirical, it claims to be an experience true and proper'.[143] And the author of *Theologia Crucis* asks: 'if the action of God always and only takes place *sub contraria specie*, does the danger not exist of religious life, life of faith, coming to nothing?'[144]

Luther's *extra nos* was meant to express the transcendence of God and thus offer an *objective* basis for Christians being sure of living under his grace. However, it has at times been interpreted in such a way that divine assurance is to some degree being excluded from all human registers, and even made independent of the sacraments and the life of the Church.

---

142 The classic study remains that of W. von Löwenich, *Theologia Crucis* . . . , op. cit., pp. 103–117 (Italian translation, cit.). The position of this author, however, is by no means shared by the unanimity of modern Luther scholars. 143 Ibid., pp. 143f. 144 Ibid., p. 144.

Concluding reflection

It should now be clear that the contemporary debate on justification moves on two distinct though related fronts, one hermeneutical or methodological, related to 'fundamental theology', the other doctrinal or thematic, more at home in the area of 'systematic theology'. Let us call them respectively the 'message' and the 'doctrine' of justification.

The 'message' of justification is identified with the primary thrust of Christianity itself, the 'essence' of the Christ-event, vitally expressing the need to consider every aspect of Christian life, both personal and ecclesial, in the light of the fundamental preponderance of divine action, initiative and mercy, of the priority of saving grace. In a sense it could be said that the 'message' of justification as such has no thematic content, and thus does not lend itself directly to systematic theological reflection; it corresponds rather to the inner, unitary simplicity of authentic Christianity. Luther and the Reformers attempted to place this message at the forefront of personal and ecclesial Christian life.

Understandably, however, difficulties began to surface, both in Luther's own theology and in later reformed theologies, when the 'message' of justification took on a thematic profile as it was applied to a variety of concrete human, social and ecclesial situations. As the 'message' of justification was concretized, or reflected upon thematically, it consolidated as a 'doctrine' of justification; specifically, it became a doctrine of grace, a Christian anthropology, an ecclesiology, an ethics.

In chapter five, we have considered different aspects of the centrality of the 'message' of justification taken as a hermeneutical or criteriological principle for assessing and correcting the life of the Church and the spirituality of Christians, to be applied with a view to ensuring that the magnanimity of God's pardon is not conditioned or blocked by manifold manifestations of the very sinfulness it is meant to heal. *Non est abbreviata manus Domini!* (Is 59:1): God's saving power cannot and must not and cannot be constrained by human clumsiness or sinfulness. In its penetrating reflection on the many areas of Church life which may need to be examined and perhaps corrected under the light of the 'message' of justification, the recent Lutheran-Catholic document *Church and Justification* shows that Catholics and Lutherans see eye-to-eye on this front, in principle if not always in practice. In fact Luther's own teaching constitutes a incisive reminder to all Christians of the need to retain a pure and simple trust in God's justifying and sanctifying action in the Spirit, not relying on their works, or successes, or projects. The American document *Justification by Faith* expresses this in the following terms: 'Our entire hope of justification and salvation rests on Christ Jesus and on the gospel whereby the good

news of God's merciful action in Christ is made known; we do not place our ultimate trust in anything other than God's promise and saving work in Christ.'[1]

In chapter six we have seen, however, that many points of tension between Catholics and Lutherans still remain in respect of the 'doctrine' of justification. In somewhat crude and approximate terms, the differences may be summarized as follows.
Freedom in Protestant theology is the same thing as liberation from the slavery of
sin, exclusively the work of grace, that is, 'salvation', whereas for Catholics freedom,
besides, is natural to that faculty (the human will) by which even the sinner is in a
position to accept and embrace divine grace (or reject it), and in that way 'cooperate' in being saved. *Sin* in Protestant thought tends to be, as it were, constitutional
(or original) in man, and is virtually identified with the sinful concupiscence remaining even after Baptism. In Catholic theology, it is a spiritual state resulting
from a wayward exercise of human free will situated in time and space, from *refusing*
God's grace and therefore *forfeiting* his friendship. In keeping with this understanding
of sin, *grace* for Protestants tends to be expressed in actualistic or dynamic terms, as
the direct action of Christ's Spirit on humans which keeps sinfulness 'at bay'; whereas
for Catholics grace involves a 're-creation' of the human subject as a result of the
pouring out of God's grace, destroying sin though not sinful inclination, made possible by a 'native' openness to grace, as distinct from a (Protestant) 'native' opposition to it. Finally, for Protestant theology, *'good works'* are such because at heart they
are 'divine', that is, they are the fruit and outcome of God's grace in man; for Catholics
good works are also driven and made possible by God's grace but directly involve
the action of the human subject in all his or her faculties.

FORMAL AND MATERIAL CONSENSUS[2]

It is commonly held nowadays that while Catholics and Protestants retain the *same
fundamental message* of justification, more or less as described, they teach *different
doctrines* of justification.[3] As a result it is considered logical and legitimate to affirm
that, whereas all believing Christians should agree on the fundamental 'message' of
their faith, they would be free to differ on particular doctrinal issues.[4]

However, this approach and assessment is not entirely satisfactory, above all because if the 'message' of justification has little or no thematic content of its own, it is

---

1 USA 157; also in USA 4.   2 In this part I will follow the reflections already presented at the II
Symposium of Theology at the Pontifical Athenaeum of the Holy Cross in Rome, held in March
1996, entitled 'L'uomo giustificato, nuova creatura in Cristo. Una riflessione intorno all'attuale
dibattito ecumenico', in J.M. Galván (ed.), *La giustificazione in Cristo* . . . , op. cit., pp. 129–164.
3 Cf. for example A.E. McGrath, 'Der articulus iustificationis als axiomatischer Grundsatz des
christlichen Glaubens', in *Zeitschrift für Theologie und Kirche* 81 (1984) 383–394.   4 Cf. C.E.
Braaten, 'Prolegomena of Christian Dogmatics', in C.E. Braaten and R.W. Jenson, *Christian Dogmatics*, 2 vols, Philadelphia 1984, vol. 1, pp. 5–78, especially pp. 51–59.

of little practical or theological use. Commenting on the American document, *Jus-tification by Faith*, a Lutheran Evangelical Church report had the following to say: 'the common statement does not distinguish as clearly as it might between agree-ment *that* the gospel is the critical norm of all churchly belief and practice, and agreement on *what* should result from application of that norm in particular cases. Or one could say it does not distinguish adequately between the specification of the gospel as *critical norm* and the application of that norm . . . *Particular application of the gospel as critical norm* represents the greatest area of uncertainty in the justifica-tion statement.'[5]

For Luther himself the lived experience of justification, of pure, simple Christi-anity, quickly crystallized as a clearly delineated systematic doctrine (with its an-thropology, ecclesiology, sacramentology, ethics and spirituality) which he consid-ered plainly incompatible with the theology and Christian praxis of his time, and sufficient to warrant a breakup of the Christian Church with a view to recuperating 'authentic' Christianity. And the point is that Luther had little 'tolerance' for differ-ences in doctrine because he saw clearly that 'doctrines' were intimately bound up with the fundamental vision of justification, with the inner 'message' of Christian-ity. He would have sided more resolutely, I should think, with the notion of 'organic unity' than with that of 'hierarchy of truths'.[6]

In order for any serious form of ecumenical dialogue be undertaken, or any worth-while ecumenical agreement to be entered into in the area of justification, it should be clear that *formal agreement* (in this case in respect of the 'message' of justifica-tion) would be meaningless if not tempered by and organically related to an ample *material agreement* on the doctrinal particulars of Christian anthropology, ecclesiology etc. And *vice versa*: agreement on Christian anthropology, which comprises the greater part of recent common statements on justification, itself needs to be exam-ined in the light of the fundamental 'message' of justification, the 'essence' of Chris-tianity. In other words, it is not sufficient to seek agreement on one front or the other, whether methodological/fundamental or doctrinal/systematic. Ecumenical agreed statements up to the present moment certainly provide ample doctrinal con-vergence between Catholics and Lutherans, and take it for granted that both under-stand the 'message' of the faith in the same way. But a lot remains to be done in order to reach a more thoroughgoing integration between the 'message' and the 'doctrine' of justification, offering the possibility of a doctrinal agreement at both at a 'formal' and 'material' level.

To overcome the dilemma and tension between these two aspects of theological and ecclesial endeavour which, to some degree, move and live on different planes, I

5 T. Rausch, *Responses to the US Lutheran-Roman Catholic Statement on Justification*, op. cit., p. 348. Emphasis added.   6 Cf. Conc. Vat. II, Decr. *Unitatis redintegratio*, no. 11. E. Jüngel spoke forcefully of the relationship between the 'form' and the 'content' of revelation (cf. E. Jüngel, *Gottes Sein ist im Werden. Verantwortliche Rede vom Sein Gottes bei Karl Barth, eine Paraphrase*, Tübingen 1965, pp. 87–90).

believe it is necessary *to reflect upon common fundamental elements of the Christian Gospel in which the 'message' and the 'doctrine' of justification are simultaneously grounded.* Three particularly relevant aspects could be profitably considered, the ecclesiological, the Christological, the creational/anthropological.

JUSTIFICATION AND ECCLESIOLOGY

It is clear that the 'message' of justification, especially in its use as a hermeneutical or criteriological principle, is closely linked to the reality and life of the Church, for its function will be to ensure that the believer is placed in the closest possible contact with the saving, pardoning power of Christ's Spirit.[7]

Yet the same thing can be said of the 'doctrine' of justification. A growing awareness has developed in recent decades that any Christian anthropology, or theology of grace and justification, if divorced from ecclesiology, runs the risk of becoming and remaining individualistic and distorted.[8] And if individualistic, then exclusive of man's social dimension, and therefore, sooner or later, irrelevant and meaningless. To an important degree, while philosophical and secularized anthropologies were paying full attention to the social and intersubjective dimensions of human beings, a marked tendency towards individualization was all the more noticeable in traditional treatises on justification and grace, among both Catholics and Protestants.

We have already examined the far-reaching findings of biblical exegesis in respect of the profoundly ecclesiological (and hence missionary) implications of St Paul's doctrine of 'justification by faith alone'.[9] The fact is of course that the social dimension of salvation and justification is essential, not accidental, to Christian anthropology, as it is to any anthropology. In the same way as humans not only 'produce' society (in this sense society can be said to relate to man accidentally), but *are produced* by society (ontologically, personally, culturally), so also Christians produce the Church (which becomes, as a result, a *congregatio fidelium*, a community of believers) but also, inseparably, *are produced* (or constituted as Christians) by the Church (as a kind of *sacramentum salutis*). The Christian as such can as much be saved 'outside the Church' as a human being can exist independently of society and human nature.

Of course in real terms, Christians are 'made believers' by the action of Christ's

7 'In fact nowadays the doctrine of justification is decided in the doctrine of the Church; that is the best test for the meaning of the *articulus stantis et cadentis ecclesiae* .... The Catholic Church must explain the "mediation" of the Church in a way that does not interrupt the direct contact of the believer with God.' (O.-H. Pesch, 'Gottes Gnadenhandeln als Rechtfertigung des Menschen', op. cit., p. 864). 8 On the necessity of contextualizing the doctrine of justification ecclesiologically, cf. W. Pannenberg, *Systematische Theologie*, vol. 3, Göttingen 1993, p. 9; S. Pemsel-Maier, *Rechtfertigung durch Kirche? Das Verhältnis von Kirche und Rechtfertigung in Entwürfen der neueren katholischen und evangelischen Theologie*, Würzburg 1991. 9 Cf. pp. 169–185 above.

Spirit, in such a way that the fundamental 'social' or communional quality of their *being Christian* is based entirely on their communion with *the* Communion of persons, the Father, the Son and the Holy Spirit. In that sense, humans are 'alone', (or better, *'dialogically' alone*), before their Creator, Redeemer and Sanctifier, in a foundational relationship that nothing or nobody can substitute. And in that sense, the 'message' of justification as a criteriological principle will always insist on the priority and unsubstitutable quality of God's saving and sanctifying action in Christ, and on the wholly personal, conscientious and untouchable faith response required of the individual Christian.

However since Christ's action in the Spirit establishes a dialogue between beings of a radically different nature, one the Creator, the other a creature, the question of the *created mediations*, or 'objective conditions of possibility' for man's immediate personal contact with God, must be taken into account. The entire thrust of the dialogue statement *Church and Justification*, for example, lies in its attempt to clarify the precise way in which the Church, as a visible institution founded by Christ (with its sacraments, ministry and preaching), is actually involved in the sanctifying and convoking action of Christ's Spirit.[10] Christ's Spirit acts, the Church 'acts' as well; but how do the two 'actions' relate? How do they coalesce and interact? Does the Church (in administering the sacraments, in preaching, etc.) do half the work, and Christ's Spirit the rest? Is the Church an essential (God-willed) instrument of divine action, or is it an accidental sign, result or manifestation of God's saving power?

One of the ways in which *Church and Justification* presents this linkup between the 'actions' of Christ's Spirit and that of the Church is in a section dealing with the *visible* and *invisible (or hidden) character* of the Church.[11] The classical, if only apparent, opposition between Lutherans and Catholics on this point is well known. For the former the Church, place of encounter of man with God, is an invisible reality, 'dwelling in the Spirit, in an "unapproachable" place';[12] for the latter it is 'just as visible and palpable as the Republic of Venice', in the words of Robert Bellarmine.[13] Obviously the traditional antithesis between the two explanations is simplistic and has long since been overcome. Nowadays Catholics and Lutherans admit peacefully that the Church, being a congregation of believers convoked by the Spirit, is visible, and is also invisible or hidden, insofar as the invisible action of the Spirit is decisive.[14]

---

10 Cf. P. O'Callaghan, 'The Mediation of Justification and the justification of Mediation . . . ', op. cit., passim.   11 Cf. ibid., pp. 198–208; CJ 135–147.   12 M. Luther, *Enarratio in Genesis* (WA 40/2: 106), in CJ 135. cf. the important study of E. Rietschel, *Das Problem der unsichtbar sichtbaren Kirche bei Luther: Darstellung und Lösungsversuch*, Leipzig 1932.   13 R. Bellarmine, *Disputatio de conciliis et ecclesia III*, 2, in CJ 135.   14 Speaking of revelation in the context of the relationship between the Church visible and hidden, S. Rostagno says: 'L'invisibilità della chiesa è per Lutero l'ultima, sostanziale *latenza* della rivelazione stessa in questo mondo e per questo mondo. Si tratta di una certa riservatezza dell'autocomunicazione di Dio, che resta un evento di carattere peculiare segreto ed inconfondibile, quasi *intimior intimo meo* . . .' ('Ecclesia abscondita. Appunti su un

However, a certain contrast and tension can be said to remain between Lutherans and Catholics in terms of the *nature* and *consistency* of the link-up which really bonds the action of Christ's Spirit (grace) and the action of the Church (preaching, administering the sacraments, etc.). This tension relates directly in turn to a certain Christological tension that may be perceived between the two positions, specifically in respect of the doctrine of the Incarnation.

JUSTIFICATION AND CHRISTOLOGY

Catholic theology tends to express its vision of the 'Incarnation' of the Word, its Christology, in the following terms. God, transcendent, ineffable and hidden to our eyes, sends his own Son, the Word, to save humanity. In Christ, God becomes incarnate, human; in him, God's own Image, God makes himself visible and tangible to humans also made 'in the image and likeness of God.'[15] As a result, the same Word incarnate extends, as it were, this visibilization or exteriorization through the Church, his Body, *Christus prolungatus*,[16] which becomes, in virtue of its head, already a kind of saved and divinized reality, or 'sacrament of salvation'. In other words, what was hidden and interior has become visible, exterior, tangible and audible in Christ and his Church. Or better, perhaps, the action of Christ's Spirit has become *bound irrevocably* to the tangible action of the Church.[17] Obviously the gift of faith is required in order to perceive the action of Christ's Spirit behind the action of the

concetto controverso', in *Studi Ecumenici* 6 (1988) 183–192, here, pp. 186f.). And B. Gherardini describes Lutheran doctrine on the matter in a similar fashion: 'nella Chiesa Dio è come nell'umanità del Verbo incarnato: nascosto e rivelato; operante, oggi nella Parola e nel sacramento come allora nell'umanità assunta, lo stesso perdono e la stessa salvezza; il 'fatto' (l'incarnazione del Verbo, l'unione ipostatica, l'opera salvifica) e la sua attiva 'testimonianza' (la Chiesa con la Parola ed il sacramento). Si tratta dunque del medesimo 'Deus absconditus-revelatus' in due distinte forme, che però non ne pregiudicano, anzi ne incanalano la "communicatio idiomatum" ' (*Creatura Verbi. La Chiesa nella teologia di Martin Lutero*, Rome 1994, p. 345). 15 Cf. Gen 1:27. 'La teologia patristica dei secoli II–IV sottolineò l'intimo legame dell'incarnazione col carattere personale di Cristo come immagine, parola e Unigenito del Padre invisibile. L'invisibilità del Padre coincide col suo carattere personale di principio-senza-principio. Il Padre, essendo in se stesso assolutamente invisibile, si rivela agli uomini in quanto si riflette pienamente nella sua immagine personale e intradivina. Tale autorivelazione consustanziale del Padre fonda la sua rivelazione per mezzo della sua parola personale incarnata: l'incarnazione presuppone il carattere personale intratrinitario di Cristo come rivelazione immanente del Padre' (J. Alfaro, *Rivelazione cristiana, fede e teologia*, Brescia 1986, p. 78). Cf. also A. Orbe, *Hacia la primera teología de la procesión del Verbo*, Rome 1958; C. Greco, 'Gesù Cristo, icona del Dio invisibile', in C. Greco (ed.), *Cristologia e antropologia*, Roma 1994, pp. 156–180. 16 Cf. J.M.-R. Tillard, 'Vers une nouvelle problématique de la "Justification" ', in *Irénikon* 55 (1982) 185–198 (here pp. 188f.). R. Frieling, 'Zu den Beziehungen zwischen protestantischen und katholischen Christen', in *Epd-Interview*, 36 (1984) 15, has noted that the ecclesiology of the *Christus prolungatus* is particularly characteristic of Catholicism. 17 Cf. Y.M.-J. Congar, 'Considérations historiques sur la rupture du XVI siécle dans ses rapports avec la réalisation catholique de l'unité', in *Chrétiens en dialogue. Contributions catholiques a l'Œcuménisme*, Paris 1964, pp. 409–435, who explains how the ecclesiology in the first millennium insisted on the solidity of the union between heaven and earth.

Church etc., but the key point is that such faith does not involve merely *going beyond the Church's action*, beyond what is created, considered Platonically perhaps as an obstacle to divine action. Rather the Christian, in believing, *perceives* God's saving action inseparably from the tangible action of Christ and the Church.

In other words, the Christian does not believe 'in' the action of Christ's Spirit ('Credo *in* Deum') in spite of the visible and concrete action of Christ and the Church; rather he or she believes in God, believing at the same time *that* the *tangible mediates the ineffable*, making it present, palpable and human. I say 'at the same time', and this point is critical, because the very same reality (the Incarnation of the Word, the Son becoming 'one of us') which reveals the divine gift of justifying faith, at the same time and inseparably makes *human acceptance* of that gift possible. That is to say: the objective pledge of the merciful magnanimity of God, which is the very heart of the 'message' of justification, is none other than the Incarnation of the Word, articulated in human grammar, perpetual union between divine action and the action of Christ and the Church. In that sense, the 'message' of justification can never be divorced from its tangible manifestations, the Church, the sacraments and the preached word, that is, from central elements of the 'doctrine' of justification.

Through the Incarnation of the Word, God's saving action has become bound irrevocably to the tangible reality of the Church's action. Hence, faith in the God who saves and personal 'assurance' of the presence of saving grace that follows such faith, is simply inseparable from belonging exteriorly to a believing community,[18] from employing the 'means of grace'.[19] In real terms, the Church, and not the individual member of the faithful, becomes, in Christ, the *fundamental believing subject*, and the individual's attachment to the Church cannot be distinguished objectively from his or her act of faith and union with the risen Lord. In other words, the personal dialogue of faith 'I-God' belongs objectively to the foundational spousal dialogue 'Church-Christ', as much as the soul does to the body.[20] In the words of Nichols, 'the Church mediates God by immediating him'.[21]

---

18 In the *Catholic Catechism for Adults* of the German Bishops' Conference we read: 'In the Lutheran doctrine of individual faith certitude is presented a concern which has become essential in the modern age: the modern problem of certitude. Rejecting the doctrine of individual certitude of faith (DH 1563–1564), the Council of Trent makes reference to the Catholic solution of the problem of certitude: certitude is only possible in the community of the Church, in the mutual encouragement and comfort of grace and hope which comes from it, as well as being carried along by the single "we" of the faith and of hope' (*Katholischer Erwachsenen-Katechismus. Das Glaubensbekenntnis der Kirche*, Bonn 1985, III, 1.3.3.4, p. 247). 19 'Les moyens de grâce ... apparaissent au service de la décision intérieure de foi qui garantira l'actualisation de la Promesse ... Ils ne sont pas extérieurs à l'expérience de la grâce ... Ils appartiennent à la chair même du mystére de l'Église en son être de grâce ... L'Église est, a sa mesure (et toujours dans sa soumission absolue à l'Esprit du Seigneur), agent de la justification' (J.M.-R. Tillard, 'Vers une nouvelle problématique de la "Justification" ', op. cit., pp. 191–192). 20 The comparison between body/soul and visible Church / invisible Church is Luther's (cf. his *Von der Papsttum zu Rom*, 1520: WA 6: 297). 21 Nichols expresses the overall meaning of Trent's Decree on justification in two stages: 'First, the Catholic Christian as an experiencing subject is never separate from the life of the Church. He or she is nourished experientially by this life, which consists in a celebration of faith and of the sacraments

Of course the historico-empirical aspect of the Church does not fully express its rich and divine *realitas complexa*, just as the humanity of Christ does not express the entirety of the divine-human reality of the Word made flesh. But just as the humanity of Christ is the humanity of God, and human contact with it, listening, touching, seeing (*fides Christi*) is union with God, righteousness, by the same logic, visible contact with the Church, by word and sacrament, is contact with Christ, and therefore salvation (*iustitia Dei*).

JUSTIFICATION AND CREATION

Consideration of the reality of the Incarnation of God's Word, taken in all its seriousness, helps us appreciate that each and every creature (man especially), though visible and corruptible, is created by the Father 'for Christ' (cf. Col 1:16) in possession of a kind of 'iconic quality',[22] and from the moment of creation is *primed to visibilize the invisible*. Too much insistence on the hidden and interior aspect of salvation, of the intrinsic ambiguity or unreliability of the Church's structures or of Christian spiritualities, too relentless an application of the 'message' of justification to the life of the Church and all its activities, may not only condition the God-willed mediating rôle the Church and creatures play,[23] but may also call into question the value and meaning of the supreme divine gesture (the Incarnation of the Word) that has definitively expressed God's perpetual will to save mankind, to justify the sinner.

In other words, the fact of the Incarnation of God's Word in Christ goes beyond the mere condemnation of sin and salvation of the sinner. It also offers a confirmation of the value of created reality, created 'in', 'through' and 'for' the eternal Word who has became incarnate, Jesus Christ, crucified and risen. Note the inseparability of the 'doctrine' of Christian justification through Christ from the 'message' of justification: the reality of the Incarnation of the Word speaks inseparably *both* of the

---

of faith together with all those who co-participate in such celebration. Second, the Christian, nourished in this way, is also directly open to the transcendent God. *The Church mediates God by immediating him*, by making him (through his own Word and grace) immediately present to each of her members' (A. Nichols, 'Experience', in *The Shape of Catholic Theology*, Edinburgh 1991, pp. 235–247, here p. 244). 22 On the background to the patristic doctrine of man as an image of God in Christ, cf. C. von Schönborn, *L'icône du Christ: fondements théologiques*, Paris 1986. 23 The theological value of 'secularity' and of the created world, on the basis of the Incarnation of the Word, is at the very heart of the spiritual reflection of Blessed Josemaría Escrivá. cf. for example his homily 'Christ present among Christians', in *Christ is Passing By . . .* , op. cit., nos. 102–116; especially nos. 105; 109; 112; also 'Passionately Loving the World', in *Conversations with Mgr. Escrivá de Balaguer*, Dublin 1980, nn. 113–123; especially nos. 114–116; *The Forge . . .* op. cit., no. 703. Cf. in particular the studies of P. Rodríguez, 'Omnia traham ad meipsum: il significato di Giovanni 12,31 nell'esperienza spirituale di mons. Escrivá de Balaguer', in *Annales Theologici* 6 (1992) 5–34; A. Aranda, 'Il cristiano "alter Christus, ipse Christus" ', in M. Belda et al. (eds.), *Santità e mondo: atti del Convegno teologico di studi sugli insegnamenti del beato Josemaría Escrivá*, Vatican City 1994, pp. 101–147 (English translation forthcoming).

eternal confirmation and tangible pledge of the magnanimity and unconditionality of God's mercy towards humankind, and of the tangible presence of saving grace in the Church, *Christus prolungatus*.

Note also that since the very origins of humanity and the universe are closely linked to the action of the same eternal Word who has become forever human in Christ the Saviour, the authentic exercise of human freedom and the primordial sinlessness of the human condition are not incompatible with the Lutheran affirmation of *solus Christus*. The exercise of human freedom and the fundamental goodness of human nature relate entirely to Christ, and can never be considered autonomously from him, because they are founded on him and constituted through him. Besides, there is no reason why humans, created in the Word, cannot be 'recreated' in Christ, that is ontologically regenerated or transformed by the selfsame Word made incarnate, made children of God in Christ through the Spirit. A dynamic/actualistic understanding of grace must give away sooner or later to one which allows for the possibility of a real regeneration of sinful man. In sum, if Christ is taken as the eternal Word, through whom all things were made, and who became forever one of the human race to save us from our sins in making us children of God, then Luther's doctrine of *solus Christus omnia*[24] is perfectly acceptable.

In brief terms, the 'message' of justification naturally tends to have its own *doctrinal* presuppositions. Above we saw how, as a criteriological principle, it must proclaim the goodness of God not only as the one who redeems, but also as the one who creates and re-creates. Therefore, it must not consider man only as a sinner, but also as one primed at creation to be, forever, a child of God.[25] Both the 'message' and 'doctrine' of justification constitute, in reality, a kind of 'applied Christology'.[26]

Contemporary Lutheran reflection on justification and its Christological underpinnings, inspired not only in Pauline exegesis but also in the theology of John and Irenaeus, has developed a view of justification quite in keeping with the radical, founding quality of the doctrine of the Incarnation just described, and with an Christ-oriented view of created reality.[27]

---

24 Cf. pp. 161–163. **25** Cf. pp. 206–208. **26** The explicit revindication of the priority of Christology over the doctrine of justification is due in no small measure to the major work of the Lutheran H.G. Pöhlmann, *Rechtfertigung: die gegenwärtige kontroverstheologische Problematik der Rechtfertigungslehre zwischen der evangelisch-lutherischen und der römisch-katholischen Kirche*, Gütersloh 1971. **27** On the efforts of Lutheran theologians to recuperate the centrality and Christological dimension of the doctrine of creation in relation to that of justification, cf. R. Prenter, *Schöpfung und Erlösung. Dogmatik II: Die Erlösung*, Göttingen 1960; G. Wingren, *Creation and Gospel: The New Situation in European Theology*, New York 1979; idem., *Man and the Incarnation: a Study in the Biblical Theology of Irenaeus*, Edinburgh/London 1959. R.R. Reno, speaking of the 'Christological conditions' of the gospel (Incarnation of the Word from the Virgin Mary, the crucifixion of Christ by Pontius Pilate, etc.), says: 'These conditions do not violate or undermine the unconditional offer of justification by faith. On the contrary, they are the very conditions entailed by God's unconditional love . . . The very logic of the gospel promise presupposes and creates these enduring conditions (not explosions!) within the human realm . . . Justification involves a rebirth made possible by a *permanent and triumphant* divine presence on this side of the divide. We

However, a more classical Lutheran vision, put forward for example in the works of W. von Löwenich and G.O. Forde, firmly anchored to the *theologia crucis* of Paul rather than to the *theologia gloriae* of John and Irenaeus, tends to consider the Incarnation of the Word more as a *hiding* of God than as his revelation, offers a somewhat dialectic vision of the relationship between God and man, and as a result a more ambiguous view of created reality. The Incarnation, considered in the light of the *theologia crucis*, tends to confirm that God is a *Deus absconditus*, a hidden divinity,[28] quite in keeping with the idea that the essential ecclesiality of the Church, what makes of a body of believers the Body of Christ, is invisible. In this context, the

are reborn because of God's willingness to accept the human condition, not in spite of it ('The doctrine of justification: Lutheran lessons for Anglicans in search of confessional integrity', in *Pro Ecclesia* 3 (1994) 455–482, here pp. 471–472). This author, in opposition to the works of G.O. Forde (*Justification by faith: A Matter of Life and Death*, 1990) draws on an analysis of D.S. Yeago who considers the question of justification in the light of the Christology of Irenaeus ('Gnosticism, antinomianism, and reformation theology. Reflections on the costs of a construal', in *Pro Ecclesia* 2 (1993) 37–49). According to Yeago, 'for Luther, it is inadequate to say that "the divine appears through the humanity of the Christ". On the contrary, the divine is found in the particular flesh and blood of Jesus Christ, and it is the singular form of this flesh and blood that we must imprint on our hearts to be saved. Here as elsewhere, Luther's rhetoric strains to articulate the utter, undialectical identity of the Son of God with the particular man born of Mary . . . The reality of the incarnation grounds the reality of holiness: God has truly given his own life to humankind in the concrete flesh and blood of his Son Jesus, and so we may be truly 'deified by grace' (as the Fathers teach) through our *conformation* to that flesh and blood' (ibid., p. 47f.). Luther speaks in this way on some occasions. For example in Thesis 23 of the *Heidelberg Disputation*, speaking of Christ, he said: 'If you touch my flesh, you are not touching mere flesh or blood; you are touching the flesh and blood which deify (*gottert*), that is, give the character and power of the divinity' (WA 1: 355). cf. also S. Rostagno, 'Coerenza del sistema e questione della verità in Ireneo', in *Studi Ecumenici* 10 (1992) 227–241.   28 J.A. Möhler in his work *Symbolik oder Darstellung der dogmatischen Gegensätze der Katholiken und Protestanten in ihren öffentlichen Bekenntnisschriften*, Regensburg 1873 (English translation: *Symbolism: or Exposition of the Doctrinal Differences between Catholics and Protestants as evidenced by their Symbolical Writings*, London 1906) comments, in a somewhat polemical fashion, that Luther had difficulties with John's doctrine of the Incarnation, and indicates the linkup between the nature of the Incarnation and that of the Church: 'If Luther had managed to understand fully the concept of the Incarnation of the Logos, he would surely have understood the Church as a educating institution, such as he never did in a clear fashion' (*Symbolik . . .*, op. cit., no. 48, p. 424). Augustine, commenting on the text of Jn 5:26 ('For as the Father has life in himself, so he has granted the Son also to have life in himself'), exclaims: 'the invisible Father with the likewise invisible Son has made this Son visible, sending him to the world' (*De Trinitate II*, 5: 9). And Luther adds to Augustine's comment: 'What a strange conclusion' (*Handbermersungen*: WA 9: 17). In his commentary on the Prologue of John's Gospel, Luther insists on the true humanity, flesh, blood and bone, of Jesus, but gives it a different theological value than does Augustine. On Jn 1:14 ('And the Word was made flesh'), he says: 'he became flesh, to reveal the weakness of mortality, because Christ took on mortal human nature, which, after the sin of the human race, is submitted to the terrible wrath and judgement of God. And this weak and mortal flesh has experienced and suffered this wrath in Christ' (*Auslegung des ersten und zweiten Kapitels Iohannis in Predigen*, 1537-8: WA 46: 632). Luther goes on to relate this text and its interpretation with two texts of Paul which clearly express the humiliation and *kénosis* of God in Christ, Gal 3:13 and 2 Cor 5:21.

object of Christian faith would seem to be what is *hidden* (the salvific action of God in Christ) *in spite of* the tangible, that is, independently of the historico-empirical action of the Church and of the apparently contingent experience of the individual Christian.

In the heel of the hunt, the root of the contrast probably lies in a different understanding of the nature of human sinfulness. The classical Lutheran 'message' *and* 'doctrine' of justification are both driven by the notion that *human beings are sinners* and remain so even when justified. Thus the subject of Christian theology, as we saw, would be God saving and man the sinner; the object of justifying grace would be man the sinner. Catholic doctrine, conversely, avoids considering Christian theology and the workings of saving grace *exclusively* in the context of sin and salvation, but rather considers one and the other in the context of the foundational 'iconic' quality of all created beings, of the Incarnation of God's own Word 'through whom all things were made', of the true divine filiation of Christian believers.

Bibliography

I. PRIMARY SOURCES

1. Collected works

Cereti, G., Voicu, S.J. and Puglisi, J.F. (eds.), *Enchiridion Œcumenicum*, 4 volumes (Dehoniane, Bologna 1986–1996).
Corpus Christianorum, Series Latina (Turnholt, 1953 ff.).
Corpus scriptorum ecclesiasticorum Latinorum (Vienna, 1866 ff.).
Denzinger, J., *Enchiridion symbolorum definitionum et declarationum de rebus fidei et morum (Kompendium der Glaubensbekenntnisse und kirchlichen Lehrentscheidungen)*, ed. P. Hünermann, (Herder, 3 Freiburg i. B. 1991).
Lietzmann, H., Bornkamm, H., Volz, H. and Wolf, E., *Die Bekenntnisschriften der evangelisch-lutherischen Kirche* (Vandenhoeck & Ruprecht, Göttingen 1967) Eng. translation in T.G. Tappert et al., (ed.), *The Book of Concord: the Confessions of the Evangelical Lutheran Church*, Fortress, Minneapolis 1988.
Migne, J.-P., *Patrologia cursus completus, series Latina*, 221 vols (Paris 1844–64);
—— *Patrologia cursus completus, series Graeca*, 162 vols (Paris 1857–66).

2. Medieval and Reformation Authors

Bellarmine, R., *Opera Omnia*, 12 vols, ed. J. Fèvre (Paris 1870–1874).
Biel, G., *Quaestiones de justificatione*, ed. C. Feckes (Aschendorff, Münster 1929).
Bonaventure, *Opera omnia*, 10 vols (Quaracchi 1882–1910).
Calvin, J., *Opera omnia quae supersunt*, 59 vols, Brunswick 1863–1900 (Eng. translation of the *Institutiones christianae* in *Institutes of the Christian religion*, 2 vols, Eerdmans, Grand Rapids 1979 f.).
Contarini, G., 'Epistola de iustificatione' (1541), in *Corpus Catholicorum*, vol. 7.
Davenant, J., *A treatise on Justification*, or *Disputatio de Iustitia Habituali et Actuali* (1631) (London 1844).
Domingo de Soto, *De Natura et Gratia* (Paris 1549).
Duns Scotus, *Opera omnia*, ed. C. Balic (Roma 1950 ff.); *Commentaria Oxoniensia*, 2 vols (Quaracchi 1912–14).
Eck, J., *Apologia pro principibus catholicis* (1543).
Erasmus, D., *Opera omnia*, 10 vols, ed. J. Clericus (Lugduni Batavorum, 1703–6).
Gropper, J., *Enchiridion Christianae Institutiones* (Cologne 1536).
Hooker, J., 'A learned discourse of Justification', in W. Speed Hill, L. Yeandle and E. Grislis (eds.), *The Folger Library Edition of The Works of Richard Hooker*, vol. 5 (Belknap, Cambridge (Mass.)/London 1990), pp. 105–69.
Lombard, P., *Libri IV Sententiarum*, 2 vols (Quaracchi 1916).
Luther, M., *Dicata super Psalterium* (1513–16, WA 3–4).
——*Die Glossen über den Römerbrief* (1515–16, WA 57: 5–127).
——*Die Scholien über den Römerbrief* (1515–16, WA 57: 131–232).
——*Die Vorlesung über den Römerbrief* (1515–16, WA 56: 3–528).
——*Disputatio contra theologia scholastica* (1517, WA 1: 220–8).
——*Sermo die S. Matthiae* (1517, WA 1: 138–41).

——*Acta Augustana* (1518, WA 2: 1–26).

——*Heidelberg Dispute* (1518, WA 1: 350–65).

——*Resolutiones Disputationum et indulgentiarum virtute* (1518, WA 1: 530–628).

——*Disputatio Johannis Eccii et Martin Lutheri Lipsiae habita* (1519, WA 2: 250–83).

——*In ep. Pauli ad Galatas Comm.* (1519, WA 2: 436–618).

——*Resolutiones Lutherianae super propositionibus suis Lipsiae disputis* (1519, WA 2: 388–435).

——*Sermo de duplici iustitia* (1519, WA 2: 143–52).

——*Assertio omnium articulorum M. Lutheri per bullam Leonis X* (1520, WA 7: 94–151).

——*De captivitate Babylonica Ecclesiae* (1520, WA 6: 497–573).

——*Disputatio de fide infusa et acquista* (1520, WA 6: 84–98).

——*Ein Sermon von dem Neuen Testament, das ist von der heilige Messe* (1520, WA 6: 349–78).

——*Tractatus de bonis operibus* (1520, WA 6: 196–276).

——*Von dem Papsttum zu Rom* (1520, WA 6: 277–324).

——*Rationis Latomianae confutatio* (1521, WA 8: 43–128).

——*De Servo Arbitrio* (1525, WA 18: 603–787).

——*Vorlesung über Iesaias* (1527-30, WA 31/2: 1–585).

——*Der Große Katechismus* (1529, WA 30/1: 123–238).

——*De loco iustificationis* (1530, WA 30/2: 652–76).

——*In ep. S. Pauli ad Galatas Comm.* (1531–35, WA 40/1: 33–40/2: 184).

——*Ennaratio in Ps 2* (1532-, WA 40/2: 192–312).

——*Ennaratio in Ps 51* (1532-, WA 40/2: 313–470).

——*Sermo 1* (1532, WA 36: 416–30).

——*Sermo 2* (1532, WA 36: 430–42).

——*Sermo 36* (1532, WA 36: 255–70).

——*Ennaratio in Genesis* (1535-, WA 40/2: 1–428).

——*Thesen de fide* (1535, WA 39/1: 44–53).

——*Articuli Smalcaldae* (1537–38, WA 50: 192–254).

——*Auslegung des ersten und zweiten Kapitels Iohannis in Predigen* (1537-38, WA 46: 538–789).

——*Die Promotionsdisputation von Palladius und Tileman* (1537, WA 39/1: 198–263).

——*Zirkulardisputation de veste nuptiali* (1537, WA 39/1: 264–333).

——*Die dritte Disputation gegen die Antinomer* (1538, WA 39/1: 486–584).

——*Expositio in Ps 125* (1538, WA 40/3: 152–73).

——*Expositio in Ps 130* (1538, WA 40/3: 335–76).

——*Von den Konziliis und der Kirche* (1539, WA 50: 488–653).

——*Von den Juden und ihren Lügen* (1543, WA 53: 417–522).

——*Von den lezten Worten Davids* (1543, WA 54: 28–100).

——Preface to Latin works (1545, WA 54: 176-187).

——Correspondence (*Briefwechsel*) (WA Br).

——German Bible (*Deutsch Bibel*) (WA DB).

——Tabletalk (*Tischreden*) (WA Tr).

Löscher, V.E., *Timotheus Verinus* (Wittenberg 1718).

Melanchthon, P., *Opera Omnia*, 28 vols, in *Corpus Reformatorum, Brunswick 1834-1860; Werke in Auswahl*, 9 vols, ed. R. Stupperich (Gütersloh 1951–75).

Strigel, V., *Loci theologici*, 4 vols, ed. Petzel (Neustadt 1581–1584).

Thomas Aquinas, *Opera Omnia*, 31 vols (Roma 1882–1947).

Vega, A. de, *Opusculum de iustificatione* (Venice 1546).

3.   Ecumenical and Official Documents

Sixteenth Century

Apologia Confessionis Augustanae (1530), in H. Lietzmann et al. (eds.), *Die Bekenntnisschriften*, pp. 141–404 (Eng. translation in T.G. Tappert et al., (ed.), *The Book of Concord*, pp. 97–285).

Confessio Augustana (1530), in H. Lietzmann et al. (eds.), *Die Bekenntnisschriften*, pp. 44–137 (Eng. translation in T.G. Tappert et al., (ed.), *The Book of Concord*, pp. 23–96).

Confutatio Confessionis Augustanae (1530), in *Corpus Catholicorum* 33, ed. H. Immenkötter (Aschendorff, Münster 1979) (Eng. translation in J.M. Reu (ed.), *The Augsburg Confession: a Collection of Sources with an Historical Introduction* (St Louis 1966), pp. 348–83).

Concilium Tridentinum, Decretum de Justificatione (1547), in DH 152–1583 (Eng. translation in J. Neuner and J. Dupuis, *The Christian Faith*, pp. 554–70).

Formula Concordiae. Solida Declaratio (1577) in H. Lietzmann et al. (eds.), *Die Bekenntnisschriften*, pp. 735–1100 (Eng. translation in T.G. Tappert et al., (ed.), *The Book of Concord*, pp. 463–636).

Twentieth Century

Anderson, H.G., Murphy, T.A. and Burgess, J.A. (eds.), 'Justification by faith', in *Lutherans and Catholics in Dialogue VII* (Augsburg, Minneapolis 1985), pp. 8–74.

ARCIC-II, *Salvation and the Church. An Agreed Statement by the Second Anglican-Roman Catholic International Commission* (Church House Publishing/Catholic Truth Society, London 1987) (also in *One in Christ* 23 (1987) 157–72).

Arnoldshainer Konferenz (AKf), in Various authors, *Lehrverurteilungen im Gespräch*, pp. 17–56.

Blancy, A. and Jourjon, M. (eds.), *Pour la Communion des Églises. L'apport du Groupe des Dombes, 1937–1987* (Centurion, Paris 1988).

Canadian Lutheran-Anglican Dialogue, *Report and Recommendations – April 1986* (Toronto-Winnipeg 1986).

Catholic-Lutheran Discussion Group in Norway, 'Justification', in *Church Information Service* (Oslo 1991).

Church of England-Evangelical Lutheran Church in Germany-Federation of Evangelical Churches in the German Democratic Republic, 'On the Way to Visible Unity; Meissen 1988', in *Mid-Stream* 29 (1990) 153–65.

Comité Mixte Catholique-Protestant en France, *Choix Éthiques et communion ecclésiale* (Cerf, Paris 1992).

Congregation for the Doctrine of the Faith, 'Observations and Commentary on ARCIC-II's "Salvation and the Church" (18.11.1988)', in *Origins* (1988) 429–34.

English Roman Catholic-Methodist Committee, 'Justification – A Consensus Statement', in *One in Christ* 28 (1992) 87–91.

Evangelical Lutheran Church in America, 'An Evaluation of the Lutheran-Catholic Statement "Justification by Faith"', in *One in Christ* 29 (1993) 342–49.

Facharbeitskreise Faith-And-Order und Catholica-Fragen, in Various authors, *Lehrverurteilungen im Gespräch*, pp. 161–99.

Gemeinsame Römisch-katholische/ Evangelisch-lutherische Kommission, 'Das Evangelium und die Kirche' (Malta 1972), in *Lutherische Rundschau* 22 (1972) 344–62.

Gemeinsame Römisch-katholische/ Evangelisch-lutherische Kommission, *Kirche und Rechtfertigung: das Verständnis der Kirche im Licht der Rechtfertigungslehre* (13.9.1993), (Bonifatius/O. Lembeck, Paderborn /Frankfurt a. M. 1994). Eng. translation: Lutheran-Roman Catholic Joint Commission, *Church and justification: understanding the Church in the light of the doctrine of justification* (Report of the third phase of Lutheran-Roman Catholic international dialogue) (Lutheran World Federation, Geneva/ Pontifical Council for Promoting Christian Unity, Rome 1994), in *Information service* 86 (1994) 128–81 and *Catholic International* 6 (1995) 329–47.

Hale, J. (ed.), *Proceedings of the Fourteenth World Methodist Conference Honolulu, Hawaii, July 21–28 1981* (World Methodist Council, Lake Junaluska 1982).

John Paul II, *Address to Members of the Evangelical Church*, Magonza (17.11.1980), in *Insegnamenti di Giovanni Paolo II, III/ 2* (1980) (Città del Vaticano 1980), pp. 1253–1257.

——Enc. *Ut Unum Sint* (1995) (Libreria Editrice Vaticana, Città del Vaticano 1995).

——Address 'Eine zukunftsträchtige Ökumene kann es nur geben, wenn wir uns selbstlos der Wahrheit stellen' (22.6.1996), no. 4, in *L'Osservatore Romano, Documenti* (26.6.1996), p. 4.

Joint Lutheran-Methodist Commission, *The Church, Community of grace, Lutheran World Federation* (Geneva 1984), no. 23–7.

Lutheran Church-Missouri Synod, 'A Response to the US Lutheran-Roman Catholic Dialogue Report VII, "Justification by Faith"', extracts in *One in Christ* 29 (1993) 349–53.

Lutheran World Federation, 'Justification today', in *Lutheran World* 12 (1965) 1, suppl., 1–11.

Lutheran-Reformed Joint Commission, *Towards Christian Fellowship, Lutheran World Federation-WARC* (Geneva 1989).

Lutheran-United Methodist Bilateral Consultation, 'A Lutheran-United Methodist Statement on Baptism', in *Perkins Journal* 34 (1981) 2–6.

Meyendorff, J. and Tobias, R. (eds.) (Canonical Orthodox Bishops in the Americas-Evangelical Lutheran Church in America-Lutheran Church, Missouri Synod), 'Christ "in us" and Christ "for us" in Lutheran and Orthodox Theology', in *Salvation in Christ: a Lutheran-Orthodox dialogue* (Augsburg, Minneapolis, 1992).

National Conference of Catholic Bishops, 'An Evaluation of the Lutheran-Catholic Statement: "Justification by Faith"', in *Ecumenical Trends* 19 (1990) 53–8; also in *One in Christ* 29 (1993) 335–42.

Ökumenischer Arbeitskreis Evangelischer und Katholischer Theologen (K. Lehmann and W. Pannenberg, eds.), 'Rechtfertigung des Sünders', in *Rechtfertigung, Sakramente und Amt im Zeitalter der Reformation und heute (1985): 'Lehrverurteilungen-kirchentrennend?'*, Vandenhoeck und Ruprecht/Herder (Göttingen/Freiburg i. Br. 1986), pp. 35–75 (Eng. translation: K. Lehmann and W. Pannenberg, 'The Justification of the Sinner', in *The Condemnations of the Reformation Era. Do they still divide?* (Fortress, Minneapolis 1990), pp. 29–69).

Oeyen, C., 'Auf dem Weg zu einer evangelisch/alt-katholischen Eucharistie-Vereinbarung', in *Ökumenische Rundschau* 34 (1985) 362–4.

Paul VI, Motu Proprio *Sanctitas clarior* (19.3.1969), in *Acta Apostolicae Sedis* 61 (1969) 150.

Reformed/Roman Catholic International Dialogue, *Towards a Common Understanding of the Church*, (WARC, Geneva 1991).

K. Schwarz, *Rechtfertigung und Verherrlichung (Theosis) des Menschen durch Jesus Christus* (Fünfter bilateraler theologischer Dialog zwischen der Rumänischen Orthodoxen Kirche und der Evangelischen Kirch in Deutschland vom 18. bis 27. Mai 1988 in Kloster Kirchberg/Sulz am Neckar) (Missionshandlung, Hermannsburg 1995), pp. 7–200.

Sekretariat der Deutschen Bischofskonferenz, 'Stellungnahme der Deutschen Bischofskonferenz zur Studie "Lehrverurteilungen – kirchentrennend?"' (4.2.1994), in *Die deutschen Bischöfe*, no. 52, Bonn 1994.

Various authors, 'An Invitation to Action', in J.E. Andrews and J.A. Burgess (eds.), *The Lutheran Reformed Dialogue*, vol. 3 (Fortress, Philadelphia 1984), pp. 9–13.

Various authors, 'Communique on the 4th Theological Conversations between Representatives of the Russian Orthodox Church and the Evangelical Lutheran Church of Finland', in *Journal of the Moscow Patriarchate* 1977/9, pp. 60 f.

Various authors, 'Gemeinsame Stellungnahme zum Dokument "Lehrverurteilungen-kirchentrennend?"', common statement of the Protestant Churches of Germany (6.11.1994: AKf, VELKD, DNK), in *Ökumenische Rundschau* 44 (1995) 99–102 (Eng. translation in *Lutheran Quarterly* 9 (1995) 359–64).

Various authors, 'Konsens in Sicht? Der Entwurf einer lutherisch-katholischen Erklärung zur Rechtfertigungslehre', in *Herder Korrespondenz* 50 (1996) 302–6.

Various authors, *Lehrverurteilungen im Gespräch. Die ersten offiziellen Stellungnahmen aus den evangelischen Kirchen in Deutschland* (Vandenhoeck & Ruprecht, Göttingen 1993).

Various authors, 'The Leuenberg Agreement', in W.G. Rusch and D.F. Martensen, *The Leuenberg Agreement and Lutheran-Reformed Relationships. Evaluation by North American Theologians* (Augsburg, Minneapolis 1989), pp. 139–54.

Various authors, 'Vereinbarung über eine gegenseitige Einladung zur Teilnahme an der Feier der Eucharistie', in *Ökumenische Rundschau* 34 (1985) 365–7.

Various authors, *The Report of the Lutheran-Episcopal Dialogue*, second series: 1976–80 (Forward

Movement, Cincinnati 1981).

Various authors, 'Konsens in Sicht? Der Entwurf einer lutherisch-katholischen Erklärung zur Rechtfertigungslehre', in *Herder Korrespondenz* 50 (1996) 302–6.

Vereinigte Evangelisch-Lutherische Kirche Deutschlands (VELKD), in Various authors, *Lehrverurteilungen im Gespräch*, pp. 57–160.

II. OTHER WORKS CITED

Alfaro, J., 'Justificación barthiana y justificación católica', in *Gregorianum* 39 (1958) 757–69.

——'Certitude de l'espérance et certitude de la grâce', in *Nouvelle Revue Théologique* 94 (1972) 3–42.

——*Rivelazione cristiana, fede e teologia* (Queriniana, Brescia 1986).

Allison, C.F., 'The Pastoral and Political Implications of Trent on Justification', in *One in Christ* 24 (1988) 110–27.

Alonso, J.M., 'Relación de causalidad entre la gracia creada e increada en santo Tomás de Aquino', in *Revista Española de Teología* 6 (1946) 3–59.

Alsted, J.H., *Theologia scholastica didacta* (Hannover 1618).

Althaus, P., *Die christliche Wahrheit. Lehrbuch der Dogmatik* (C. Bertelsmann, Gütersloh 1952).

——*Die Theologie Martin Luthers* (Mohn, Gütersloh 1962). Eng. translation: *The Theology of Martin Luther* (Fortress, Philadelphia 1975).

——*Luther und die Rechtfertigung* (Darmstadt 1971).

Anderson, H.G., Murphy, T.A and Burgess, J.A. (eds.), 'Justification by faith', in *Lutherans and Catholics in Dialogue VII* (Augsburg, Minneapolis 1985).

Andresen, C. (ed.), *Handbuch der Dogmen- und Theologiegeschichte*, 3 vols (Vandenhoeck & Ruprecht, Göttingen 1980–1986).

Aranda, A., 'Il, cristiano "alter Christus, ipse Christus"', in M. Belda et al. (eds.), *Santità e mondo: atti del Convegno teologico di studi sugli insegnamenti del beato Josemaría Escrivá* (Libreria Editrice Vaticana, Città del Vaticano 1994), pp. 101–47.

——'Dio ha assunto in Cristo il peccato dell'uomo', in J.M. Galván (ed.), *La giustificazione in Cristo*, pp. 211–25.

Auer, J., 'Textkritische Studien zur Gnadenlehre des Alexander von Hales', in *Scholastik* 15 (1940) 63–75.

——*Die Entwicklung der Gnadenlehre in der Hochscholastik, mit besonderer Berücksichtigung des Kardinals Matteo d'Acquasparta* (Herder, Freiburg i. Br. 1942), 2 vols.

——'Die "skotistische" Lehre von der Heilsgewißheit. Walter von Chatton, der erst "Skotist"', in *Wissenschaft und Weisheit* 16 (1953) 1–19.

Avis, P., 'Reflections on ARCIC-II', in *Theology* 90 (1987) 451–60.

Barclay, J.M.G., 'Paul and the Law: Observations on Some Recent Debates', in *Themelios* 12/1 (1986) 5–15.

——Obeying the Truth: A Study of Paul's Ethics in Galatians (T. & T. Clark, Edinburgh 1988).

Barclay, R., *An Apologie for the True Christian Divinity* (Manchester 1869).

Bardenas, R., *Christ the End of the Law. Romans 10:4 in Pauline Perspective* (JSOT, Sheffield 1985).

Barrett, C.K., *Paul. An Introduction to his Thought* (Chapman, London 1994).

Barth, H.-M., *Wie ein Segel sich entfalten. Selbstverwirklichung und christliche Existenz* (Munich 1979).

——'L'uomo secondo Martin Lutero. Alcune osservazioni sulla "Disputatio de Homine" (1536)', in *Studi Ecumenici* 1 (1983) 209–28.

——'Giustificazione e identità', in *Protestantesimo* 51 (1996) 116–30.

Barth, H.-M. (ed.), *Das Regensburger Religionsgespräch im Jahr 1541* (F. Pustet, Regensburg 1992).

Barth, K., *Nein! Antwort an E. Brunner*, 1934.

——*Evangelium und Gesetz* (Ch. Kaiser, Munich 1935).

——Church Dogmatics 2/2: *The Doctrine of God*; Church Dogmatics 4/1: *The Doctrine of Recon-*

ciliation (T. & T. Clark, Edinburgh 1956/57).

——*Die protestantische Theologie im 19. Jahrhundert, Evangelischer Verlag* (Zurich 1947). Eng. translation: *Protestant theology in the nineteenth century: its background & history* (Judson Press, Valley Forge 1973).

Basse, M., *Certitudo Spei. Thomas von Aquins Begründung der Hoffnungsgewißheit und ihre Rezeption bis zum Konzil von Trient* (Vandenhoeck & Ruprecht, Göttingen 1993).

Baumgartner, C., 'Concupiscence', in *Dictionnaire de Spiritualité* 2 (1953) 1343–1373.

Baur, F.C., *Brevis disquisitio in Andreae Osiandi de iustificatione doctrinam* (Berlin 1831).

Baur, J., *Salus Christiana: die Rechtfertigungslehre in der Geschichte des christlichen Heilsverständnisses* (G. Mohn, Gütersloh 1968).

—— *Einig in Sachen Rechtfertigung?: zur Prüfung des Rechtfertigungskapitels der Studie des Ökumenischen Arbeitskreises evangelischer und katholischer Theologen: 'Lehrverurteilungen-kirchentrennend?'* (J.C.B. Mohr (P. Siebeck), Tübingen 1989).

Bavaud, G., 'La doctrine de la justification d'après Saint Augustin', in *Revue des Études augustiniennes* 5 (1959) 21–32.

——'La doctrine de la justification d'après Calvin et le Concile de Trent', in *Verbum Caro* 22 (1968) 83–92.

——'La justification par la foi. Quelle est la racine de la divergence entre catholiques et protestants?', in *Nova et Vetera* 68 (1993) 250–62.

——'Le fruit d'un dialogue entre luthériens et catholiques: Le mystère de l'Église et celui de la justification', in *Nova et Vetera* 70 (1995) 50–65.

Bayer, O., *Promissio. Geschichte der reformatorischen Wende in Luthers Theologie* (Vandenhoeck & Ruprecht, Göttingen 1971).

Beachy, A.J., *The concept of Grace in the Radical Reformers* (B. de Graaf, Nieuwkoop 1977).

Beck, N., *The Doctrine of Faith: a study of the Augsburg Confession and contemporary ecumenical documents* (Concordia, St Louis 1987).

Becker, J.C., *Paul the Apostle. The Triumph of God in Life and Thought* (T. & T. Clark, Edinburgh 1989).

Becker, K.J., *Die Rechtfertigungslehre nach Domingo de Soto: Das Denken eines Konzilsteilnehmers vor, in und nach Trient* (Analecta Gregoriana, Roma 1967).

Beer, T., *Der fröhliche Wechsel und Streit* (Johannes Verlag, Einsiedeln 1980).

——'La "theologia crucis" de Lutero', in *Scripta Theologica* 16 (1984) 747–80.

Beinert, W., 'Den einen Glauben zur Ehre Gottes bekennen', in *Ökumenische Rundschau* 43 (1994) 37–46.

——'Do the condemnations of the Reformation era still confront the contemporary ecumenical partners?', in *Lutheran Quarterly* 8 (1994) 53–70.

Beintker, M. et al. (eds.), *Rechtfertigung und Erfahrung. Für Gerhard Sauter zum 60. Geburtstag* (Ch. Kaiser/Güterslohvorlesung, Gütersloh 1995).

Bellini, A., 'La giustificazione per la sola fede', in *Communio* (ed. it.) 38 (1978) 30–73.

Belluci, D., *Fede e giustificazione in Lutero. Un esame teologico dei 'Dicta super Psalterium' e del Commentario sull'Epistola ai Romani* (1513–1516), Roma 1963.

Benrath, G.A., 'Jakob Böhme', in C. Andresen (ed.), *Handbuch der Dogmen- und Theologiegeschichte*, vol. 2, pp. 603–7.

Bergendorff, C., 'Justification and Sanctification: Liturgy and Ethics', in P.C. Empie and J.I. McCord, *Marburg Revisited*, pp. 118–27.

Berkhof, H., *200 Jahre Theologie. Ein Reisebericht* (Neukirchener Verlag, Neukirchen-Vluyn 1985).

Bertram, R.W., 'Faith alone justifies. Luther on "Iustitia fidei"', in H.G. Anderson et al. (eds.), *Justification by faith*, pp. 172–84.

Billing, E., *Our Calling* (Philadelphia 1964).

Birmelé, A., *Le salut en Jésus Christ dans les dialogues oecuméniques* (Cerf/Labor et fides, Paris 1986).

Bizer, E., *Fides ex auditu. Eine Untersuchung über die Entdeckung der Gerechtigkeit Gottes durch Martin Luther* (Buchhandlung des Erziehungsvereins, Neukirchen 1958).

——*Theologie der Verheißung: Studien zur theologischen Entwicklung des jungen Melanchthon 1519–1524* (Buchhandlung des Erziehungsvereins, Neukirchen 1964).

Blank, J., *Paulus: Von Jesus zum Christentum. Aspekte der paulinischen Lehre und Praxis* (Kösel, Munich 1982).

Blaumeiser, H., *Martin Luthers Kreuzestheologie: Schlüssel zu seiner Deutung von Mensch und Wirklichkeit* (Bonifatius, Paderborn 1995).

Blumenberg, H., *Die Legimität der Neuzeit* (Frankfurt a. M. 1966).

Bof, G., 'Giustificazione', in *Nuovo Dizionario di Teologia, Supplemento*, (Paoline, Cinisello Balsamo 1983), pp. 1992–2004.

Bogdahn, M., *Die Rechtfertigungslehre Luthers im Urteil der neueren katholischen Theologie: Möglichkeiten und Tendenzen der katholischen Lutherdeutung in evangelischer Sicht* (Vandenhoeck & Ruprecht, Göttingen, 1971).

Böhme, J., *The Way to Christ* (Paulist, New York 1978).

Boisset, J., 'Justification et sanctification chez Calvin', in W.H. Neuser (ed.), *Calvinus Theologus: Die Referate des Congrès Européen des recherches Calviniennes (1974)* (Neukirchener Verlag, Neukirchen-Vluyn 1976), pp. 131–48.

Bonhöffer, D., *Widerstand und Erbegung. Briefe und Aufzeichnungen aus der Haft* (Chr. Kaiser, Munich 1970).

Bonnardiére, A.-M. la, 'Le verset paulinien Rom., v. 5 dans l'œuvre de saint Augustin', in Various authors, *Augustinus Magister*, vol. 2, pp. 657–65.

Bornkamm, G., *Paul* (Harper, San Francisco 1971).

Bornkamm, H., 'Justitia dei in der Scholastik und bei Luther', in *Archiv für Reformationsgeschichte* 39 (1942) 1–46.

——'Zur Frage der "Iustitia Dei" beim jungen Luther', in *Archiv für Reformationsgeschichte* 52 (1961) 16–29; 53 (1962) 1–60.

Boulding, M.C., 'The ARCIC Agreement on Salvation and the Church', in *Doctrine and Life* 39 (1989) 452–8.

Bousset, W., *Die Religion des Judentums im späthellenistischen Zeitalter* (Mohr, Tübingen 1966) (orig. 1925).

Bouttier, M., *En Christ. Étude d'exégèse et de théologie pauliniennes* (Presses Universitaires de France, Paris 1962).

Bovati, P., *Re-establishing justice: legal terms, concepts and procedures in the Hebrew Bible* (Academic Press, Sheffield 1994) (orig. 1986).

Braaten, C.E., *Justification: the Article by which the Church Stands or Falls* (Fortress, Minneapolis 1990).

Braaten, C.E. and Jenson, R.W., *Christian Dogmatics*, 2 vols (Augsburg/Fortress, Philadelphia 1984).

Brandenburg, A., *Martin Luther gegenwärtig. Katholische Lutherstudien* (Paderborn 1967).

Brauch, M.T., 'Perspectives on "God's righteousness" in recent German discussion', in E.P. Sanders, *Paul and Palestinian Judaism*, pp. 523–42.

Braunisch, R., *Die Theologie der Rechtfertigung im 'Enchiridion' (1538) des Johannes Gropper: Sein kritischer Dialog mit Philipp Melanchthon* (Aschendorff, Münster 1974).

Brena, G.L., 'Teologia della creazione e della redenzione', in *Civiltà Cattolica*, quad. 3490 (1995/IV) 366–78.

Breuning, W. and Hägglund, B., 'Sin and Original Sin', in G.W. Forell and J.F. McCue, *Confessing One Faith*, pp. 94–116.

Breytenbach, C., *Versöhnung. Eine Studie zur paulinischen Soteriologie* (Neukirchener Verlag, Neukirchen-Vluyn 1989).

Brinkman, M.E., *Justification in Ecumenical Debate. Central Aspects of Christian Soteriology in Debate* (Interuniversity Institute for Missiology and Ecumenical Research, Utrecht 1996).

Bruce, F.F., 'Paul and the Law in Recent Research', in B. Lindars (ed.), *Law and Religion. Essays on the Place of the Law in Israel and Early Christianity* (Cambridge 1988), pp. 115–25.

Brunner, E., *Natur und Gnade. Zum Gespräch mit Karl Barth* (Mohr, Tübingen 1934).

——*Der Mensch im Widerspruch* (Zwingli Verlag, Zürich 1937).

——*Die christliche Lehre von Schöpfung und Erlösung* (Zwingli Verlag, Zurich 1950).

Brunner, P., 'Die Rechtfertigungslehre des Konzils von Trient', in E. Schlink and H. Volk (eds.), *Pro veritate: Ein theologischer Dialog* (Aschendorff, Münster 1963), pp. 59–69 (also published as P. Brunner, *Pro Ecclesia. Gesammelte Aufsätze zur dogmatischen Theologie* (Lutherisches Verlagshaus, Hamburg 1962–1966), vol. 2, pp. 141–69).

Bruskewitz, F.W., *The Theology of Justification of Reginald Cardinal Pole*, Dott. Diss. P.U.G., (Rome 1969).

Buchanan, J., *The Doctrine of Justification. An Outline of its history in the Church and of its exposition from Scripture* (The Banner of Truth Trust, London 1961) (orig. 1867).

Bultmann, R., 'Die Geschichtlichkeit des Daseins und der Glaube: Antwort an Gerhardt Kuhlmann', in *Zeitschrift für Theologie und Kirche* 11 (1930) 339–64.

——'Das Problem der Hermeneutik' (1950), in *Glauben und Verstehen*, vol. 2, pp. 211–23.

——*Theology of the New Testament*, 2 vols (Scribner, New York 1951–1955).

——*Primitive Christianity in a Contemporary Setting* (Thames and Hudson, London 1956).

——*Glauben und Verstehen*, 4 vols, Mohr, Tübingen 1958–1965.

——*Jesus Christ and Mythology* (SCM, London 1960).

——'Δικαιοσύνη Θεου' in *Journal of Biblical Literature* 83 (1964) 12–16.

——'Καυχάομαι', in G. Kittel and G. Friedrich (eds.), *Theological Dictionary of the New Testament*, vol. 3 (Eerdmans, Grand Rapids 1965), pp. 648–54.

——*Geschichte und Eschatologie* (Mohr, Tübingen 1964).

Burgess, J.A. (ed.), *The Role of the Augsburg Confession: Catholic and Lutheran views* (Fortress, Philadelphia 1991).

Burgess, J.A. and Inglehart, G.A. (eds.), 'Lutheran-Baptist Dialogue', in *American Baptist Quarterly* 1 (1982) 103–12.

Burgess, J.A. and Nelson, F.B. (eds.), 'Lutheran-Conservative/Evangelical Dialogue', in *Covenant Quarterly* 41 (1983) 1–99.

Buri, F., *Die Bedeutung der ntl. Eschatologie für die neuere protestantische Theologie* (M. Niehans, Zurich 1935).

Burnaby, J., *'Amor Dei'. A Study of the Religion of St Augustine* (Hodder & Stoughton, London 1938).

Buzzi, F., 'La teologia di Lutero nelle "Lezioni sulla lettera ai Romani"(1515–1516)', in *La Lettera ai Romani* (Paoline, Cinisello Balsamo 1991), pp. 5–180.

—— *Il Concilio di Trento (1545–1563). Breve introduzione ad alcuni temi teologici principali* (Glossa, Milano 1995).

Byrne, B., *Sons of God, seed of Abraham: a Study of the Idea of the Sonship of God of all Christians in Paul against the Jewish Background* (Diss. Pont. Istituto Biblico, Rome 1979).

Camelot, T., 'Sacramentum fidei', in Various authors, *Augustinus Magister*, vol. 2, pp. 891–6.

Campbell, D.A., *The Rhetoric of Righteousness in Romans* 3.21–6 (JSOT, Sheffield 1992).

Cannon, W.R., *The Theology of John Wesley, with Special Reference to the Doctrine of Justification* (Abingdon, New York 1946).

Capánaga, V., 'La deificación en la soteriología agustiniana', in Various authors, *Augustinus Magister*, vol. 2, pp. 745–54.

——'Interpretación agustiniana del amor. Eros y Agape', in *Augustinus* 18 (1973) 213–78.

Capdevila i Montaner, J.-M., *Liberación y divinización del hombre*, vol. 2: *Estudio sistemático* (Secretariado Trinitario, Salamanca 1994).

Cassese, M. (ed.), *Augusta 1530: il dibattito Luterano-Cattolico: la confessione augustana e la confutazione pontifica* (Libreria Facoltà Biblica Internazionale, Milan 1981).

——'L'uomo nuovo e le buone opere secondo Martin Lutero', in *Studi Ecumenici* 1 (1983) 247–76.

Cassidy, E.I., 'The Pontifical Council for Promoting Christian Unity in 1993', in *One in Christ* 30 (1994) 199–215.

Cavallera, F., 'La session VI du concile de Trente', in *Bulletin de littérature ecclésiastique* 44 (1943)

229–38; 45 (1944) 220–31; 46 (1945) 54–6; 47 (1946) 103–12.

——'Le Décret du concile de Trente sur la justification', in *Bulletin de littérature écclésiastique* 49 (1948) 21–31; 51 (1950) 65–76; 146–68.

——'La Session VI du concile de Trente. Foi et justification', in *Bulletin de littérature écclésiastique* 53 (1952) 99–108.

Cerfaux, L., 'Justice, Justification', in *Dictionnaire de la Bible, Supplément* 4 (1949) 1471–96.

——*Le Chrétien dans la théologie de saint Paul* (Cerf, Paris 1954).

Chadwick, H., 'Justification by Faith: a Perspective', in *One in Christ* 20 (1984) 191–225.

Chantraine, G., *Érasme et Luther, libre et serf arbitre* (Lethielleux/Presses universitaires, Paris/Namur 1981).

Chubb, T., 'The True Gospel of Jesus Christ', in *Posthumous Works*, vol. 2 (London 1748).

Colombo, G., 'Dove va la teologia sacramentaria', in *La Scuola Cattolica* 102 (1974) 673–717.

——'Sull'antropologia teologica', in *Teologia* 20 (1995) 223–60.

Colzani, G., 'La dottrina della giustificazione alla prova della storia. La proposta barthiana ed il dibattito ecumenico', in *Annales Theologici* 10 (1996) 119–46.

Congar, Y.M.-J., 'Regards et réflexions sur la christologie de Luther', in A. Grillmeier and H. Bacht, *Das Konzil von Chalkedon, Geschichte und Gegenwart*, vol. 3 (Echter Verlag, Würzburg 1954), pp. 457–86.

——'Considérations historiques sur la rupture du XVI siècle dans ses rapports avec la réalisation catholique de l'unité', in *Chrétiens en dialogue. Contributions catholiques a l'œuménisme* (Cerf, Paris 1964), pp. 409–35.

——*Martin Luther. Sa foi, sa réforme. Etudes de théologie historique* (Cerf, Paris 1983).

Conzelmann, H., 'Die Rechtfertigungslehre des Paulus: Theologie oder Anthropologie?', in *Evangelische Theologie* 28 (1968) 389–404.

——*An Outline of the Theology of the New Testament* (SCM, London 1969).

Copleston, F., *History of Philosophy*, vols 6 and 7 (Burns & Oates, London 1947).

Cornely, R., *Epistula ad Romanos* (Paris 1896).

Cranfield, C.E.B., 'St Paul and the Law', in *Scottish Journal of Theology* 17 (1964) 43–68.

——'Has the Old Testament Law a Place in Christian Life? A Response to Professor Westerholm', in *Irish Biblical Studies* 15 (1993) 50–64.

Cremer, H., *Die paulinische Rechtfertigungslehre in Zusammenhange ihrer geschichtlichen Voraussetzungen* (Gütersloh 1900).

Cristiani, L., 'Stancaro', in *Dictionnaire de Théologie Catholique* 14 (1953) 2558–61.

Cura Elena, S. del, 'Radicación trinitaria de la "Koinônia" eclesial. Dios Trinitario e Iglesia en el documento del diálogo católico-luterano "Iglesia y Justificación" (1993)', in *Salmanticensis* 42 (1995) 211–34.

D'Arcy, M.C., *The Mind and Heart of Love: Lion and Unicorn, a Study in Eros and Agape* (Faber and Faber, London 1954).

Dahl, N.A., *Studies in Paul. Theology for the Early Christian Mission* (Augsburg, Minneapolis 1977).

Dantine, W., 'Das Dogma im tridentinischen Katholizismus: Die Lehre von der Rechtfertigung', in C. Andresen (ed.), *Handbuch der Dogmen- und Theologiegeschichte*, vol. 2, pp. 453–64.

Davies, W.D., *The Setting of the Sermon on the Mount* (University Press, Cambridge 1964).

——*Paul and Rabbinic Judaism. Some Rabbinic Elements in Pauline Theology* (SPCK, London 1965) (orig. 1948).

——'Paul and the People of the New Testament', in *New Testament Studies* 24 (1977–78) 4–39.

Degenhardt, J.J., Willebrands, J., Döring, H., Schulz, H.J., Gaßmann, G., Hünermann, P. and Urban, H.J., *Die Sakramentalität der Kirche in der ökumenischen Diskussion* (Möhler Institut, Paderborn 1983).

Deißmann, A., *Paulus: eine kultur- und religionsgeschichte Skizze* (Tübingen 1925).

Denifle, H., *Die abendländischen Schriftausleger bis Luther über 'Iustitia Dei' [Rom I.17] und 'Iustificatio'* (Mainz 1905).

Deutsche Bischofskonferenz, *Katholischer Erwachsenen-Katechismus. Das Glaubensbekenntnis der Kirche* (Verband der Diüzesen Deutschlands, Bonn 1985).

Dianich, S., *Ecclesiologia. Questioni di metodo e una proposta* (Paoline, Cinisello Balsamo 1993).

Dobbeler, A. von, *Glaube als Teilhabe. Historische und semantische Grundlagen der paulinischen Theologie und Ekklesiologie des Glaubens* (J.C.B. Mohr (P. Siebeck), Tübingen 1987).

Drane, J.W., *Paul, Libertine or Legalist? A Study in the Theology of the Major Pauline Epistles* (SPCK, London 1975).

Ducay, A., 'Croce e giustificazione nella Chiesa. Una lettura ecumenica alla luce della soteriologia giovannea', in J.M. Galván (ed.), *La giustificazione in Cristo*, pp. 248–59.

Dulles, A., 'Justification in contemporary Catholic theology', in H.G. Anderson et al. (eds.), *Justification by faith*, pp. 256–77.

Dunn, J.D.G., 'Jesus – Flesh and Spirit: an Exposition of Romans 1.3-4', in *Journal of Theological Studies* 24 (1973) 44–9.

——*Romans* (Word Biblical Commentary 38) (Word Books, Dallas 1988).

——*Jesus, Paul and the Law: studies in Mark and Galatians* (SPCK, London 1990).

——'The Justice of God. A Renewed Perspective on Justification by Faith', in *Journal of Theological Studies* 43 (1992) 1–22.

——*The Theology of Paul's Letter to the Galatians* (University Press, Cambridge 1993).

——'Paul's Conversion – A Light to Twentieth Century Disputes', in O. Hofius (ed.), *Evangelium-Schriftauslegung-Kirche* (Vandenhoeck & Ruprecht, Göttingen 1996).

——'4QMMT and Galatians', in *New Testament Studies* 43 (1997) 147–53.

Dunn, J.D.G. (ed.), *Paul and the Mosaic Law* (J.C.B. Mohr (P. Siebeck), Tübingen 1996).

Dunn, J.D.G. and Suggate, A.M., *The Justice of God. A Fresh Look at the Old Doctrine of Justification* (Paternoster Press, Carlisle 1993), pp. 7–48.

Dupont, J., 'The Conversion of Paul, and its Influence on his Understanding of Salvation by Faith', in W.W. Gasque and R.P. Martin (eds.), *Apostolic History and the Gospel* (Festschrift F. F. Bruce) (Eerdmans, Grand Rapids 1970), pp. 176–94.

Ebeling, G., 'Die Anfänge von Luthers Hermeneutik', in *Zeitschrift für Theologie und Kirche* 48 (1951) 172-230 (summarized in English as 'The New Hermeneutics and the young Luther', in *Theology Today* 21 (1964) 34–46).

——*Das Wesen des christlichen Glaubens* (Mohr, Tübingen 1959).

——*Evangelische Evangelienauslegung. Eine Untersuchung zu Luthers Hermeneutik* (Wissenschaftliche Buchgesellschaft, Darmstadt 1962) (orig. 1942).

——*Theologie und Verkündigung. Ein Gespräch mit Rudolf Bultmann* (Mohr, Tübingen 1963).

——*Wort Gottes und Tradition: Studien zu einer Hermeneutik der Konfessionen* (Vandenhoeck & Ruprecht, Göttingen 1964).

——*Luther, Einführung in sein Denken* (Mohr, Tübingen 1964). Eng. translation: *Luther: An Introduction to his Thought* (Collins, London 1970).

——'Gewißheit und Zweifel: Die Situation des Glaubens im Zeitalter nach Luther und Descartes', in *Zeitschrift für Theologie und Kirche* 64 (1967) 282–324.

——*Einführung in die theologische Sprachlehre* (J.C.B. Mohr (P. Siebeck), Tübingen 1971).

——*Lutherstudien*, 3 vols (Mohr, Tübingen 1971–89).

——*Dogmatik des christlichen Glaubens*, 3 vols (J.C.B. Mohr (P. Siebeck), Tübingen 1979).

——*Martin Lutero. L'itinerario e il messaggio* (Claudiana, Torino 1988), pp. 78–88.

——*Wort und Glaube*, 4 vols (J.C.B. Mohr (P. Siebeck), Tübingen 1960–94).

Ehses, S., 'Johannes Groppers Rechtfertigungslehre auf dem Konzil von Trient', in *Römische Quartalschrift* 20 (1906) 175–88.

Empie, P.C. and McCord, J.I., *Marburg Revisited: A Reexamination of Lutheran and Reformed Traditions* (Fortress, Minneapolis 1966).

England, R.G., 'Salvation and the Church: A Review Article', in *Churchman* 101 (1987) 49–57.

Enslin, M.S., *Reapproaching Paul* (Fortress, Philadelphia 1972).

Ernst, W., *Gott und Mensch am Vorabend der Reformation. Eine Untersuchung zur Moralphilosophie und -theologie bei Gabriel Biel*, St. Benno-Verlag (Leipzig 1972).

Eschweiler, K., *Die zwei Wege der neueren Theologie. Georg Hermes – M.J. Scheeben. Eine kritische Untersuchung des Problems der theologischen Erkenntnis* (B. Filser, Augsburg 1926).

Escrivá, J., *The Way* (Four Courts, Dublin 1987).

——'Passionately Loving the World', in *Conversations with Mgr. Escrivá de Balaguer* (Four Courts, Dublin 1980), no. 113–23.

——*Christ is Passing By* (Four Courts, Dublin 1982).

——*Furrow* (Four Courts, Dublin 1988).

——*The Forge* (Four Courts, Dublin 1988).

Estrada-Barbier, B., 'La fede e le opere a confronto con il giudaismo', in J.M. Galván (ed.), *La giustificazione in Cristo*, pp. 63–72.

Evard, A., *Étude sur les variations du dogme de la prédestination et du libre arbitrie dans la théologie de Melanchthon* (Laval 1901).

Falk, H., *Jesus the Pharisee. A new look at the Jewishness of Jesus* (Paulist, New York 1985).

Feckes, C., *Die Rechtfertigungslehre des Gabriel Biel und ihre Stellung innerhalb der nominalistischen Schule* (Aschendorff, Münster 1925).

Ferrara, O., *Gasparo Contarini et ses missions* (Michel, Paris 1956).

Fitzmyer, J.A., 'Crucifixion in Ancient Palestine, Qumran Literature and the New Testament', in *Catholic Biblical Quarterly* 40 (1978) 493–513.

——*Romans. A New Translation with Introduction and Commentary* (Anchor Bible, no. 33) (Doubleday, New York 1992).

Flick, Z. and Alszeghy, M., *Il vangelo della grazia* (Libreria Editrice Fiorentina, Firenze 1964).

Forde, G.O., *The Law-Gospel Debate: an interpretation of its historical development* (Augsburg, Minneapolis 1969).

——'Forensic Justification and Law in Lutheran Theology', in H.G. Anderson et al. (eds.), *Justification by faith*, pp. 278–303.

——'Justification by faith alone', in *Dialog* 27 (1988) 260–7.

——*Justification by faith: A Matter of Life and Death* (Sigler Press, Philadelphia 1990).

Forell, G.W., 'Law and Gospel', in P.C. Empie and J.I. McCord, *Marburg Revisited*, pp. 128–40.

Forell, G.W. and McCue, J.F., *Confessing One Faith: a joint commentary on the Augsburg Confession by Lutheran and Catholic theologians* (Augsburg, Minneapolis 1982).

Forget, J., 'Déisme', in *Dictionnaire de Théologie Catholique* 4 (1910) 232–43.

Fragnito, G., *Gasparo Contarini: un magistrato veneziano al servizio della cristianità* (Leo S. Olschki, Firenze 1988).

Frieling, R., 'Zu den Beziehungen zwischen protestantischen und katholischen Christen', in *Epd-Interview* 36 (1984) 15.

Frölich, K., 'Justification Language in the Middle Ages', in H.G. Anderson et al. (eds.), *Justification by Faith*, pp. 143–61;

Galván, J.M. (ed.), *La giustificazione in Cristo* (Atti del II Simposio Internazionale della Facoltà di Teologia del Pontificio Ateneo della Santa Croce, 14–15 marzo 1996) (Libreria Editrice Vaticana, Città del Vaticano 1997).

——'La giustizia di Dio, sorgente della giustificazione', in J.M. Galván (ed.), *La giustificazione in Cristo*, pp. 117–28;

García Martínez, F., *The Dead Sea Scrolls Translated: The Qumran Texts in English* (Brill, Leiden 1994).

Gaßmann, G., 'The Church as Sacrament, Sign and Instrument. The Reception of this ecclesiological understanding in ecumenical debate', in *Church, Kingdom, World*, Faith & Order Paper, no. 130 (Geneva 1986), pp. 1–17.

——'Lutheran-Catholic Agreement on Justification (I): a Historical Breakthrough', in *Ecumenical Trends* 25 (1996) 82–5.

——'Lutheran-Catholic Agreement on Justification (II): The Ecclesiological Dimension', in *Ecumenical Trends* 25 (1996) 97–103.

——'La dimensione ecclesiologica della giustificazione. Una prospettiva luterana', in J.M. Galván (ed.), *La giustificazione in Cristo*, pp. 165–86.

Gaston, L., 'Paul and the Torah', in A.T. Davies (ed.), *Antisemitism and the Foundations of Christianity* (Paulist, New York 1979), pp. 48–71.

Geiger, M., 'The Leuenberg agreement – A step forward and a beginning', in *Reformed World* 33 (1974) 160–6.

Gherardini, B., *Theologia crucis: l'eredità di Lutero nell'evoluzione teologica della Riforma* (Paoline, Roma 1978).

——*Creatura Verbi. La Chiesa nella teologia di Martin Lutero* (Vivere in, Rome 1994).

——'"Articulus stantis et cadentis ecclesiae"', in *Annales Theologici* 10 (1996) 109–17.

Gibbs, J. and Gaßmann, G. (eds.), *Anglican-Lutheran Dialogue: The Report of the Anglican-Lutheran European Regional Commission Helsinki 1982* (SPCK, London 1983).

Gibbs, L.W., 'Richard Hooker's Via Media Doctrine of Justification', in *Harvard Theological Review* 74 (1981) 211–20.

Giovanni, G. di, 'Free Choice and Radical Evil. The Irrationalism of Kant's Moral Theory', in G. Funke and T.M. Seebohm (eds.), *Proceedings of the Sixth International Kant Congress II/2* (Washington 1989), pp. 311–25.

Glare, P.G.W., *Oxford Latin Dictionary* (University Press, Oxford 1984).

Gnilka, J., 'La dottrina paolina della giustificazione: legge, giustificazione, fede', in *Annales Theologici* 10 (1996) 93–108.

Goeser, R.J., 'Commentary on U.S. Roman Catholic-Lutheran Statement on Justification', in *Ecumenical Trends* 13 (1984) 81–5.

Gonzáles Rivas, S., 'Los teólogos salmantinos y el decreto de la justificación', in *Estudios Eclesiásticos* 21 (1947) 147–70.

Grane, L., *Contra Gabrielem: Luthers Auseinandersetzung mit Gabriel Biel in der Disputatio contra scholasticam theologiam 1517* (Gyldenhal, Kopenhagen 1962).

——'Gregor von Rimini und Luthers Leipziger Disputation', in *Scottish Journal of Theology* 22 (1968) 29–49.

Grech, P., 'La nuova ermeneutica: Fuchs e Ebeling', in *Associazione Biblica Italiana, Esegesi ed ermeneutica. Atti della XXI Settimana Biblica* (1968) (Paideia, Brescia 1972), pp. 71–90.

Greco, C., 'Gesù Cristo, icona del Dio invisibile', in C. Greco (ed.), *Cristologia e antropologia*, (AVE, Rome 1994), pp. 156–80.

Greschat, M., *Melanchthon neben Luther: Studien zur Gestalt der Rechtfertigungslehre zwischen 1528 und 1537* (Luther-Verlag, Witten 1965).

——'Der Ansatz der Theologie Martin Bucers', in *Theologische Literaturzeitung* 103 (1978) 81–96.

Gritsch, E.W. and Jenson, R.W., *Lutheranism: The Theological Movement and its Confessional Writings* (Fortress, Philadelphia 1976).

Gross, J., *Entwicklungsgeschichte des Erbsündendogmas seit der Reformation* (E. Reinhardt, Munich 1972).

Grossi, V., 'La giustificazione secondo Girolamo Seripando nel contesto dei dibattiti tridentini', in *Analecta Augustiniana* 41 (1978) 6–24.

Guérard des Lauriers, M.L., 'Saint Augustin et la question de la certitude de la grâce au Concile de Trente', in Various authors, *Augustinus Magister*, vol. 2, pp. 1057–67.

Gundry, R.H., 'Grace, Works, and Staying Saved in Paul', in *Biblica* 66 (1985) 1–38.

Gutiérrez, G., 'Un capítulo de teología pretridentino: el problema de la justificación', in *Miscelánea Comillas* 4 (1945) 7–31.

Gutiérrez Miras, D., 'Hieronymi Seripandi scripti', in *Latinitas* 12 (1964) 142–52.

Gyllenkrok, A., *Rechtfertigung und Heiligung in der frühen evangelischen Theologie Luthers* (A.B. Lundequistska Bokhandeln/Otto Harrassowitz, Uppsala/Wiesbaden 1952).

Häcker, P., *Das Ich im Glauben bei Martin Luther* (Styria, Graz/Wien 1966).

Haikola, L., 'Melanchthons und Luthers Lehre von der Rechtfertigung', in *Luther und Melanchthon: Referate und Berichte des Zweitens Internationalen Kongresses für Lutherforschung* (Göttingen 1961), pp. 89–103.

Häring, T., *ΔΙΚΑΙΟΣΥΝΗ ΘΕΟΥ bei Paulus* (Tübingen 1896).

Härle, W., 'Lehrverurteilungen-kirchentrennend in der Rechtfertigungslehre?', in *Materialdienst des Konfessionskundlichen Instituts Bensheim* 38 (1987) 123–7.

Harnack, A., *Dogmengeschichte III* (5 ed.) (Mohr, Tübingen 1931).

Harnack, T., *Luthers Theologie mit besonderer Beziehung auf seine Versöhnungs- und Erlösungslehre*, 2 vols, 1862–85.

Hauser, M., '"L'autonomia del mondo": un concetto promettente nella teologia della giustificazione', in *Studi Ecumenici* 14 (1996) 223–31.

Hazard, P., *La crise de la conscience européenne* (1680–1715), 3 vols (Boivin, Paris 1935).

Hefner, J., *Die Entstehungsgeschichte der Trienter Rechtfertigungsdekrete: ein Beitrag zur Geschichte des Reformationszeitalters* (Schöningh, Paderborn 1909).

Heidegger, M., *Sein und Zeit* (Niemeyer, Tübingen 1927).

——*Unterwegs zur Sprache* (V. Klostermann, Frankfurt a. M. 1985).

Heine, H., *Religion and Philosophy in Germany* (Beacon Press, Boston 1959).

Heitmüller, W., *Luthers Stellung in der Religionsgeschichte des Christentums* (Marburg 1917).

Hengel, M., *Between Jesus and Paul* (SCM, London 1983).

Hennig, G., *Cajetan und Luther: ein historischer Beitrag zur Begegnung von Thomismus und Reformation* (Calwer, Stuttgart 1966).

Henninger, J., *S. Augustinus et doctrina de duplici iustitia. Inquisitio historico-critica in opinionem Hieronymi Seripandi (1493–1563) de justificatione ejusque habitudinem ad doctrinam S. Augustini* (Diss. Dott. PUG, Rome 1935).

Hermann, R., *Zum Streit um die Überwindung des Gesetzes. Erörterungen zu Luthers Antinomerthesen* (Weimar 1958).

——'Willensfreiheit und gute Werke im Sinne der Reformation', in *Gesammelte Studien zur Theologie Luthers und der Reformation* (Vandenhoeck & Ruprecht, Göttingen 1960), pp. 44–76.

——*Luthers These 'Gerecht und Sünder zugleich'* (Mohn, Gütersloh 1960).

Heynck, V., 'Untersuchungen über die Reuelehre der tridentinischen Zeit', in *Franziskanische Studien* 29 (1942) 25–44; 120–50; 30 (1943) 53–73.

——'A Controversy at the Council of Trent concerning the Doctrine of Duns Scotus', in *Franciscan Studies* 9 (1949) 181–258.

——'Der Anteil des Konzilstheologen Andreas de Vega O.F.M. an dem ersten amtlichen Entwurf des Trienter Rechtfertigungsdekretes', in *Franziskanische Studien* 33 (1951) 49–81.

——'Zur Kontroverse über die Gnadengewißheit auf dem Konzil von Trient', in *Franziskanische Studien* 37 (1955) 1–17; 161–88.

——'Die Bedeutung von "mereri" und "promereri" bei dem Konzilstheologen Andreas de Vega', in *Franziskanische Studien* 50 (1968), 224–38.

Hill, E.D., *Edward, Lord Herbert of Cherbury* (Twayne Publishers, Boston 1987).

Hirsch, E., *Die Theologie des Andreas Osiander und ihre geschichtliche Voraussetzung* (Vandenhoeck & Ruprecht, Göttingen 1919).

Hobbes, T., *Leviathan* (Collier Books, New York 1962) (orig. London 1651).

Holl, K., *Gesammelte Aufsätze zur Kirchengeschichte* (Mohr, Tübingen 1921–28), 3 vols.

——'Die Rechtfertigungslehre in Luthers Vorlesung über den Römerbrief mit besonderer Rücksicht auf die Frage der Heilsgewißheit', in *Gesammelte Aufsätze*, vol. 1, pp. 111–54.

——'Luthers Bedeutung für den Fortschritt der Auslegungskunst', in *Gesammelte Aufsätze*, vol. 1, pp. 544–82.

Holte, R., *Béatitude et Sagesse. Saint Augustin et le problème de la fin de l'homme dans la philosophie ancienne* (Études Augustiniennes, Paris 1962).

Hooker, M.D., 'Paul and "Covenental Nomism"', in M.D. Hooker and S.G. Wilson (eds.), *Paul and Paulinism. Essays in honour of C.K. Barrett* (SPCK, London 1982), pp. 47–56.

Hornig, G., 'Der englische Deismus', in C. Andresen (ed.), *Handbuch der Dogmen- und Theologiegeschichte*, vol. 3, pp. 115–25.

——'Der Pietismus', in C. Andresen (ed.), *Handbuch der Dogmen- und Theologiegeschichte*, vol. 3, pp. 97–115.

Hotchkin, F.J., 'Reflections on dialogue and justification', in *Ecumenical Trends* 13 (1984) 62–4.

Howard, G., 'Christ the End of the Law: the Meaning of Romans 10:4', in *Journal of Biblical Literature* 88 (1969) 331–7.

Hübner, H., 'Existentiale Interpretation der paulinischen "Gerechtigkeit Gottes". Zur Kontroverse R. Bultmann-E. Käsemann', in *New Testament Studies* 21 (1974/75) 462–88.

——'Pauli Theologiae Proprium', in *New Testament Studies* 26 (1980) 455–73.

——*Das Gesetz bei Paulus* (Vandenhoeck & Ruprecht, Göttingen 1980); English translation, *Law in Paul's thought: a Contribution to the Development of Pauline Theology* (T. & T. Clark, Edinburgh 1986).

Hughes, P.E., *The Reformation in England*, vol. 2: *Religio depopulata*, (Hollis & Carter, London 1953).

——*Faith and Works: Cranmer and Hooker on justification* (Morehouse-Barlow, Wilton 1982).

Hultgren, G., *Le Commandement d'amour chez Augustin. Intérpretation philosophique et théologique d'aprés les écrits de la période 386–400* (Vrin, Paris 1939).

Hünermann, F., 'Die Rechtfertigungslehre des Kard. Kaspar Contarini', in *Theologische Quartalschrift* 102 (1921) 1–22.

Huthmacher, H., 'La Certitude de la grâce au Concile de Trente', in *Nouvelle Revue Théologique* 65 (1933) 213-226.

Iammarrone, G., 'Gesù Cristo Riconciliatore e Redentore in Martin Lutero', in *Miscellanea Francescana* 96 (1996) 425–54.

Illanes, J.L., *Cristianismo, historia, mundo* (EUNSA, Pamplona 1972).

——'Teología Sistemática de Paul Tillich', in *Scripta Theologica* 6 (1974) 711–54.

Innerarity, D., *Dialéctica de la modernidad* (Rialp, Madrid 1990).

Iserloh, E., 'Gratia et donum, giustificazione e santificazione secondo lo scritto di Lutero contro il teologo lovaniense Latomus (1521)', in Various authors, *Lutero e la riforma. Contributi a una comprensione ecumenica* (Morcelliana, Brescia 1977), pp. 129–53.

Iwand, H.J., *Rechtfertigungslehre und Christusglaube: eine Untersuchung zur Systematik der Rechtfertigungslehre Luthers in ihren Anfängen* (Chr. Kaiser, Munich 1966) (original 1930).

——*Nachgelassene Werke*, vol. 5: *Luthers Theologie* (Ch. Kaiser, Munich 1974).

Jaubert, A., *La notion d'alliance dans le judaïsme, aux abords de l'ère chrétienne* (Seuil, Paris 1963).

Jeanrond, W.G., *Introduction à l'herméneutique théologique* (Cerf, Paris 1995).

Jedin, H., *Studien über die Schriftstellertätigkeit Albert Pigges* (Münster 1931).

——*Girolamo Seripando. Sein Leben und Denken im Geisteskampf des 16. Jahrhunderts* (Rita Verlag, Würzburg 1937).

——*Kardinal Contarini als Kontroverstheologe* (Aschendorff, Münster 1949).

——*A History of the Council of Trent* (T. Nelson, Edinburgh 1961), 2 vols.

——'Le Concile de Trente fut-il un obstacle a la réunion des chrétiens?', in Various authors, *Union et désunion des chrétiens* (Desclée de Brouwer, Paris 1963), pp. 79–94.

Jeremias, J., *The Central Message of the New Testament* (SCM, London 1965).

Joest, W., *Gesetz und Freiheit: Das Problem des tertius usus legis bei Luther und die neutestamentliche Paränese* (Vandenhoeck & Ruprecht, Göttingen 1956).

——'Die tridentinische Rechtfertigungslehre', in *Kerygma und Dogma* 9 (1963) 41–59.

——*Ontologie der Person bei Luther* (Vandenhoeck & Ruprecht, Göttingen 1967).

Johnson, J.F., *Justification according to the Apology of the Augsburg Confession and the Formula of Concord*, in H.G. Anderson et al. (eds.), *Justification by faith*, pp. 185–99.

Jolivet, R., *La notion de substance. Essai historique et critique sur le développement des doctrines d'Aristote à nos jours* (Beauchesne, Paris 1929).

Jorrisen, H., 'Kritische Erwägungen zur Stellungnahme der Deutschen Bischofskonferenz zur Studie "Lehrverurteilungen-kirchentrennend?"', in *Catholica* 48 (1994) 267–78.

Journet, C., 'Le mystère de la sacramentalité. Le Christ, l'Église, les sept sacrements', in *Nova et Vetera* 49 (1974) 161–214.

Jüngel, E., *Paulus und Jesus: eine Untersuchung zur Präzisierung der Frage nach dem Ursprung der Christologie* (Mohr, Tübingen 1962).

——*Gottes Sein ist im Werden. Verantwortliche Rede vom Sein Gottes bei Karl Barth, eine Paraphrase* (Mohr, Tübingen 1965).

——'Die Kirche als Sakrament?', in *Zeitschrift für Theologie und Kirche* 80 (1983) 432-457.

Kähler, M., *Zur Lehre von der Versöhnung* (Leipzig 1898).

Kandler, K.H., 'Rechtfertigung-Kirchentrenned', in *Kerygma und Dogma* 36 (1990) 325–47.

Kant, I., 'Religion innerhalb der Grenzen der bloßen Vernunft', in *Kants gesammelte Schriften*, vol. 6 (W. de Gruyter, Berlin 1969). Eng. translation, *Religion within the Limits of Reason Alone* (Harper and Row, New York 1960).

Käsemann, E., *Leib und Leib Christi: eine Untersuchung zur paulinischen Begrifflichkeit* (Mohr, Tübingen 1933).

——*Exegetische Versuche und Besinnungen* (Vandenhoeck & Ruprecht, Göttingen 1960). Eng. translation, *Essays on New Testament themes* (SCM, London 1964).

——'Gottesgerechtigkeit bei Paulus', in *Zeitschrift für Theologie und Kirche* 58 (1961) 367–78. Eng. translation: '"The Righteousness of God" in Paul', in *New Testament Questions of Today*, pp. 168–82.

——*New Testament Questions of Today* (Fortress, Philadelphia 1969).

——*Perspectives on Paul* (Fortress, Philadelphia 1971).

——*Commentary on Romans* (SCM, London 1980).

Kasper, W., 'Grundkonsens und Kirchengemeinschaft. Zum Stand des ökumenischen Gespräches zwischen katholischer und evangelisch-lutherischer Kirche', in *Theologische Quartalschrift* 167 (1987) 161–81.

Keck, L.E., 'The Law and "the Law of Sin and Death" (Rom. 8:1–4). Reflections on the Spirit and Ethics in Paul', in J.L. Crenshaw and S. Sandmel (eds.), *The Divine Helmsman. Studies on God's Control of Human Events* (Ktav, New York 1980), pp. 41–57.

Kertelge, K., *'Rechtfertigung' bei Paulus. Studien zur Struktur und zum Bedeutungsgehalt des paulinischen Rechtfertigungsbegriffs* (Aschendorff, Münster 1967).

——'Zur Deutung des Rechtfertigungsbegriffs im Galaterbrief', in *Biblische Zeitschrift* 12 (1968) 215;

Kim, S., *The Origins of Paul's Gospel* (J.C.B. Mohr (P. Siebeck), Tübingen 1983).

Klaiber, W., *Rechtfertigung und Gemeinde. Ein Untersuchung zum paulinischen Kirchenverständnis* (Vandenhoeck & Ruprecht, Göttingen 1982).

Klein, G., 'Gottes Gerechtigkeit als Thema der neuesten Paulus-Forschung', in Various authors, *Rekonstruction und Interpretation* (Munich 1969), pp. 225–36.

——'Ein Sturmzentrum der Paulusforschung', in *Verkündigung und Forschung* 33 (1988) 40–56.

Klenicki, L., 'Exile and Return: Moments in the Jewish Pilgrimage to God (Responding to the Shoah)', in *Annales Theologici* 10 (1996) 485–503.

Knox, J., *Chapters in a Life of Paul* (Adam & Charles Black, London 1954).

Knox, R., *Enthusiasm: a Chapter in the History of Religion* (Clarendon Press, Oxford 1950).

Köberle, J., *Sünde und Gnade im religiösen Leben des Volkes Israel bis auf Christentum. Ein Geschichte des vorchristlichen Heilsbewußtseins* (Beck, Munich 1905).

Kohls, E.W., *Die Theologie des Erasmus* (Reinhardt, Basel 1966), 2 vols.

Kölbing, P., 'Studien zur paulinischen Theologie', in *Theologische Studien und Kritiken* 68 (1895) 7–51.

König, J., *Jews and Christians in Dialogue. New Testament Foundations* (Westminster Press, Philadelphia 1979).

Köster, H., 'Urstand, Fall und Erbsünde von der Schrift in der Scholastik', in M. Schmaus et al. (eds.), *Handbuch der Dogmengeschichte*, Herder, Freiburg i. Br./Basel/Wien 1951 ff., vol. 2/3, b.

Kösters, R., 'Luthers These "Gerecht und Sünder zugleich"', in *Catholica* 33 (1964) 48–77.

Krause, R., *Die Predigt der späten deutschen Aufklärung* (Calwer, Stuttgart 1965).

Kriechbaum, F., *Grundzüge der Theologie Karlstadts: Eine systematische Studie zur Erhellung der Theologie Andreas von Karlstadts* (Hamburg 1967).

Kröger, M., *Rechtfertigung und Gesetz: Studien zur Entwicklung der Rechtfertigungslehre beim jungen Luther* (Vandenhoeck & Ruprecht, Göttingen 1968).

Krüger, F., *Bucer und Erasmus: Eine Untersuchung zum Einfluß des Erasmus auf die Theologie Martin Bucers* (Wiesbaden 1970).

Kühl, E., *Der Brief des Paulus an die Römer* (Quelle & Meyer, Leipzig 1913).

Kuhlman, G., 'Zum theologischen Problem der Existenz: Fragen an Rudolf Bultmann', in *Zeitschrift für Theologie und Kirche* 10 (1929) 28–57.

Kühn, U. and Pesch, O.H. 'Rechtfertigung im Disput. Eine freundliche Antwort an Jörg Baur', in *Ökumenische Rundschau* 37 (1988) 22–46.

Kühn, U. and Pesch, O.H., 'Rechtfertigung im Disput. Eine freundliche Antwort an Jörg Baur' (J.C.B. Mohr (P. Siebeck), Tübingen 1991).

Küng, H., *Justification: the Doctrine of Karl Barth and a Catholic Reflection* (T. Nelson, New York 1964).

Küry, U., *Die Altkatholische Kirche, ihre Geschichte, ihre Lehre, ihr Anliegen* (Evangelisches Verlagswerk, Stuttgart 1966).

Kuss, O., *Der Römerbrief* (Pustet, Regensburg 1957).

Laemmer, H., *Die Vortridentinisch-katholische Theologie des Reformations-Zeitalters aus den Quellen dargestellt* (G. Schlawitz, Berlin 1858).

Lagrange, M.-J., *L'Epître aux Romains* (Lecoffre/J. Gabalda, Paris 1950).

Lambrecht, J., 'Gesetzesverständnis bei Paulus', in K. Kertelge (ed.), *Das Gesetz im Neuen Testament* (Herder, Freiburg i. Br. 1986), pp. 86–127.

Landgraf, A.M., *Dogmengeschichte der Frühscholastik, I: Gnadenlehre* (Pustet, Regensburg 1952–3).

Lange, D., et al., *Überholte Verurteilungen?: Stellungnahme gegenüber 'Lehrverurteilungen-kirchentrennend?'; Die Gegensätze in der Lehre von Rechtfertigung, Abendmahl und Amt zwischen dem Konzil von Trient und der Reformation – damals und heute*, (Vandenhoeck & Ruprecht, Göttingen 1991). Eng. translation of the section on justification: D. Lange et al., 'An Opinion on "The Condemnations of the Reformation Era". Part One: Justification', in *Lutheran Quarterly* 5 (1991) 1–62.

Lehmann, K. (ed.), *Lehrverurteilungen-kirchentrennend? Materialien zu den Lehrverurteilungen und zur Theologie der Rechtfertigung* (Herder, Freiburg i. Br. 1989).

Lehmann, K. and Pannenberg, W., 'Lehrverurteilungen and kirchentrennend?' (Vandenhoeck und Ruprecht/Herder, Göttingen/Freiburg i. Br. 1986) (Eng. translation: 'The Justification of the Sinner', in *The Condemnations of the Reformation Era. Do they still divide?* (Fortress, Minneapolis 1990).

Leith, J.H., 'Creation and Redemption; Law and Gospel in the Theology of John Calvin', in P.C. Empie and J.I. McCord, *Marburg Revisited*, pp. 141–51.

Lemonnyer, R., 'Justification', in *Dictionnaire de Théologie Catholique* 8/2 (1925) 2058–75.

Lerch, D., *Heil und Heiligung bei John Wesley* (Zürich 1941).

Lessing, E., '"Lehrverurteilungen-kirchentrennend?": zur Bedeutung und zu den Grenzen eines ökumenischen Dokuments', in *Ökumenische Rundschau* 45 (1996) 24–38.

Lienhard, M., 'Christologie et humilité dans la "Theologia Crucis" du Commentaire de l'Epître aux Romains de Luther', in *Revue d'histoire et de philosophie religieuses* 42 (1962) 304–15.

——*Au coeur de la foi de Luther: Jésus Christ* (Desclée, Paris 1991).

Lietzmann, H., Bornkamm, H., Volz, H. and Wolf, E., *Die Bekenntnisschriften der evangelisch-lutherischen Kirche* (Vandenhoeck & Ruprecht, Göttingen 1967).

Lindström, H., *Wesley and Sanctification: A Study in the Doctrine of Salvation* (London 1956).

Lipgens, W., *Kardinal Johannes Gropper (1503–1559) und die Anfänge der katholischen Reform in Deutschland* (Aschendorff, Münster 1951).

Locke, J., 'The Reasonableness of Christianity', in *The Works of John Locke*, vol. 7 (Scientia, Aalen 1963).

Lohff, W., *Die Konkordie reformatorischer Kirchen in Europa* (O. Lembeck, Frankfurt a. M. 1985).

Lohmeyer, E., *Probleme paulinischer Theologie*, (W. Kohlhammer, Stuttgart 1955).

Lohse, B., 'Das Konkordienbuch', in C. Andresen (ed.), *Handbuch der Dogmen- und Theologiegeschichte*, vol. 2, pp. 138–64.

——'Die Auseinandersetzung mit den 'Schwärmern'. . . mit den Antinomern', in C. Andresen (ed.), *Handbuch der Dogmen- und Theologiegeschichte*, vol. 2, pp. 27–33; 39–45.

——'Grundzüge der Theologie Melanchthons', in C. Andresen (ed.), *Handbuch der Dogmen- und*

Theologiegeschichte, vol. 2, pp. 69–81.

——'Innerprotestantische Lehrstreitigkeiten', in C. Andresen (ed.), *Handbuch der Dogmen- und Theologiegeschichte*, vol. 2, pp. 102–38;

Lorenz, R., *Die unvollendete Befreiung vom Nominalismus: Martin Luther und die Grenzen hermeneutischer Theologie bei Gerhard Ebeling* (J.C.B. Mohr (P. Siebeck), Gütersloh 1973).

Löser, W., 'Lehrverurteilungen-Kirchentrennend', in *Catholica* 41 (1987) 177–96.

Lottin, O., *Psychologie et morale aux XIIème et XIIIème siècles*, vol. 4 (Abbaye du Mont-Cesar, Louvain 1954).

Löwenich, W. von, *Luthers Theologia Crucis* (Luther-Verlag, Witten 1967).

——*Duplex iustitia: Luthers Stellung zu einer Unionsformel des 16. Jahrhunderts* (F. Steiner, Wiesbaden 1972).

Luthe, H. (ed.), *Christus-begegnung in der Sakramenten* (Butzon & Bercker, Kevelaer 1981).

Lutz, J., *Unio und Communio. Zum Verhältnis von Rechtfertigungslehre und Kirchenverständnis bei Martin Luther. Eine Untersuchung zu ekklesiologisch relevanten Texten der Jahre 1519–1528* (Bonifatius, Paderborn 1990).

Lyonnet, S., 'De "iustitia Dei" in Epistola ad Romanos', in *Verbum Domini* 25 (1947) 23–34.

Maccoby, H., *The Mythmaker: Paul and the Invention of Christianity* (Weidenfeld & Nicolson, London 1986).

Mackenson, H., 'Contarini's Theological Role at Ratisbon in 1541', in *Archiv für Reformationsgeschichte* 51 (1960) 36–57.

Maffeis, A., 'La giustificazione nel dialogo ecumenico. Chiarificazioni e nodi irrisolti', in *Rassegna di Teologia* 37 (1996) 623–45.

——'Santità della chiesa e mediazione della salvezza', in *Studi Ecumenici* 14 (1996) 209–22.

Mannermaa, T., 'Einig in Sachen Rechtfertigung?: eine lutherische Stellungnahme zu Jörg Baur', in *Theologische Rundschau* 55 (1990) 326–35.

Manns, P., 'Absolute and Incarnate Faith: Luther on Justification in the Galatians' Commentary of 1531–1535', in J. Wicks (ed.), *Catholic Scholars Dialogue with Luther*, pp. 121–56.

Manschreck, C.L., *Melanchthon, the Quiet Reformer* (New York 1958).

Marco, A. di, 'Δικαιοσυνη, Δικαιωμα, Δικαιωσις''', in *Laurentianum* 24 (1983) 46–75.

Maritain, J., 'Luther, or The Advent of the Self', in *Three reformers: Luther, Descartes, Rousseau* (Sheed & Ward, London 1966), pp. 3–50.

Marlé, R., *Bultmann et l'interprétation du Nouveau Testament* (Aubier/Montaigne, Paris 1966).

——*Parler de Dieu aujourd'hui. La théologie herméneutique de G. Ebeling* (Cerf, Paris 1975).

Maron, G., *Kirche und Rechtfertigung: eine kontroverstheologische Untersuchung, ausgehend von den Texten des Zweiten Vatikanischen Konzils* (Vandenhoeck & Ruprecht, Göttingen 1969).

Marquardt, M., 'Evangelische Kirchengemeinschaft. Inhalt und Ergebnisse der lutherisch-methodistischen Lehrgespräche', in *ökumenische Rundschau* 35 (1986) 401–15.

Marranzini, A., *Dibattito Lutero-Seripando* (Morcelliana, Brescia 1981).

Martens, G., *Die Rechtfertigung des Sünders – Rettungshandeln Gottes oder historisches Interpretament? Grundentscheidungen lutherischer Theologie und Kirche bei der Behandlung des Themas 'Rechtfertigung' im ökumenischen Kontext* (Vandenhoeck & Ruprecht, Göttingen 1992).

Martikainen, E., 'Die Leuenberger Lehrgespräche in ökumenischer Perspektive', in *Kerygma und Dogma* 33 (1987) 23–31.

Martin, B.L., *Christ and the Law in Paul* (Brill, Leiden 1989).

Martin, R., 'La question du péché originel dans saint Anselme', in *Revue de Sciences Philosophiques et Théologiques* 5 (1911) 735–49.

Mateo-Seco, L.F., *M. Lutero. Sobre la libertad esclava* (Magisterio Español, Madrid 1978).

Matheson, P., *Cardinal Contarini at Regensburg* (Clarendon Press, Oxford 1972).

Maurer, W., *Der junge Melanchthon zwischen Humanismus und Reformation, vol. 2: Die Theologe* (Vandenhoeck & Ruprecht, Göttingen 1969).

McGrath, A.E., 'Karl Barth and the Articulus Iustificationis: the Significance of his Critique of Ernst Wolf within the Context of his Theological Method', in *Theologische Zeitschrift* 39 (1983) 349–61.

——'Der articulus iustificationis als axiomatischer Grundsatz des christlichen Glaubens', in *Zeitschrift für Theologie und Kirche* 81 (1984) 383–94.

——'Karl Barth als Aufklärer? Der Zusammenhang seiner Lehre vom Werke Christi mit der Erwählungslehre', in *Kerygma und Dogma* 30 (1984) 273–83.

——*Luther's Theology of the Cross* (B. Blackwell, Oxford 1985).

——'John Calvin and Late Medieval Thought: A Study in Late Medieval Influences upon Calvin's Theological Thought', in *Archiv für Reformationsgeschichte* 77 (1986) 58–78.

——*The Making of Modern German Christology: From the Enlightenment to Pannenberg* (B. Blackwell, Oxford 1986).

——*Iustitia Dei. A History of the Christian Doctrine of Justification*, 2 vols (University Press, Cambridge 1986).

——*ARCIC-II and Justification: an evangelical assessment of 'Salvation and the Church'* (Latimer House, Oxford 1987).

——*The Intellectual Origins of the European Reformation* (B. Blackwell, Oxford 1987).

——'Justification: The New Ecumenical Debate', in *Themelios* 13 (1988) 43–8.

McSorley, H.J., 'Was Gabriel Biel a Semipelagian?', in L. Scheffczyk (ed.), *Wahrheit und Verkündigung* (Festschrift M. Schmaus) (Schöningh, München 1967), vol. 2, pp. 1109–20.

——*Luther: Right or Wrong?: an ecumenical-theological study of Luther's major work The Bondage of the Will* (Newman/ Augsburg, New York /Minneapolis 1969).

Meeks, W.A., *The First Urban Christians. The social world of the Apostle Paul* (Yale University Press, New Haven (CT) 1983).

Meißinger, K.A., *Der katholische Luther* (Leo Lehnen, Munich 1952).

Menoud, P.H., 'Revelation and Tradition: The Influence of Paul's Conversion on his Theology', in *Interpretation* 7 (1953) 131–41.

Merz, H., *Historia vitae et controversiae V. Strigelii* (Tübingen 1732).

Meyer, H., 'Le dialogue entre l'Église catholique romaine et la fédération luthérienne mondiale', in *Positions luthériennes* 20 (1972) 179–93.

——'The doctrine of Justification in the Lutheran Dialogue with Other Churches', in *One in Christ* 17 (1981) 86–116.

——'Ekklesiologie im ökumenischen Gespräch und der katholisch/lutherische Dialog über "Kirche und Rechtfertigung"', in *Kath. Nachrichtenagentur- Ökumenische Information* no. 1 (5 January 1994) 5–16.

——'Der katholisch/lutherische Dialog über "Kirche und Rechtfertigung"', in *Materialdienst der ökumenischen Centrale* I/II, (1995), 68–82.

Meyer, H. (ed.), *The Augsburg Confession in Ecumenical Perspective* (Stuttgart 1979).

Meyer, H. and Gaßmann, G. (eds.), *Rechtfertigung im ökumenischen Dialog; Dokumente und Einführung* (O. Lembeck/J. Knecht, Frankfurt a. M. 1987).

Meyer, H., Schütte, H., Mund, H.-J. (eds.), *Katholische Anerkennung des Augsburgischen Bekenntnisses?: ein Vorstoß zur Einheit zwischen katholischer und lutherischer Kirche* (O. Lembeck/J. Knecht, Frankfurt a. M. 1977).

Meyer, H. and Vischer, L. (eds.), *Growth in Agreement. Reports and Agreed Statements of Ecumenical Conversations on a World Level*, Paulist/World Council of Churches (New York/Geneva 1984).

Michaelson, G.E., *Fallen Freedom. Kant on radical Evil and moral Regeneration* (University Press, Cambridge 1990).

Michel, O., *Der Brief an die Römer* (Vandenhoeck & Ruprecht, Göttingen 1963).

Miegge, G., *Lutero, vol. 1: L'uomo e il pensiero fino alla Dieta di Worms, 1483–1521* (Claudiana, Torre Pellice 1946).

Möhler, J.A., *Symbolik oder Darstellung der dogmatischen Gegensätze der Katholiken und Protestanten in ihren öffentlichen Bekenntnisschriften* (G.J. Manz, Regensburg 1873). Eng. translation: *Symbolism: or Exposition of the Doctrinal Differences between Catholics and Protestants as evidenced by their Symbolical Writings* (Gibbings, London 1906).

Möller, C., 'La grâce et la justification', in *Lumen Vitae* 19 (1964) 532–44.

Moo, D.J., 'Paul and the Law in the Last Ten Years', in *Scottish Journal of Theology* 40 (1987) 287–307.

Moore, G.F., 'Christian Writers on Judaism', in *Harvard Theological Review* 14 (1921) 197–254.

——*Judaism in the First Centuries of the Christian Era: The Age of Tannaim* (Harvard University Press, Cambridge (Mass.) 1950), 2 vols (orig. 1927–30).

Morales, J., 'Le vie del progresso ecumenico nella dottrina della giustificazione', in J.M. Galván (ed.), *La giustificazione in Cristo*, pp. 260–7.

Moreau, E.P., 'Loi divine et loi naturelle selon Hobbes', in *Revue Internationale de Philosophie* 33 (1979) 443–51.

Moreno Garcia, A., *La sabiduría del Espíritu: sentir en Cristo* (Diss. Pont. Univ. Gregoriana, Rome 1995).

Morerod, C., *Cajetan et Luther en 1518: édition, traduction et commentaire des opuscules d'Augsbourg de Cajetan* (Éditions Universitaires, Fribourg (Suisse) 1994).

Morgan, T., *The Moral Philosopher*, vol. 1 (London 1738).

Mosheim, L. von, *Elementa theologiae dogmaticae* (Nuremberg 1758).

Mostert, W., 'Scriptura sacra sui ipsius interpres. Bermerkungen zum Verständnis der Heiligen Schrift bei Luther', in *Lutherjahrbuch* 46 (1979) 60–96.

Mouroux, J., *L'expérience chrétienne: Introduction à une théologie* (Aubier, Paris 1952).

Mühlen, K.H. zur, *Nos extra nos. Luthers Theologie zwischen Mystik und Scholastik* (J.C.B. Mohr (P. Siebeck), Tübingen 1972).

Müller, A.V., *Luther und Tauler auf ihren theologischen Zusammenhang neu untersucht* (Berne 1918).

Müller, C., *Gottes Gerechtigkeit und Gottes Volk: Eine Untersuchung zu Römer 9–11* (Göttingen 1964).

Müller, G., *Die Rechtfertigungslehre: Geschichte und Probleme* (G. Mohn, Gütersloh 1977).

Müller, G. and Pfnür, V., 'Justification-Faith-Works', in G.W. Forell and J.F. McCue, *Confessing One Faith*, pp. 117–46.

Müller, H.M., 'Keine romantische Verbrüderung. Mit der "Confessio Augustana" auf dem Weg zur Einheit', in *Lutherische Monatschefte* 21 (1982) 23–6.

Munck, J., *Paul and the Salvation of Mankind* (SCM, London 1959).

Mussner, F., *Traktat über die Juden* (Kösel, Munich 1979).

Neuner, J. and Dupuis, J. (eds.), *The Christian Faith in the Doctrinal Documents of the Catholic Church* (Collins, London 1982).

Neuser, H.W., *Die Vorbereitung der Religionsgespräche von Worms und Regensburg 1540/41* (Neukirchener Verlag, Neukirchen-Vluyn 1974).

Neusner, J., *Judaism. The Evidence of the Mishnah* (Chicago 1981).

Neveut, E., 'Peut-on avoir a certitude d'être en état de grâce?', in *Divus Thomas* (Piacenza) 37 (1934) 321–49.

Nichols, A., *The Shape of Catholic Theology* (T. & T. Clark, Edinburgh 1991).

Niesel, W., 'Calvin wider Osianders Rechtfertigungslehre', in *Zeitschrift für Kirchengeschichte* 46 (1982) 410–30.

Nygren, A., *Eros und Agape: Gestaltwandlungen der christlichen Liebe* (Bertelsmann, Gütersloh 1930), 2 vols.

——*Der Römerbrief* (Vandenhoeck & Ruprecht, Göttingen 1954).

O'Callaghan, P., 'The Holiness of the Church in "Lumen Gentium"', in *Thomist* 52 (1988) 673–701.

——'Il realismo e la teologia della creazione', in *Per la filosofia* 12 (1995) 98–110.

——'The Mediation of Justification and the justification of Mediation. Report of the Lutheran/Catholic Dialogue: "Church and Justification: Understanding the Church in the Light of the Doctrine of Justification" (1993)', in *Annales Theologici* 10 (1996) 147–211.

——'"That everything may be for his glory": the Paternity of God, Christ's own perspective', in Various authors, *Preparing for the year 2000* (Urbi et Orbi Communications, New Hope / Rome 1996), pp. 207–18.

——'L'uomo giustificato, nuova creatura in Cristo. Una riflessione intorno all'attuale dibattito ecumenico', in J.M. Galván (ed.), *La giustificazione in Cristo*, pp. 129–64.

Oberman, H.A., 'Facientibus quod est in se est Deus non denegat gratiam. Robert Holcot O.P. and the Beginnings of Luther's Theology', in *Harvard Theological Review* 55 (1962) 317–41.
——*The Harvest of Medieval Theology: Gabriel Biel and Late Medieval Nominalism* (Harvard University Press, Cambridge (Mass.) 1963).
——'Das tridentinische Rechtfertigungsdekret im Lichte spätmittelalterlicher Theologie', in *Zeitschrift für Theologie und Kirche* 61 (1964) 251–82.
——'"Iustitia Christi" and "Iustitia Dei": Luther and the Scholastic Doctrines of Justification', in *Harvard Theological Review* 59 (1966) 1–26.
——'Headwaters of the Reformation: Initia Lutheri-Initia Reformationis', in H.A. Oberman (ed.), *Luther and the Dawn of the Modern Era* (Brill, Leiden 1974), pp. 40–88.
——*Wurzeln des Antisemitismus. Christenangst und Judenplage im Zeitalter von Humanismus und Reformation* (Severin und Siedler, Berlin 1981).
Ocáriz Braña, F., *Hijos de Dios en Cristo: introducción a una teología de la participación sobrenatural* (EUNSA, Pamplona 1972).
Occhipinti, G. (ed.), *Storia della Teologia, vol. 3: da Pietro Abelardo a Roberto Bellarmino* (Dehoniane, Bologna 1996).
Odero, J.M., *La fe en Kant* (EUNSA, Pamplona 1992).
Oepke, A., *Die Missionspredigt des Apostels Paulus. Eine biblisch-theologische und religionsgeschichtliche Untersuchung* (Hinrichs, Leipzig 1920).
——'Δικαιοσυνη Θεου' bei Paulus in neuer Beleuchtung', in *Theologische Literaturzeitung* 78 (1953) 257–63.
Olivier, D., 'Les deux sermons sur la double et la triple justice', in *Ôcumenica* 3 (1968) (Centre d'Etudes Œuméniques de Strasbourg, Neuchâtel), pp. 39–69.
——*La Foi de Luther: la cause de l'Évangile dans l'Église* (Beauchesne, Paris 1978).
Olzarán, J., *Documentos inéditos tridentinos sobre la justificación* (Fax, Madrid 1957).
Orbe, A., *Hacia la primera teología de la procesión del Verbo* (Analecta Gregoriana, Rome 1958).
Outler, A.C. (ed.), *John Wesley* (Oxford University Press, New York 1964).
Ozment, S.E., *Homo spiritualis: a comparative study of the anthropology of Johannes Tauler, Jean Gerson and Martin Luther (1509–16) in the context of their theological thought* (Brill, Leiden 1969).
Pannenberg, W., *Anthropology in Theological Perspective* (Westminster Press, Philadelphia 1985).
——*Systematische Theologie*, 3 vols (Vandenhoeck & Ruprecht, Göttingen 1988–1993). Engl. translation, *Systematic Theology*, 3 vols (T. & T. Clark, Edinburgh 1991–96).
——'Die Rechtfertigungslehre im ökumenischen Gespräch', in *Zeitschrift für Theologie und Kirche* 88 (1991) 232–46;
——'Müssen sich die Kirchen immer noch gegenseitig verurteilen?', in *Kerygma und Dogma* 38 (1992) 311–30.
Pannenberg, W. and Schneider, T. (eds.), *Lehrverurteilungen-kirchentrennend?: Antworten auf kirchliche Stellungnahmen* (Vandenhoeck und Ruprecht, Göttingen 1994).
Pas, P., 'La doctrine de la double justice au Concile de Trente', in *Ephemerides Theologiae Lovanensis* 30 (1954) 5–53.
Pawlikowski, J.T., *Christ in the Light of Christian-Jewish Dialogue* (Paulist, New York 1982).
Pelikan, J., 'The Origins of the Subject-Object Antithesis in Lutheran Theology', in *Concordia Theological Monthly* 21 (1950) 94–104.
——*Jesus through the Centuries. His Place in the History of Culture* (Yale University Press, New Haven 1985).
Pelster, F., 'Das Leben und die Schriften des Oxforder Dominikanerlehrers Richard Fishacre (d. 1248)', in *Zeitschrift für Katholische Theologie* 54 (1930) 518–53.
Pemsel-Maier, S., *Rechtfertigung durch Kirche? Das Verhältnis von Kirche und Rechtfertigung in Entwürfen der neueren katholischen und evangelischen Theologie* (Würzburg 1991).
Penna, R., 'Il problema della legge nelle lettere di San Paolo', in *L'Apostolo Paolo. Studi di esegesi e teologia* (Paoline, Cinisello Balsamo 1991), pp. 496–518.
Penzel, K., 'How to transcend the two classical positions of Lutheranism and Methodism', in *Perkins Journal* 34 (1981), 35–42.

Pesch, O.-H., *Theologie der Rechtfertigung bei Martin Luther und Thomas von Aquin* (Matthias-Grünewald, Mainz 1967).

——'Gottes Gnadenhandeln als Rechtfertigung des Menschen', in Various authors, *Mysterium Salutis IV/2: Das Heilsgeschehen in der Gemeinde: Gottes Gnadenhandeln* (Benzinger, Einsiedeln 1973), pp. 831–920.

——'Neuere Beiträge zur Frage nach Luthers "Reformatorischer Wende"', in *Catholica* 37 (1984) 66–133;

——'Rechtfertigung und Kirche. Die kriteriologische Bedeutung der Rechtfertigungslehre für die Ekklesiologie', in *Ökumenische Rundschau* 37 (1988) 22–46.

Peter, C.J., 'Justification by faith and the need for another critical principle', in H.G. Anderson et al. (eds.), *Justification by faith*, pp. 304–15.

——'A Moment of Truth for Lutheran-Catholic Dialogue', in *Origins* 17 (1987/88) 537–41.

Peters, A., *Rechtfertigung* (G. Mohn, Gütersloh 1984).

Pfaff, E., *Die Bekehrung des hl. Paulus in der Exegese des 20. Jahrhundert* (Diss. Pont. Univ. Gregoriana, Rome 1942).

Pfnür, V., *Einig in der Rechtfertigungslehre?: die Rechtfertigungslehre der 'Confessio Augustana' (1530) und die Stellungnahme der katholischen Kontroverstheologie zwischen 1530 und 1535* (F. Steiner, Wiesbaden 1970).

——'Zur Verurteilung der reformatorischen Rechtfertigungslehre auf dem Konzil von Trient', in *Annuarium Historiae Conciliorum* 8 (1976) 407–28.

——*Die Einigung bei den Religionsgesprèchen von Worms und Regensburg 1540/41: Eine Täuschung?*, (G. Mohn, Gütersloh 1980).

Pfürtner, S., *Angoisse et certitude de notre salut: Luther et Saint Thomas au-delà des oppositions traditionelles* (Centurion, Paris 1967); English translation, *Luther and Aquinas on Salvation* (Sheed & Ward, New York 1964).

Philips, G., 'La justification luthÄreienne et la Concile de Trente', in *Ephemerides Theologiae Lovanensis* 47 (1971) 340–58.

—— 'Saint Augustin a-t-il connu une "grâce créée"?', in *Ephemerides Theologiae Lovanensis* 47 (1971) 97–116.

——*L'union personnelle avec le Dieu vivant. Essai sur l'origine et le sens de la grâce créée* (University Press, Leuven 1974).

Pieper, J., *Über die Liebe* (Kösel, München 1972).

Piette, M., *John Wesley in the Evolution of Protestantism* (Sheed & Ward, New York 1937).

Pini, G., 'Vocazione di Paolo o conversione', in L. Padovese (ed.), *Atti del I Simposio di Tarso su San Paolo Apostolo* (Pontificio Ateneo Antoniano /Istituto francesano di spiritualità, Rome 1993), pp. 47–63.

Pinomaa, L., *Sieg des Glaubens. Grundlinien der Theologie Luthers* (Vandenhoeck & Ruprecht, Göttingen 1964).

Pitta, A., *Disposizione e messaggio della Lettera ai Galati: analisi retorico-letteraria* (Diss. Pont. Istituto Biblico, Rome 1992).

Pohlmann, H., *Hat Luther Paulus endeckt? Eine Frage zur theologischen Besinnung* (Berlin 1959).

Pöhlmann, H.G., *Rechtfertigung: die gegenwaertige kontroverstheologische Problematik der Rechtfertigungslehre zwischen der evangelisch-lutherischen und der römisch-katholischen Kirche* (G. Mohn, Gütersloh 1971).

Prat, F., *La théologie de Saint Paul*, 2 vols (Beauchesne, Paris 1927–30).

Prenter, R., *Man and the Incarnation: a Study in the Biblical Theology of Irenaeus* (Oliver & Boyd, Edinburgh/London 1959).

——*Schöpfung und Erlösung. Dogmatik II: Die Erlösung* (Vandenhoeck & Ruprecht, Göttingen 1960).

——*Der barmherizge Richter. Iustitia Dei passiva in Luthers 'Dictata super Psalterium' 1513–1515* (Universitetsforlaget i Aarhus, Copenhagen 1961).

Preus, J.S., *From Shadow to Promise* (Belknap Press, Cambridge (Mass.) 1969).

Quimron, J. and Strugnell, E., *Qumran Cave 4 - V* (Clarendon Press, Oxford 1994).

Raem, H.-A., 'Beachtlicher Beitrag zur Versöhnung der getrennten Christen, Gutachten des Einheitsrates zur deutschen Studie "Lehrverurteilungen-kirchentrennend?"', in *Kath. Nachrichtenagentur-ökumenische Information*, no. 26 (23 June 1993) 13–16.
——'Katholische und lutherische Lehrverurteilungen – weiterhin kirchentrennend?', in *Una Sancta* 49 (1994) 302–7.
——'The Third Phase of Lutheran-Catholic Dialogue (1986-1993)', in *Information Service* 86 (1994) 189–97.
——'I rapporti con i Luterani nell'anno 1995', in *L'Osservatore Romano* 22–23 January 1996, p. 7.
Rahner, K., *Theological Investigations* (Darton, Longman & Todd, London 1974), 20 vols.
——*Kirche und Sakramente* (Herder, Freiburg i. Br. 1960).
——'Some Implications of the Scholastic Concept of Uncreated Grace', in *Theological Investigations*, vol. 1, pp. 319–46.
——'Questions of a Controversial Theology on Justification', in *Theological Investigations*, vol. 4, pp. 189–218.
——'The Word and the Eucharist', in *Theological Investigations*, vol. 4, pp. 253-281.
——'"Just and Sinner"', in *Theological Investigations*, vol. 6, pp. 218–30.
Räisänen, H., *Paul and the Law* (J.C.B. Mohr (P. Siebeck), Tübingen 1983).
Randellini, L., 'L'ermeneutica esistenziale in Bultmann', in Various authors, *Esegesi ed ermeneutica. Atti della XXI Settimana Biblica dell'Associazione Biblica Italiana* (1968) (Paideia, Brescia 1972), pp. 35–70.
Rausch, T., 'Responses to the US Lutheran-Roman Catholic Statement on Justification', in *One in Christ* 29 (1993) 333–53.
Reitzenstein, R., *Die hellenistischen Mysterienreligionen nach ihren Grundgedanken und Wirkungen* (Teubner, Leipzig 1927).
Reno, R.R., 'The doctrine of justification: Lutheran lessons for Anglicans in search of confessional integrity', in *Pro Ecclesia* 3 (1994) 455–82.
Reumann, J., *'Righteousness' in the New Testament: 'Justification' in the United States Lutheran-Roman Catholic Dialogue; with responses by Joseph A. Fitzmyer; Jerome D. Quinn* (Fortress/Paulist, Philadelphia/New York 1982).
——'"Justification by Faith" in the Lutheran-Roman Catholic Dialogue and Beyond: Reflections over a Decade', in *Lutheran Forum* 23 (1989) 21–4.
Rich, A., *Die Anfänge der Theologie Huldrych Zwinglis* (Zürich 1949).
Riecke, B., 'Paulus über das Gesetz', in *Theologische Zeitschrift* 41 (1985) 237–57.
Rietschel, E., *Das Problem der unsichtbar sichtbaren Kirche bei Luther: Darstellung und Lösungsversuch* (Heinsius Nachfolger, Leipzig 1932).
Riga, P.G., 'Created Grace in St Augustine', in *Augustinian Studies* 3 (1972) 113–30.
Ritschl, A.B., 'Die Rechtfertigungslehre des Andreas Osiander', in *Jahrbücher für deutsche Theologie* 2 (1857) 785–829.
——*Geschichte des Pietismus*, 3 vols (A. Marcus, Bonn 1880–1886).
——*Die christliche Lehre von der Rechtfertigung und Versöhnung*, 3 vols (A. Marcus, Bonn 1882–88). Eng. translation, *The Christian Doctrine of Justification and Reconciliation* (Edinburgh 1871).
Rivière, J., *Le dogme de la Rédemption. Étude théologique* (G. Gabalda, Paris 1914).
——'Justification: le Concile de Trente', in *Dictionnaire de Théologie Catholique* 8/2 (1925) 1964–1992.
——'Quelques antécédents patristiques de la formule: "facienti quod est in se"', in *Revue de Sciences Réligieuses* 7 (1927) 93–7.
——'Mérite', in *Dictionnaire de Théologie Catholique* 10 (1928) 574–785.
Rivkin, E., *What Crucified Jesus?* (Nashville 1984).
Rodríguez, P., 'Omnia traham ad meipsum: il significato di Giovanni 12,31 nell'esperienza spirituale di mons. Escrivá de Balaguer', in *Annales Theologici* 6 (1992) 5–34.
——'La Iglesia, "creatura evangelii"', in *Diálogo ecuménico* 31 (1996) 375–99.
——'La dimensione ecclesiologica della giustificazione. Una prospettiva cattolica', in J.M. Galván (ed.), *La giustificazione in Cristo*, pp. 187–207.

Rogge, J., *Johannes Agricolas Lutherverständnis unter besonderer Berücksichtigung des Antinomismus* (Berlin 1960).

Roloff, J., *Die Kirche im Neuen Testament* (Vandenhoeck & Ruprecht, Göttingen 1993).

Rondet, H., *Le péché originel dans la tradition patristique et théologique* (Fayard, Paris 1967).

Roo, W.A. van, *Grace and Original Justice according to St Thomas Aquinas* (Analecta Gregoriana, Rome 1955).

Rostagno, S., 'Ecclesia abscondita. Appunti su un concetto controverso', in *Studi Ecumenici* 6 (1988) 183–92.

——'Coerenza del sistema e questione della verità in Ireneo', in *Studi Ecumenici* 10 (1992) 227–41;

——'Consenso tra cattolici e luterani', in *Protestantesimo* 51 (1996) 64–6.

Rovira Belloso, J.M., *Trento. Una interpretación teológica* (Herder, Barcelona 1979).

Rückert, H., *Die Rechtfertigungslehre auf dem Tridentinischen Konzil* (A. Marcus & E. Weber, Bonn 1925).

——*Die theologische Entwicklung Gasparo Contarinis* (A. Marcus & E. Weber, Bonn 1926).

——'Promereri: Eine Studie zum tridentinischen Rechtfertigungsdekret als Antwort an H.A. Oberman', in *Zeitschrift für Theologie und Kirche* 68 (1971) 162–94.

Ruiz de la Peña, J.L., *El don de Dios. Antropología teológica especial* (Secretariado Trinitario, Santander 1991).

Ruokanen, M., *Hermeneutics as an Ecumenical Method in the Theology of Gerhard Ebeling* (Luther-Agricola Gesellschaft, Helsinki 1982).

Sagués, J., 'Un libro pretridentino de Andrés de Vega sobre la justificación', in *Estudios Eclesiásticos* 20 (1946) 175–209.

Sanders, E.P., *Paul and Palestinian Judaism. A Comparison of Patterns of Religion* (SCM, London 1977).

——*Paul, the Law, and the Jewish People* (Fortress, Philadelphia 1983).

——*Jesus and Judaism* (SCM, London 1985).

——*Judaism. Practice and Belief* (SCM, London 1992).

Santmire, H.P., 'Justification in Calvin's 1540 Romans Commentary', in *Church History* 33 (1963) 294–313.

Santos-Noya, M., *Die Sünden- und Gnadenlehre des Gregor von Rimini* (P. Lang, Frankfurt a. M. 1990).

Sartori, L., 'Chiesa e giustificazione', in *Protestantesimo* 51 (1996) 131–52.

Sattler, D., 'Neue Urteile zu den alten Lehrverurteilungen; die evangelischen Kirchen in Deutschland und die Studie des ökumenischen Arbeitskreises', in *Catholica* 49 (1995) 98–113.

Schedler, G., 'Hobbes on the Basis of Political Obligation', in *Journal of the History of Philosophy* 15 (1977) 165–70.

Scheeben, M.J., *I misteri del cristianesimo* (Morcelliana, Brescia 1960) (orig. 1865).

Scheffczyk, L., 'Urstand, Fall und Erbsünde von der Schrift bis Augustin', in M. Schmaus et al. (eds.), *Handbuch der Dogmengeschichte* (Herder, Freiburg i. Br. /Basel/Vienna 1951 ff.), vol. 2/3 a.

Schian, M., *Orthodoxie und Pietismus in Kampf um die Predigt* (Giessen 1912).

Schierse, F.J., 'Das Trienter Konzil und die Frage nach der christlichen Gewißheit', in G. Schreiber (ed.), *Das Weltkonzil von Trient: Sein Werden und Wirken*, pp. 145–67.

Schillebeeckx, E., *Christ the Sacrament of Encounter with God* (Sheed and Ward, London 1963).

Schleiermacher, F.D.E., *The Christian Faith* (T. & T. Clark, Edinburgh 1989); orig., *Der christliche Glaube*, 2 vols (W. de Gruyter, Berlin 1960).

Schlier, H., *Der Römerbrief*, Herder, Freiburg i. Br. 1977.

Schlömann, M., *Natürliches und gepredigtes Gesetz bei Luther. Ein Studie zur Frage nach der Einheit der Gesetzesauffassung Luthers mit besonderer Berücksichtigung seiner Auseinandersetzung mit der Antinomern* (Berlin 1961).

Schmid, H., *The Doctrinal Theology of the Evangelical Lutheran Church* (Minneapolis n/d).

Schmid, H., *Zwinglis Lehre von der göttlichen und menschlichen Gerechtigkeit* (Zwingli Verlag, Zurich 1959).

Schmidt, M., *Wiedergeburt und neuer Mensch: Gesammelte Studien zur Geschichte des Pietismus* (Luther-Verlag, Witten 1969).

Schmidt, S., 'S. Pauli "iustitia Dei" notione iustitiae, quae in V.T. et apud S. Paulum habetur, dilucidata', in *Verbum Domini* 37 (1959) 96–105.

Schnackenburg, R., 'Die paulinische Theologie', in *Lexikon für Theologie und Kirche*, 2nd ed., vol. 8, 220–8.

Schneider, T., 'The Dialogue Report in the Present Ecumenical Context: A Comment on "Church and Justification"', in *Information Service* 86 (1994) 182–8.

Schoeps, H.J., *Paulus. Die Theologie des Paulus im Lichte der jüdischen Religionsgeschichte* (Mohr, Tübingen 1959).

Scholz, H., *Eros und Caritas. Die platonische Liebe und die Liebe im Sinne des Christentums* (Max Niemeyer, Halle 1929).

Schönborn, C. von, *L'icône du Christ: fondements théologiques* (Cerf, Paris 1986).

Schott, E., *Fleisch und Geist nach Luthers Lehre unter besonderer Berücksichtigung des Begriffs 'totus homo'* (Leipzig 1928).

Schreiber, G., (ed.), *Das Weltkonzil von Trient: Sein Werden und Wirken*, 2 vols (Herder, Freiburg i. Br. 1951).

Schreiner, T.R., 'The Abolition and Fulfillment of the Law in Paul', in *Journal for the Study of the New Testament* 35 (1989) 47–74.

——*The Law and its Fulfillment. A Pauline Theology of the Law* (Baker, Old Rapids 1993).

Schultz, S., 'Zur Rechtfertigung aus Gnade in Qumran und bei Paulus', in *Zeitschrift für Theologie und Kirche* 56 (1959) 155–85.

Schupp, J., *Die Gnadenlehre des Petrus Lombardus*, Herder, Freiburg i. Br. 1932.

Schütte, H. (ed.), *Einig in der Lehre von der Rechtfertigung!: mit einer Antwort an Jörg Baur* (Bonifatius, Paderborn 1990).

——'"Articulis stantis et cadentis ecclesiae": der Rechtfertigungsartikel in der Bedeutung für die Kirche', in *Bausteine für die Einheit der Christen* 36 (1996) 16–21.

Schwager, R., 'Die fröhliche Wechsel und Streit', in *Zeitschrift für katholische Theologie* 105 (1983) 27–66.

Schweitzer, A., *Die Religionsphilosophie Kants in der Kritik der reinen Vernunft bis Religion innerhalb der Grenzen der bloßen Vernunft*, Freiburg i. Br. 1899;

——*Geschichte der paulinischen Forschung von der Reformation bis auf die Gegenwart* (Mohr, Tübingen 1911).

——*The Mysticism of Paul the Apostle* (London 1956) (orig. 1931).

Scott, D.A., '"Salvation and the Church" and theological truth-claims', in *Journal of Ecumenical Studies* 25 (1988) 428–36.

Seifrid, M.A., *Justification by Faith: the origin and development of a central Pauline theme* (Brill, Leiden 1992).

Selig, C.A., *Vollständige Historie der Augsburger Confession* (Halle 1730), 2 vols.

Semmelroth, O., *Die Kirche als Ur-Sakrament* (J. Knecht, Frankfurt a. M. 1953).

Siggins, J.D.K., *Martin Luther's Doctrine of Christ* (Yale University Press, New Haven 1970).

Stakemeier, A., 'Die theologischen Schulen auf dem Trienter Konzil während der Rechtfertigungsverhandlung', in *Theologisches Quartalschrift* 117 (1936) 188–207; 322–50; 446–504.

——*Glaube und Rechtfertigung. Das Mysterium der christlichen Rechtfertigung aus dem Glauben dargestellt nach den Verhandlungen und Lehrbestimmungen des Konzils von Trient* (Herder, Freiburg i. Br. 1937).

——*Das Konzil von Trient über die Heilsgewißheit* (F.H. Kerle, Heidelberg 1949).

Steinbart, G.S., *System der reinen Philosophie oder Glückseligkeitslehre des Christentums* (Züllichau 1778).

Stendahl, K., 'The Apostle Paul and the Introspective Conscience of the West', in *Harvard Theological Review* 56 (1963) 199–215 (reprinted in K. Stendahl, *Paul among Jews and Gentiles and other essays* (Augsburg/ Fortress, Philadelphia 1987), pp. 78–96.

Stephens, W.P., *The Holy Spirit in the Theology of Martin Bucer* (University Press, Cambridge 1970).

Stöckle, B., *Die Lehre von der erbsündlichen Konkupiszenz in ihrer Bedeutung für das christliche Leibethos* (Buch-Kunstverlag, Ettal 1954).

Strecker, G., 'Befreiung und Rechtfertigung. Zur Stellung der Rechtfertigungslehre in der Theologie des Paulus', in J. Friedrich, W. Pöhlmann and H. Conzelmann, *Rechtfertigung* (*Festschrift für E. Käsemann zum 70. Geburtstag*) (Vandenhoeck & Ruprecht, Göttingen 1976), pp. 479–508.

Stuhlmacher, P., *Gerechtigkeit Gottes bei Paulus* (Vandenhoeck & Ruprecht, Göttingen 1966).

——'"Das Ende des Gesetzes': Über Ursprung und Ansatz der paulinischen Theologie', in *Zeitschrift für Theologie und Kirche* 67 (1970) 14–39.

Stupperich, R., *Der Humanismus und die Wiedervereinigung der Konfessionen* (Leipzig 1936).

——'Der Ursprung des Regensburger Buches von 1541 und seine Rechtfertigungslehre', in *Archiv für Reformationsgeschichte* 36 (1939) 88–116.

——*Melanchthon* (W. de Gruyter, Berlin 1960).

——'Die Rechtfertigungslehre bei Luther und Melanchthon 1530–1536', in Various authors, *Luther und Melanchthon: Referate und Berichte des Zweitens Internationalen Kongresses für Lutherforschung* (Vandenhoeck & Ruprecht, Göttingen 1961), pp. 73–88.

Subilia, V., *La Giustificazione per Fede* (Paideia, Brescia 1976).

Tabet, M.A., 'Rm 10,4 nel dialogo ebraico-cristiano', in J.M. Galván (ed.), *La giustificazione in Cristo*, pp. 83–100.

Tanzella-Nitti, G., *Mistero trinitario ed economia della grazia. Il personalismo soprannaturale di M.J. Scheeben* (Armando, Roma 1997).

Tavard, G., *Justification: An Ecumenical Study*, (Ramsey/ Paulist, New York 1983).

——'The Contemporary Relevance of Justification by Faith', in *One in Christ* 21 (1985) 131–38.

——'Justification in Dialogue', in *One in Christ* 25 (1989) 299–310;

Teetaert, A., 'Le péché originel d'aprés Abélard', in *Estudis Franciscans* 40 (1928) 23–54.

Thackery, H. St John, *The Relation of St Paul to Contemporary Jewish Thought* (Macmillan, London 1900).

Thielman, F., *From Plight to Solution. A Jewish Framework for Understanding Paul's View of the Law in Galatians and Romans* (Brill, Leiden 1989).

——*Paul and the Law: A Contextual Approach*, Intervarsity, Downers Grove (Ill.) 1994.

Thompson, W.M., 'Viewing Justification through Calvin's Eyes', in *Theological Studies* 57 (1996) 447–66.

Thyen, H., *Studien zur Sündenvergebung im Neuen Testament und ihren alttestamentlichen und jüdischen Voraussetzungen* (Vandenhoeck & Ruprecht, Göttingen 1970).

Tillard, J.M.-R., 'Vers une nouvelle problématique de la "Justification"', in *Irénikon* 55 (1982) 185–98.

Tillich, P., 'Rechtfertigung und Zweifel', from *Vorträge der theologischen Konferenz zu Gießen* (1924), in *Gesammelte Werke, Evangelisches Verlagswerk* (Stuttgart 1970), vol. 8, pp. 85–100.

——*Systematic Theology*, 3 vols (University of Chicago Press, Chicago 1951–63).

—— *The Protestant Era* (University of Chicago Press, Chicago 1963).

—— *The Shaking of the Foundations* (Penguin Books, Harmondsworth 1969).

——*Theology of Culture* (Oxford University Press, New York 1964).

Tindal, M., *Christianity as old as the creation* (G. Gawlick, ed.) (Frommann Verlag, Stuttgart-Bad Cannstatt 1967).

Töllner, J.G., *Der thätige Gehorsam Christi untersucht* (Breslau 1768).

Torrance, J.B., 'Marburg revisited – an evaluation', in *Lutheran World* 14/3 (1967) 67–70.

Torrance, T.F., 'Justification: its radical nature and place in reformed doctrine and life', in *Scottish Journal of Theology* 13 (1960) 225–46.

Trapè, A., *S. Agostino. Introduzione alla dottrina della grazia, vol. 1: Natura e grazia* (Città Nuova, Rome 1987).

Trütsch, J., 'Facienti quod in se est Deus non denegat gratiam', in *Lexikon für Theologie und Kirche* 3 (1959) 1336 f.

Turner, H.E.W., 'Justification by Faith in Modern Theology', in M.E. Glasswell and E.W. Fasholé-

Luke, New Testament Christianity for Africa and the World (SPCK, London 1974).

Tyson, J.B., '"Works of the Law" in Galatians', in *Journal of Biblical Literature* 92 (1973) 423–31.

Ullrich, L., 'Genesis und Schwerpunkte des katholisch-lutherischen Dialogdokumentes "Kirche und Rechtfertigung"', in *Catholica* 50 (1996) 1–22.

Vajta, V., 'Sine Meritis. Zur kritischen Funktion der Rechtfertigunglehre', in *Œumenica* 3 (1968) 146–97.

Valentini, D., 'A Contribution to the Reading of the ARCIC-II Statement on "Salvation and the Church"', in *Information Service* 63 (1987) 41–53.

Vannini, M., 'La teologia mistica', in G. Occhipinti (ed.), *Storia della Teologia, vol. 3: da Pietro Abelardo a Roberto Bellarmino*, pp. 263–90.

Various authors, *Augustinus Magister. Congrès International Augustinien* (Études Augustiniennes, Paris 1954), 3 vols.

Various authors, *Thesaurus Linguae Latinae*, vol. 7/2 (G. Teubneri, Leipzig 1979).

Vercruysse, J., 'Luther's Theology of the Cross at the Time of the Heidelberg Disputation', in *Gregorianum* 57 (1976) 523–48.

——'Da Lutero a Calvino', in G. Occhipinti (ed.), *Storia della Teologia*, pp. 389–404.

Vignaux, P., *Justification et prédestination au XIV siécle: Duns Scot, Pierre d'Auriole, Guillaume d'Occam, Grégoire de Rimini* (E. Leroux, Paris 1934).

——'Luther lecteur de Gabriel Biel', in *Église et théologie* 22 (1959) 33–52.

——*De saint Anselme à Luther* (Vrin, Paris 1976).

Villalmonte, A. de, 'Andrés de Vega y el proceso de la justificación según el Concilio Tridentino', in *Revista Española de Teología* 5 (1945) 311–74.

Vorster, H., 'Ende gut, alles gut?: zur Rücknahme der reformatorischen Verurteilungen gegenüber der heutigen römisch-katholischen Lehre', in *Ökumenische Rundschau* 44 (1995) 92–8.

——*Das Freiheitsverständnis bei Thomas von Aquin und Martin Luther* (Vandenhoeck & Ruprecht, Göttingen 1965).

Waelhens, A. de, *La philosophie de Martin Heidegger* (Editions de l'Institut Supérieur de Philosophie, Louvain 1943).

Wagner, H. von, 'Kirche und Rechtfertigung: zum Dokument aus der dritten Phase des katholisch-lutherischen Dialogs (1993)', in *Catholica* 48 (1994) 233–41.

Walz, A., 'La giustificazione tridentina. Nota sul dibattito e sul decreto conciliare', in *Angelicum* 28 (1951) 97–138.

Weber, F.W., *System der altsynagogalen palästinischen Theologie aus Targum, Midrasch und Talmud, 1880* (revised as *Jüdische Theologie auf Grund des Talmud und verwandter Schriften* (Leipzig 1897), edited by F. Delitzsch and G. Schnedermann (Olms, Hildesheim 1975).

Weder, H., *Das Kreuz Jesu bei Paulus* (Vandenhoeck & Ruprecht, Göttingen 1981).

Wegenast, K., *Das Verständis der Tradition bei Paulus und in den Deuteropaulinen* (Neukirchen 1962)

Wendebourg, D., '"Kirche und Rechtfertigung". Ein Erlebnisbericht zu einem neueren ökumenischen Dokument', in *Zeitschrift für Theologie und Kirche* 93 (1996) 84–100.

Wenz, G., *Einführung in die evangelische Sakramentenlehre*, Wissenschaftliche Buchgesellschaft (Darmstadt 1988).

Wernle, P., *Der Christ und die Sünde bei Paulus* (Freiburg i. Br./Leipzig 1897).

Wesley, J., *Standard Sermons* (London 1920).

Westerholm, S., *Israel's Law and the Church's Faith. Paul and his Recent Interpreters* (Eerdmans, Grand Rapids 1988).

——*Jesus and Scribal Authority* (CWK Gleerup, Lund 1978).

Wicks, J., 'Justification and Faith in Luther's Theology', in *Theological Studies* 44 (1983) 3–29.

——'Living and Praying as Simul Iustus et Peccator', in *Gregorianum* 70 (1989) 521–48.

——'U.S. Bishops Welcome Document on Justification', in *Ecumenical Trends* 19 (1990) 49–52.

——*Luther's reform: studies on conversion and the Church* (P. von Zabern, Mainz 1992).

——'Holy Spirit – Church – Sanctification: insights from Luther's Instructions on the Faith', in *Pro Ecclesia* 2 (1993) 150–72.

Wicks, J. (ed.), *Catholic Scholars Dialogue with Luther* (Loyola University Press, Chicago 1970).

——*Cajetan responds: a reader in reformation controversy* (The Catholic University of America Press, Washington 1978).

Wilkens, E., *Rechtfertigung als Freiheit: Paulusstudien* (Neukirchener Verlag, Neukirchen-Vluyn 1974).

——*Evangelisch-katholischer Kommentar zum Neuen Testament*, 3 vols (Benzinger, Zurich 1978).

Wilkens, E. (ed.), *Helsinki 1963; Beiträge zum theologischen Gespräch des Lutherischen Weltbundes. Im Auftrage des Deutschen Nationalkomitees des Lutherischen Weltbundes* (Lutherisches Verlagshaus, Berlin/Hamburg 1964).

Wilpert, P., 'Begierde', in *Reallexikon für Antike und Christentum*, vol. 2 (Hiersemann, Stuttgart 1950), pp. 63–78.

Wingren, G., *Theology in Conflict: Nygren, Barth, Bultmann* (Oliver and Boyd, Edinburgh/London 1958).

——*Man and the Incarnation: a study in the biblical theology of Irenaeus* (Oliver & Boyd, Edinburgh/London 1959).

——*Schöpfung und Gesetz* (Vandenhoeck & Ruprecht, Göttingen 1960).

——*Creation and Gospel: The New Situation in European Theology* (New York 1979).

Wolf, E., *Staupitz und Luther: Ein Beitrag zur Theologie des Johannes von Staupitz und deren Bedeutung für Luthers theologischen Werdegang* (Leipzig 1929).

——'Die Rechtfertigungslehre als Mitte und Grenze reformatischer Theologie' (1949), in *Pereginatio*, vol. 2 (Chr. Kaiser, München 1965), pp. 11–21.

Wood, H.G., 'The Conversion of Paul: its Nature, Antecedents and Consequences', in *New Testament Studies* 1 (1954–55) 276–82.

Wrede, W., *Paulus* (Tübingen 1907).

Wright, J.R., 'Martin Luther: An Anglican Ecumenical Appreciation', in *Anglican and Episcopalian History* 56 (1987) 320–23.

——'"Salvation and the Church". A Response to David Scott', in *Journal of Ecumenical Studies* 25 (1988) 437–44.

Xiberta, B., 'La causa meritoria de la justificación en las controversias pretridentinas', in *Revista Española de Teología* 5 (1945) 87–106.

Yeago, D.S., 'Gnosticism, antinomianism, and reformation theology. Reflections on the costs of a construal', in *Pro Ecclesia* 2 (1993) 37–49.

Ziesler, J.A., *The Meaning of Righteousness in Paul. A Linguistic and Theological Enquiry* (Cambridge University Press, New York-London 1972).

Zumkeller, A., 'Erbsünde, Gnade und Rechtfertigung im Verständnis der Erfurter Augustinertheologen des Spätmittelalters', in *Zeitschrift für Kirchengeschichte* 92 (1981) 39–59.

Index